State and Religion

With its increasingly secular and religiously diverse population, Australia faces many challenges in determining how the State and religion should interact. Australia is not unique in facing these challenges. States worldwide, including common law countries with shared legal and religious heritages, have also been faced with the question of how the State and religion should relate to one another. Countries such as the United Kingdom, Canada, New Zealand and the United States have all had to grapple with how to manage the State–religion relationship in the present day.

This book provides a comprehensive historical review of the interaction of the State and religion in Australia. It brings together multiple examples of areas in which the State and religion interact and reviews these examples across Australia's history from settlement through to the present day. The book sets this story within a wider theoretical context via an examination of theories of State–religion relationships as well as a comparison with other similar common law jurisdictions.

The book demonstrates how the solutions arrived at in Australia are uniquely Australian owing to Australia's unique legal system, religious demographics and history. However, this is just one possible outcome among many that have been tried in common law liberal democracies.

Renae Barker is a lecturer in the Law School and Honorary Research Fellow in the Centre for Muslim States and Societies at the University of Western Australia. She is a member of Bishop in Council and Trustee in the Anglican Diocese of Bunbury and a member of the legislation drafting committee for the Anglican Diocese of Perth. Renae has an LLB and Bachelor of Economics from Murdoch University and PhD from the University of Western Australia.

Law and Religion

The practice of religion by individuals and groups, the rise of religious diversity, and the fear of religious extremism, raise profound questions for the interaction between law and religion in society. The regulatory systems involved, the religion laws of secular government (national and international) and the religious laws of faith communities, are valuable tools for our understanding of the dynamics of mutual accommodation and the analysis and resolution of issues in such areas as: religious freedom; discrimination; the autonomy of religious organisations; doctrine, worship and religious symbols; the property and finances of religion; religion, education and public institutions; and religion, marriage and children. In this series, scholars at the forefront of law and religion contribute to the debates in this area. The books in the series are analytical with a key target audience of scholars and practitioners, including lawyers, religious leaders, and others with an interest in this rapidly developing discipline.

Series Editor: Professor Norman Doe, Director of the Centre for Law and Religion, Cardiff University, UK

Series Board:
Carmen Asiaín, Professor, University of Montevideo
Paul Babie, Professor and Associate Dean (International), Adelaide Law School
Pieter Coertzen, Chairperson, Unit for the Study of Law and Religion, University of Stellenbosch
Alison Mawhinney, Reader, Bangor University
Michael John Perry, Senior Fellow, Center for the Study of Law and Religion, Emory University

Titles in this series include:

Religious Expression in the Workplace and the Contested Role of Law
Andrew Hambler

Women's Rights and Religious Law
Domestic and International Perspectives
Fareda Banda and Lisa Fishbayn Joffe

State and Religion

The Australian Story

Renae Barker

Routledge
Taylor & Francis Group

LONDON AND NEW YORK

First published 2019
by Routledge
2 Park Square, Milton Park, Abingdon, Oxon OX14 4RN

and by Routledge
711 Third Avenue, New York, NY 10017

Routledge is an imprint of the Taylor & Francis Group, an informa business

© 2019 Renae Barker

British Library Cataloguing-in-Publication Data
A catalogue record for this book is available from the British Library

Library of Congress Cataloging-in-Publication Data
Names: Barker, Renae, author.
Title: State and religion : the Australian story / Renae Barker.
Description: New York, NY : Routledge, 2018. |
   Series: Law and religion | Includes index.
Identifiers: LCCN 2018007392 | ISBN 9781138684539 (hardback)
Subjects: LCSH: Religion and state—Australia. | Religious law and
   legislation—Australia. | Freedom of religion—Australia.
Classification: LCC KU2162 .B37 2018 | DDC 342.9408/52—dc23
LC record available at https://lccn.loc.gov/2018007392

ISBN: 978-1-138-68453-9 (hbk)
ISBN: 978-1-315-54375-8 (ebk)

Typeset in Galliard
by Apex CoVantage, LLC

Thank you to the three boys in my life, Calvin, Elijah and Jethro. Calvin, you have been my rock for so long. Elijah, you have joined us recently and have been the light of our lives. Jethro, you are so new but your little kicks and squirms while I typed reminded me why I wrote this book.

Contents

PART III
Conclusion   323

List of illustrations

Figure

Tables

1 Introduction

Modern Australia is a secular nation, with no State church and a very high level of both religious freedom and diversity. The State and religion are two very separate entities, but this does not mean that they do not interact. In recent years there have been a number of instances where the State has interacted in some way with religion. For example, religious based political parties such as the Christian Democrats[1] have run for, and been successful, in winning seats at both State and federal elections.[2] While not religious themselves many political parties have official policy positions on religious issues such as religion and education. The Greens, for example, include in their National education policy '[a] secular public education system free from religious proselytising and materials that discriminate on the basis of race, sexuality or gender.'[3] There have been a number of high profile court cases such as *Commissioner of Taxation (Cth) v Word Investments Ltd*,[4] *Williams v The Commonwealth*,[5] *Monis v The Queen*[6] and *Attorney General for the State of South Australia v Corporation of the City of Adelaide*[7] which have involved some element of interaction between the State and religion. Growing concern over sexual abuse in the Roman Catholic Church has led to three governmental inquires, including the recently completed Royal Commission into Institutional Responses to Child Sexual Abuse.[8] The issue of freedom of religion has also

---

1 See Christian Democratic Party, *Home Page* <www.cdp.org.au/.> As at January 2018 Rev Hon Fred Nile MLC ED LTh MLC is the only parliamentary representative from the Christian Democratic Party. He sits in the New South Wales upper House.
2 Prior to 2017, the Family First party had members in the National parliament. In 2017 they merged with the Australian Conservative party. While neither were officially religious, both had strong connections with Christianity.
3 The Greens, *Education* <https://greens.org.au/policies/education.>
4 (2008) 236 CLR 204.
5 [2012] HCA 23 (20 June 2012).
6 [2013] HCA 4 (27 February 2013).
7 [2013] HCA 3 (27 February 2013).
8 Royal Commission into Institutional Responses to Child Sexual Abuse, *Home Page* <www.childabuseroyalcommission.gov.au/>; Parliament of Victoria, Committees, *Inquiry into the Handling of Child Abuse by Religious and Other Organisations* <www.parliament.vic.gov.au/fcdc/inquiries/inquiry/340>; Special Commissions of Inquiry, *Special Commission of Inquiry*

loomed large during the same-sex marriage postal survey, subsequent parliamentary debate and passage of the *Marriage Amendment (Definition and Religious Freedoms) Act 2017* (Cth) amending the *Marriage Act 1986* (Cth).

Religion in Australia

Australians have a complex relationship with belief and un-belief.[9] As Australian historians Manning Clarke and John Thornhill have famously characterised it, religion in Australia is a 'whisper in the mind and a shy hope in the heart.'[10] Traditionally 'Australians tended to be suspicious of too-overt religiosity, shying away, for example, from American-style civil religion and avoiding anything resembling "God bless America" political rhetoric.'[11] This may however be changing, with an increasing percentage of the population self-identifying as having no religion. It may be for this reason that traditional religious groups feel 'under threat.' At the same time Australians are increasingly becoming emboldened to wear their religious beliefs, or lack thereof, on their sleeves.

In the 2016 census, 30.1% of the Australian population self-identified as having no religion, up from 22.3% in the 2011 census.[12] Despite some claims that this has now made 'no religion' the largest 'religious' group in Australia,[13] those self-identifying as Christian still make up the largest grouping with 52.1% of the population. While this is a significant drop from the 2011 number of 61.1%, Christians still make up over half of the Australian population. The remainder was made up of those belonging to a minority faith (8.2%) and those who chose not to answer the question (9.6%).[14]

---

into matters relating to the Police investigation of certain child sexual abuse allegations in the Catholic Diocese of Maitland-Newcastle <www.specialcommissions.justice.nsw.gov.au/Pages/sisa/default.aspx.>

9 See Renae Barker, *Religion and the Census: Australia's Unique Relationship to Faith and Unbelief* (5 July 2017) ABC, Religion and Ethics <www.abc.net.au/religion/articles/2017/07/05/4696888.htm>; Renae Barker, *Australians have an increasingly complex, yet relatively peaceful, relationship with religion* (21 December 2016) The Conversation <https://theconversation.com/australians-have-an-increasingly-complex-yet-relatively-peaceful-relationship-with-religion-70328>.

10 See Gary Bouma, *Australian Soul: Religion and Spirituality in the 21st century* (Cambridge University Press, 2006) 2.

11 Marian Maddox, *God under Gillard: Religion and politics in Australia* (10 November 2011) ABC, Religion and Ethics <www.abc.net.au/religion/articles/2011/11/10/3360973.htm.>

12 Australian Bureau of Statistics, *Religion In Australia, 2016* (23 October 2017) <www.abs.gov.au/ausstats/abs@.nsf/Lookup/by%20Subject/2071.0~2016~Main%20Features~Religion%20Article~80>.

13 See, for example, Tosca Lloyd, *The message in the Census: End Australia's Christian bias* (27 June 2011) The Sydney Morning Herald, Comment <www.smh.com.au/comment/the-message-in-the-census-end-australias-christian-bias-20170627-gwzdz5.html.>

14 Australian Bureau of Statistics, above n 12; the religion question is the only optional question on the Australian census. Those who choose not to answer the question may do so for a variety of reasons including religious ones. For a more details discussion of the religious

It is traditional, when reporting Australian census data, to split Christianity into various sub-groups. In 2016, for example, Catholics made up 22.6% of the population while Anglicans accounted for 13.3%. However, other religious groups are rarely sub-divided in this way. Islam (2.6%), for example, could be split into Sunni and Shia. Judaism (0.4%) could be split into Orthodox, Reformed and Conservative. Buddhism (2.4%) could similarly be split into different schools. Given the relatively small number of those self-identifying as belonging to each of these religions, such splitting would produce tiny numbers and would arguably be unhelpful. While there may be some utility in splitting Christianity into sub-groups, care must be taken when using the data which has been split in this way, particularly when making comparisons to those who self-identify as having no religion. The no religion group could also be split into multiple sub groups such as atheists, agnostics and humanists.[15] Those identifying as having no religion are not a homogenous group and may self-identify as having no religion for a range of reasons. As identified by Joseph Baker and Buster Smith, 'the need for subcategories arises out of the fact that claiming no religion is an identity question that essentially determines whether an individual claims to be part of an established religious group.'[16] This is different from positively claiming to be atheist or agnostic. 'Atheists make a definitive claim that God does not exist, while agnostics assert that such knowledge is beyond the realm of human capacity; they do not affirm or deny they exist.'[17]

It is important not to overstate what statistics can tell us about the religiosity of Australians. By its very nature census data about religious belief can only tell us how people self-identify. The census data can tell us nothing about how religious (or irreligious) a person is. Just as saying that 52.1% of the population are Christian does not mean that all of those people attended church last Sunday, nor does stating that 30.1% of the population have no religion mean that none of them will ever have any interaction with religion. Many may have attended religious schools, accepted assistance from a religious charity, had an operation in a hospital run by a religion or received services from a religious service provider.

Finally, it is not uncommon for Australians to have a distorted view of the religious beliefs of their fellow Australians. A 2014 poll conducted by IPSOS Mori revealed that Australian's believed that Muslims accounted for around 20% of the population, nine times reality.[18] In reality those self-identifying as Muslim make

---

question in the Australian census see Tom Frame, *Losing My Religion: Unbelief in Australia* (University of NSW Press, 2009) ch 5.

15 See Glenn M. Vernon, 'The Religious "Nones": A Neglected Category' (1968) 7(2) *Journal for the Scientific Study of Religion* 219.

16 Joseph Baker and Buster Smith, 'None Too Simple: Examining Issues of Religious Nonbelief and Nonbelonging in the United States' (2009) 48(4) *Journal for the Scientific Study of Religion* 719, 720.

17 Ibid. 721.

18 Michael Safi, 'Australians think Muslim population is nine times greater than it really is', *The Guardian* (online), 30 October 2014 <www.theguardian.com/australia-news/datablog/2014/oct/30/australians-think-muslim-population-nine-times-greater>.

up just 2.6% of the population.[19] Contrary to claims made by controversial politician Pauline Hanson, Australia is not in danger of being 'swamped by Muslims.'[20]

Existing literature

Interactions between the State and religion in Australia are not just a modern phenomenon. Examples of this interaction can be found across Australia's history. These interactions have been examined and analysed by a number of authors. However, this examination has tended to be fragmented. Rather than examining the interaction across Australia's history, academic work in this area has focused on specific time periods, events or issues. For example, Marion Maddox's *God Under Howard* focuses on the interaction of the Howard Government with religion.[21] Similarly, the focus of Richard Ely's *Unto God and Caesar* is on the period 1891 to 1906, with a particular focus on religion and Federation.[22] Even John Stradbroke Gregory's *Church and State,* which covers the period 1788 to 1972, is not comprehensive in that the focus is on Victoria since its separation from New South Wales rather than on Australia as a whole.[23] More common are works dealing with specific issues or events such as David Marr's *The High Price of Heaven,*[24] Frank Brennan's *Acting on Conscience,*[25] Don Smart's *Federal Aid to Australian Schools*[26] and Jean Ely's *Contempt of Court.*[27] While some of these works deal with the relationship over a significant period of time most do not, and all are limited to the particular issues or event they are dealing with.

In addition to scholarship which specifically addresses the interaction between the State and religion, there are numerous works which look at the history of Australia generally or at issues, events or religions in Australia specifically. While these works do not deal specifically with the issue of the interaction between the State and religion, they do touch upon this issue, where it is relevant to their more general discussion. Tom Frame's *Losing My Religion* is an example

19 Australian Bureau of Statistics, above n 12.
20 Commonwealth, *Parliamentary Debates,* Senate, 14 September 2016, 937–944 (Pauline Hanson).
21 Marion Maddox, *God Under Howard: The Rise of the Religious Right in Australian Politics* (Allen & Unwin, 2005); John Howard led the Liberal Coalition Government in Australia from 1996 to 2007.
22 Richard Ely, *Unto God and Caesar: Religious Issues in The Emerging Commonwealth 1891–1906* (Melbourne University Press, 1976); Australia Federated on 1 January 1901.
23 John Stradbroke Gregory, *Church and State: Changing Government Policies Towards Religion in Australia, with Particular Reference to Victoria Since Separation* (Cassell Australia, 1973).
24 David Marr, *The High Price of Heaven* (Allen and Unwin, 1999).
25 Frank Brennan, *Acting on Conscience: How Can We Responsibly Mix Law, Religion and Politics* (University of Queensland Press, 2007).
26 Don Smart, *Federal Aid to Australian Schools* (University of Queensland Press, 1978).
27 Jean Ely, *Contempt of Court: Unofficial Voices from the DOGS Australian High Court Case 1981* (Dissenters Press, 2010).

of scholarship of this type. His book focuses on the issues of changing levels of religiosity and religious affiliation in Australia. In doing so he touches upon government policies towards religion and therefore the interaction between the State and religion.[28] There are also numerous works analysing the development of colonial, State and federal education policies such as Alan Barcan's *History of Australian Education*,[29] John Cleverley's *The First Generation*,[30] Albert Austin's *Australian Education 1788–1900*[31] and Douglas Alan Jeck's *Influences in Australian Education*.[32] In analysing education in Australia more generally, these authors touch upon the interaction of the State and religion in relation to education specifically. Works dealing with the history of religion in Australia generally or specific religious denominations also touch upon the interaction between the State and religion as part of their more general discussions. Examples include Ian Breward's *A History of the Australian Churches*,[33] John Barrett's *That Better Country*,[34] Timothy Suttor's *Hierarchy and Democracy in Australia 1788–1870*[35] and Ross Border's *Church and State in Australia 1788–1872* which, despite its tittle, deals specifically with the constitutional development of the Church of England rather than the issue of the wider relationship between the State and religion.[36] This book draws on these works in addition to material which deals specifically with the interaction between the State and religion to fill the gaps left by the fragmented nature of the scholarship in this area.

Even when these areas of scholarship are synthesised, gaps still remain in the overall picture of the interaction of the State and religion across Australia's history. This is particularly evident in relation to both the earliest and the most recent interactions of the State and religion. The relationship between the State and religion is an area of constant change. As highlighted above, there have been a number of recent events which have brought that interaction between the State and religion in Australia to greater public attention. Where possible, these recent events have been included with reference to upcoming reports, government enquires and predicted changes to the law. The law and policy positions outlined in the book are correct as of January 2018.

---

28 Tom Frame, above n 14.
29 Alan Barcan, *A History of Australian Education* (Oxford University Press, 1980).
30 John Cleverley, *The First Generation: School and Society in Early Australia* (Sydney University Press, 1971).
31 Albert Gordon Austin, *Australian Educatio,n 1788–1900: Church, State and Public Education in Colonial Australia* (Pitman, 1961).
32 Douglas Alan Jecks (ed), *Influences in Australian Education* (Carroll's Pty Ltd, 1974).
33 Ian Breward, *A History of the Australian Churches* (Allen and Unwin, 1993).
34 John Barrett, *That Better Country: The Religious Aspects of Life in Eastern Australia, 1835–1850* (Melbourne University Press, 1966).
35 Timothy Lachlan Suttor, *Hierarchy and Democracy in Australia 1788–1870: The Formation of Australian Catholicism* (Melbourne University Press, 1965).
36 Ross Border, *Church and State in Australia, 1788–1872: A Constitutional Study of the Church of England in Australia* (Society for Promoting Christian Knowledge, 1962).

Organised religion vs. individual religious belief

The interaction between the State and religion is often described as being between State and church. This term has not been used in this book. Although most of the interactions between the State and religion considered in this book are interactions between the State and organised religion, this is not the only way in which these two bodies can interact. Some actions of the State will have a greater impact on individual adherents than on organised religion. For example, the legislation restricting the wearing of full-face coverings in public is an inter-action between the State and the individual practice of Muslim women. While a religious organisation may advocate on behalf of these women, the actual legal interaction is not between the State and the religious organisation, but between the State and the individual women. To exclude this type of interaction would be to exclude an important aspect of the interaction between the State and religion, that of the individual adherent. For this reason, the phrase State and Church is inappropriate.

The phrase State and church is also inappropriate because the term 'church' is usually only associated with the Christian religion.[37] While Christianity has been the dominant religion for much of Australia's history, this book is not just about Christianity and the State. With the increasing diversity of Australia's religious community, it is just as accurate to say that there is an interaction between Mosque and State, Temple and State, or Synagogue and State.

Religion and culture

There is a fine line between religion and culture, particularly in relation to religious practice. It is not uncommon for there to be debate around whether a particular practice is religious or cultural. This has particular relevance in relation to arguments relating to freedom of religion. If a practice is cultural rather than religious, then it will not attract the protection of human rights instruments that guarantee freedom of religion. Nor will arguments for the continuation of that practice necessarily have the same moral force. This is not to say that all manifestations of religion should be permitted just because they are religious rather than cultural. As will be discussed in Chapter 2, freedom of religion is not an absolute right. The manifestation of religious beliefs is often subject to limitations in the interests of protecting others or society. Rather, once a practice has been identified as religious, the arguments which can and should be had about whether the State can and should restrict or protect the practice are different if they are religious than if they are considered to be 'purely' cultural.[38]

---

37 See, for example, the definition of 'Church' in Oxford Dictionaries, *Church* (2018) <http://oxforddictionaries.com/definition/english/church?q=Church>.

38 Cultural rights are protected at international law, but tend to be less well recognised than freedom of religion. See Athanasios Yupsanis, 'The Concept and Categories of Cultural

It has occasionally been argued that a belief or practice is only religious if it is held or manifested by all people of that faith. The debate regarding the wearing of full face veils by some Muslim women is an example of the religion vs. culture debate.[39] While some conceptualise the practice as religious, others have argued that it is cultural.[40] Another practice which is often argued to be cultural rather than religious is female genital mutilation (FGM). On its website Human Rights Watch states that FGM 'is erroneously linked to religion' and that the link to religion is flawed. However, they also state that 'some adherents of . . . religions believe the practice is compulsory for followers of the religion.'[41] The difficulty is that for many religions practices within the religion vary wildly. Christianity is notorious for the variety that can be found within that faith alone.[42] Just because orthodox adherents of a particular faith do not engage in a particular practice does not necessarily mean the practice is not a manifestation of a religious belief by another adherent. Nor does the fact that orthodox adherents of a faith manifest their belief in a particular way mean that all people who engage in that behaviour are necessarily doing so for religious reasons.[43] As a result, what is a religious practice for one person may be a cultural practice for another, or even just an expression of personal preference. The celebration of Christmas in Australia is a prime example. For many it is a Christian religious holiday and the various activities associated with it are undertaken for religious reasons. By contrast, for other Australians it is a cultural holiday with the focus on family and friends rather than on religious observance.

When is a law interacting with religion?

It is not always clear on the face of a law that it has any effect on religion. For example, without knowing that Jehovah's Witnesses object to blood transfusions, laws permitting medical practitioners to administer blood transfusions to children without parental consent do not appear to have anything to do with religion. The High Court has interpreted the word 'for' in Section 116 of the *Australian Constitution* to require that a law have the purpose of prohibiting the free exercise of religion before it will infringe that provision. However, when considering

Rights in International Law – Their Broad Sense and the Relevant Clauses of the International Human Rights Treaties' 2009–2010(2) 37 *Syracuse Journal of International law and Commerce* 207.

39 Renae Barker, 'Rebutting the Ban the Burqa Rhetoric: A Critical Analysis of the Arguments for a Ban on the Islamic Face Veil in Australia' (2016) 37(1) *Adelaide Law Review* 191, 197–201.

40 See Samina Yasmeen, 'Australia and the Burqa and Niqab Debate: The Society, the State and Cautious Activism' (2013) 25(3) *Global Change, Peace and Security* 251, 258.

41 Human Rights Watch, *Q&A on Female Genital Mutilation* (16 June 2010) <www.hrw.org/news/2010/06/16/qa-female-genital-mutilation.>

42 *R v Secretary of State for Education and Employment and others ex parte Williamson* [2005] UKHL 15 (24 February 2005) [56].

43 Ibid. [30]–[35].

whether a law interacts with religion the consideration needs to go beyond the purpose of the law. The effect of the law must also be considered. The effect of a law can go far beyond its purpose. Sometimes this effect is acknowledged by law makers, as was the case with blood transfusion laws. This may not always be the case. It is plausible that laws whose purpose does not appear to have any relationship with religion can affect religion in some way. This is becoming more and more likely with the increasingly diverse religious community in Australia.

Beliefs of individual religions

In some cases discussed in this book it is necessary to outline the beliefs of the religion under consideration. For example, in the cases in Chapter 7, this is done to explain how the relevant law restricts the practice or beliefs of a particular religion. In some cases, the religions under consideration are controversial, and their belief systems poorly understood by non-adherents. It is not the purpose of this book to explain in detail the historical background, beliefs or practices of any of the religions under consideration. Nor is it the purpose of this book to give a detailed theological account of any of the beliefs considered. Where the history, beliefs, or practices of the religion are relevant, there is a concise explanation of the relevant belief or practice. However, the author is not an adherent to any of the religious beliefs under examination.[44] While every effort has been taken to correctly represent the beliefs of the various religions considered by this book, some errors may have occurred. Any errors in the description of the various beliefs and practices are inadvertent.

State

In Australia the term 'State' can be used in two distinct contexts. First, it can be used to refer to the six States, formed from the original six colonies that make up the Federation of Australia. Second, the term can be used to refer to the State as a concept made up of the three tiers of government (federal, State and local), and the three branches of government (executive, legislative and judicial). The book will use, where relevant, the term 'State' in both contexts. The use of the term in the phrase the 'State and religion' refers to the second of these contexts. It is the relationship with religion in this broader context that this book seeks to explore.

It must, however, be recognised that what constitutes the 'State' in the broad context has changed since European colonisation. In modern Australia it encompasses the executive, the legislature and the judiciary within a federal structure. The early colonial structure was very different. The State was in effect made up entirely of an executive consisting of the Colonial Governors and their officials, along with the Colonial Secretary in the United Kingdom. Over the course of the nineteenth century this gradually changed to include first a partially, then

---

44 The author is a member of the Anglican Church of Australia.

wholly, elected legislature and a structured judiciary. In 1901 this changed again to include a federal legislature, executive, and judiciary, along with the existing colonial structures. Due to the long-term historical nature of this book, all of these different phases of 'State' are included.

Indigenous spirituality

The book does not deal with changes in the relationship between the State and religion in relation to Australian Indigenous spirituality. Indigenous spirituality and its relationship with the State is a complex issue, owing to the unique place of Indigenous Australians as Australia's First Peoples, the traumas suffered by Indigenous peoples as a result of colonisation,[45] and the interconnectedness of Indigenous spirituality with all aspects of Indigenous life as a result of their holistic world view.[46] Further the issue of Indigenous spirituality cannot be separated from the broader issues of decolonisation and the recognition of Indigenous peoples' rights. As a result, a complete understanding of the interaction between the State and Indigenous spirituality deserves to be dealt with in its own right, and not conflated with other issues arising from the interaction between the State and religion.

Moral and ethical judgments

In the study of the relationship between the State and religion, learned minds may differ on the desirability of many laws and changes in law considered by this book. It is not the purpose of this book to make moral or ethical judgments about the law and changes in law. Readers are invited to draw their own conclusions as to the appropriate level of interaction between the State and religion.

Book structure

The book is divided into two parts. Part I, consisting of Chapters 2 through 5, sets out the theoretical, legal and historical context in which the relationship between the State and religion has developed in Australia. Chapter 2 examines various theoretical models of the relationship between State and religion and places the Australian relationship with in that theoretical frame work. Chapters 3 and 4 examine two potential 'beginnings' for the State–religion relationship: the arrival of the first fleet in 1788 and Federation in 1901. Chapter 3 considers whether or not the Church of England came to Australia as the established church of the new colony and if so when this came to an end. Chapter 4 then

---

45 Many Indigenous people refer to Australia Day, celebrated on the day the First Fleet arrived in Australia (26 January), as Invasion Day.

46 See Ambelin Kwaymullina and Blaze Kwaymullina, 'Learning to Read the Signs: Law in an Indigenous Reality' (2010) 34(2) *Journal of Australian Studies* 195.

examines the history, impact and interpretation of Section 116 of the *Australian Constitution*, the so-called 'freedom of religion' clause, which came into effect on 1 January 1901. Finally, Chapter 5 sets the modern Australian relationship between the State and religion within the wider international context with a particular focus on the impact the lack of a Bill or Charter of rights has had on that relationship in Australia, when compared to other jurisdictions with a similar legal and religious heritage.

Part II of the book looks specifically at the State and religion relationship in Australia. Chapter 6 examines three contemporary issues: terrorism, same-sex marriage and the Royal Commission into Institutional Responses to Child Sexual Abuse. The remaining chapters, 7 through 9, each examine one area of the relationship between the State and religion tracing that relationship from the early Australian colony through to modern day Australia. Chapter 7 looks at restrictions on religions, Chapter 8 on religion and education and Chapter 9 examines State funding of religion. These chapters are intended to give historical context to the Australian State–religion relationship and in particular highlight how that relationship has changed and evolved over Australia's 200 plus-year history.

The book concludes with a final section which draws together some of lessons to be learned from where the Australian relationship between the State and religion has been and where it may be going.

Part I
Theory and context

2 Theories of State–religion relationships

Introduction

What is religion? What does it mean for a State to be secular? How should we classify the relationship between the State and religion in Australia, both today and in the past? These are fundamental questions in understanding the relationship between the State and religion, not only in Australia but in any State. In Australia, the concept of a secular nation is often contrasted with that of a Christian/religious nation – suggesting that Australia must be either one or the other.[1] As outlined in the first chapter, in the most recent census 60.3% of the population self-identified as having a religion with 52.1% self-identifying as Christian.[2] At the same time the number of people self-identifying as having no-religion is on the rise.[3] Section 116 of the *Australian Constitution* prohibits the federal government from establishing a State church, yet the federal government provides significant financial assistance to religious schools and tax exemptions to religious organisations. Australia has a complex and unique relationship with belief and unbelief.[4]

The answer to the question of whether Australia is a secular or Christian/religious nation is not just a theoretical one. It has real currency in the context of ongoing debates in Australian society. Issues such as assisted dying, LGBTIQ+

1 Tom Frame, *Losing My Religion Unbelief in Australia* (University of New South Wales Press, 2009), 281–283.
2 *Religion in Australia – 2016 Census Data Summary* (28 June 2017) Australian Bureau of Statistics <www.abs.gov.au/ausstats/abs@.nsf/Lookup/by%20Subject/2071.0~2016~Main%20Features~Religion%20Data%20Summary~70>.
3 *2016 Census data reveals "no religion" is rising fast* (27 June 2017) Australian Bureau of Statistics <www.abs.gov.au/AUSSTATS/abs@.nsf/mediareleasesbyReleaseDate/7E65A144540 551D7CA258148000E2B85?OpenDocument>.
4 Renae Barker, *Religion and the Census: Australia's Unique Relationship to Faith and Unbelief* (5 July 2017) Australian Broadcasting Corporation www.abc.net.au/religion/articles/2017/07/05/4696888.htm; Renae Barker, *Australians have an increasingly complex, yet relatively peaceful, relationship with religion* (21 December 2016) The Conversation<https://theconversation.com/australians-have-an-increasingly-complex-yet-relatively-peaceful-relationship-with-religion-70328>.

rights, terrorism laws, how to deal with historical instances of child sexual abuse by religious organisations, along with many others, all invite a critique of the relationship between the Australian State and religion. How you see that relationship, both in terms of what it should be and what it is, can influences the terms with which you engage with these debates. It frames not only your response but also how you respond to those who take a different view.

In order to be able to understand if Australia is a secular or Christian/religious nation, or perhaps both, it is necessary to understand the theory which underlies such an enquiry.

However, the majority of this book focuses on practical examples of the interaction between the State and religion in the Australian context. It is at this micro level of individual laws and their impact on individuals and religious organisations that the State and religion interact on a daily basis. However, that interaction needs to be understood in the wider macro and theoretical context of State–religion relationships. Therefore, before examining specific laws, changes in those laws and the consequences of those changes for the relationship of the State and religion in Australia, it is important to examine the underlying theory in order to set the laws and policies considered in later chapter in their proper context.

This chapter begins by examining the meaning of the term 'religion' in the legal context – an important first step in understanding the State–religion relationship. It then goes on to examine different models of State–religion relationship, including a discussion of secularism, before applying these models to Australia. Finally, the chapter examines the important issue of freedom of religion, its foundations in Australia and the limits that the law may place on that freedom.

What is a 'religion'?

The term religion is notoriously difficult to define.[5] As Latham CJ put it in *Adelaide Company of Jehovah's Witnesses Inc v Commonwealth*,[6] 'it would be difficult, if not impossible, to devise a definition of religion which would satisfy the adherents of all the many and various religions which exist, or have existed in the world.'[7] However this has not prevented judges, politicians, theologians, philosophers, anthropologists, sociologists, psychologists and a myriad of other disciplines from attempting to do so. Inevitably the definitions arrived at vary from discipline to discipline and from context to context.[8] What is a useful definition

---

5 W. Cole Durham and Elizabeth A Sewell, 'Definition of Religion' in James A Serritella (ed), *Religious Organizations in the United States: A Study of Identity, Liberty, and the Law* (Carolina Academic Press, 2006) 3, 3–7; Russell Sandberg, *Religion, Law and Society* (Cambridge University Press, 2014), 30–38; Rex Ahdar and Ian Leigh, *Religious Freedom in the Liberal State* (Oxford University Press, 2nd ed, 2013) 139–140.

6 (1943) 67 CLR 116.

7 Ibid. 123.

8 Robert Crawford, *What is Religion?* (Routledge, 2003) 3; Ian Ellis-Jones, *Beyond the Scientology Case* (PhD Thesis, University of Technology Sydney, 2007) ch 1.

in one context will not work for other purposes.[9] Richard Dawkins' definition of religion as a virus is virtually useless to a judge trying to determine whether a particular set of beliefs are covered by Section 116 of the *Australian Constitution.* On the other hand, it makes Dawkins' point very succinctly.[10] This is not to say that interdisciplinary approaches should not be adopted, but that the purpose for which the definition is to be used must be taken into account in constructing it.[11]

In attempting to identify changes in the relationship between the State and religion, defining religion is vital. Without a working definition there are no outer boundaries which help to delineate when the State is interacting with religion and when it is interacting with some other worldview. If the definition is too wide it may be possible to find 'great reservoirs of religious sentiment in an apparently secular society'[12] and therefore overestimate the amount of interaction between the State and religion. On the other hand, a definition that is too narrow risks missing many of the interactions that take place been the State and new, novel and unpopular religions.[13]

The way in which the State defines religion is itself an important interaction between the State and religion. The State's definition of religion has the power to exclude and include; to make legitimate or illegitimate religions which falls inside or outside its definition.[14] If the State defines religion narrowly then it may exclude belief systems that are generally accepted as religious. The State may even deliberately seek to define religion narrowly with this very purpose in mind. The treatment of witchcraft[15] and the Church of Scientology in Australia are particularly poignant examples of the State attempting to define religion in such a way as to exclude belief systems from the category of religion.

In 2000, during the debate to repeal the laws banning the practice of Witchcraft in Queensland, the Deputy Leader of the Opposition, Lawrence Springborg, commented that:

> The abolition of the provision also arguably suggests that the occult, witchcraft and so on are acceptable social practices, perhaps on a par with religions.

---

9 W. Cole Durham Jr and Brett G. Scharffs, *Law and Religion: National, International and Comparative Perspectives* (Wolters Kluwer, 2010), 44.

10 Richard Dawkins, 'Viruses of the Mind' in Bo Dahlbom (ed), *Dennett and his Critics* (Blackwell, 1993) 13.

11 See Sandberg, above n 5, 28–52.

12 Steve Bruce, *God is Dead: Secularization in the West* (Blackwell, 2002), 199.

13 Sandberg, above n 5, 29.

14 Ibid. 38–39; Renae Barker, 'Scientology the Test Case Religion' (2015) 40(4) *Alternative Law Journal* 275, 278–279.

15 For a discussion of witchcraft in Australia see Lynne Hume, *Witchcraft and Paganism in Australia* (Melbourne University Press, 1997); Lynne Hume, 'Exporting Nature Religions: Problems in Praxis Down Under' (1999) 2(2) *Nova Religio: The Journal of Alternative and Emergent Religions* 287; Lynne Hume, 'Witchcraft and the Law in Australia' (1995) 37 *Journal of Church and State* 135; Human Rights and Equal Opportunities Commission, *Article 18 Freedom of Religion and Belief* (Commonwealth of Australia, 1998), 60–64.

I do not believe that the majority of organised religions, let alone the general community, would accept that they are to be regarded as on par with witchcraft, but that is a consequence of such an approach.[16]

Earlier, in 1973, Commonwealth Senator Edgar Prowse expressed concern that the recognition of Scientologists under the *Marriage Act 1961* (Cth) may lead to witchcraft also being recognised as a religion.[17]

The Church of Scientology has also been subject to attempts to define it out of the category of 'religion.' As will be discussed in more detail in Chapter 7, in the 1960s the Victorian Government initiated an inquiry into the Church of Scientology, known as the Anderson Report. The report found, *inter alia*, that Scientology was not a religion. Based on this report Victoria, Western Australia and South Australia attempted to ban the practice of Scientology. In Victoria the States continued insistence that Scientology was not a religion eventually led to the famous High Court case *Church of the New Faith v Commissioner of Pay Roll Tax (Vic)*[18] (the *Scientology Case*) which is the basis of the legal definition of religion in Australia.

Approaches to defining religion

As identified above, context is important in determining the appropriate definition of religion. The purpose of this book is to examine legal interactions between the State and religion. Therefore, the most appropriate definition in this context is a legal one. However, caution must be exercised in using the State's own definition. As the Courts form part of the State this must be kept in mind in what follows. In order to minimise problems associated with using the State's definition, multiple definitions from multiple jurisdictions are considered.

The Courts have adopted three types of definitions of religion: functional, substantive and analogical.[19] Given the fame of the *Scientology Case*, it is tempting to believe that the legal definition of religion has been settled in Australia; however, the case has been criticised for failing to deliver a unified definition of religion.[20] An example of each of the three types of definitions can be found in the case. This has not stopped State entities such as the Australian Tax Office (ATO) and Australian Bureau statistics (ABS) from relying on the case.[21]

---

16 Queensland, *Parliamentary Debates*, Legislative Assembly, 10 November 2000, 4323 (Lawrence Springborg).
17 Commonwealth of Australia, *Parliamentary Debates*, Senate, 13 March 1973, 351 (Edgar Prowse).
18 *Church of the New Faith v Commissioner of Pay Roll Tax (Vic)* (1983) 154 CLR 120.
19 Durham and Scharffs, above n 9, 40; see also Durham and Sewell, above n 5, 3; Ahdar and Leigh, above n 5, 145.
20 Ellis-Jones, above n 8, ch 3.
21 See *Part 10: Religious Institutions and Services* (18 November 2013) Australian Taxation Office <www.ato.gov.au/Business/GST/In-detail/GST-issues-registers/Charities-consultative-

Functional definitions

Functional definitions define religion from the viewpoint of an individual adherent, focusing on the role religion plays in the adherent's life.[22] The most well-known legal definitions which adopt a functionalist approach are found in the United Sates conscientious objector/free exercise cases.[23] In *United States v Seeger*[24] the United States Supreme Court found that in determining whether a given belief was religious the Court needed to determine:

> whether a given belief that is sincere and meaningful occupies a place in the life of its possessor parallel to that fulfilled by the orthodox belief in God of one who clearly qualifies for the exemption.[25]

Justice Murphy's definition of religion in the *Scientology Case* is a functional definition. Justice Murphy determined that:

> any body which claims to be religious, whose beliefs or practices are a revival of, or resemble earlier cults, is religious. Any body which claims to be religious and to believe in a supernatural Being or Beings, whether physical and visible . . . or a physical invisible God or spirit, or an abstract God or entity is religious.. . . Any body which claims to be religious, and offers a way to find meaning and purpose in life, is religious.[26]

Functionalist definitions have been criticised as too wide. They have the potential to include a multitude of secular, political and social belief systems which occupy a similar place to religion, but which ultimately most people would not consider to be religious in the ordinary sense of the word.[27] In *Welsh v United States*[28] the Court found that purely ethical and moral beliefs, which Welsh himself did not consider religious, qualified as a religion.[29] The main difficulty with functional definitions is that they include belief systems that are 'parallel' to 'orthodox belief systems' and as Dillon J pointed out in *Barralet v Attorney General* 'parallels, by definition, never meet.'[30]

committee-resolved-issues-document/?page=32>; *Australian Standard Classification of Religious groups, 2011: About the Classification* (28 July 2011) Australian Bureau of Statistics <www.abs.gov.au/ausstats/abs@.nsf/Lookup/1266.0main+features102011>.

22 Durham and Scharffs, above n 9, 46; Ahdar and Leigh, above n 5, 145–146.

23 *United States v Seeger*, 330 US 163 (1965); *Welsh v United States*, 398 US 33 (1970).

24 330 US 163 (1965).

25 Ibid. 165–166.

26 Ibid.

27 Durham and Scharffs, above n 9, 24; Ahdar and Leigh, above n 5, 146–148.

28 398 US 33 (1970).

29 See Frank S Ravitch, *Law and Religion, a Reader: Cases, Concepts, and Theory* (Thomson West, 2nd ed, 2004) 581.

30 *Barralet v Attorney General* [1980] 3 All ER 918, 924 (Dillon J).

One context where a wide definition may be helpful is in relation to freedom of religion provisions. Not only would a wide definition be more likely to include new, novel and unpopular religions, it is most likely to cover those belief systems and individuals which espouse or desire freedom from religion. However, such a wide definition may not be strictly necessary, even in this context. International freedom of religion provisions such as Article 18 of the Universal Declaration of Human Rights covers 'freedom of thought, conscience and religion.' [31] Even where this is not the case freedom of religion provisions can be interpreted widely enough to encompass the freedom not to have a religion. For example, in Australia Latham JC commented that:

> The prohibition in s. 116 operates not only to protect the freedom of religion, but also to protect the right of a man to have no religion. . ... Section 116 proclaims not only the principle of toleration of all religions, but also the principle of toleration of absence of religion.[32]

Substantive definitions

Substantive definitions, also called essentialist definitions, attempt to identify the essence or core concepts of religion.[33] Legal definitions which have taken this approach have tended to include a requirement that there be a belief in a Supreme Being or God. This has been the traditional approach in the United Kingdom. In *Barralet v Attorney General* Dillon J concluded that:

> Religion . . . is concerned with man's relations with God, and ethics are concerned with man's relations with man.. . . It seems to me that two of the essential attributes of religion are faith and worship; faith in a god and worship of that god.[34]

Similarly in *R v Register General; ex parte Segerdal* Lord Denning MR found that '[r]eligious worship means reverence or veneration of God or of a Supreme Being.'[35]

Courts in the United States have also deployed substantive definitions in the past. For example, in *Davis v Beason* the Unites States Supreme Court held that:

> The term religion has reference to one's views of his relations to his creator, and to the obligations they impose of reverence for his being and character, and of obedience to his will.[36]

---

31 *Universal Declaration of Human Rights*, GA Res 217A (II) UN GAOR, 3rd sess, 183rd plen mtg, UN Doc A/810 (10 December 1948) art 18.
32 *Adelaide Company of Jehovah's Witnesses Incorporated v The Commonwealth* (1943) 67 CLR 116, 123 (Latham CJ).
33 Durham and Scharffs, above n 9, 45; Ahdar and Leigh, above n 5, 148.
34 *Barralet v Attorney General* [1980] 3 All ER 918, 924 (Dillon J).
35 *R v Register General; ex parte Segerdal* [1970] 2 QB 697, 707 (Denning MR).
36 *Davis v Beason*, 133 US 333, 341–342 (Field J) (1890).

In *United States v MacIntosh* Hughes CJ and Holmes J found that '[t]he essence of religion is belief in a relation to God involving duties superior to these arising from human relations.'[37]

If functionalist definitions are too wide, then substantive definitions are too narrow. In focusing on the need for belief in God they effectively exclude non-theistic religions such as non-theistic Buddhism. Substantive definitions are also criticised for attempting to find a single essence or core idea which is common to all religions. Critics argue that the attempt is misconceived as no such single characteristic exists.[38]

More recently substantive definitions have moved away from an emphasis on belief in God. They focus instead on the supernatural. The definition proposed by Mason ACJ and Brennan J in the *Scientology Case* is a substantive definition which has replaced God with the supernatural. They determined that:

> for the purpose of the law, the criteria of religion are twofold, belief in a supernatural Being, Thing or Principle; and second, the acceptance of canons of conduct in order to give effect to that belief, although canons of conduct which offend against the ordinary laws are outside the area of any immunity, privilege or right conferred on the grounds of religion.[39]

In including supernatural things and principles, Mason ACJ and Brennan J have expanded the traditional substantive definition beyond theistic religions.

In 2004 the Supreme Court of Canada adopted a similar approach. In *Syndicate Northcrest v Anselem* the Court held that:

> Defined broadly, religion typically involves a particular and comprehensive system of faith and worship. Religion also tends to involve the belief in a divine, superhuman or controlling power. In essence, religion is about freely and deeply held personal convictions or beliefs connected to an individual's spiritual faith and integrally linked to one's self-definition and spiritual fulfilment, the practices of which allow individuals to foster a connection with the divine or with the subject or object of that spiritual faith.[40]

While employing slightly different language, referring to divine, superhuman and controlling power rather than supernatural, the focus is still on the essence of religion. What it is, in this case, is the non-natural.

More recently the Supreme Court in the United Kingdom explicitly rejected the use of the term supernatural 'because it is a loaded word which can carry

---

37 *United States v MacIntosh*, 283 US 605, 633–644 (Holmes J and Hughes CJ) (1931).
38 Durham and Scharffs, above n 9, 45.
39 *Church of the New Faith v Commissioner of Pay-roll Tax (Vic)* (1983) 154 CLR 120, 136 (Mason ACJ and Brennan J).
40 *Syndicate Northcrest v Anselem* [2004] 2 SCR 551, 576 [39] (Iacobucci J).

a variety of connotations.'[41] Instead Lord Toulson, with whom the rest of the Court agreed, determined that:

> I would describe religion in summary as a spiritual or non-secular belief system held by a group of adherents, which claims to explain mankind's place in the universe and relationship with the infinite, and to teach its adherents how they are to live their lives in conformity with the spiritual understanding associated with the belief system.[42]

Analogical definitions

A third option is analytical definitions, sometimes called the family resemblance approach, which attempts to define religion by identifying a list of criterion that are common to many religions. Rather than insisting that there is an essential core that all religions share, the analytical approach accepts that not all religions will exhibit all of the characteristics, but the presence of one or more is a strong indication that the belief system under consideration is in fact a religion.[43]

The most famous example of a legal definition based on analogy is that articulated by Adams J in *Malnak v Yogi*[44] and *Africa v Commonwealth of Pennsylvania*.[45] Justice Adams identified three indicia that could be used in determining if a particular set of beliefs constitutes a religion:

> First, a religion addresses fundamental and ultimate questions having to do with deep and imponderable matters. Second, a religion is comprehensive in nature; it consists of a belief-system as opposed to an isolated teaching. Third, a religion often can be recognised by the presence of certain formal and external signs . . . that may be analogized to accepted religions. Such signs might include formal services, ceremonial functions, the existence of clergy, structure and organisation, efforts at propagation, observance of holidays and other similar manifestations associated with traditional religions.[46]

However, he emphasised that '[a]lthough these indicia will be helpful, they should not be thought of as a final test for religion.'[47]

---

41 *R v Registrar General of Births, Deaths and Marriages* [2013] UKSC 77, [57] (Lord Toulson).
42 Ibid.
43 Durham and Scharffs, above n 9, 47.
44 592 F 2d 197 (3rd Cir, 1979); for a discussion of *Malnak v Yogi* see Sarah Barringer, 'The New Age and the New Law' in Leslie Griffin (ed), *Law and Religion: Cases in Context* (Aspen Publishers, 2010) 11.
45 *Africa v Commonwealth*, 662 F 2d 1025 (3rd Cir, 1981).
46 Ibid. 1035 (Adams J).
47 *Malnak v Yogi*, 592 F 2d 197, 210 (3rd Cir, 1979).

In the *Scientology Case* Wilson and Dean JJ adopted an analytical approach, identifying five indicia 'derived by empirical observation of accepted religions':[48]

> One of the most important indicia of a religion is that the particular collection of ideas and/or practices involves belief in the supernatural, that is to say, belief that reality extends beyond that which is capable of perception by the senses. . . .. Another is that the ideas relate to man's nature and place in the universe and his relation to things supernatural. A third is that the ideas are accepted by adherents as requiring or encouraging them to observe particular standards or codes of conduct or to participate in specific practices having supernatural significance. A fourth is that, however loosely knit and varying in beliefs and practices adherents may be, they constitute an identifiable group or identifiable groups. A fifth, and perhaps more controversial, indicium . . . is that the adherents themselves see the collection of ideas and/or practices as constituting a religion.[49]

They considered that

> [n]o one of the above indicia is necessarily determinative of the question whether a particular collection of ideas and/or practices should be objectively characterised as 'a religion'. They are no more than aids in determining that question and the assistance derived from them will vary according to the context in which the question arises.[50]

This approach was approved of by Lord Toulson in *R v Registrar General of Births, Deaths and Marriages*[51] although ultimately the definition he adopted had more in common with substantive approaches than analogical ones.

Models of State–religion relationships

Once religion has been defined the next challenge is to define how the religions that exist within a State interact with that State. Numerous typologies have been presented which attempt to classify the various current and historic State–religion relationships. Inevitably the form they take and the way in which they classify the various forms of State–religion relationships depend upon the purpose for which the typology is derived. For example, the typology presented by Carl Esbeck in *A Typology of Church-State Relations in Current American Thought*[52] is inevitably

48 *Church of the New Faith v Commissioner of Pay-roll Tax (Vic)* (1983) 154 CLR 120, 174 (Wilson and Deane JJ).
49 Ibid. 174.
50 Ibid.
51 *R v Registrar General of Births, Deaths and Marriages* [2013] UKSC 77, [57] (Lord Toulson).
52 Carl Esbeck, 'A Typology of Church-State Relations in Current American Thought' (1988) 15 (1) *Religion & Public Education* 3.

narrower than many others in that it focuses primarily on State–religion relationships which either exist or are argued for in the United States of America. Darryn Jensen presents just two categories, monism and pluralism.[53] His argument is that it is a mistake to assume that secularization 'is a necessary concomitant of political modernization'[54] and that it is similarly a mistake 'to regard religiosity and secularity as opposite poles.'[55] A common purpose behind typologies presented in the literature is to evaluate which model of State–religion relationship has the greatest potential to promote freedom of religion.[56]

It is not the purpose of this chapter to present a new typology of State–religion interactions. Instead this chapter synthesis existing typologies, drawing primarily from those presented by Rex Ahdar and Ian Leigh in *Religious Freedom in the Liberal State*,[57] W. Cole Durham and Brett G. Scharffs in *Law and Religion; National, International, and Comparative Perspectives*[58] and Jerone Tempermann in *State–religion Relationships and Human Rights Law*[59] with reference to others where appropriate.

This chapter also does not suggest which of the models of State–religion relationship is to be preferred. Which model of State–religion relationships is most suitable for any particular time or place is in large part dependent on a myriad of factors including, but not limited to, the historical development of the interaction in that State, the political system in place in a particular State, whether there is a dominant religious group or groups and the particular beliefs of that group or groups. Further as Ahdar and Leigh explained '[c]riticism or defence of a particular model will reflect one's largely unarticulated premises concerning the purpose of the Church . . . the role of the state, and so on.'[60] It is also important to note that it is not possible to select a model of State–religion relationship which is ever truly 'neutral.' As Carl Esbeck puts, 'there is no truly neutral position concerning these matters, for all models of church/state relations embody substantive choice.'[61] Further, as Darryn Jensen explains,

---

53 Darryn Jensen, 'Classifying Church-state Arrangements' in Nadirsyah Hosen and Richard Mohr (eds) *Law and Religion in Public Life: The Contemporary Debate* (Routledge, 4th ed, 2011) 15.

54 Ibid. 16.

55 Ibid. 17.

56 See Durham and Scharffs, above n 9, 113–122; W. Cole Durham Jr, 'Perspectives on Religious Liberty: A Comparative Framework' in Johan D. van der Vyver and John Witte Jr (eds), *Religious Human Rights in Global Perspective: Legal Perspectives* (Martinus Nijhoff Publishers, 1st ed, 1996) 1; Jeroen Temperman, *State–religion Relationships and Human Rights Law: Towards a Right to Religiously Neutral Governance* (Brill, 2010).

57 Ahdar and Leigh, above n 5, ch 4.

58 Durham and Scharffs, above n 9, 113–122; Durham and Scharffs' model draws heavily on that presented in Durham, above n 56, 1; Ahdar and Leigh, above n 5.

59 Jeroen Temperman, *State–religion Relationships and Human Rights Law: Towards a Right to Religiously Neutral Governance* (Brill, 2010).

60 Ahdar and Leigh, above n 5, 87.

61 Carl H Esbeck, 'A Constitutional Case for Governmental Cooperation with Faith-based Social Service Providers' (1997) 46(1) *Emory Law Journal* 1, 5.

[t]he existence of political community is predicated upon the widespread acceptance of political values which determine where the line is to be drawn between matters of public concern and matters of private concern and how disagreements about matters of public concern are to be resolved. The most liberal of states is not a neutral state but a minimally committed state.[62]

Somewhat confusingly, one of the models presented below is most commonly referred to as the 'neutrality' model. This is the model which has largely been endorsed by the European Court of Human Rights.[63] However this model is not neutral in the sense of being free from value judgments about religion and its place in society rather it is neutral in the sense that the State attempts to be neutral as between different faiths.

It is important to note that the models of State and religion interaction presented in this chapter should be seen as part of a continuum.[64] Any particular State at any particular point in time may be in transition from one to another. Many of the models are related to one another. A State may have attributes of two or even more of the models considered.[65] As will be discussed in more detail below, this is true for Australia. In modern Australia there are examples of laws that point to the relationship between the State and religion having attributes of structural separation, formal neutrality and pragmatic pluralism.

Theocracy, erastianism and religious establishment

At one end of the spectrum are models in which the State and religion have a very high level of positive interaction. In theocracies and erastianism the State and religion are in effect fused while in States with established religions the State singles out a particular religion or sect for special treatment and support.[66]

In a theocracy, religion is supreme and the purpose of the State is to support and further the religion. Often there is no separation between civic and religious rulers and, where there are, the civic leaders are subject to religious rulers.[67] Modern examples include Iran and Afghanistan under the Taliban.[68] The erastianism[69] model is the flip side of a theocracy. Rather than the State supporting and furthering religion, in the erastianism model religion supports and furthers the State. Ahdar and Leigh give the example of modern China where the State

---

62 Jensen, above n 53, 15, 19.
63 Ahdar and Leigh, above n 5, 113.
64 Ahdar and Leigh, above n 5, 88–89.
65 Durham and Scharffs, above n 9, 113.
66 Ahdar and Leigh, above n 5, 90–91, 100–109.
67 Ahdar and Leigh, above n 5, 90; Durham and Scharffs, above n 9, 18; Temperman, above n 59, 12–13.
68 Ahdar and Leigh, above n 5, 90.
69 Also called Caesaropapism.

defines official religious groups and these religious groups are obliged to carry out policies of the government.[70]

In States with an established religion or church the State identifies one religion, sect or denomination (or sometimes a small number) for formal recognition and support.[71] Durham and Scharrffs separate out different models of State and religion interaction in this portion of the spectrum into Established Church, Religious Status Systems, Historically favoured and endorsed Church and Preferred set of Religions.[72] Temperman divides this portion of the spectrum into four categories State religions[73] and State churches,[74] State support[75] and State acknowledgment.[76]

However, the exact term given is largely irrelevant, what all of these models have in common is a relatively high level of positive interaction between the State and a specific religion or sect.[77] This is usually accompanied with some form of official recognition of the religions status, be that as an official State religion or church or as the religion of the majority of the population or as a church with historical importance for the relevant State.

Pluralism and neutrality models

In the middle of the spectrum are models of State–religion interaction which are less than establishment but in which the State and religion are not entirely separate. Some of these models would fit the definition of 'secular' depending on how that term is defined. Others would fall far short of this description. Ahdar and Leigh identify three types of models which fall into this spectrum of the continuum: pluralist models, neutrality models and the competitive market model.[78] Temperman identifies accommodation of religion, both specified and unspecified[79] and Non-Identification[80] in this part of the spectrum. What these models have in common is a cooperation, interaction or accommodation of religion, without treating any one religion or church in a preferential way.[81]

In a pluralist model, the State 'attempts an even-handed co-operation with all religions and worldviews held by individuals and groups in society.'[82] Therefore,

---

70 Ahdar and Leigh, above n 5, 91.
71 Ibid.
72 Durham and Scharffs, above n 9, 118–119.
73 Temperman, above n 59, 32–33.
74 Ibid. 44.
75 Ibid. 66–67.
76 Ibid. 72–73.
77 See also Stephen V. Monsma and J. Christopher Soper, *The Challenge of Pluralism: Church and State in Five Democracies* (Rowman & Littlefield Publishing Group, 1st ed, 1997), 11.
78 Ahdar and Leigh, above n 5, 109–122.
79 Temperman, above n 59, 94.
80 Ibid. 103.
81 Ibid. 93.
82 Ahdar and Leigh, above n 5, 109.

unlike separationist models, discussed below, religion is not seen as something that must be relegated to the private sphere. Instead the State supports religion, in all its forms, in the public sphere.[83] Pluralism most closely aligns with Temperman's unspecified accommodation which involves State support for all religions. By contrast, specific accommodation singles out specific religions for State support.[84] As a result specified accommodation is more closely aligned to plural establishment.[85]

Ahdar and Leigh split pluralism into two forms: principled and pragmatic. The primary difference is the reason the State adopts pluralism. In the case of principled pluralism, the State adopts pluralism as a deliberate choice, as a principle to be upheld and promoted.[86] Monsma and Soper argue that the Netherlands is an example of this kind of pluralism.[87] Pragmatic pluralism on the other hand is adopted as a pragmatic response to a plural society in which a number of religions already exist.[88]

Neutrality[89] models also have elements of State–religion interaction somewhere between establishment and separation. The European Court of Human Rights currently endorses this approach.[90] In *Refah Partisi (The Welfare Party) v Turkey* the Court emphasised that:

> [t]he Court has frequently emphasised the State's role as the neutral and impartial organiser of the exercise of various religions, faiths and beliefs, and stated that this role is conducive to public order, religious harmony and tolerance in a democratic society. It also considers that the State's duty of neutrality and impartiality is incompatible with any power on the State's part to assess the legitimacy of religious beliefs . . . and that it requires the State to ensure mutual tolerance between opposing groups.[91]

In neutrality models the State attempts to take a neutral stance towards religion, treating all equally, favouring none. While pluralism models also support secular worldviews, their inclusion is more explicit in neutrality models. As long as secular worldviews are in some way 'like' religion, such as atheism and humanism, then the State should be neutral as between these worldviews and religion

---

83 Stephen Monsma and J. Christopher Soper, *The Challenge of Pluralism: Church and State in Five Democracies* (Rowman & Littlefield Publishing Group, 2nd ed, 2009), 11–12.

84 Temperman, above n 59, 94.

85 For a discussion of Plural Establishment see Renae Barker, 'Under Most Peculiar Circumstances: The Church Acts in the Australian Colonies as a Study of Plural Establishment' (2016) 3(3) *Law & History* 28.

86 Ibid. 85–87.

87 Monsma and Soper, above n 83, ch 3.

88 Ahdar and Leigh, above n 5, 111–112.

89 Note as discussed above 'neutrality' here does not donate that there are no value judgments inherent in the decision by the State to adopt this kind of interaction with religion.

90 Ahdar and Leigh, above n 5, 113.

91 *Refah Partisi (The Welfare Party) v Turkey* (2003) 37 EHRR [91].

as much as between different religious worldviews.[92] Temperman's Non-identification model could also be described as a 'neutrality model.' In his typology non-identification occurs where 'a state does not establish or support one specific religion (or accommodate various religions simultaneously in a manner as outlined above), yet neither does it position itself as a clear-cut secular or separationist state.'[93]

Ahdar and Leigh again identify two types of neutrality models; formal and substantive neutrality. Formal neutrality requires the State to be 'religion blind.' In effect religion is an irrelevant consideration in any decision by the State. As long as the purpose of a particular law is not to restrict religion then it is permissible, even if the effect is to restrict religion. Substantive neutrality requires the State to actively engage in a policy of neutral treatment for all religions. The aim is not to make adherence to any one religion more difficult as a result of State action.[94]

The final model, identified by Ahdar and Leigh, which falls into the middle of the spectrum, is the competitive market model. It is similar to both substantive neutrality and the pluralist models but focuses on religion being a matter of private choice. In this model, the State encourages a free market place of religions in which individuals can choose which religious belief or non-belief is 'best.' Like a more traditional market the absence of monopolies allows a variety of forms of religion to flourish with a consequently high level of religiosity. Ahdar and Leigh identify the United States of America as a State with this model.[95]

Separation of church and State

At the other end of the spectrum from theocracies, erastianism and established religion models are separationist models.[96] In these models religion and the State are separate and inhabit separate spheres, usually conceptualised as private and public respectively. These models are often described as secular.[97] Temperman for example argues that 'maintaining a secular status necessitates a significant degree of separation; whilst upholding the separation between the State and religion presupposes a fairly secularist government.'[98] However as will be discussed below pluralism and neutrality models may also be described as secular depending on the definition of secular you adopt.[99]

---

92 Ahdar and Leigh, above n 5, 113–115.
93 Temperman, above n 59, 103.
94 Ahdar and Leigh, above n 5, 115–119.
95 Ibid. 119–122; for a discussion of this model see also Jianlin Chen, 'Money and Power in Religious Competition: A Critique of the Religious Free Market' (2014) 3(2) *Oxford Journal of Law and Religion* 212.
96 Ahdar and Leigh, above n 5, 92–94; Temperman, above n 59, 121–124
97 See, eg, Temperman, above n 59, 111–113.
98 Temperman, above n 59, 111.
99 See for example Charles Taylor's three forms of secularism; Charles Taylor, *A Secular Age* (Belknap Press of Harvard University Press, 2007), 2–3; see also Tom Frame, *Losing My Religion Unbelief in Australia* (University of New South Wales Press, 2009), 281–283.

While Temperman separates out separation of church and State and separation of religion and State, in practice this amounts to much the same thing.[100] Ahdar and Leigh, however, split separationist models into two substantively different concepts; structural and transvaluing separation. Structural separation requires that the institutions of the State and religion be formally separate.[101] Formal separation can be based on a desire to protect the State from undue interference by religion or conversely to protect religion from corruption by the State.[102] As a result separationist models of this kind can be established on both secular and religious principles. Ahdar and Leigh identify France's policy of *Laïcité* as an example of this kind of separation.[103]

Transvaluing separation requires the State to actively seek to remove all religious influences from the public sphere. Public life is seen as a religion free zone. While this model is not necessarily hostile to religion, it is also not neutral. The State deliberately adopts secularism. This may, as Temperman observes, 'in practice translate into instances of religious scepticism or ideological secularism.[104] Ahdar and Leigh[105] further caution there is a danger that removal of religion from the public sphere can evolve into an anti-religious stance.

Durham and Scharffs add an additional two models to this end of the spectrum: secular control regimes and abolitionist States.[106] Temperman similarly adds additional categories to this end of the spectrum, Secular world views[107] and negative identification, although the only State he identifies with the later model is North Korea.[108]

Unlike the separationist regimes described above, these models are almost necessarily anti-religious. In a secular control regime, the State adopts freedom from religion, as opposed to freedom of religion. In effect secularism becomes the established religion.[109] Temperman's secular world view model is similar in that the State adopts secularism or a secular world view as official State doctrine.

> In other words, state secularism does not come down to an official rejection of religion. State secularism denotes an intention on the part of the state to not affiliate itself with religion, to not consider itself a priori bound by religious principles (unless they are reformulated into secular state laws) and to not seek to justify its actions by invoking religion.. . . By contrast, secularism as a philosophical notion can indeed be construed as an ideological defence

---

100 Temperman, above n 59, 123–124.
101 Ahdar and Leigh, above n 5, 93–94.
102 Ibid. 73.
103 Ibid.
104 Temperman, above n 59, 112.
105 Ahdar and Leigh, above n 5, 97–100.
106 Durham and Scharffs, above n 9, 120–121.
107 Temperman, above n 59, 139.
108 Ibid. 143–145.
109 Durham and Scharffs, above n 9, 120.

of the secular cause, which might include criticism of or scepticism towards religion. Thus, states that are 'ideologically secular' and that declare secular worldviews the official state doctrine give evidence, explicitly or by implication, of judgements about the value of religion within society.[110]

While secular world views would not consider themselves to be religious, as observed by Ninian Smart, secular world views such as communism and Marxism have much in common with religion.[111] Darryn Jensen similarly groups secular world views of this type along with religious States in his concept of religious-ethnic monism.[112]

> Religious-ethical monism is the idea that political community ought to be coextensive with religious *communion* or, at the very least, there is room for only one paramount system of values with in each political community.. . . A Communist state is a monistically committed state because it enthrones a single philosophy as the paramount basis for ordering the life of the community and marginalizes or suppresses alternative philosophies.[113]

As a result, models of this type have much in common with the established religion model discussed above. Abolitionist States take this a step further. In this model the State actively aims to eliminate religion, not simply suppress or actively discriminate against it. Durham and Scharffs identify Albania during the soviet era is an example of this kind of regime.[114]

The spectrum

In the forgoing discussion the various models have been presented as a spectrum moving from a very high level of interaction between the State and religion at one end to a relatively low level of interaction at the other. This would seem to imply a linear relationship and suggest that those models at one end have the least in common with models at the other end. In some regards this is correct. If the relationship is viewed purely in terms of how positively the State interacts with religion, then theocracies have almost nothing in common with abolitionist States. This is not the only way to view the model. Durham has suggested that rather than viewing the various models on a linear spectrum they should be viewed as a loop.[115]

In States with either an extreme positive (theocracies, erastianisms) or extreme negative (secular worldview, secular control regimes and abolitionist States) there

110 Temperman, above n 59, 140.
111 Ninian Smart, *The World's Religions* (Cambridge University Press, 1st ed, 1992) 21–28.
112 Jensen, above n 53, 15, 19–21.
113 Ibid. 19.
114 Durham and Scharffs, above n 9, 120–121.
115 Durham, above n 56, 18–25.

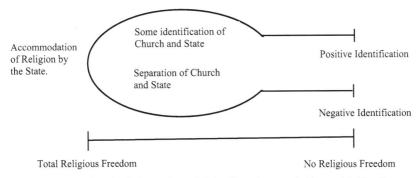

Source: based on W Cole Durham Jr, 'Perspectives on Religious liberty: A comparative Framework in Johan D van der Vyver and John Witte Jr, *Religious Human Rights in Global Perspective: Legal Perspectives* (Martinus Nijhoff Publishers, 1996)1, 18 figure 3

Figure 2.1 State and religion relationship loop

is very little freedom of religion and a very strong association between the State and the chosen world view, be that religious or anti-religious. As one moves around the loop from positive association, through various degrees of accommodation and cooperation (pluralism, neutrality etc.) and back towards negative association the level of interaction between religion and the State decreases. Religious freedom, by contrast first increases as you move away from extreme positive association, through the various forms of accommodation and cooperation but then decreases again as you move around the bottom of the loop back towards the more negative forms of association with religion.[116]

As a result, optimum freedom of religion lies somewhere in the middle of the traditional State–religion typology spectrum. However where exactly that point lies will depend on a number of factors and may differ for different States.[117] Durham himself identifies accommodationist regimes as those most able and most likely to optimize freedom of religion.[118]

Secularism

Just as there is considerable debate about the meaning of the term 'religion' there is also debate about the term 'secularism.' Adding to the confusion is the fact that the terms secular, secularism and secularisation are often confused and used interchangeably.[119] Russell Sandberg described the difference between the three terms in the following way:

116 Ibid.
117 Durham and Scharffs, above n 9, 117.
118 Durham, above n 56, 1, 24.
119 Sandberg, above n 5, 56–57.

The term 'secular' refers to a category that can be distinguished from the religious. The term 'secularisation' describes a 'process of religious change', usually alleging that there has been a decline over time in religious behaviour. And the worldview of 'secularism 'refers to an ideology, a theoretical and often political or philosophical posture, which promotes secularity. Yet, the terms 'secularisation' and 'secularism' are often treated as if they are synonymous.[120]

This section is primarily concerned with secularism, as described by Sandberg. However, the secularisation thesis will be touched upon briefly.

Charles Taylor identifies three different forms of secularism.[121] First, secularism can mean the removal of God and religion from the public sphere. Taylor argues that under this model:

> as we function within various spheres of activity . . . the norms and principles we follow, the deliberations we engage in, generally don't refer us to God or to any religious beliefs; the considerations we act on are internal to the 'rationality' of each sphere.[122]

This form of secularism does not necessarily correlate with a decrease in religious belief by the population, although the two phenomena can coincide. Taylor's second form of secularism addresses the issue of the level of religiosity of the population. It involves 'the falling off of religious belief and practice, in people turning away from god, and no longer going to Church.'[123] In this form secularism can occur even where the State still supports religion. Taylor argues this has already taken place in much of Western Europe.[124] The third form of secularism, and the one explored and promoted by Taylor in his book *A Secular Age*, 'consists . . . of a move from a society where belief in God is unchallenged and indeed, unproblematic, to one in which it is understood to be one option among others, and frequently not the easiest to embrace.'[125] In societies which operate under this form of secularism, believing is an option. Societies could be highly religious from an individual's point of view, in terms of Taylor's second form of secularism, while still being secular. In this sense Taylor's third form is like his first: non-belief of the population is not a precondition. However, in the third form religion is not removed from the public sphere, rather it is just once voice amongst many.

Ahdar and Leigh present a different typology of the different forms secularism can take. They suggest that secularism as a political philosophy can be divided

---

120 Ibid.
121 Taylor, above n 99, 2–3; see Frame, above n 99, 281–283.
122 Taylor, above n 99, 2.
123 Ibid.
124 Ibid.
125 Ibid. 3.

into two forms; benevolent or hostile.[126] In benevolent or soft secularism, the State 'refrains[s] from adopting and imposing *any* established beliefs – whether they be conventional religious or non-religious (atheistic) beliefs – upon its citizens'[127] [emphasis in original]. By contrast, in hostile secularism 'the state actively pursue[s] a policy of established unbelief.'[128] While these two forms have similarities with Taylor's third and first forms respectively they are also different from them. Taylor's definitions of secularism focuses on the society, while Ahdar and Leigh's focuses on the policy of the government.

The form of secularism that is adopted influences the types of arguments that can be made in support of continued secularisation. For example, arguments against the continued wholesale tax exemptions for religious organisations take multiple forms with different underlying assumptions about secularism. An argument that the State should remove all tax exceptions from religious organisations, as to do otherwise is to effectively subsidise believers, assumes secularism in terms of Taylor's type one or two. This argument focuses on the removal of religion from the public sphere and on the increase in the number of non-believers in the population who are now subsidising the believers through their taxes. Another option is to instead argue that tax exemptions should be extended to other worldviews, such as atheism and secular humanism.[129] This argument adopts Taylor's third form of secularism, that belief is just one option among many.

It is tempting to see the secular and the religious as being in opposition to one another and to equate secularism with atheism.[130] However, supporters of secularism argue that secularism and atheism are two separate concepts and that one does not necessarily mean the other. Rather secularism is a 'neutral' position.[131] This last point is debatable. Regardless of whether or not secularism and atheism should be seen as synonymous, religion and secularism should not be seen as two polar opposites. Instead they should be seen as two sides of the one coin.

Rather than seeing the debate as being between religion and secularism the debate should be seen as being between two worldviews. In many cases these worldviews will be religion and secularism or even atheism. In earlier decades the debate would have been between Protestantism and Catholicism. The debate itself is not different, it is just that the parties have changed and arguably a new party has joined the conversation. The debate remains focused on the place of religion in society. When the debate was between Protestants and Catholics the debate centred on the form that religion should take. The debate between

---

126 Ahdar and Leigh, above n 5, 95.
127 Ibid.
128 Ibid. 96.
129 New South Wales Anti-Discrimination Board, *Discrimination and Religious Conviction* (New South Wales Anti-Discrimination Board, 1984), 172.
130 Frame, above n 99, 272.
131 See Max Wallace, *Secularism is not Atheism* (10 November 2008) Online Opinion – Australia's E-journal of Social and Political Debate <www.onlineopinion.com.au/view.asp?article=8139&page=0>.

religionists and secularists focuses more on the place of religion but the form is also still important, particularly if the various religious positions are viewed as worldviews and secularism as just another worldview.

The traditional secularisation thesis argued that the decline of religious belief and the influence of religions in the public, political and social spheres was an inevitable consequence of modernity. '[T]hat changes associated with modernity, including economic growth, urbanisation, greater geographical and social mobility and the rise of technology and science, effectively undermined and marginalised religion and brought on secularism.'[132] However as Gary Bouma and others have observed,

> secular societies are not irreligious, anti-religious or lacking in spirituality. Whatever theories of secularism predicted, it has become extremely clear at the opening of the twenty-first century that spirituality is not in decline [and] that religion is growing in strength in most parts of the world.[133]

While some still maintain the inevitability of secularization, others have re-interpreted the thesis suggesting that it is just one option on the path of history, and not necessarily an irreversible one. Alternatively, as Taylor has suggested, true secularisation has not taken place at all, rather there has simply been a re-organisation or re-composition of religion and belief into new forms.[134]

Can secularism be neutral? Is it, as Max Wallace has argued, 'neither religious nor anti-religious, but simply neutral.'[135] Certainly it would be difficult to describe hostile secularism as identified by Leigh and Ahdar as neutral towards religion, but as has been identified above this is not the only form secularism can take. Leigh and Ahdar argue that even benevolent secularism is not neutral in the same way that any other political philosophy is not neutral.[136] As they put it, '[n]o philosophy, unless it is content with its own destruction, is indifferent to or accepting of tenants that directly contradict or undermine its own central premises.'[137] Secularism, therefore, could not accept a State–religion relationship based on the model of theocracy or erastianism but most of the other models presented above can be 'secular' – depending upon how they are implemented and the form of secularism adopted.

132 Frame, above n 99, 281.
133 Gary Bouma, *Australian Soul: Religion and Spirituality in the Twenty-first Century* (Cambridge University Press, 2006), 5; see also Sandberg, above n 5, 57–58.
134 James Beckford, *Social Theory and Religion* (Cambridge University Press, 2003); Frame, above n 99, 282; Charles Taylor, *Problems Around the Secular* (2 November 2007) The Immanent Frame – Secularism, Religion and the Public Sphere <http://blogs.ssrc.org/tif/2007/11/02/problems-around-the-secular/.>
135 Wallace, above n 131.
136 Ahdar and Leigh, above n 5, 97–98.
137 Ibid. 97.

Ultimately whether or not a nation is secular will depend on the definition of secularism adopted and the argument an individual, religious organisation or government wishes to advance. If secularism itself is not neutral, then neither is the choice as to which version you adopt as the benchmark.

Australia

In *The Challenge of Pluralism* Stephen V Monsma and J Christopher Soper argue that Australia has been through four different models of State–religion relationship: establishment, plural establishment, liberal separationism and pragmatic pluralism.[138] This section briefly examines the relationship between the State and religion in Australia in light of the various models presented above. While this section agrees with Monsma and Soper that Australia has transitioned between multiple different models of State–religion relationship it also suggests that a more nuanced approach in required, especially in relation to modern Australia.

Establishment

While Australia has never had a theocracy, it is arguable that both the erastianism and establishment models were present in Australia in the early colonial period. The relationship between the early Australian Governors and chaplains plays out as an erastianism model, at least in terms of how some of the early Governors saw this relationship. Many of the early Governors saw the role of the chaplains as moral policemen. They were to support the State in maintaining order and control. Manning Clark characterised the relationship between Rev Johnson, the first chaplain in the colony, and Governor Phillip in the following way. 'Where he [Johnson] saw religion as the divine medium for eternal salvation, the Governor treasured it as a medium of subordination, and esteemed a chaplain according to the efficacy of his work as a moral policeman.'[139] Governor Macquarie's treatment of the chaplains also shows evidence of an erastian worldview. It was his practice to require that chaplains read government notices during mass. When one of the chaplains refused, Macquarie wrote to the Secretary of State for the colonies setting out his view of the matter:

> At present it is my opinion that whatever has a tendency to benefit the community in a material degree (as was the object of the Order in question) cannot be improper to be made public during the time of religious worship.[140]

---

138 Monsma and Soper, above n 83, 93; Monsma and Soper's analysis focuses primarily on pragmatic pluralism.

139 Manning Clark, *A History of Australia* (Melbourne University Press, 1962) vol 1, 75.

140 Governor Macquarie, 'Despatch from Governor Macquarie to Earl Bathurst, 24 May 1814' in Frederick Watson (ed), *Historical Records of Australia Series I* (Library Committee of the Commonwealth Parliament, 1914–1925) vol 8, 255–256.

While the early Australian colony may not have formally operated under an erastian model, the Governors at least seem to have operated under an assumption that the role of religion was to support the operations of the State.

The question of whether Australia has ever had an established church is debatable. As will be discussed in more detail in Chapter 3, whatever the technical legal case may be, the Governors, and later the Legislative Council, treated the Church of England as the established church of the colony.[141] Even if formal *de jure* establishment cannot be established less formal *de facto* establishment can be. Throughout much of the nineteenth century the State supported the Christian churches via direct grants and the funding of religious schools.

De facto establishment came to an end sometime in the late 1800s. The exact date is difficult to pin down for a number of reasons. First, different colonies moved at different rates. Second, the move away from plural establishment was a gradual process.[142] As a result it is difficult to determine exactly where the relationship crossed the line and ceased being most accurately described as establishment and began to be more accurately described by some other model. Third, if Murphy J's formulation of what constitutes establishment as articulated in the DOGS case is accepted then Australia has never been in a position without established religion. Murphy J described establishment as 'forbidd[ing] not only a national church, and any preference to one religion over other, but also sponsorship or support (including financial support) of any religion'[143] [emphasis added]. The character of that establishment may have changed but as later chapters will demonstrate in relation to education and funding there are no periods where the State has not provided at least some support for religion.[144]

Pluralism and neutrality

Monsma and Soper argue that modern Australia best fits the pragmatic pluralism model.[145] In particular they describe Australia's education system which provides funding to non-government schools, including religious schools, as an example of pragmatic pluralism.[146] As will be discussed in Chapter 8, State funding for religious schools was re-introduced in Australia in response to a perceived crisis in Roman Catholic education. The State did not introduce funding in order to positively support a religiously plural society but rather to gain votes from the growing Roman Catholic minority and to stave off the perceived funding crisis

---

141 Ross Border, *Church and State in Australia 1788–1872 A Constitutional Study of the Church of England in Australia* (Society for Promoting Christian Knowledge, 1962) 41.

142 Renae Barker, 'Under Most Peculiar Circumstances: The Church Acts in the Australian Colonies as a Study of Plural Establishment' (2016) 3(3) *Law & History* 28, 52.

143 *Attorney General (Vic); ex rel Black v The Commonwealth* (1981) 146 CLR 559, 622–623 (Murphy J).

144 Ibid. 622–624 (Murphy J).

145 Monsma and Soper, above n 83, ch 4.

146 Ibid. 107–115.

faced by Roman Catholic schools. This would seem to support an argument that, at least in relation to education, Australia's pluralism is a matter of practicality, not principle.

Pragmatic pluralism can also be seen in tax exemptions granted to religious organisations. Despite repeated suggestions that these exemptions should be limited in some way they continue to be available to all religions for almost all their activities. The argument for some limitation has been particularly strong in relation to the commercial activities of religions however in most circumstances no restrictions have been imposed on the exemptions. The reason however is not a matter of principle. As one parliamentarian argued, as long ago as 1936, 'any decision to compel religious institutions to pay income tax upon trading profits would react harshly upon an organisation which is doing great service to the poor of Australia.'[147] In other words it is more practical to allow pluralism, even to those religions whose activities are of doubtful benefits to continue to receive tax exemptions.

Simply describing Australia as operating under a pragmatic pluralist model does not tell the whole story. As identified above, the models presented in this chapter operate on a continuum and a State may have features of more than one model. Modern Australia would seem to fit this description. As well as exhibiting traits associated with pragmatic pluralism the State–religion relationship in Australia also exhibits traits from the two neutrality models.

The Australian High Court adopts formal neutrality in its interpretation of Section 116 of the *Australian Constitution*. As will be discussed in more detail in Chapter 4, the High Court has interpreted the use of the word 'for' in Section 116 to mean purpose. As a result, a law will only infringe the 'freedom of religion clause' of Section 116 if it has the purpose of restricting the free exercise of religion. The State is in effect 'religion blind' as a result of focusing on the purpose of the law rather than its effect. Facial neutral laws which have a disproportionate effect on adherents of particular religions are also evidence of formal neutrality. Laws about face coverings and blood transfusions to minors arguably fall into this category.

Substantive neutrality can be seen in exemptions for religious organisations in anti-discrimination legislation. Religious organisations receive exemptions from some provisions of the *Sex Discrimination Act 1984* (Cth),[148] the *Age Discrimination Act 2004 (Cth)*,[149] The *Australian Human Rights Commission Act 1986* (Cth)[150] along with various State-based anti-discrimination Acts.[151] While these exemptions could be seen as privileging religion they can also be seen as the State

---

147 Commonwealth, *Parliamentary Debates*, Senate, 20 May 1936, 1894 (Alexander John McLachlan).
148 *Sex Discrimination Act 1984* (Cth) s 37.
149 *Age Discrimination Act 2004* (Cth) s 35.
150 *Australian Human Rights Commission Act 1986* (Cth) s 3.
151 *Anti-Discrimination Act 1977* (NSW) s 56; *Anti-Discrimination Act 1991* (Qld) s 109; *Anti-Discrimination Act 1996* (NT) s 51; *Anti-Discrimination Act 1998* (Tas) div 8; *Discrimination Act 1991* (ACT) ss 32–33, 44, 46; *Equal Opportunity Act 1984* (SA) ss 50,

attempting to make sure that adherence to any one religion is not more difficult as a result of anti-discrimination laws.[152]

Separation

In theory, Section 116 the *Australian Constitution* could form the foundation of a structural separation model. However, Section 116 has not been interpreted as requiring the establishment of a 'wall of separation.' On paper, Australia may have a model of structural separation, if the State ever wished to utilise that model, but in effect the level of interaction between the State and religion is too high to fit this model. The one time in Australia's history when Australia might have been said to have structural separation was during the period between the removal of State aid to religious schools in the late 1800s and its reintroduction in 1964. At least in relation to education there was in effect formal separation between the State and religion. Monsma and Soper describe this period of Australia's State–religion relationship as liberal separation.[153] However, State funding, via tax exemptions, continued during this period as did other practices such as prayers in Federal Parliament.[154] If the State–religion relationship in Australia does not follow a structural separationist model it is even further removed from transvaluing separation.

A secular control or abolitionist model also seems unlikely to accurately reflect the State–religion relationship in Australia. While there is some anti-religious sentiment, this can be seen most acutely in debate surrounding issues such as LGBTIQ+ rights and discrimination, the Royal Commission into Institutional Handling of Child Sex Abuse and terrorism. However, these negative sentiments appear to be directed toward a specific religion that is 'at fault' rather than at religion in general. As Bouma has pointed out, Australians tend to have 'a notion of fair play, [the] equal worth of human dignity and live and let live' attitude. [155] This is a far cry from a secular control or abolitionist model.

Freedom of religion

Freedom of religion is recognised as a fundamental human right in multiple international human rights instruments[156] along with numerous national constitutions

85ZM, 85ZN; *Equal Opportunity Act* 1984 (WA) ss 72–73; *Equal Opportunity Act 2010* (Vic) ss 82–84.

152 Ahdar and Leigh, above n 5, 116–118.

153 Monsma and Soper, above n 83, ch 3.

154 See Richard Ely, *Unto God and Caesar: religious issues in the emerging Commonwealth* (Melbourne University Press, 1976) 117–124.

155 Gary Bouma, *Mosques and Muslim Settlement in Australia* (Australian Government Publishing Service, 1994) 90.

156 *Universal Declaration of Human Rights*, GA Res 217A (II) UN GAOR, 3rd sess, 183rd plen mtg, UN Doc A/810 (10 December 1948) art 18; *International Covenant on Civil*

and bills of rights.[157] Article 18 of the Universal Declaration of Human Rights states:

> Everyone has the right to freedom of thought, conscience and religion, this right includes freedom to change his religion or belief, and freedom, either alone or in community with others and in public or private, to manifest his religion or belief in teaching, practice, worship and observance.[158]

Australia is infamously the only western liberal democracy without a bill of rights.[159] Australia is a State party to several international human rights instruments which include freedom of religion including the Covenant on Civil and Political Rights. However; international law instruments are not automatically incorporated into domestic law.[160] Freedom of religion, as expressed in international law, has so far not been incorporated into Australian domestic law.[161]

Victoria and the Australian Capital Territory have enacted legislative bills of rights which incorporate freedom of religion.[162] The Tasmanian Constitution also incorporates freedom of religion.[163] These are weak protections. They only operate within the territories of Victoria, the ACT and Tasmania and as ordinary acts of Parliament which may be displaced by later acts. Freedom of religion in Australia is therefore protected, almost solely, by Section 116 of the *Australian Constitution*. This so called 'freedom of religion provision' is both much less and much more than a guarantee of freedom of religion. It is much less in that the concept of freedom of religion as protected by Section 116 has been interpreted narrowly. It is much more in that protecting freedom of religion is just one limb of the four so called limbs of Section 116.

---

and Political Rights, opened for signature 19 December 1966, 999 UNTS 171 (entered into force 23 March 1976) art 18; *Convention for the Protection of Human Rights and Fundamental Freedoms*, opened for signature 4 November 1950, 213 UNTS 221 (entered into force 3 September 1953) art 9; see also Natan Lerner, 'Religious Human rights Under the United Nations' in Johan D van der Vyer and Hohn Witte Jr (eds), *Religious Human Rights in Global Perspective Legal Perspectives* (Martinus Nijoff Publishers, 1st ed, 1996) 79.

157 See, eg, *United States Constitution* amend I; *Canada Act 1982* (UK) c 11, sch B Pt I ('Canadian Charter of Rights and Freedoms) s 2(a); *New Zealand Bill of Rights Act 1990* (NZ).

158 *Universal Declaration of Human Rights*, GA Res 217A (II) UN GAOR, 3rd sess, 183rd plen mtg, UN Doc A/810 (10 December 1948) art 18.

159 David Erdos, *Delegating Rights Protection: The Rise of Rights in the Westminster World* (Oxford University Press, 2010), ch 8.

160 *Nulyarimma v Thompson* [1999] FCA 119, [20]; see also Chief Justice Robert French, 'Oil and water? – International Law and Domestic Law in Australia' (Speech delivered at the Brennan Lecture, Bond University, 26 June 2009).

161 Human Rights and Equal Opportunities Commission, *Article 18 Freedom of Religion and Belief* (Commonwealth of Australia, 1998).

162 *Human Rights Act 2004* (ACT) s 14; *Charter of Human Rights and Responsibilities Act 2006* (Vic) s 14.

163 *Constitution Act 1934* (Tas) s 46.

While freedom of religion is only weakly protected by domestic law in Australia, Australians still enjoy a relatively high level of religious freedom.[164] This is not to say that there have not been instances where religious freedom of individuals and groups has been restricted. Several instances of restrictions on religious practice are discussed in this book. However, the outcomes have not been materially different from States which have express freedom of religion provisions incorporated into domestic law.

Limiting freedom

Most human rights instruments, which include freedom of religion, protect the freedom of belief absolutely. For example, Article 18(1) of the International Covenant on Civil and Political Rights and Article 9(1) of the European Convention on Human Rights contain a freedom of religion provision in a material similar form to Article 18 of the Universal Declaration of Human Rights. This includes the right to change those beliefs.[165]

The right to manifest this belief is also protected. However, this right is often subject to limitations, the wording of which varies between conventions. For example, Article 18(3) of the Covenant on Civil and Political Rights states that:

> Freedom to manifest one's religion or beliefs may be subject only to such limitations as are prescribed by law and are necessary to protect public safety, order, health, or morals or the fundamental rights and freedoms of others.

Similar qualifications can be found in other international law instruments.[166] For example Article 9(2) of the European Conventions on Human Rights states:

> No restrictions shall be placed on the exercise of these rights other than such as are prescribed by law and are necessary in a democratic society in the interests of national security or public safety, for the prevention of disorder or crime, for the protection of health or morals or for the protection of the rights and freedoms of others. This Article shall not prevent the imposition of lawful restrictions on the exercise of these rights by members of the armed forces, of the police or of the administration of the State.

Similarly, in Australia freedom of religion has never meant license. In order for religious freedom to exist there must be a free society. This means that some

164 Kevin Boyle and Juliet Sheen (eds), *Freedom of Religion and Belief: A World Report* (Routledge, 1997) 166–175.
165 Lerner, above n 156, 95.
166 See, eg, *Universal Declaration of Human Rights*, GA Res 217A (II) UN GAOR, 3rd sess, 183rd plen mtg, UN Doc A/810 (10 December 1948) art 29; *United Nations Declration on the Elimination of All Forms of Intolerance and of Discrimination on Religion or Belief*, GA Res 36/55, UN GAOR, 36th sess, 73rd plen mtg (25 November 1981).

restrictions need to be placed on freedom. As Latham CJ observed in the *Jeho-vah's Witness Case*

> It is consistent with the maintenance of religious liberty for the state to restrain actions and courses of conduct which are inconsistent with the main-tenance of civil government or prejudicial to the continued existence of the community.[167]

This division, between the absolute protection of belief and the limited protec-tion of manifestation of belief is known as the action-belief dichotomy.[168] The application of Article 9 of the European Convention on Human Rights is par-ticularly illustrative. The provision has been used to permit laws which ban the wearing of Islamic head scarves by teachers[169] and university students[170] in the interests of secularism. More recently the European Court of Human Rights has upheld France's ban on the wearing of facial coverings in public, including those worn for religious reasons such as the niqab and burqa, on the basis of the mini-mum requirement of 'living together' or *le vivre ensemble*.[171] The laws in question did restrict freedom of religion; however, the Strasburg Court felt that these laws were 'necessary in a democratic society.'

In determining whether a law restricting religious freedom is 'necessary in a democratic society' the Court determines whether the restrictions imposed on freedom to manifest religious belief are proportionate to the aim the law seeks to achieve. A recent example of this process can be seen in *Eweida and Oth-ers v United Kingdom*.[172] The case concerned four applicants, all of whom were Christian, who contended that they had been prevented from manifesting their religious beliefs. Two of the applicants (Eweida and Chaplin) claimed that their right to manifest their religion had been infringed when they were prevented from wearing a Christian cross at work.[173]

In the case of Eweida, the Court found that too much weight had been given to her employer's desire to display a certain image. It therefore concluded that

167 *The Adelaide Company of Jehovah's Witnesses Inc v The Commonwealth* (1943) 67 CLR 116, 131.
168 Gabriel Moens, 'The Action-Belief Dichotomy and Freedom of Religion' (1989–1990) 12 *Sydney Law Review* 195, 197.
169 *Dahlab v Switzerland* (European Court of Human Rights, Second Section, Application No 42393/98, 15 February 2001).
170 *Leyla Şahin v Turkey* (2005) 44 EHRR 99.
171 *SAS v France* (European Court of Human Rights, Grand Chamber, Application No 43835/11, 1 July 2014) 4–5, 17, 55, 57.
172 *Eweida and Others v United Kingdom* (European Court of Human Rights, Fourth Section, Application Nos 48420/10, 59842/10, 51671/10 and 36516/10, 15 January 2013).
173 Ian Leigh and Andrew Hambler, 'Religious Symbols, Conscience, and the Rights of Oth-ers' (2014) 3(1) *Oxford Journal of Law and Religion* 2, 3–5.

there had been a breach of Article 9.[174] By contrast, in the case of Chaplin the Court found that there had been no breach of Article 9, even though the manifestation of religion, in this case the wearing of a small Christian cross, was practically identical to Eweida. In Chaplin's case the competing interest was health and safety in the context of a hospital. Chaplin's employer was concerned that her cross might be grabbed by patients or touch open wounds.[175] The Court determined that the measures taken by Chaplin's employer were not disproportionate and that in the case of health and safety 'domestic authorities must be allowed a wide margin of appreciation.'[176] In Chaplin's case, unlike Eweida's, the Court was in effect satisfied that such restrictions on the manifestation of religion was necessary in a democratic society in the interests of public safety, for the protection of public order, health or morals, or for the protection of the rights and freedoms of others.

Another example of this balancing process can be seen in the United Kingdom House of Lords decision; *R v Secretary of State for Education and Employment and others ex parte Williamson*.[177] The case considered the use of corporal punishment at privately funded Christian schools. The teachers and parents considered the use of 'loving corporal correction' to be essential.[178] While the Court accepted that corporal punishment was a manifestation of religious belief the Court also found that restriction of this manifestation of belief was necessary in a democratic society.[179] While all of the judges undertook a balancing exercise, Baroness Hale's is a particularly good example of the Court weighing the rights and freedoms of others against the freedom of religion. She explicitly weighed the right of children to be free from violence in education as expressed in a number of documents on children's rights against freedom of religion of the parents and teachers. In light of this she concluded that 'it is quite impossible to say that Parliament was not entitled to limit the practice of corporal punishment in all schools in order to protect the rights and freedoms of all children.' She also commented that '[i]f a child has a right to be brought up without institutional violence, as he does, that right should be respected whether or not his parents and teachers believe otherwise.'[180]

In neither *Eweida* nor *Williamson* did the Court deny that the belief in question was religious, nor did the Court deny that the manifestation of that belief

---

174 *Eweida and Others v United Kingdom* (European Court of Human Rights, Fourth Section, Application Nos 48420/10, 59842/10, 51671/10 and 36516/10, 15 January 2013) [89]–[95].

175 Ibid. [98].

176 Ibid. [99]–[100].

177 [2005] UKHL 15 (24 February 2005); the decision concerned the *Human Rights Act 1998* (UK) which incorporates the European Convention of Human Rights into domestic law.

178 *R v Secretary of State for Education and Employment and others ex parte Williamson* [2005] UKHL 15 (24 February 2005) [10] (Lord Bingham).

179 Ibid. [49]–[50], [79]–[86].

180 Ibid. [86].

had been restricted. Rather the Court accepted that the restrictions on that manifestation were necessary in a democratic society.

Different jurisdictions use different terminology to express this balancing process and at what point it will be acceptable to limit religious freedom in favour of the freedom of others or the interests of society and the State as a whole. In Australia, Latham CJ used the term 'undue infringement'[181] rather than 'necessary in a democratic society' as used in the European Convention. Whatever the term used, the effect is the same. Courts must weigh up the infringement to freedom of religion against the harm the law is trying to prevent and determine if such infringement is 'undue' or 'necessary.' As a result, freedom to manifest religion is never absolute. Rather it must be balanced against the rights and freedoms of others. While Australia does not have an express right to freedom of religion this process is still undertaken by legislators and judges when considering issues relating to the restriction of manifestations of religion. This process can be seen in the debate surrounding the wearing of the niqab and burqa. However, without an express freedom of religion contained in a bill of rights there is a danger that this balancing process may be missed in future debates.

Conclusion

This brings us back to the question first articulated in the introduction to this chapter – is Australia a secular or a Christian/religious nation?

As this chapter has argued, whether or not a nation is secular in part depends upon the form of secularism that is adopted as the benchmark. But it also depends upon what is meant by 'nation.' Nation can mean State, referring to the formal aspects of government and in this sense a nation will be secular if there is at least some separation between the State and religion. This does not necessarily need to be as formal as a declaration in a State's constitution as in the United States and France, particularly if Taylor's third form or Ahdar and Leigh's benevolent secularism is the benchmark. In the model presented by Durham and Scharffs, set out above, a State is secular anywhere on the right-hand side of the loop, although secularism is only achieved halfway along the bottom arm of the loop. However, nation can also refer to the people or society. In this sense the formal relationship between the State and religion is irrelevant. The State may be at either extreme a theocracy or an abolitionist State and the people may be secular. This is Taylor's second form of secularism. While this form is arguably more likely in the bottom half of Durham and Scharffs' loop, it is not impossible to imagine a situation where the State maintains a formal and close relationship with religion while its people turn their backs on God.

In Australia those advancing the argument that Australia is a secular nation most often point to Section 116 of the *Australian Constitution*. While this

---

181 *The Adelaide Company of Jehovah's Witnesses Inc v The Commonwealth* (1943) 67 CLR 116, 131 (Latham CJ).

section does prevent the establishment of a State church in Australia in practice its application has been very narrow. As will be discussed in later chapters, the existence of Section 116 has not prevented a close and sometimes intimate relationship between the State and religion in Australia. Those who argue that Australia is a Christian/religious nation point to census statistics which show a historical dominance of Christianity that has continued into the twenty-first century.[182] If Australia is a secular nation, then it is one where the majority of people have not turned their backs on religion, even if the numbers doing so are increasing with each census.[183] If Australia is a Christian/religious nation then it is one without a State church and without a formal role for religion and religious leaders in government. Those advancing these two apparently mutually exclusive positions are arguing at cross purposes. They do not have the same definition of secularism let alone nation. Perhaps the best explanation is that Australia is both. It is secular in that there is no State church and it is religious, even arguably Christian, in that religion and faith continue to play an important part in the lives of many of its citizens including its political leaders.

It is in this context that Australia has been able to create a county in which individuals are relatively free to exercise their own faith, without freedom of religion being protected in a bill of rights. As this book will show, not all Australians have been free to exercise all elements of their faith. However, freedom of religion, even in countries with a bill of rights, does not mean license. Limits have always been placed on the manifestation of religion. The situation in Australia has been no different. In some instances, Australia has arguably reached less restrictive accommodations of controversial religious practices than countries with a bill of rights.[184]

The remainder of the book moves from looking at these wider macro issues of State–religion relationships to considering the relationship at a micro level. It is at this micro level that individual adherents and religious organisations interact with the State on a daily basis, and therefore the focus of this book. However, in considering the specific laws and changes in those laws, the macro theoretical context in which these changes take place needs to be kept in mind. Ultimately, the micro changes build together to form macro changes which can in time effect the wider context of the State–religion relationship.

---

182 *Cultural Diversity in Australia: Reflecting a Nation: Stories from the 2011 Census* (21 June 2012) Australian Bureau of Statistics <www.abs.gov.au/ausstats/abs@.nsf/Lookup/2071. 0main+features902012-2013>.

183 Renae Barker, *Religion and the Census: Australia's Unique Relationship to Faith and Unbelief* (5 July 2017) ABC Religion & Ethics <www.abc.net.au/religion/articles/2017/07/05/4696888.htm.>

184 Compare for example Australia's laws relating to the burqa with those in Europe and with the European Court of Human Right's decisions relating to the Islamic head scarf.

3   In the beginning

Introduction

Most faiths have an origin story, an explanation of how the world began. The Christian Bible begins with the words:

> In the beginning when God created the heavens and the earth the earth was formless void and darkness covered the face of the deep, while a wind from God swept over the face of the waters.[1]

When Europeans arrived in Australia they did not find a 'formless void.' Instead they found a land inhabited by hundreds of Indigenous Nations each with their own unique history, law, culture, language and origin stories.[2] However, Australia's first European settlers did not recognise this, instead declaring Australia to be *Terra Nullius*, a legal fiction which was not overturned until 1992, in the landmark Indigenous land rights case *Mabo v Queensland*,[3] over 200 years after the arrival of the First fleet in 1788. As a result, it was the United Kingdom laws and religion which defined the relationship between the emerging State and religion in the early days of the Australian colony. The exact nature of the relationship between the State and religion in the early colonial period has been a matter of debate.

It is often assumed that the Church of England was the established church in the early days of the Australian colony. Monsma and Soper, for example, describe Australia as having passed through four different State–religion relationships: the first of which was establishment.[4] In an oft quoted passage[5] from the 1948 High

---

1   Genesis 1: 1–2 (New Revised Standard Version).
2   Vicki Grieves, Aboriginal Spirituality: Aboriginal Philosophy, the Basis of Aboriginal Social and Emotional Wellbeing (Cooperative Research Centre for Aboriginal Health, 2009).
3   (1992) 175 CLR 1.
4   Stephen V. Monsma and J. Christopher Soper, *The Challenge of Pluralism: Church and State in Five Democracies* (Rowman & Littlefield Publishing Group, 2nd ed, 2009) 93.
5   See, for example, Luke Beck, 'The Establishment Clause of the Australian Constitution: Three Propositions and A Case Study' (2014) 35(2) *Adelaide Law Review* 225, 249; John Gilchrist,

Court decision of *Wylde v Attorney General of New South wales*, Dixon J asserts that:

> Notwithstanding judicial statements of a contrary tendency, the better opinion appears to be that the Church of England came to New South Wales as the established church and that it possessed that status in the colony for some decades.[6]

However, this view is not universal. Prior to Dixon's J proclamation above, Australian Courts had found that the Church of England was not and had never been the established church.[7] Others, such as Priestly JA in *Scandrett v Dowling*,[8] have taken a middle ground, accepting that the Church of England may have been treated as if it was the established church while questioning the correctness of this assertion.[9] This chapter analyses these divergent views and examines the evidence on which they are based.

What is establishment?

Before being able to determine if Australia ever had an established church, it is necessary to work out what that means. The majority, if not all, typologies of State–religion relationships contain a category for established churches and/or religions. However, as Ogilvie explains, it is a 'concept [that] is vague, imprecise and ever changing.'[10] He concludes that, in relation to the established church in England, there are:

> Two correlative propositions concerning the essential nature of 'establishment' in England.. . . First, an established church is that single church within a country accepted and recognised by the state as the truest expression of the Christian faith. Secondly, the state's recognition of its established church places upon the state a legal duty to protect, preserve and defend the church, if necessary to the exclusion of all others.[11]

'The Extent to Which the Prerogative Right of the Crown to Print and Publish Certain Works Exists in Australia' (2012) 11(2) *Canberra Law Review* 32, 35; Tom Frame, *Church and State: Australia's Imaginary Wall* (University of New South Wales Press, 1st ed, 2006) 48; Tom Frame, *Losing My Religion Unbelief in Australia* (University of New South Wales Press, 2009) 56.

6 *Wylde v Attorney General for New South Wales* (1948) 78 CLR 224, 284 (Dixon J).

7 *Ex parte Ryan* (1855) 2 Legge 876; *Ex parte The Rev George King* (1861) 2 Legge 1307; *Ex parte Collins* [1889] The Weekly Notes 85; *Nelan v Downes* (1917) 23 CLR 546.

8 (1992) 27 NSWLR 483.

9 *Scandrett v Dowling* (1992) 27 NSWLR 483, 492.

10 M. H. Ogilvie, 'What is a Church by Law Established?' (1990) 28(1) *Hall Law Journal* 179, 196.

11 M. H. Ogilvie, 'What is a Church by Law Established?' (1990) 28(1) *Hall Law Journal* 179, 198.

While Ogilvie's definition focuses on establishment in a Christian context, establishment is not an exclusively Christian concept. Today many of the most prominent examples of establishment are found in the Islamic world.[12] Further, while Ogilvie's definition focuses on formal or constitutional establishment, this is not the only possible definition of establishment. Less formal arrangements, where the State recognizes or privileges a church or religion, may also be considered to be establishment.[13] Justice Murphy in his dissenting judgment in *Attorney General (Vic); ex rel Black v. The Commonwealth*[14] (*DOGS* case) considered that establishment included providing any sponsorship or support, including financial, to any religion.[15] Nor is exclusion of all others always necessary. Today the Church of England continues to be the formally established Church of England,[16] however this does not mean that other churches and religions are excluded.[17] As a signatory to the European Convention on Human Rights, the United Kingdom is bound by Article 9 which guarantees freedom of religion to all, not just the established church and its adherents.[18] In its broadest sense, establishment, therefore, involves the recognition, support or privileging of a church or religion/s by the State whether or not that recognition, support or privileging is formally recognised in the State's Constitution or other founding documents.

Such a wide definition will, of course, capture States which would not normally be considered to have an established church or religion. It is therefore useful to divide establishment into sub-categories which recognize that establishment can playout in different ways in different States.

The first distinction which can be drawn is between those States with an established church as opposed to those with an established religion.[19] Many religions are divided into numerous sects or denominations. Often with significant divergence between them – although an outsider would still consider all of them to fit within the one religion. Within Christianity for example there is remarkable variety 'from the Southern Baptist snake handlers to the Russian Orthodox Church,

---

12 See, for example, Jan Michiel Otto, *Sharia Incorporated: A Comparative Overview of the Legal Systems of Twelve Muslim Countries in Past and Present* (Amsterdam University Press, 2010).

13 See, for example, Rex Ahdar and Ian Leigh, *Religious Freedom in the Liberal State* (Oxford University Press, 2nd ed, 2013) 116. See also Chapters 8 and 9 for an in-depth discussion of how Australia continues to establish religion in that the federal government continues to financially support religion via programs such as tax exemptions, funding to religious schools and funding of religious chaplains in government and non-government schools.

14 (1981) 146 CLR 559.

15 Ibid. 622–624.

16 Ahdar and Leigh, above n 13, 113–114.

17 For a discussion of the position of the Church of England see Rex Ahdar and Ian Leigh, *Religious Freedom in the Liberal State* (Oxford University Press, 2nd ed, 2013) 101–103.

18 *Human Rights Act 1998* (UK) which incorporates the *Convention for the Protection of Human Rights and Fundamental Freedoms*, opened for signature 4 November 1950, 213 UNTS 221 (entered into force 3 September 1953).

19 Jeroen Temperman, *State–religion Relationships and Human Rights Law: Towards a Right to Religiously Neutral Governance* (Brill, 2010).

from the Quakers to the Roman Catholics.'[20] Similarly Islam can be divided into five major schools, four Sunni and one Shia,[21] although this only hints at the complex diversity with in Islam. A State can therefore establish just one sect or denomination within the broader category of any one religion or establish the whole of a religion. Temperman has observed that the former, establishing a single State church, is exclusively a Christian phenomenon,[22] although he does acknowledge that, in the case of State religions, 'occasionally a religion in its entirety is *de jure* established whilst a specific denomination is *de facto* preferentially treated.'[23]

A State may also choose between single and plural establishment. In the former, the State establishes a single religion or church while plural establishment 'involves the state recognizing, supporting and /or promoting multiple nominated religions.'[24] Plural establishment itself could be further divided,[25] at least at a theoretical level, into those States which establish several specific sects or denominations which fall within the one religion,[26] those which establish multiple sects or denominations coming from more than one religion,[27] States which establish multiple religions[28] and States which establish religion generally without singling out specific religions.[29]

Establishment within any of the sub-categories identified above can be further divided into *de jure* and *de facto* establishment depending upon the level of formality with which the State establishes a religion or church. *De jure* establishment requires the formal constitutional or other legal recognition of the established church/es or religion/s.[30] Formal *de jure* establishment may be further divided

---

20 Renae Barker, 'Rebutting the Ban the Burqa Rhetoric: A Critical Analysis of the Arguments for a Ban on the Islamic face Veil in Australia' (2016) 37(1) *Adelaide Law Journal* 191, 200.
21 Jamila Hussain, Islam: Its Laws and Society (Federation Press, 3rd ed, 2011) 39.
22 Temperman, above n 19, 44.
23 Temperman, above n 19, 32–33.
24 Renae Barker, 'Under Most Peculiar Circumstances': The Church Acts in the Australian Colonies as a Study of Plural Establishment' (2016) 3(3) *Law & History* 28, 35–36; see also Veit Bader, 'Religions and States A New Typology and a Plea for Non-Constitutional Pluralism' (2003) 6(1) *Ethical Theory and Moral Practice* 55, 68.
25 Ahdar and Leigh, above n 13, 104.
26 Finland currently has two national churches, the Evangelical Lutheran Church of Finland and the Finnish Orthodox Church; see Veit Bader, 'Religions and States: A New Typology and a Plea for Non-Constitutional Pluralism' (2003) 6(1) *Ethical Theory and Moral Practice* 55, 68.
27 Germany recognises "three main historical religious communities – Evangelical, catholic, and Jewish", see Ahdar and Leigh, above n 13, 104; the Chinese government recognises Buddhism, Catholicism, Islam, Protestantism and Taoism as religions although '[t]he official governmental position is that religion will ultimately die out. . .' and although 'Communist party members are expected to be atheist, the state or any of its organs are not allowed to actively compel citizens to become atheists.' See Temperman, above n 19, 141.
28 Bader, above n 26, fn 19.
29 Ahdar and Leight, above n 13, 116.
30 Ahdar and Leigh, above n 13, 104.

into those States with strong or weak establishment, depending on the extent to which the formal establishment is compatible with the continued existence of other religions within the State.[31] In the case of strong *de jure* establishment the aim is to create 'religion-national cultural monism.'[32] Freedom of religion and *de facto* recognition or support of other church/es or religion/s is neither permissible nor possible. By contrast, weak establishment is compatible with pluralism. While specified church/es or religion/s are officially established, such an establishment must 'be compatible with *de jure* and *de facto* religious freedom and religious pluralism.'[33]

The State may also have *de facto* established church/es or religion/s. While the State's constitution and other establishing documents may not formally establish a church or religion

> [o]ne particular faith may be favoured by the state in practice due to its numerical or cultural dominance in that country. Alternatively, the state may promote a generic form of religion by passing laws and implementing public policies that reflect the broad tenets and ideals of a religion.[34]

States may also have symbolic, as opposed to substantive, establishment. The sub- categories of establishment outlined above have so far assumed that establishment of State church/es or religion/s will have some substantive effect, however this may not necessarily be the case.[35] The preamble of the *Australian Constitution*, for example, contains the words 'humbly relying on the blessing of Almighty God.'[36] Similarly, the preamble of the *Canadian Constitution* commences with 'Whereas Canada is founded upon principles that recognize the supremacy of God and the role of law . . .'[37] Neither of these symbolic acknowledgments of a deity have much, if any, substantive impact on the laws or the relationship between the State and religion of either State.

The definition outlined above is also arguably too wide to be applied to non-establishment or separation clauses such as Section 116 of the *Australian Constitution* or the United States of America's Constitutional First Amendment.[38] In Australia the High Court was asked to consider the meaning of establishment, in the context of Section 116 in the *DOGS* case. Justice Gibbs identified four

---

31 Bader, above n 26, 67–68.
32 Ibid. 68; for a discussion of monism see Darryn Jensen, 'Classifying Church-state arrangements' in Nadirsyah Hosen and Richard Mohr (eds), *Law and Religion in Public Life: The Contemporary Debate* (Routledge, 4th ed, 2011) 15.
33 Bader, above n 26, 68.
34 Ahdar and Leigh, above n 13, 105.
35 Ibid. 104.
36 *Australian Constitution* preamble.
37 *Canada Act 1982* (UK) c 11, sch B pt 1 ('*Canadian Charter of Rights and Freedoms*') preamble.
38 For a discussion of non-establishment clauses see Temperman, above n 19, 115–121.

potential meanings for the term; '[1] to protect by law . . . [2] to confer on a religion or a religious body the position of a state religion or a state church . . . [3] to support a church in the observance of its ordinances and doctrines . . . [4] to found or set up a new church or religion.'[39] He concluded that in the context of Section 116 it is the second of these, 'confer[ing] on a religion or a religious body the position of a state religion or a state church,' which is most appropriate.[40] The remainder of the majority judges similarly found that 'establishing' in the context of Section 116 required the creation, to a greater or lesser extent, of a State church or the privileging of one religion to the exclusion of all others.[41] By contrast, the Supreme Court of the United States has taken a wider approach to the question of what constitutes establishment in the context of the First Amendment of the *Constitution of the United Sates.* Justice Black in *Everson v Board of Education* determined that the non-establishment clause meant that

> neither a state nor the Federal Government can set up a church. Neither can pass laws which aid one religion, aid all religions, or prefer one religion over another. Neither can force nor influence a person to go to or to remain away from church against his will or force him to profess a belief or disbelief in any religion. No person can be punished for entertaining or professing religious beliefs or disbeliefs, for church attendance or non-attendance. No tax in any amount, large or small, can be levied to support any religious activities or institutions, whatever they may be called, or whatever form they may adopt to teach or practice religion. Neither a state nor the Federal Government can, openly or secretly, participate in the affairs of any religious organizations or groups, and vice versa. In the words of Jefferson, the clause against establishment of religion by law was intended to erect 'a wall of separation between church and State.[42]

This is much more in line with Murphy J's definition of establishment than the majority of the Australian High Court.[43] Part of the difference in interpretation no doubt lies not in the word establishment itself but in whether the relevant constitutional provision is interpreted to refer to the establishment of a religion or any religion.

---

39 *Attorney General (Vic); ex rel Black v. The Commonwealth* (1981) 146 CLR 559, 595–597 (Gibbs J).
40 Ibid. 603–604.
41 Ibid. 610 (Stephen J), 612 (Mason J), 653 (Wilson J).
42 *Everson v Board of Education*, 2330 US 1, 15–16 (Black J) (1947).
43 Justice Murphy drew heavily on American jurisprudence in his judgment in *Attorney General (Vic); ex rel Black v. The Commonwealth* (1981) 146 CLR 559 while the majority rejected the use of American precedent in determining the meaning and scope of section 116 of the *Australian Constitution.*

Did Australia have an established church?

Whether or not Australia ever had, or in fact still has, an established church or religion largely depends upon which of the various sub-categories you include in that inquiry. As already identified, Australia today has a form of symbolic establishment as a result of the reference to Almighty God in the preamble of the *Australian Constitution*. However, the substantive effect of that symbolic establishment is so weak as to be almost non-existent. Furthermore, Murphy J's definition, which closely equates to *de facto* plural establishment of religion generally, would seem to imply that Australia continues to establish religion in that the federal government continues to financially support religion via programmes such as tax exemptions,[44] funding to religious schools and funding of religious chaplains in government and non-government schools.[45] However, as outlined in the previous chapter, neither of these forms of establishment are necessarily incompatible with pluralism or secularism. The remainder of this chapter will therefore evaluate whether or not Australia ever had a formal *de jure* establishment of any specified church/es or religion/s with particular focus on the early colonial period.

The most likely church to have been the established church in the Australian colonies is the Church of England. Its successor in Australia today is the Anglican Church of Australia, which is a voluntary association. At the time of settlement, and today, the Church of England was the established church of England, although it has never been the established church of the United Kingdom.[46] The question therefore is whether in being transported to the colonies of Australia, the Church of England retained its status as an established church or whether on arrival it became a voluntary association, or something else.

Case law

The question of whether Australia ever had an established church has been considered judicially on a number of occasions.[47] The conclusions reached have been mixed. Those cases decided prior to Federation all find that the Church of England was not and had never been the established church of the Australian colonies.[48] By contrast, in *Wylde v Attorney General for New South Wales*, decided in 1948, both Latham CJ and Dixon J conclude that the Church of England was

---

44 See Chapter 9.
45 See Chapter 8.
46 *Scandrett v Dowling* (1992) 27 NSWLR 483, 523 (Priestley JA).
47 In addition, a number of cases have considered the legal position of the Church of England in other colonies (eg New Zealand, South Africa) see, for example, *R v Eton College* (1857) 120 ER 228; *Long v Bishop of Cape Town* (1863) 15 ER 756; *Re the Bishop of Natal* (1865) 16 ER 43; *Bishop of Natal v Gladstone* (1866) LR 3 Eq 1.
48 *Ex Parte Ryan* (1855) 2 Legge 876; *Ex parte The Rev George King* (1861) 2 Legge 1307; *Ex parte Collins* [1889] The Weekly Notes 85.

the established church in the colony at the time of settlement and lost this legal status over time. One primary difference between this and the earlier judgments is the immediacy of the issue. In the pre-Federation period, the issue of establishment and dis-establishment was a live issue, not only in Australia but around the Empire. As Mason J explained in the *DOGS case*, in reference to the citizens of the Australian colonies at the time of Federation:

> They were acutely familiar with the relationship between church and state in England and Wales, Scotland and Ireland. They were aware that the Church of England, the Church of Scotland and the Church of Ireland respectively were referred to as 'the Established Church'. And they had followed the move to disestablish the Church of England, a move which had generated great political controversy in the first half of the century. To them the issue of establishment was by no means remote. It was a burning question because a large proportion of the Australian population in the second half of the nineteenth century consisted of Nonconformists and Roman Catholics who had suffered from religious discrimination in their homelands.[49]

A finding therefore that the Church of England was or had been the established church of the Australian colonies was more likely to have a practical impact in the pre-Federation cases. By contrast, by the time *Wylde v Attorney General for New South Wales* was decided, the Church of England had ceased being the established church at least a century earlier, if it ever had been. In *Scandrett v Dowling,* decided in 1992, the courts appear to have moved to a more central position, accepting that the Church of England may have been treated as the established church in the early colony while casting doubt as to the correctness of this assumption as a matter of law.

Ex Parte Ryan (1855)

Ex Parte Ryan[50] concerned whether a person engaged under the *Masters and Servants Act* could lawfully refuse to work on a day prescribed as a holiday by his religion. In this case a Roman Catholic refused to work on the feast of Epiphany.[51] Under the *Holy Days and Fasting Days Act 1551* (5 &6) Ewd 6 c 3 the Feast of Epiphany and other feast days were prescribed as days of rest.[52] The question for the court therefore was whether this English Act applied in the colony of New South Wales.

---

49 *Attorney General (Vic); ex rel Black v. The Commonwealth* (1981) 146 CLR 559, 616–617 (Mason J).
50 (1855) 2 Legge 876.
51 6 January.
52 *Ex Parte Ryan* (1855) 2 Legge 876, 876.

The Court held that the *Holy Days and Fasting Days Act 1551* (5 &6) Ewd 6 c 3 was not, and had never been, in force in the colony.

> [I]t was clearly inapplicable to the circumstances of the Colony. It was an Act passed at the time that the Legislature of England was exerting itself for the maintenance of an [sic] uniformity of religion. The object of this Act was to compel such uniformity on all hands.. . . In Scotland this law had never been applicable, as the Presbyterian religion was the established faith; and this Colony being a colony from the United Kingdom, this reason alone would prevent the law being here enforced. But where the professors of all religions were placed upon a footing of equality, a law obviously passed for the maintenance of a dominant church was clearly not applicable.[53]

Ex parte The Rev George King (1861)

As a result of his grievance at not being appointed Dean of the Cathedral Church of St. Andrew in Sydney, of which he was the parish priest, Rev George King proceeded to physically bar the Right Reverend Frederic Barker, Doctor in Divinity, Bishop of Sydney from entering to conduct an ordination service. In response, the Bishop instructed his Chancellor, Sir William Westbrook Burton, to cite Rev King to appear before him and answer charges in accordance with terms set out in the Bishop's letter's patent.[54] Rev King disputed Bishop Barker's authority to summons and try him in accordance with his letter's patent. In finding in favour of Rev King, the Court held that the ecclesiastical law of the Church of England, and thus the power of the Bishop to constitute a tribunal under his letters patent, had no application in the colony of New South Wales.

In coming to their conclusion both Dickinson CJ and Wise J referred to Blackstone's proclamation on the reception of law in a settled colony.[55]

> if an uninhabited country be discovered and planted by English subjects, all the English laws then in being, which are the birthright of every subject, are immediately then in force. But this must be understood with very many and very great restrictions. Such colonists carry with them only so much of the English law as is applicable to their own situation and the condition of an infant colony : such for instance as the general rules of inheritance and of protection from personal injuries. The artificial refinements and distinctions incident to the property of a great and commercial people; the laws of police and revenue (such especially as are enforced by penalties) ; the mode of maintenance for the established clergy, the jurisdiction of spiritual Courts,

---

53 *Ex Parte Ryan* (1855) 2 Legge 876, 879.
54 *Ex parte The Rev George King* (1861) 2 Legge 1307, 1309–1310.
55 Note the assignation of Australia as a settled colony relied on the declaration of *Terra Nullius* a legal fiction which was overturned in *Mabo v Queensland [No 2]* (1992) 175 CLR 1.

and a multitude of other provisions, are neither necessary nor convenient for them, and therefore are not in force. What shall be admitted and what rejected, at what times, and under what restrictions, must, in case of dispute, be decided in the first instance by their own provincial judicature, subject to the revision and control of the King in Council: the whole of their constitution being also liable to be new-modelled and reformed by the general superintending power of the Legislature in the mother country.[56]

Dickinson CJ therefore concluded that a Bishop in the Australian colonies:

though appointed by the British monarch, and ordained and consecrated by an English private and metropolitan, is not a bishop of the Church establishment of England, but a bishop over Christian persons and congregations in this portion of the Queen's dominions, who hold the same opinions on doctrine, ritual, and Church government, as are entertained in England and Ireland by the members of the United Church as there by law established. He is a bishop, moreover, here over those only who voluntarily submit to his jurisdiction.[57]

As a result, he concluded that 'the King's Ecclesiastical Law of England has no applicability to the circumstances of [the] colony.[58] Wise J similarly found that the Church of England was not, and had never been, the established church of the colony. He drew particular attention to the position of those from Scotland immigrating to the new colony as opposed to their English brethren if the Church of England had in fact become the established church, drawing on language from Lord Blackstone's commentary on reception of laws.

Whatever difficulty there may be in defining what laws are so introduced, I think one safe test is whether the particular law would equally affect all persons in the colony. Tried by this test, no ecclesiastical law could be applicable to the colony. Such law, in its origin, was based upon the principle that the Church was national, and all citizens were equally bound by its laws, when sanctioned by the State – that is, by the King's ecclesiastical law. But the legal rights of a Scotchman are bound up with the existence of Presbyterianism as his national Church, and how could a colony, open alike to Englishmen and Scotchmen be governed by a law which should be applicable only to a portion of its inhabitants? Just as a Scotchman, on his arrival in the colony, ceases to enjoy any rights peculiarly Scotch – so an Englishman, being a member of the Church of England, loses all legal rights which are incapable of being shared by his fellow colonists.[59]

---

56 See *Ex parte The Rev George King* (1861) 2 Legge 1307, 1313 (Dickinson J), 1323 (Wise J).
57 Ibid. 1311.
58 Ibid. 1314 (Dickinson CJ).
59 Ibid. 1324 (Wise J).

Ex parte Collins (1889)

In *Ex parte Collins* the court considered whether a pamphlet titled 'The Law of Population: its consequences and its bearing upon human conduct and morals' by Annie Besant was an obscene book and therefore its sale contravened Section 2 of the *Obscene Publication Prevention Act 1880*.[60] Chapter 3 of the book '[advocated and described] different means of checking the increase of population by preventing the natural result which follows sexual intercourse taking effect.'[61] In concluding that the book was not an obscene publication Windeyer J commented that:

> In an empire, the sovereign of which rules over more non-Christians that Christians, it has become an obsolete fiction that Christianity is part of the common law.[62]

While not saying so explicitly this would seem to suggest that Christianity, and therefore the Church of England, was not the established church, if it ever had been.

Nelan v Downes (1917)

In *Nelan v Downes*[63] the High Court considered whether a testamentary gift of £50 to say Catholic mass was charitable. As the Court observed, 'The Sum involved is not large, but the principle at stake is of the utmost importance in view of the frequency of such testamentary gifts.'[64] English decisions had held that such gifts were 'for superstitious uses, and therefore void.'[65] Barton J, however rejected the applicability of English laws relating to superstitious gifts stating:

> But I do not think that the law of England as to superstitious uses applies in Victoria, or elsewhere in Australia. Of course, the express terms of the Statute 1 Edw. VI. c. 14 relate to circumstances which do not apply in this country, and the English decisions which have followed it in this regard are founded on analogy. This is a country without any established Church. Within its bounds, all religions are on an equal footing. The Act of Edw. VI. was clearly passed in the interests of the Reformed Church as against those of the Roman Catholic, the previous State Church of England.[66]

---

60 *Ex parte Collins* [1889] The Weekly Notes 85, 85, 88.
61 Ibid. 86.
62 Ibid. 88 (Windeyer J).
63 *Nelan v Downes* (1917) 23 CLR 546.
64 Ibid. 549 (Barton J).
65 Ibid.
66 Ibid. 550 (Barton J).

The reference here is to the state of the law at the time of the decision, which was after Federation and well after any establishment of the Church of England came to an end. However, he then goes onto quote from *Yeap Chah Neo v Ong Chen Neo*, in relation to Penang:[67]

> the law of England must be taken to be the governing law, so far as it is applicable to the circumstances of the place, and modified in its application by these circumstances. This would be the case in a country newly settled by subjects of the British Crown; and, in their Lordships' view, the charters referred to, if they are to be regarded as having introduced the law of England into the colony, contain in the words' 'as far as circumstances will admit' the same qualification. In applying this general principle, it has been held that Statutes relating to matters and exigencies peculiar to the local condition of England, and which are not adapted to the circumstances of a particular colony, do not become a part of its law, although the general law of England may be introduced into it.[68]

Barton J then goes on to state that '[t]here can be no doubt that the same thing is true as to Australia,'[69] This would seem to imply that not only was the law of superstition not applicable to Australia but also the underlying reasoning of that law, the establishment of the Church of England.

Wylde v Attorney General for New South Wales (1948)

In *Wylde v Attorney General for New South Wales*[70] (the *Red Book* case) the High Court, in a split (2:2) decision, dismissed an appeal from the judgment of Roper CJ of the Supreme Court of New South Wales granting an injunction preventing the Bishop of Bathurst, Arnold Thomas Wylde, from permitting, *inter alia*, a book known as *The Holy Eucharist* commonly referred to as the *Red Book*, from being used to conduct services in Anglican churches within the diocese of Bathurst. The cases primarily revolved around the issue of the terms of the trusts under which the properties, including the churches, were held and in which the *Red Book* was being used. Given the ecclesiastical nature of the case the High Court justices were not pleased to be called upon to resolve this dispute in a civil court. As Rich J wryly commented:

> The subject of this unhappy controversy is only fit for a domestic forum and not for a civil court. Unfortunately it is not an example of 'Charity' in the New Testament sense or of the command to love one another. The dispute

67 LR 6 PC 381.
68 *Nelan v Downes* (1917) 23 CLR 546, 550–551 (Barton J).
69 Ibid. 551 (Barton J).
70 (1948) 78 CLR 224.

illustrates a saying of Dean Swift that 'we have just enough religion to hate, but not enough to make us love one another.'[71]

Williams J similarly commented:

I have found this appeal difficult and distasteful, difficult because a civil court has to adjudicate in a suit which involves questions of ecclesiastical law with which it is not familiar, and distasteful because it is unfortunate that a suit of this sort should have reached a civil court at all.[72]

In the preceding New South Wales Supreme Court judgment,[73] Roper CJ, sitting in equity, gave an outline of the history of the Church of England in New South Wales, to which Latham CJ referred with approval.[74] Roper CJ then concluded that 'originally the Church of England as it was established in England was the established Church in New South Wales, and that by a gradual process comprising a number of events it became disestablished.'[75] He lists a number of events as part of that process including the dissolving of the Church and Schools Corporation, the provision of funds in the colony's constitution for the benefit of a number of religions (State aid), the grant of responsible government and the withdrawal of State aid.[76]

In the High Court's decision both Latham CJ and Dixon J similarly concluded that the Church of England had at least begun its life in the colony of New South Wales as the established church of the colony. Latham CJ concluded that:

When New South Wales was occupied the Church of England was recognised and treated as teaching the State religion, and the chaplains of the church were paid from public funds.[77]

While Dixon J concluded:

Notwithstanding judicial statements of a contrary tendency, the better opinion appears to be that the Church of England came to New South Wales as the established church and that it possessed that status in the colony for some decades.[78]

---

71 Ibid. 273 (Rich J).
72 Ibid. 297 (Williams J).
73 *Attorney General v Wylde* (1948) 48 SR (NSW) 366; see also the Full Supreme Court Judgment *Solicitor General v Wylde* (1945) 46 SR (NSW) 83.
74 *Wylde v Attorney General for New South Wales* (1948) 78 CLR 224, 253 (Latham CJ), 298 (Williams J).
75 *Attorney General v Wylde* (1948) 48 SR (NSW) 366, 381 (Roper CJ).
76 Ibid.
77 *Wylde v Attorney General for New South Wales* (1948) 78 CLR 224, 257 (Latham CJ).
78 Ibid. 284 (Dixon J).

He offers a number of pieces of evidence for this conclusion including that the chaplains were part of the civil establishment, the Governor's instruction included the celebration of public worship and that Australia lay with in the territory of the Eat India Company's charter and therefore was part of the Bishopric of Calcutta.[79] While he provides no date for the end of Establishment, commenting that '[i[t is not easy to trace the steps by which the result was reached,'[80] it ended at the latest with the 'grant of representative government and the separation of the colonies.'[81]

Attorney General (Vic); ex rel Black v The Commonwealth (1981)

While the *DOGS Case* primarily considered the meaning of establishment in Section 116 of the *Australian Constitution* the question of whether or not Australia ever had an established church was referred to in passing by Stephen J:

> Australia's colonial history does indeed disclose, first, something at least approaching official recognition of the Church of England; followed, however, by a general recognition of a wide variety of denominations, accompanied by impartial financial assistance to all their churches and schools; then, in the latter part of the nineteenth century, there occurred a move towards complete separation of church and state, with the abolition of all financial aid to churches and to church schools.[82]

Scandrett v Dowling (1992)

On 7 March 1992 the first women were ordained as priests in the Anglican Church of Australia in Perth Western Australia by the Right Reverend Peter Carnley, Archbishop of Perth.[83] The ordination only occurred after much legal wrangling and the delay of the intended first ordination of women on 2 February 1992 announced by the Right Reverend Owen Dowling Bishop of the Anglican Diocese of Canberra Goulburn.[84] Bishop Dowling's announcement was met with legal challenge by those opposed to the ordination of women to the priesthood, and as a result of an injunction, the intended ordination was delayed until the legal issues in dispute could be determined.[85] In *Scandrett v Dowling* the New

---

79 Ibid.
80 Ibid. 285–286 (Dixon J).
81 Ibid. 286 (Dixon J).
82 *Attorney General (Vic); ex rel Black v. The Commonwealth* (1981) 146 CLR 559, 607–608 (Stephen J).
83 Peter Carnley, 'The Perth Ordination Reflecting on Law and Grace' in Elaine Lindsay and Janet Scarfe (eds), *Preachers, Prophets and Heretics Anglican Women's Ministry* (UNSW Press, 2012) 165.
84 *Scandrett v Dowling* (1992) 27 NSWLR 483, 486 (Mahoney JA).
85 *Scandrett v Dowling* (1992) 27 NSWLR 483, 486–487 (Mahoney JA); The Perth ordination also faced legal challenge but was permitted to go ahead, see Peter Carnley, 'The Perth Ordination Reflecting on Law and Grace' in Elaine Lindsay and Janet Scarfe (eds), *Preachers, Prophets and Heretics Anglican Women's Ministry* (UNSW Press, 2012) 165, 169–172.

South Wales Court of Appeal lifted the injunction in effect permitting the ordination to go ahead. The cases however are notable as much for what it is not about as what it is about. As Priestly JA observed:

> The publicity this case has had in some of its stages must have made many people think that it is about whether women can be ordained as priests in the Anglican Church. The men who have brought the case say that it is about no such thing; it is not about a claim by men that God has willed that one half of humanity is unfit, in all social conditions and for all time, for a religious office which is important to a great many people, male and female; what it is about, they say, is their rights as Church members and members of various bodies in the Church's organisation to get a secular court to enforce what they say is the proper interpretation of the Church's Constitution.[86]

Similar Mahoney JA commented:

> The plaintiffs' claim is, and is only, that they may not be ordained without the prior approval of the General Synod of the Church. It is not to be inferred that the plaintiffs or any of them are of the view that the ordination of women is in accordance with the will of Christ, as disclosed in the Bible or otherwise, or that the functions of the priesthood are of their nature such that they may, now or ever, be performed by women. The views of the plaintiffs in relation to matters such as these have not been in issue and so are not relevant in the proceeding as it has finally been dealt with.[87]

In reaching their conclusions both Priestly JA and Mahoney JA examined the legal status of the Anglican Church of Australia including the historical development of that status. In relation to the question of whether the Church of England was the established church in the Australian colonies, Mahoney JA concluded that:

> It is not, I think, clear whether those concerned saw the bodies set up as in fact or in law part of the Church of England which was the established church in England ... separate bodies in communion with . . . the Church of England in England, or separate bodies having rules similar or analogous to those of the Church of England.. . . It may well be that, as the decided cases suggest, those concerned did not then recognise that the Church of England was a body which, as an established church, was confined to the relevant part of the United Kingdom.[88]

---

86 *Scandrett v Dowling* (1992) 27 NSWLR 483, 512 (Priestley JA).
87 Ibid. 488 (Mahoney JA).
88 Ibid. 492 (Mahoney JA).

Priestly JA primarily considered the development of the legal status of the Church of England in Australia, and other colonies, from the mid-1800s. As he observed, the legal status of the Church of England, its Bishoprics and legal powers of its Bishops was being questioned from at least the late 1840s throughout the 1850s and into the 1860s.[89] What can be seen from these debates is that, at least by the early 1860s, it was largely accepted that the Church of England in Australia was not the established church in the Australian colonies. What still needed to be resolved was where that left the Australian church in relation to the Church of England in England and the English statute, ecclesiastical and common law regulating the Church of England. In relation to the specific issue of whether or not the Church of England had been the established church in the very early Australian colony, Priestly JA commented:

> It may well be that, as the decided cases suggest, those concerned did not then recognise that the Church of England was a body which, as an established church, was confined to the relevant part of the United Kingdom."[90]

However, he goes onto say:

> it is now clearly established by judicial decision that the bodies set up outside the relevant parts of the United Kingdom were or became, in the sense to which I have referred, not established churches but voluntary associations.[91]

In Priestly JA's view, those in the early colony may have thought the Church of England was the established church of the colony and may have behaved in that way, but later judicial examination has shown this assumption to be wrong. This is in stark contrast to Dixon J's proclamation that 'better opinion' is that the Church of England was the established church of the colony.[92]

The last date for single establishment

While the case law is mixed on the question of whether the Church of England ever was the established church in the Australian colonies, they all agree, that if it ever had this character, it lost it at some point. Roper J, in *Attorney General v Wylde*, suggests that '[c]learly it was no longer an established church after the abolition of State aid to religion in 1862. In some respects, it was not fully established after the enactment of 7 Wm IV, No 3 [1936].[93] Probably it ceased to be the established church before the introduction of responsible government in

---

89 Ibid. 522–562 (Priestley JA).
90 Ibid. 492 (Priestley JA).
91 Ibid.
92 *Wylde v Attorney General for New South Wales* (1948) 78 CLR 224, 284 (Dixon J).
93 *An act to promote the building of Churches and Chapels and to provide for the maintenance of Ministers of Religion in New South Wales.*

1850.'[94] A fourth potential date is the dissolution of the Church and Schools Corporation in 1833,[95] which, although alluded to by Roper J in his earlier discussions, was not included as a potential date for the end of establishment. We therefore have at least four potential dates to choose from as the end date for any potential establishment of the Church of England in the colony of New South Wales: the dissolution of the Church and schools Corporation in 1833, the initiation of State aid to multiple religions in 1836, the grant of responsible government in 1850 or the removal of State aid in 1862.

It is relatively well accepted that the Australian colonies went through a period of *de jure* plural establishment courtesy of the provision of State aid to multiple Christian denominations, under the *Church Acts,* in combination with constitutional provisions providing a set sum for public worship.[96] The first of the *Church Acts* was introduced in New South Wales in 1836 and provided funds to the 'Three Grand Divisions of Christianity'; the Church of England, Roman Catholic Church and Presbyterian Church.[97] Funds were available for the maintenance of a minister of religion and the building of church buildings on a co-contribution basis.[98] Other colonies followed suit introducing their own *Church Acts* or inheriting them on separation from New South Wales.[99] State aid came to an end in New South Wales with the revocation of that colony's *Church Act* in 1962.[100] However, it took much longer in other colonies with Western Australia not removing State aid until 1895.[101]

The existence of *de jure* plural establishment from 1836 is inconsistent with the continued existence of *de jure* establishment of a single State church; namely the Church of England. While the Church of England continued to be established, if it had previously been so, beyond 1836 it did so as one of three Christian denominations recognized, supported and promoted by the State. This leaves the tantalizing question of the status of the Church of England before this date.[102]

---

94 *Attorney General v Wylde* (1948) 48 SR (NSW) 366, 381.

95 For a discussion of the Church and Schools Corporation see Chapter 8.

96 See, for example, Renae Barker, 'Under Most Peculiar Circumstances': The Church Acts in the Australian Colonies as a Study of Plural Establishment' (2016) 3(3) *Law & History* 28; Stephen v Monsma and J Christopher Soper, *The Challenge of Pluralism: Church and State in Five Democracies* (Rowman & Littlefield Publishing Group, 2nd ed, 2009) 93, 96–99.

97 Frederick Watson (ed), *Historical Records of Australia Series 1* (Library Committee of the Commonwealth Parliament, 1914–1925) vol 17, 226–228.

98 *Church Act 1836* (NSW) s 1.

99 Renae Barker, 'Under Most Peculiar Circumstances': The Church Acts in the Australian Colonies as a Study of Plural Establishment' (2016) 3(3) *Law & History* 28.

100 Ibid. 43–44.

101 Ibid. 48.

102 The end date for plural establishment is usually given as the mid-1860s – coinciding with the removal of State aid in New South Wales. However, the date for removal of State aid across the colonies varies and other interactions between the State and religion such as funding for religious schools makes the exact date for the end of plural establishment difficult to pin down, see Renae Barker, 'Under Most Peculiar Circumstances': The Church

The Church of England before the Church Acts

Just as judicial opinion varies as to whether the Church of England was the established church of colonial New South Wales, commentators have also expressed mixed opinions.[103] In *Attorney General v Wylde*,[104] Roper CJ quotes the opinion of Henry Lowther Clarke in *Constitutional Church Government*[105] that 'the Church of England came to Australia as a State religion.'[106] Although Dixon J did not specifically refer to Clarke's opinion in the subsequent High Court decision he cites much of the same evidence as Roper CJ. Other commentators have expressed a contrary view. Archbishop Eris O'Brien, for example was of the opinion that although the Church of England had an effective monopoly for the first 30 years of colonisation 'with all the rights, privileges and endowments of an established Church' its claim to be so was illegal.[107] This is more in line with the view expressed by Mahoney JA in *Scandrett v Dowling*.[108] After evaluating the evidence and O'Brien's view, Border concludes that 'the evidence both of history and of law clearly supports the case that in the early colonial period of New South Wales the Church of England was . . . the Established Church in fact as well as in theory.'[109]

Which opinion is to be preferred ultimately rests on which definition of establishment you adopt and therefore what evidence you will accept as being sufficient to prove the case that either the Church of England was or was not the established church of colonial New South Wales. '[T]he Home Government, the Colonial Office, the Governors, the Legislative Council of New South Wales, and the responsible Churchmen both clerical and law all held that the Church of England was established in New South Wales in the early period.'[110] Given that those at the time believed and behaved as if the Church of England was the established church, it is incumbent on those who assert otherwise to establish their case.

Two main arguments can be advanced against a finding that the Church of England was the established church. First the there is no official proclamation,

---

Acts in the Australian Colonies as a Study of Plural Establishment' (2016) 3(3) *Law & History* 28.

103 Brian Fletcher, 'The Anglican Ascendancy 1788–1835' in Bruce Kaye (ed), *Anglicanism in Australia A History* (Melbourne University Press, 2002) 7, 16; Ross Border, *Church and State in Australia 1788–1872 A Constitutional Study of The Church of England in Australia* (Society for Promoting Christian Knowledge, 1962) 51.

104 (1948) 48 SR (NSW) 366.

105 Henry Lowther Clarke, *Constitutional Church Government in the Dominions Beyond the Seas and in Other Parts of the Anglican Communion* (Society for Promoting Christian Knowledge, 1924) 77.

106 *Attorney General v Wylde* (1948) 48 SR (NSW) 266, 380 (Roper CJ).

107 Eris O'Brien, *The Foundation of Australia* (Angus and Robertson, 2nd ed, 1950) 44; see also Eris O'Brien, *The Dawn of Catholicism in Australia Vol II* (Angus and Robertson, 1928) 210–216.

108 *Scandrett v Dowling* (1992) 27 NSWLR 483, 492 (Mahoney JA).

109 Border, above n 103, 62.

110 Ibid. 59.

statute or other document establishing the Church of England in New South Wales, second that at the time of reception of English law into Australia, the establishment of the Church of England was not 'applicable to their own situation and the condition of an infant colony.'[111]

No formal legal documents

The first argument that can be advanced against the existence of a formal *de jure* establishment is the lack of official documentation establishing the Church of England. There are no formal legal documents which explicitly state that the Church of England was the established church of New South Wales at the time of settlement. Governor Phillip's instructions did include an admonition to 'enforce a due observance of religion . . . and that you do take such steps for the due celebration of publick [sic] worship as circumstances permit.'[112] While an assumption may be made that this was envisaged to be worship according to the rituals of the Church of England, given the only clergy in the colony was Rev Richard Johnston the words themselves do not go that far. They do however place matters spiritual within the purview of the Governor. An earlier draft of Phillips instructions would have put the matter beyond doubt. The instruction included the admonition:

> especially you shall take care that the Lord's Day be devoutly and duly observed that the Book of Common Prayer as by Law established in this Kingdom be read each Sunday and Holy day, and the Blessed sacraments be administered, according to the Rites of the Church of England.[113]

This would have more firmly associated the infant colony in New South Wales with the Church of England.

The absence of any formal statement as to the establishment of the Church of England at the time of settlement may not however be as significant as it would first seem. As Gregory observes, as part of his assertion that the Church of England was the established church, '[t]here was no explicit statement to this effect – it was too obvious to require it.'[114] Later legal documents such as the charter for the Church and Schools Corporation, the *Registration of Births Deaths and Marriages Act 1826* and the *Licensed Publicans Act 1825* along with the inclusion of

---

111 Sir William Blackstone, *Commentaries on the Laws of England in Four Books, vol. 1* (1753) 107.

112 James Cook (author), Britton Alexander and Frank Murcott Bladen (eds), *Historical Records of New South Wales* (Government Printer, 1892–1901) vol 1, pt 2, 90.

113 Governor Phillips, *Governor Phillips Instructions 25 April 1787 (UK)* (26 July 2017) Documenting a Democracy www.foundingdocs.gov.au/resources/transcripts/nsw2_doc_1787. pdf 7.

114 J.S. Gregory, *Church and State Changing Government Policies towards Religion in Australia: with Particular Reference to Victoria since Separation* (Cassell Australia, 1973) 6.

Archdeacon Scott in the first Legislative Council in 1824 all point towards the establishment of the Church of England.

As discussed in Chapter 8, the Church and Schools Corporation was established in 1826. Under the Corporation one seventh of all land was to be vested in the Corporation for the provision of education and religion in the colony by the Church of England. According to the words of the Corporation's charter it was established to make 'an adequate provision for the support of the Established Church of England throughout the Colony, and for the Education of Youth in the principles of the Church.'[115] These words leave little doubt as to the status those creating the Corporation believed the Church of England to have, and intended it to have, into the future. The Church and Schools Corporation was however short lived. The Roman Catholics, led by Father Joseph Therry, and the Presbyterians, led by Dr John Dunmore Lang, were vocal opponents of the Church and Schools Corporation.[116] They objected to the Corporation on both religious and economic grounds. In Lang's estimation, the Corporation was responsible for,

> repressing emigration, discouraging improvement, secularizing the Episcopal Clergy, and thereby lowering the standard and morals and religion throughout the Territory.[117]

While Lang's main objections appear to be economic, Rev Therry was concerned that the Church of England monopoly created by the Corporation would exclude poor Catholic children from education:

> it may be inferred, that public provision is to be made for Protestant parochial schools exclusively; and that the children of the Catholic poor are to be either excluded from the salutary benefits of education, or compelled or enticed to abandon the truly venerable religion of their ancestors.[118]

115 Frederick Watson (ed), *Historical Records of Australia Series 1* (Library Committee of the Commonwealth Parliament, 1914–1925) vol XI, 438.
116 Bernard Keith Hyams and Bob Bessant, *Schools for the People? An Introduction to the History of State Education in Australia* (Longman, 1972) 18–19; Albert Gordon Austin, *Select Documents in Australian Education 1788–1900* (Sir Isaac Pitman & Sons Ltd, 1963) 26–28.
117 John Dunmore Lang, 'John Dunmore Lang enclosed in Lindesay to Goderich 18 November 1831' in Albert Gordon Austin, *Select Documents in Australian Education 1788–1900* (Sir Isaac Pitman & Sons Ltd, 1963) 26–27.
118 Joseph Therry, 'Therry to Editor of the *Sydney Gazette* 14 June 1825' in Albert Gordon Austin, *Select Documents in Australian Education 1788–1900* (Sir Isaac Pitman & Sons Ltd, 1963) 27.

As a result of these criticisms and the continued reliance of the Church of England on the colonial office for funding,[119] the Corporation was dissolved in 1833.[120]

The *Licensed Publicans Act 1825*[121] and *Parish Registers Act 1826*[122] both included provisions making the clergy of the Church of England part of the formal administrative mechanisms of the law.[123] The *Licensed Publicans Act 1825* required publicans to get a certificate of good character signed by the Minister for the Church of England,[124] the Chief Constable and three respectable house-keepers.[125] The *Parish Registers Act 1826* made the Church of England ministers of each Parish the official registrar of baptisms, marriages and burials. Where a baptism, marriage or burial was conducted by a religious minister, other than a Church of England clergyman, the person conducting the service was required to provide a certificate to the local Church of England minister and pay a fee of one shilling.[126] Further evidence of the treatment of the Church of England as the established church for the purposes of the Act can be found in the reference to the Church of England ministers as the 'established Ministers' in the Act.[127]

Finally, the position of the senior Church of England clergy on the first Legislative Council would indicate that the Church of England was the established church of the colony. Since the arrival of the first fleet the Church of England clergy formed part of the administrative structure of the colony. The Rev Richard Johnston, and later Rev Samuel Marsden and subsequent clergymen, served as civil magistrates.[128] Johnston, for example, sat on the first civil trial to take place in the colony[129] and Marsden has become infamous as the 'flogging parson' in reference to the severe sentences he imposed.[130] O'Brien is critical of the role of the

119 Goderich, 'Goderich to Darling, 14 February 1831' in Albert Gordon Austin, *Select Documents in Australian Education 1788–1900* (Sir Isaac Pitman & Sons Ltd, 1963) 30–31; Third Report of the Commissioner for inquiry into the receipt and Expenditure of the Revenues in the Colonies and Foreign Possession, *Great Britain and Ireland Parliamentary Documents Vol 5 1826–1838,* 1 November 1830, 74–76; Goderich, 'Goderich to Darling, 14 February 1831' in Frederick Watson (ed), *Historical Records of Australia Series 1* (Library Committee of the Commonwealth Parliament, 1914–1925) vol 16, 81.
120 Austin, above n 116, 31. For their answer to this question, see Chapter 5.
121 6 Geo 4 No. 4.
122 6 Geo 4 No. 21.
123 Gregory, above n 114, 10; Border, above n 103, 56–57.
124 Where a Church of England Minister officiated with in the district where a publican wanted to be granted their license.
125 *Licensed Publicans Act 1825*, 6 Geo 4 No. 4, s 5.
126 *Parish Registers Act 1825*, 6 Geo 4 No. 21, s 8–9.
127 See *Parish Registers Act 1825*, 6 Geo 4 No 21, s 8.
128 K. J. Cable, *Johnson, Richard (1753–1827)* Australian Dictionary of Bibliography http://adb.anu.edu.au/biography/johnson-richard-2275; A. T. Yarwood, *Marsden, Samuel (1765–1838)* Australian Dictionary of Bibliography http://adb.anu.edu.au/biography/marsden-samuel-2433.
129 For an account of the case see Jeremy Stoljar, *The Australian Book of Great Trials: The cases that Shaped a Nation* (Pier 9, 1st ed, 2011) ch 1.
130 Eris O'Brien, *The Foundation of Australia* (Angus and Robertson, 2nd ed, 1950) 45.

clergy as magistrates as in his view it 'made the church part of the governmental machine and prevented it from criticizing the penal system.'[131]

In 1823, the *Judicature Act 1823* (27 Geo. III C.2) set up the Legislative Council of New South Wales made up of people appointed by the Governor. In 1824, the Church of England clergyman Archdeacon Scott was appointed to the Council. A decade later he was replaced by his successor Archdeacon Broughton, later the first Anglican Bishop of Australia, who retained his position until 1842.[132] The presence of Church of England clergy in the Legislature points to a practice of treating the Church of England as the established church. It mirrors the position of Bishops in the House of Lords in England and was a privilege not afforded to clergy of other denominations, even after the State began to provide funding to them under the *Church Act*. While Rev Dunmore Lange, the Presbyterian minister, did sit in the Legislative Council, he did so as an elected member, not on the basis of his position as a member of the clergy within the colony.[133]

Not applicable to the colony

The second argument that can be advanced to rebut the assertion that the Church of England was the established church in early colonial New South Wales is that English laws relating to its establishment were not 'applicable to their own situation and the condition of any infant colony.' As a result, these laws were not received into the colony and thus did not form part of the laws of Australia. O'Brien, for example, bases his assertion that the Church of England was not the established church of Australia on this argument.[134]

In *Cooper v Stuart*[135] the Privy Council held that the colony of New South Wales was a settled colony. As a result, the law of England, as at the time of settlement, prevailed until it was abrogated or modified.[136] As Lord Blackstone puts it 'all the English laws then in being, which are the birth-right of every subject, are immediately there in force.'[137] However, this general principle is qualified. Not all of the laws of England are applicable to a newly settled colony. As such only these laws which are 'applicable to their own situation and the condition of any infant

131 Ibid.
132 Gregory, above n 114, 25.
133 D. W. A Baker, *Lang, John Dunmore (1799–1878)* Australian Dictionary of Bibliography http://adb.anu.edu.au/biography/lang-john-dunmore-2326.
134 Eris O'Brien, *The Dawn of Catholicism in Australia Vol II* (Angus and Robertson, 1928) 210–216.
135 (1880) 14 App Cas 286.
136 Ibid. 291.
137 Alex C. Castles, *An Introduction to Australian Legal History* (The Law Book Company Limited, 1971) 10–11 Cf Sir William Blackstone, *Commentaries on the Laws of England in Four Books, vol. 1* (1753) 107.

colony'[138] in fact apply.[139] Lord Blackstone goes onto suggest that amongst the laws which may not apply to a newly settled colony are 'the modes and maintenance of the established Church' and 'the jurisdiction of spiritual Courts' as they are 'neither necessary nor convenient for them.'[140] Given the nature of the Australian colony as a military convict settlement, it is arguable that the laws relating to the establishment of the Church of England were not necessary nor convenient. As outlined above, this is the view taken by the judges in the early cases considering this issue.[141] It is not until the decision of Roper CJ and Dixon J in 1948 that this view is rejected.[142]

However, the date for the reception of laws into Australia may not be 1788. In his 1938 article, Evatt argues that this emphasis on the criminal jurisdiction suggests that the colony was not a true colony but a goal and the only difference between it and the goals in England was it was not in England.[143] His argument is supported by the fact that the 1787 Act setting up the civil and criminal juris-diction to apply in New South Wales outlined that the Criminal courts where to apply the criminal law of England as if the offence had been committed in England.[144] This meant that the criminal laws did not crystallize in 1788 but continued to change as the criminal law in England changed as the judges had to constantly refer back to the criminal law in England.[145] Adding weight to this argument is the passage of the *Australian Courts Act 1828*.[146] This act was designed to end confusion regarding the date of reception of laws in the Austral-ian colonies.[147] The Act, *inter alia,* set the date for reception of English law into Australia as 25 July 1828.[148] However the Act did not import all of the Laws of England only those laws 'consistent with such laws so far as the circumstances of the said colony.'[149] The exclusion of the Church of England as the established church of the colony would then rest upon a similar one as that advanced above in relation to reception of English Law in 1788.

---

138 Alex C. Castles, *An Introduction to Australian Legal History* (The Law Book Company Limited, 1971) 10–11. Cf Sir William Blackstone, *Commentaries on the Laws of England in Four Books, vol. 1* (1753) 107.

139 In *Cooper v Stuart* (1880) 14 App Cas 286, 294 the Court found that the relevant laws of England did not apply in the infant colony.

140 *Cooper v Stuart* (1880) 14 App Cas 286, 291.

141 *Ex parte Ryan* (1855) 2 Legge 876; *Ex parte The Rev George King* (1861) 2 Legge 1307; *Nelan v Downes* (1917) 23 CLR 546.

142 *Attorney General v Wylde* (1948) 48 SR (NSW) 366, 381 (Roper CJ); *Wylde v Attorney General for New South Wales* (1948) 78 CLR 224, 284 (Dixon J).

143 H. V. Evatt, 'The Legal Foundations of New South Wales' (1938) 11 *The Australian Law Journal* 421.

144 Ibid. 412.

145 Ibid. 415–416.

146 9 Geo 4, c 83.

147 Peter Butt, *Land Law* (Thomson Reuters, 6th ed, 2010) 2.

148 Alex Castles, 'The Reception and Status of English law in Australia' (1963) 2(1) *Adelaide Law Review* 1, 3.

149 *Australian Courts Act 1828*, 9 Geo 4, c 83.

The question of whether the Church of England was ever the established church was not only relevant to the Australian colony. Colonies around the empire needed to grapple with the issue. In a series of judgments, the Privy Council held that the Church of England was not the established Church of South Africa.[150] Most influentially, in 1863, in *Long v Bishop of Cape Town*, the court found the issuing of letters patient establishing the Bishopric did not also establish an ecclesiastical jurisdiction with in the colony. [151] And therefore that:

> The Church of England, in places where there is no Church established by law, is in the same situation with any other religious body – in no better, but in no worse position; and the members may adopt, as the members of any other communion may adopt, rules for enforcing discipline within their body which will be binding on those who expressly or by implication have assented to them.[152]

This argument is certainly persuasive and is the one adopted by all the courts considering the question up until *Wylde* in 1948.[153] These arguments, however, as with the argument that there are no legal documents formally establishing the Church of England, rest on a very technical understanding of the require-ments for establishment. While the establishment of the Church of England may not have been technically applicable to the circumstances of the colony this did not stop those in authority from treating the Church as if it was the established church.[154] This would seem to suggest that those in authority did consider the laws of England relating to the establishment of the Church of England as being 'applicable to the colony.' Further even if it is accepted that laws relating to the establishment of the Church of England were not technically received into the Australian colony this does not stop the Church of England being later estab-lished. As identified above, multiple colonial documents refer to or treat the Church of England as the established church.

Conclusion

As Border points out, O'Brien, Roper CJ and Dixon J may well be correct in their assertions that the Church of England was not formally the established church, but that does not change the fact that the Church of England was treated as if it was the established church. Their arguments rest on legal technicalities and while academically interesting, say little about the practical realities of a colony many

---

150 *Long v Bishop of Capetown* (1863) 15 ER 756; *Re the Bishop of Natal* (1864) 16 ER 43; *Bishop of Natal v Gladstone (1866)* LR 3 Eq 1.
151 *Long v Bishop of Capetown* (1863) 15 ER 756, 774.
152 Ibid.
153 *Ex parte Ryan* (1855) 2 Legge 876; *Ex parte The Rev George King* (1861) 2 Legge 1307; *Ex parte Collins* [1889] The Weekly Notes 85; *Nelan v Downes* (1917) 23 CLR 546.
154 *Scandrett v Dowling* (1992) 27 NSWLR 483, 492 (Priestly JA).

months away from mother England and the legal expertise to sort out such legal niceties. As Border puts it, '[i]f an innocent man is hanged, the Courts can decide that he was wrongly hanged but they cannot unhang him.'[155] Even if the Church of England was never technically the established church, saying so now does not change the fact that it was treated as such for much of the early colonial period. Even if *de jure* establishment cannot be maintained, the Church of England was certainly the *de facto* established church.

If the Church of England was not the established church this raises another question: what was the relationship between the State and religion in the early colonial period? Plural establishment did not begin until 1836 which leaves nearly 50 years, a not inconsiderable period of time, unaccounted for. Neutrality or pluralism would seem to be the most likely candidates. Separation must certainly be ruled out from the start given the high level of interaction between the State and religion already outlined in this chapter. While possible, pluralism is unlikely, at least in the initial period, as the first non-Church of England clergy did not arrive in the colony until February 1800 – however, these arrived as convicts while Rev Dixon was given permission to officiate this permission was short lived.[156] Restrictions were not finally removed on Roman Catholics until the arrival of Rev Joseph Therry and Rev Philip Conolly in May 1820.[157] While clergy or religious leaders are not necessary for a religion to exist in a given State and be included in pluralism this fact along with the other restrictions faced by Roman Catholics and all of those not belonging to the Church of England would seem to rule out pluralism.[158] This leaves neutrality, which is also unlikely. Neutrality requires the State to take an even-handed approach towards religion, favouring none over others.[159] While it is certainly true that some of the early Governors, particularly Governor Phillip, were uninterested in religion this does not mean they were neutral as between different religions.[160] In practice, the role for the Church of England in the early colony may have been more as a moral policemen than a fully-fledged State Church but it still received privileges and support not given to other religions. Further the State, at least on paper, endorsed the activities of the Church of England. For example, all convicts in the early colony, regardless of denomination, were required to attend church services conducted by the Church of England clergyman Rev Richard Johnston.[161] This leaves only establishment as a viable description for the State–religion relationship during this period.

---

155 Border, above n 103, 61.
156 Lynette Ramsay Silver, *The Battle of Vinegar Hill: Australia's Irish Rebellion, 1804* (Doubleday, 1st ed, 1989) 25.
157 Tom Luscombe, *Builders and Crusaders* (Lansdowne Press, 1st ed, 1967) 19.
158 See Chapter 7.
159 Ahdar and Leigh, above n 13, 87–92.
160 Gregory, above n 114, 5–6.
161 Luscombe, above n 157, 3.

4 Religion in the Australian Constitution

Introduction

When discussing the relationship between the State and religion in Australia reference will almost inevitably be made to Section 116 of the *Australian Constitution*, most commonly to support an assertion that Australia is a secular State. The Section states:

> The Commonwealth shall not make any law for establishing any religion, or for imposing any religious observance, or for prohibiting the free exercise of any religion, and no religious test shall be required as a qualification for any office or public trust under the Commonwealth.

This is not the only reference to religion to be found in the *Australian Constitution*. The preamble of the *Constitution* begins with the words

> WHEREAS the people of New South Wales, Victoria, South Australia, Queensland, and Tasmania, *humbly relying on the blessing of Almighty God,* have agreed to unite in one indissoluble Federal Commonwealth under the Crown of the United Kingdom of Great Britain and Ireland, and under the Constitution hereby established [emphasis added].

This chapter examines the history of both these two references to religion along with the interpretation of Section 116 by Australia's High Court.

The history and inclusion of both references to religion in Australia's *Constitution* are intimately linked. Arguably without one we would not have the other, and vice-versa. They are a tangible reminder of the compromises needed to make Federation possible. In the case of religion, the churches were adamant that they would not support Federation if God was not recognised in the nation's founding document. Whether or not the Constitutional Convention delegates and constitutional drafters personally felt that God was a necessary inclusion in the *Constitution* was largely irrelevant. As Patrick Glynn observed:

> We must, I am sure, all agree, whatever may be the decision of the Convention as to the propriety of passing the motion, that we cannot ignore the evidence afforded by the petitions of a widespread desire that the spirit of

the proposal should be accepted; we cannot pass over in silence the almost unanimous request of the members of so many creeds, of one aim and hope, that the supremacy of God should be recognised, and His blessing invoked, in the opening lines of our Constitution.[1]

However, the churches were not the only ones petitioning the Constitutional Convention on religious matters. Of equal importance were the numerous petitions seeking to keep God out of the *Constitution*.[2] The solution was to both include God in the preamble and then exclude the Commonwealth from effectively doing anything about it by the inclusion of what because Section 116.

Despite extensive academic literature on Section 116[3] there are in fact very few High Court cases dealing directly with the provision.[4] This makes understanding the meaning and application of the provision difficult and often a matter of speculation. What does emerge from the small number of cases is a reluctance by the High Court to give Section 116 an expansive application. Instead the provision has been read narrowly with each of its four 'limbs' confined to its own meaning rather than the provision being read as a 'repository of some broad statement of

1 *Official Report of the National Australasian Convention Debates*, Adelaide, 22 April 1897, 1184 (Patrick Glynn).
2 Richard Ely, *Unto God and Ceasar: Religious Issues in the Emerging Commonwealth 1891– 1906* (Melbourne University Press, 1976) 24–30, 43–44.
3 See, for example, Clifford Pannam, 'Traveling Section 116 with a U.S. Road Map' (1963) 4 *Melbourne University Law Review* 41; Stephen McLeish, 'Making Sense of Religion and the Constitution: A Fresh Start for Section 116' (1992) 18 *Monash University Law Review* 207; Tony Blackshield, 'Religion and Australian Constitutional Law' in Peter Radan, Denis Meyerson and Rosalind F Croucher, *Law and Religion: God, the State and the Common Law* (Routledge, 2005) 81.; Kate Boland, 'Interpreting the Constitutional Freedom of Religion: How Australian Courts Might Define "Religion" and Interpret the "Free Exercise" Provision in the Future' (2010) 12(3) *Constitutional Law and Policy Review* 47; Carolyn Evans, 'Religion as Politics Not Law; The Religion Clause in the Australian Constitution' (2008) 36(3) *Religion, State and Society* 283; FD Cumbrae-Stewart 'Section 116 of the Constitution' (1946) 20 *Australian Law Journal* 207; Michael Hogan, 'Separation of Church and State: Section 116 of the Australian Constitution' (1981) 53(2) *Australian Quarterly* 214; Gabriel Moens, 'The Action-Belief Dichotomy and Freedom of Religion' (1989–1990) 12 *Sydney Law Review* 195; Gabriel Moens, 'Church and State Relations in Australia and the United States: The Purpose and Effect Approaches and the Neutrality Principle' (1996) 4 *Brigham Young University Law Review* 787; Joshua Puls, 'The Wall of Separation: Section 116, the First Amendment and Constitutional Religious Guarantees' (1998) 26 *Federal Law Review* 139; Luke Beck, 'Clear Emphatic: The Separation of Church and State under the Australian Constitution' (2008) 27 *University of Tasmania Law Review* 161; note this list is far from conclusive. It is intended as sample of the literature which has been published on Section 116.
4 The only reported High Court cases which consider Section 116 as part of the *ratio* of the case are: *Krygger v Williams* (1912) 15 CLR 366; *Adelaide Company of Jehovah's Witnesses v Commonwealth* (1943) 67 CLR 366; *Attorney General (Vic); ex rel Black v The Commonwealth* (1981) 146 CLR 559; *Kruger v Commonwealth* (1997) 190 CLR 1; *Williams v The Commonwealth* (2012) 248 CLR 156.

principle concerning the separation of church and state.'[5] The discussion of the interpretation of Section 116 in this chapter therefore focuses on each of the four limbs individually, as well as highlighting the gaps in our understanding of the meaning and application of the provision.

The case law

As alluded to above, there are only a handful of High Court cases which directly address the meaning of Section 116. There are also a number of Federal Court,[6] Family Court[7] and State Supreme Court[8] decisions which consider Section 116 to various degrees as well as a small number of High Court cases which are either unreported[9] or where the comments relating to Section 116 are *in obiter.*[10]

As the High Court cases are referred to frequently in this chapter, and throughout the remaining chapters, a brief outline of the facts of each case is included here as a reference for readers.

Krygger v Williams

The High Court had its first opportunity to examine Section 116 in *Krygger v Williams.*[11] Krygger was charged with failing to render service required by Part XII of the *Defence Act 1903* (Cth). This part required Krygger to attend military training for a period of 64 hours. He failed to attend because as he stated:

> Attendance at drill is against my conscience and the word of God. If thine enemy smite thee on the one cheek turn to him the other is part of my religion. . . . anything therefore such as compulsory military training is anti-Christ, and is not following the Lord Jesus. Therefore I can have no part in the matter whatever.[12]

---

5 *Attorney General (Vic); ex rel Black v The Commonwealth* (1981) 146 CLR 559, 609 (Stephen J).

6 *Cheedy on behalf of the Yindjibarndi People v State of Western Australia* [2011] FCAFC 100 (12 August 2011).

7 *P & L* [2006] FamCA 947 (28 September 2006); *In the Matter Of: John Murray Abbott Appellant/Husband and Annette Jean Abbott Respondent/Wife Appeal* [1995] FamCA 5 (6 February 1995); *Re Lynette* [1999] FamCA 1239 (15 September 1999).

8 *Hoxton Park Residents' Action Group Inc. v Liverpool City Council* [2010] NSWSC 1312 (12 November 2010); *Gordon v Dimitriou* [1999] QCA 132 (16 April 1999); *Deputy Commissioner of Taxation v Casley* [2017] WASC 161 (16 June 2017).

9 *ICM Agriculture Pty Ltd v The Commonwealth* [2009] HCA 51 (9 December 2009); *Wurridjal v The Commonwealth of Australia* [2009] HCA 2 (2 February 2009).

10 *Judd v McKeon* (1926) CLR 380; *R v Winneke; Ex part Gallagher* (1983) 152 CLR 211.

11 (1912) 15 CLR 336.

12 *Krygger v Williams* (1912) 15 CLR 336, 367.

The legislation provided for those whose 'conscientious beliefs do not allow them to bear arms"[13] to be exempt in times of war. However, this did not apply to training and the First World War was still two years away. In times of peace, the legislation provided that those 'who are forbidden by the doctrines of their religion to bear arms shall so far as possible be allotted to non-combatant duties.'[14] This also applied in times of war. Krygger argued, among other things, that the provisions of the *Defence Act 1903* at the time were in breach of the freedom of religion limb of Section 116.

Adelaide Company of Jehovah's Witnesses v Commonwealth

In *The Adelaide Company of Jehovah's Witnesses Inc v The Commonwealth*[15] (*Jehovah's Witnesses case*) the High Court was asked to decide whether:

> s. 116 prevents the Commonwealth Parliament from legislating to restrain the activities of a body, the existence of which is, in the opinion of the Governor-General, prejudicial to the defence of the Commonwealth or the efficient prosecution of the war, if that body is a religious organization? Is the answer to this question affected by the fact that the subversive activities of such a body are founded upon the religious views of its members? Can such a body be suppressed?[16]

The case occurred in the middle of the Second World War and involved the application of the *National Security (Subversive Associations) Regulations* made by the Governor General under Section 5 of the *National Security Act 1939* (Cth)[17] to the Jehovah's Witnesses. The declaration had in effect rendered membership of the Jehovah's Witnesses unlawful and led to the seizure of their property in Adelaide. The Governor General was concerned about the beliefs and actives of the Jehovah's Witnesses for several reasons including their belief that Satan rules the world though agencies such as organized political, religious and financial organisations. And in particular that the British Empire was one such organisation, associating it with the Beast in Chapter Thirteen of Revelation.[18] As such, they were teaching beliefs prejudicial to the war effort.[19]

---

13 *Krygger v Williams* (1912) 15 CLR 336, 371; see *Defence Act 1903* (Cth) s 61(i).

14 *Krygger v Williams* (1912) 15 CLR 336, 372; see s143(3) *Defense Act 1903* (Cth), as repealed by *Defence Act 1951* (Cth) s12.

15 (1943) 67 CLR 116.

16 *The Adelaide Company of Jehovah's Witnesses Inc v The Commonwealth* (1943) 67 CLR 116, 122 (Latham CJ).

17 *National Security Act 1939* (Cth), as repealed by *Statute Law Revision Act 1950* (Cth) sch 3.

18 *The Adelaide Company of Jehovah's Witnesses Inc v The Commonwealth* (1943) 67 CLR 116, 133, 145–146.

19 A more detailed discussion of the background to the case can be found in Chapter 7.

Attorney General (Vic); ex rel Black v The Commonwealth

The only case to consider the establishment limb of Section 116 is *Attorney General (Vic); ex rel Black v The Commonwealth*[20] (*DOGS case*). The High Court was asked to consider whether payments made by the federal government to non-government religious schools, via Section 96 grants to the States, amounted to establishment of any religion. In the 1960s the federal government introduced capital grants for schools. These began as grants for specific projects which were available to both non-government and government schools. The programme later morphed into recurring capital works grants which were only available to non-government schools. In the 1970s the federal government expanded their school funding programme further by introducing per-capita grants for non-government schools, predominantly religious.[21] While the Plaintiff was the Attorney General for Victoria the case was primarily pursued by the Defence of Government Schools (DOGS) group.[22]

Kruger v Commonwealth *(1997) 190 CLR 1*

In *Kruger v Commonwealth*[23] (*Stolen Generation* case) the High Court was asked to consider whether the *Aboriginal Ordinance 1918* (NT), amongst other things, infringed Section 116. The case was brought as part of a raft of litigation by members and parents of the Stolen Generations. This case concerned five members of the Stolen Generations who had been removed from their families as children and one mother whose child had been removed.[24]

Blackshield has argued that the plaintiffs made two crucial errors which may have affected the outcome of their case in relation to their claims based on Section 116. First, the main issues of the case were reserved for decision by the Full Court before the taking of evidence. This meant that the subtleties of their argument and the effect of the *Aboriginal Ordinance 1918* (NT) could not be fully taken into account.[25] Second, the six cases all concerned members of the Stolen Generations from the Northern Territory. As a result, the Court also had to consider the operation of Section 122 of the *Constitution*. This Section gives the Commonwealth power to legislate for the territories. Unfortunately for the plaintiffs the interaction between Section 122 and other provisions of the *Constitution*, including Section 116, has not been settled by the High Court.[26]

---

20 (1981) 146 CLR 559.
21 For a more detailed discussion of the background of the case see Chapter 8.
22 See Jean Ely, *Contempt of Court: Unofficial Voices from the DOGS Australia High Court Case 1981* (Dissenters Press, 2010) for an account of the case from the perspective of members of the DOGS organisation.
23 (1997) 190 CLR 1.
24 Blackshield, above n 3, 103–104.
25 Ibid. 103–104.
26 Ibid. 105–106.

Williams v The Commonwealth *(2012) 248 CLR 156*

In 2006 the federal government introduced the National School Chaplaincy Programme (NSCP) which provided funding to both government and non-government schools for religious chaplaincy services. The programme has since been challenged twice in the High Court.[27] While in both cases the court declared the programme to be unconstitutional as a result of the funding mechanisms used by the federal government, only the first (*Williams No 1*) directly considered Section 116. The plaintiff in both cases, Ron Williams, became aware of the programme when his son came home from school singing Christian songs. After requesting his children be removed from religious education classes and attempting to move them to a school without a school chaplain, he launched a High Court challenge to the NSCP.[28] In his own words he was not 'anti-faith' but rather 'fiercely and passionately for the separation of Church and State.'[29]

While the plaintiff was successful, in having the NSCP declared unconstitutional on the basis of his non-Section 116 arguments, the programme continues in both government and non-government schools. The federal government has been able to remedy the defects in the funding mechanism identified by the High Court.[30]

History of Section 116 and God in the preamble

Andrew Inglis Clark's dream – the first draft

Andrew Inglis Clark was the first to attempt to draft a complete Constitution for Australia. He drew heavily from the *Constitution of the United States of America*.[31] Much of his Constitution can be seen as a cut and paste job from this document, with the necessary changes to make the clauses relevant to Australian conditions.[32] Clark was drawn to America and its history, particularly its political history, from an early age. Throughout his life he read American authors, followed the careers of American judges and corresponded with American friends.[33] He was even president of The American Club in Hobart, an annual dinner society which met on the anniversary of American independence to celebrate the

---

27 *Williams v The Commonwealth* (2012) 248 CLR 156; *Williams v Commonwealth (no 2)* (2014) 252 CLR 416.

28 Renae Barker, 'A Critical Analysis of Religious Aspects of the Australian Chaplaincy Cases' (2015) 4(1) *Oxford Journal of Law and Religion* 26, 41.

29 Compass, *Challenging the Chaplains* (24 October 2010) Australian Broadcasting Corporation www.abc.net.au/compass/s3024993.htm.

30 For a more detailed discussion of the background of the case see Chapter 8.

31 John La Nauze, *The Making of the Australian Constitution* (Melbourne University Press, 1972) 24–29.

32 See J Reynolds, 'A.I. Clark's American Sympathies and his Influence on Australian Federation' (1958) 32 *The Australian Law Journal*, appendix 1 for a copy of Clark's constitution.

33 Ibid. 63.

founding of the *American Constitution*.[34] It is not surprising then that when he came to draft his vision of an Australian Constitution he should draw so heavily from the *American Constitution* he so admired.

The concept of personal rights, as enshrined in the American Bill of Rights, appealed to Clark. In relation to religion, he included two clauses: Clause 46 which stated:

> The Federal Parliament shall not make any law for the establishment or support of any religion, or for the purpose of giving any preferential recognition to any religion, or for prohibiting the free exercise of any religion;

and Clause 81 which stated:

> No Province shall make any law prohibiting the free exercise of any religion.[35]

These clauses are similar in nature to Article VI s. 3 and the First Amendment of the *American Constitution*.

> The Senators and Representatives before mentioned, and the members of the several State Legislatures, and all executives and judicial officers, both of the United States, and of the several States, shall be bound by oath or affirmation to support this Constitution; but no religious test shall ever be required as a qualification to any office or public trust under the United States.
>
> Congress shall make no law respecting an establishment of religion or prohibiting the free exercise thereof

Clause 46 places a restriction on the federal government such that it would not be able to establish or support any religion nor give preferential treatment to any religion nor prohibit the free exercise of any religion. Clause 81 applies the last of these prohibitions to the States. Presumably in Clark's Federation, the States would have been free to establish a particular religion or give preferential treatment to a religion.

Initially, Clark was successful in getting this American style Bill of Rights clause into the draft constitution. At the 1891 Constitutional Convention in Sydney, the drafting committee, headed by Samuel Griffith, recommended the inclusion of Clark's Clause 81.[36] This is hardly surprising as Clark along with Kingston joined Griffith to make up the three person drafting sub-committee (Edmund Barton was also present throughout).[37] His inclusion in this group is not surprising when you consider that he was the first to attempt to draft a constitution for

---

34 Blackshield, above n 3, 62.
35 Ely, above n 2, 1.
36 The word province was amended to read 'state.'
37 Blackshield, above n 3, 66.

Australia and it is clear from the words of Bernhard Ringrose Wise, one of the New South Wales delegates, that he was respected as an expert on American constitutionalism by his fellow delegates:

> No one in Australia, not even excepting Sir Samuel Griffith, had Mr Clark's knowledge of the Constitutional history of the United States; and, when knowledge of detail is combined with zeal, its influence on the deliberative body becomes irresistible.[38]

When you take into account Griffith was to become the first Chief Justice of the High Court of Australia, this is an amazing compliment.

While Clause 46 was not included, meaning in theory both the federal government and the States could establish religions and provide preferential treatment to a particular religion, the free exercise of religion, any religion, was 'safe.'

When the Draft Constitution, prepared by Griffith, Kingston, Clark and Barton was presented, the Convention accepted the drafting committee's recommendations regarding the inclusion of Clarks clause 81 without debate.[39]

A gap of six years followed before the next Constitutional Convention in Adelaide in 1897. However, Clark was not present. Owing to ill health, he took no further active part in the Federation process after 1891. However, his influence can be seen in the nickname 'Clark's boys' given to those who carried on the cause of Federation in Tasmania.[40]

At the Adelaide Convention in 1897,[41] Clark's clause was renumbered to 109, but was otherwise left as it was. The clause was not discussed and seemed well on the way to becoming a part of the *Australian Constitution*. Again, at the Sydney Convention in 1897[42] the clause was not discussed. [43] However at the Melbourne Convention in 1898[44] it was rejected when Higgins sought to amend it.[45]

In again, out again

It is possible that Clause 109 (as it was then called) may have made it through the Melbourne Convention unscathed had Henry Bournes Higgins not sought to amend it. As it was, once Higgins started, two other delegates also sought to

---

38 Ibid. 64–65.
39 Ely, above n 2, 1.
40 Reynolds, above n 32, 66.
41 *Official Report of the National Australasian Convention Debates*, Adelaide, 22 March 1987 to 5 May 1897.
42 *Official Record of the Debates of the Australasian Federal Convention*, Sydney, 2 September 1897 to 24 September 1897.
43 Ely, above n 2, 48.
44 *Official Record of the Debates of the Australasian Federal Convention*, Melbourne, 20 January 1898 to 17 March 1898.
45 Ely, above n 2, 67.

amend the clause. As a result, Clark's Bill of Rights style Freedom of Religion was doomed.

Higgins sought to amend the clause to include the Commonwealth and prevent the use of a religious test, presumably for public office, although the amendment does not make this clear. Had Higgins' amendment been successful, Clause 109 would have read:

> Neither State nor the Commonwealth shall make any law prohibiting the free exercise of religion or imposing any religious test or observance.[46]

Brandon and Symon also sought to amend Clause 109. Brandon wanted to add the words:

> But shall prevent the performance of any such religious rites, as are of a cruel or demoralizing character or contrary to the law of the Commonwealth.

Symon wanted to remove the existing Clause 109, in favour of retaining the second part of Higgins' amendment, the restriction on the use of a religious test for public office. His proposed new Clause 109 read:

> No religious test shall be imposed as a qualification for any public office of trust in the Commonwealth or in a State.

Neither Brandon nor Symon's amendments were put to the Convention, but their proposal made the debate more confusing than it might otherwise have been. Making the debate even more confusing is the fact that the debate commenced at the end of the day on 7 February 1898 and had to run onto the next day. To add even further to the confusion, on 8 February Higgins proposed a clause which he had modified again. This time the clause he proposed read:

> A State shall not, nor shall the Commonwealth, make any law prohibiting the free exercise of any religion, or for the establishment of any religion, or imposing and religious observance.[47]

With all the chopping and changing, Clark's Bill of Rights style clause was doomed. Once the delegates started thinking negatively about the various amendments they were stuck and voted 'No' to the clause itself as well. So why didn't the convention want to strengthen the clause and why didn't they want the clause itself? To answer these questions, it is important to understand Higgins' argument for the clause.

---

46 Higgins' proposed additions are underlined.
47 Ely, above n 2, 63.

Higgins' argument for both the clause and the amendment was based on the experience in America. In particular, he referred to the result of the American Supreme Court decision which had held that America was a 'Christian Nation' with the ultimate result that the United States Congress had been able to impose Sunday observance on the World Columbian Exhibition held in 1892.[48]

The American Supreme Court decision in question was *Church of the Holy Trinity v United States* 143 US 45, which concerned an Act which restricted the employment of foreigners. The Court held that the Act was not infringed when a church employed a rector from England. The Court based its decision on the fact that the Congress could not have intended to jeopardize the employment of ministers of religion because 'America was a Christian Nation.' The Court based this assertion on a historical analysis going right back to the commissioning of Christopher Columbus.[49]

Higgins argued that if an American Court could hold that America was a 'Christian Nation' despite no such express assertion in their *Constitution*, an Australian Court could come to a similar conclusion, especially if God was referred to in the preamble of the *Australian Constitution*. Section 109, and his amendment to have it apply to the Commonwealth, would, in his opinion, prevent this from happening. He did not mention that America had Article VI and the First Amendment, on which Section 109 was based. So it is doubtful that Section 109 would have had this effect if the issue had ever arisen in Australia. It has been argued by Blackshield that Higgins misrepresented the *Church of the Holy Trinity v United States*. Blackshield argues that rather than being an authority for the proposition that America was a 'Christian Nation, the case was merely a legislative interpretation that the Act in question applied only to the employment of manual labourers.'[50]

Higgins argued that the declaration by the American Supreme Court in *Church of the Holy Trinity v United States* that America was a 'Christian Nation' had the immediate effect of providing ammunition for the Sunday observance lobbyists. As a result of heavy lobbying by such groups federal funding for the World Columbian Exhibition was granted on the condition that it not open on Sunday. Higgins did not mention that this funding ran out after only a fortnight and the exhibition opened on Sunday after that.[51]

Higgins was concerned that if Australia could be seen as a 'Christian Nation' because of the reference to God in the preamble, the federal government might be able to impose Sunday observance. His reason for objecting to such an outcome seems to be two pronged. First, some members of the community, such as

---

48 Blackshield, above n 3, 82.
49 Ibid.
50 Blackshield, above n 3.
51 Ibid. 82–83.

the Seventh-day Adventists, objected to the imposition of Sunday observance and second, that such matters should be left to the States as local custom dictated.[52]

Where Higgins' argument fell down was the fact that there was no reference to God in the *Australian Constitution*. The inclusion of God in the preamble had been discussed and rejected in Adelaide. While there had continued to be pressure for a reference to God in the preamble, at the time Higgins' amendments were discussed, God was not a part of the preamble and there was no indication that God would be. So this argument had no currency and, while a possibility, there was no immediate 'threat.'[53]

The delegates' negativity towards the clause on the Tuesday night was evident from the multiple interruptions to Higgins' speech. Higgins had only been speaking for a very short time when Gordon interrupted with "What is the honorable member's amendment?" This followed by interruptions by Symon, Fraser, Braddon, Douglas and an unidentified member. The debate about Clause 109 came at the end of the day and you can almost hear the frustration in the voices of the delegates as they interrupted with comments like: "which side are you on?", "why not leave the words out of the preamble?", "But how many votes will you lose by doing so?" and "I do not think so." On the Tuesday afternoon the delegates where clearly not in a positive frame of mind towards either the clause or the amendment.

Higgins' address to the convention the next day did not start well. It began with the following exchange:

Higgins: There is no application to the Federal Parliament at all in the clause as it stands. I intend to propose amendments which, if adopted, will make the clause read as follows:-

A state shall not, nor shall the Commonwealth, make any law prohibiting the free exercise of any religion, or for the establishment of any religion, or imposing any religious observance.

O'Connor: *The Commonwealth will have no power to do that.*
Higgins: I explained yesterday evening that, in the *Constitution of the United States*, there is a prohibition on Congress making any law for this purpose.
Symon: No.
Higgins: With all respect to the honorable member, there is.
Symons: Prohibiting religion?

The rest of the debate continued along three main themes: (1) The Commonwealth could not legislate about religion anyway; (2) the States should have the

---

52 Blackshield, above n 3; see also *Official Record of the Debates of the Australasian Federal Convention*, Melbourne, 7 February 1898, 656 (Henry Higgins).
53 This line of argument will be discussed more fully bellow.

right to legislate regarding religion; and (3) It is desirable to be able to prevent certain religious practices. The only delegate to continue to support the clause was Higgins.

The point made by O'Connor in the opening exchange with Higgins was taken up again by Barton. As far as Barton was concerned, the convention had no intention of giving the Commonwealth power to legislate with regard to religion, so there was no need to prevent it from doing so.

> I think it is, quite clear that the Commonwealth will have no power to make any law regarding religion, even if no amendment such as that which has been suggested is agreed to. The Commonwealth will have no powers except such as are given to it either expressly or by, necessary intention. [54]

As Barton pointed out, the reason the original clause had only referred to a restriction on the states was because the Commonwealth could not legislate on religion anyway.[55]

The new country that was being created was not to be a country split into States, but a collection of States coming together and agreeing to give some powers to a central government. Sections 51 and 52 of the *Australian Constitution* are the outcome of this principle. They list the matters which the Commonwealth can legislate on. Everything else is left to the States.[56] Religion is not listed in either Section 51 or 52. Barton's point has played out in the cases on Section 116 heard by the High Court. So far, no case which directly concerns Section 116 has been successful.

Barton also dismissed Higgins' argument that a court might declare Australia a 'Christian Nation' as had happened in the United States, even if a reference to God was put in the preamble:

> But the question for us to consider is whether a court like the Federal High Court or the Privy Council would ever come to such a conclusion. One would think it highly improbable.[57]

Alongside O'Connor and Barton's was the assertion that even though the Commonwealth couldn't legislate on religion, the States should have the power to. One of the ideals of Federation was that after Federation the States would have the same powers that they had before Federation. Since they were not prevented

54 *Official Record of the Debates of the Australasian Federal Convention*, Melbourne, 8 February 1898, 661 (Edmund Barton).

55 Ibid.

56 See Gabriel Moens and John Trone, *Lumb & Moens' The Constitution of the Commonwealth of Australia Annotated* (LexisNexis Butterworths, 7th ed, 2007) Chapter I Part IV.

57 *Official Record of the Debates of the Australasian Federal Convention*, Melbourne, 8 February 1898, 661 (Edmund Barton).

from legislating on religion before Federation, they should not be prevented from doing so after Federation.

Symon, Cockburn and others took up this argument:

> However, it seems to be, *prima facie*, an interference with the legislative authority of the state itself. But putting it both ways-a prohibition against the state and against the Commonwealth making any law prohibiting the free exercise of any religious faith is, I think, a little beyond what any of us is prepared to go.[58]
>
> I do not see why the states should not have the same rights of self-preservation under a Federal Constitution as they have at the present time. There is no atrocity which the human mind can devise which has not at some time or another been perpetrated under the name of religion, and the states should have the power to prevent such occurrences as those referred to by the right honorable member and others which might be mentioned *ad libitum*.[59]

Even Higgins admitted that the clause should only apply to the Commonwealth:

> Clause 109 commences- "A state shall not make any law." I agree with the honorable member that that provision should not be there. I am willing that the prohibition should extend only to the Commonwealth.[60]

However, no one moved an amendment to remove the application of the clause to the States. Of all the arguments raised against Clause 109, this was to have the longest effect. When the clause was discussed again later in the convention, it only referred to the Commonwealth. Further in 1944 and 1988 when the people where asked in referendum whether they wanted to extend Section 116 to the States, the proposal was rejected.[61]

As well as the argument, that the States could legislate on religion before Federation, so they should be able to after, was the argument that such an ability was desirable. The issue was first raised by Sir Edward Braddon on Monday evening. He was concerned about the practices of the Hindoos (sic) particularly their practices of 'sutee'[62] which he interpreted as murder, and 'churruck'[63] which he inter-

---

58 *Official Record of the Debates of the Australasian Federal Convention*, Melbourne, 8 February 1898, 659 (Josiah Symon).

59 *Official Record of the Debates of the Australasian Federal Convention*, Melbourne, 8 February 1898, 660 (Sir John Cockburn).

60 *Official Record of the Debates of the Australasian Federal Convention*, Melbourne, 8 February 1898, 662 (Henry Higgins).

61 Andrew Byrnes, Hilary Charlesworth and Gabrielle McKinnon, *Bills of Rights in Australia History, Politics and Law*, (The University of New South Wales Press, 2009) 26–27.

62 Also spelt sati – this is the practice of a widow placing herself of the funeral pyre of her husband so she can die with him.

63 Also spelt churuck – those who had vowed themselves to self-torture, submitted to be swung in the air supported only by hooks passed through the muscles over the blade-bones.

preted as barbarous cruelty.[64] Cockburn also raised the issue of the Thugs[65] and Symon and Gordon later raised the issue of Welsh faith healers whose patients died where they would not have done if conventional medical treatment had been sought.[66]

The delegates who spoke at the convention, were in no doubt that such practices existed and that they should be prevented:

> I do not think the prohibition should extend to interference with the exercise of faiths that are carried to the lengths which are objectionable from a sociological point of view.[67]
>
> The points referred to by Sir Edward Braddon last night are of the very highest importance. We may be willing to admit people professing Oriental faiths, but unwilling to permit the exercise of those faiths as those people would wish to exercise them in this country, detrimental in every possible way to the cause of religion and of freedom itself.[68]

Towards the end of the debate, Abbot also pointed out that the group which Higgins had referred to as desiring such a clause, the Seventh-day Adventists, persisted in breaking the law by working on Sundays. He also pointed out that if they were to be accommodated by allowing them to have their day of rest on a Saturday, this accommodation must be extended to other groups which may lead to six or seven such days per week. And as far as he was concerned, if the Jews could behave and simply have two days of rest, so could everyone else.[69] For Abbot, not only was freedom of religion out of the question, but so too was religious tolerance, when it came to practices 'out of the norm.'[70]

Ultimately, both Higgins' amendment and the clause itself were rejected by the convention. Unfortunately, the convention transcript does not record particular delegates' votes but from the tone of the debate it is likely that the clause was soundly rejected.

This was not the end of the story – Section 116 of the *Constitution* is testament to that. On 2 March 1898, Higgins again tried to insert a 'freedom of religion' clause into the Constitution.

These hooks were hung from a long crossbeam, which see-sawed upon a huge upright pole. Hoisted into the air by men pulling down the other end of the see-saw beam, the victim was then whirled round in a circle. The torture usually lasted 15 or 20 minutes.

64 *Official Record of the Debates of the Australasian Federal Convention*, Melbourne, 7 February 1898, 657 (Sir Edward Braddon).

65 Ibid, 657 (Sir John Cockburn) who likened practitioners of the Hindu religion as 'Thugs.'

66 *Official Record of the Debates of the Australasian Federal Convention*, Melbourne, 8 February 1898, 659 (Josiah Symon and J. H. Gordon).

67 Ibid. 659 (J. H. Gordon).

68 Ibid. 660 (Josiah Symon).

69 Ibid. 664 (Sir J. P. Abbott).

70 There was a large degree of tolerance for the different Christian religions.

The preamble got it in

The 2 March 1898 was to be a momentous day for religion. This is the day on which its position in Australia's new Federation was to be determined. The first decision concerned the preamble. Patrick McMahon Glynn again sought to have God recognised in the preamble.

On 22 April 1987 Glynn had attempted to have the words 'invoking divine providence' inserted into the Constitution. He did so in response to the large volume of petitions received by the convention delegates from Christian churches. Glynn's own dedication to the amendment he sought must be questioned given his opening statement:

> We must, I am sure, all agree, whatever may be the decision of the Convention as to the propriety of passing the motion, that we cannot ignore the evidence afforded by the petitions of a widespread desire that the spirit of the proposal should be accepted; we cannot pass over in silence the almost unanimous request of the members of so many creeds, of one aim and hope, that the supremacy of God should be recognised, and His blessing invoked, in the opening lines of our Constitution.[71]

It would seem that the need to gain votes for the Constitution was one of the driving factors. Whatever Glynn's personal feeling about inserting these words into the Constitution, his endeavour failed 17 votes to 11, with Glynn himself attempting to withdraw the motion before the vote took place.

As referred to above, this failure by Glynn may have in part lead to Higgins' defeat on 8 February 1898. Higgins argument for the inclusion of Clause 109 and its extension to the Commonwealth was based on the fact that recognising God in the preamble may lead to a judgment by the courts that Australia was a Christian nation, and that in turn may lead to the Commonwealth being able to legislate for a national day of rest. With no recognition of God in the preamble, his arguments were moot.

On 2 March 1989, Glynn again moved a motion to have God recognised in the preamble. This time he sought to have the words 'humbly relying on the Blessing of Almighty God' inserted. This phrasing was much less controversial and passed on the voices. It is unfortunate that the votes were not recorded; we will never know who switched sides.[72]

With God now recognised in the preamble, Higgins again sought to have his Clause 109 inserted into the Constitution. His proposed clause now read:

---

71 *Official Report of the National Australasian Convention Debates*, Adelaide, 22 April 1897, 1184 (Patrick Glynn).

72 For a detailed discussion of the convention debate relating to the inclusion of God in the preamble, see also Richard Ely, *Unto God and Caesar: Religious Issues in the Emerging Commonwealth 1891–1906* (Melbourne University Press, 1976), ch 4 and 10.

The Commonwealth shall not make any law prohibiting the free exercise of any religion, or for the establishment of any religion, or imposing any religious observance, and no religious test shall be required as a qualification for any office or public trust under the Commonwealth.

On this occasion, Higgins did not make a long speech, but instead referred to his comments earlier in the day with regard to the insertion of God in the preamble.[73] His arguments were in essence the same as on 8 February 1898; if the American Supreme Court could find that America was a 'Christian Nation,' despite the existence of the first amendment, then with God recognised in the *Australian Constitution* such a decision was also possible here.

Neither Higgins, nor others who spoke for the inclusion of Clause 109, had any intention that religion be free from restriction. Rather, they wanted such issues to be left to the States. In his opening remarks Higgins went to great lengths to make this point:

> My idea is to make it clear beyond doubt that the powers which the states individually have of making such laws as they like with regard to religion shall remain undisturbed and unbroken, and to make it clear that in framing this *Constitution* there is no intention whatever to give to the Federal Parliament the power to interfere in these matters. My object is to leave the reserved rights to the states where they are, to leave the existing law as it is; and just as each state can make its own factory laws, or its own laws as to the hours of labour, so each state should be at full liberty to make such laws as it thinks fit in regard to Sunday or any other day of rest. I simply want to leave things as they are. I do not want to interfere with any right the state has.[74]

Others who also emphasised the desire to leave the issue of religion to the States included Wise:

> I can conceive of no matter more fit for state control than that of religious observance.... There should not be any opening for doubt as to the power of the Commonwealth to exercise control over any religion of the state. I wish I could share Mr. Barton's optimistic views as to the death of the spirit of religious persecution. But we have seen in our own time a reoccurrence of that evil demon, which, I fear, is only scotched and not killed. At any rate, the period during which we have enjoyed religious liberty is not long enough for us to be able to say with confidence that there will be no swinging back of the pendulum to the spirit of the times from which we have only recently emerged;[75]

---

73 He had not supported Glynn's proposal.
74 *Official Record of the Debates of the Australasian Federal Convention*, Melbourne, 2 March 1898, 1769 (Henry Higgins).
75 Ibid. 1773 (Bernhard Wise).

Kingston:

> I do not think that power ought to be given to the Federal Parliament. It is a matter of purely domestic concern, with which the states are particularly qualified to deal. If we carry the amendment in the way in which it is now proposed, we shall secure to the states the power which they at present possess;[76]

and Lyne:

> [I]t is not a wise thing, where you have a number of states to deal with, to allow the Commonwealth authority to decide how Sunday should be observed. The Commonwealth authority might have that power if this provision were not inserted in the Bill.[77]

It could be argued that the emphasis on the right of the State to legislate on religion in part explains why we do not have a freedom of religion, the inclusion of what was to become Section 116 wasn't about freedom of religion, but States' rights. Although Higgins referred to the American experience and the case of *Church of the Holy Trinity v United States* he, and those who supported him, were prepared to allow Sunday observance laws as long as it was the States and not the Commonwealth who legislated for it.

The existence of the words referring to God in the preamble also influenced the inclusion of Clause 109. Higgins explained his decision to include the words 'or imposing any religious observance,' as a direct consequence of the inclusion of God in the preamble:

> The only difficulty, therefore, is in respect of these words about imposing religious observances, and that part, as I have already indicated this morning, is rendered necessary by the inclusion in the preamble of our *Constitution* of words which they have not got in the *American Constitution*.[78]

Other convention delegates also referred to their desire to allay any fears held by those who opposed the recognition of God in the preamble:

> I believe rather more wrongly than rightly-believe that the agitation for the insertion in the preamble of the words which we have inserted today is sufficient to cause alarm among citizens of certain ways of thinking, and that there is an interior design on the part of some people in the community to give the Commonwealth power to interfere with religious observances.[79]

76 Ibid. 1777 (Charles Kingston).
77 Ibid. 1777 (William Lyne).
78 Ibid. 1769 (Henry Higgins).
79 Ibid. 1773 (Bernhard Wise).

If we put in Mr. Higgins' amendment we shall remove those fears and establish a sound principle, and, I believe, will commend the Constitution to a very large number of those who at present are doubtful as to its effects.[80]

I do not wish to enter into the subject, but I felt that, and it is with a view of getting rid of any apprehension of that kind, and of securing every vote possible for this Bill, that I think it well to yield to the view that has been expressed so forcibly by Mr. Higgins.[81]

There is a great deal of force in the suggestion that, in view of the amendment in the preamble, we should make a declaration of this description in the broadest possible terms, for the purpose of allaying any apprehension that might otherwise be entertained on the subject.[82]

As can be seen from these comments, it was not a concern over freedom of religion which prompted the convention delegates to consider the feeling of those opposed to the inclusion of God in the preamble, but a desire to get their vote. The inclusion of what was to become Section 116 was not about freedom of religion, but about getting as many votes for the Constitution as possible. The same argument has been made about the inclusion of the reference to God in the preamble.

The main opposition to the inclusion of Clause 109 again came from Barton. He opposed the clause's inclusion on two grounds; first, it was unnecessary; and second, it was desirable to be able to restrict religion in some cases. Barton believed that there was no power in the Constitution for the federal government to make legislation about religion and even if it could, it wouldn't because they were living in an enlightened age. This part of his argument was essentially the same as it had been last time the clause was discussed. His new arguments came from his second ground for opposing the clause. Barton contended that including clause 109 would restrict the operation of the race power and the immigration power. As far as he was concerned, it was desirable for the Commonwealth to be able to restrict the practice of some religions:

That might be a provision that might be held to be too express in its terms, because there may be practices in various religions which are believed in by persons who may enter into the Commonwealth belonging to other races, which practices would be totally abhorrent to the ideas, not only to any Christian, but to any civilized community; and inasmuch as the Commonwealth is armed with the power of legislation in regard to immigration and emigration, and with regard to naturalization, and also with regard to the making of special laws for any race . . . inasmuch as we have all these provisions under which it would be an advisable thing that the Commonwealth,

---

80 Ibid. 1774 (Bernhard Wise).
81 Ibid. 1776 (Josiah Symon).
82 Ibid. 1776 (Charles Kingston).

under its regulative power, should prevent any practices from taking place which are abhorrent to the ideas of humanity and justice of the community; and inasmuch as it is a reasonable thing that these outrages on humanity and justice (if they ever occur) should be prohibited by the Commonwealth, it would be a dangerous thing, perhaps, to place in the Bill a provision which would take out of their hands the power of preventing any such practices.[83]

This argument seems to contradict Barton's first argument that Clause 109 was not necessary; however, he does not seem to have seen the contradiction.

At the end of the debate, Clause 109 was voted in, 25 votes to 16.

Section 116 – what does it mean?

As discussed above, Section 116 has its genesis in the *American Constitution*. In form and wording it appears on the surface to be an amalgam of America's Article VI Section 3 and the First Amendment.

> The Senators and Representatives before mentioned, and the members of the several State Legislatures, and all executives and judicial officers, both of the United States, and of the several States, shall be bound by oath or affirmation to support this Constitution; but no religious test shall ever be required as a qualification to any office or public trust under the United States.[84]
>
> Congress shall make no law respecting an establishment of religion or prohibiting the free exercise thereof.[85]

However, the interpretation of Section 116 has been much narrower than its American counterpart. In particular the High Court has held that '[t]he provision . . . cannot answer the description of a law which guarantees within Australia the separation of Church and State.'[86]

In interpreting Section 116, the High Court has divided it into four limbs or clauses: the free exercise clause, the no religious observance clause, the establishment clause and the no religious test clause. In order to make out a breach of Section 116 a party must establish a breach of one of these clauses specifically.[87] As a result the Section has never been interpreted as a 'repository of some broad statement of principle concerning the separation of church and state.'[88] Instead it has been interpreted as a limit on Commonwealth power in the areas covered by the four limbs.

---

83 Ibid. 1771–1772 (Edmund Barton).
84 *United States Constitution* art VI §3.
85 *United States Constitution* amend I.
86 *Attorney General (Vic); ex rel Black v The Commonwealth* (1981) 146 CLR 559, 652 (Wilson J).
87 Ibid. 285 (Barwick CJ), 605 (Stephen J), 654–655 (Wilson J).
88 Ibid. 609 (Stephen J).

The Commonwealth shall not . . .

Section 116 only applies to the Commonwealth. It has no application to the States and there is debate as to whether or not it applies to the territories.[89] By contrast the United States equivalent First Amendment provision has been held to apply to both the States and the federal government despite the fact that it begins with the phrase 'Congress shall make no law' which appears to be similar to the beginning of Section 116 which states 'The Commonwealth shall not make any law.' The reason for the different interpretations is the existence of the fourteenth amendment in the *American Constitution.*

The fourteenth amendment, also known as the equal protection clause, requires States to provide 'equal protection of the laws.' Its effect has been, *inter alia*, to extend the protections of the First Amendment to the States as well as the federal government. The *Australian Constitution* contains no equivalent clause, as a result Section 116 only applies to laws made by the Commonwealth.[90] Section 116 therefore acts as a limit on Commonwealth power rather than as a guarantee of freedom of religion or the separation of church and State. This has important implications for the relationship between the State and religion in Australia. As will be expanded upon in later chapters many of the areas where the State and religion interact are areas of State rather than Commonwealth responsibility.

. . . for . . .

The establishment, religious observance and free exercise limbs are all prefaced by the word 'for.' The inclusion of this three letter word has had a profound effect on the interpretation of Section 116. The American First Amendment uses the word 'respecting' rather than 'for' which in the *DOGS case* was a significant factor in the majorities' decision not to rely on American precedent in determining the meaning of the term 'establishing any religion.'[91] The version of Section 116 which was voted on and passed the Constitutional Conventions did not contain the word 'for' in relation to the free exercise clause. As originally passed the clause read:

> The Commonwealth shall not make any law prohibiting the free exercise of any religion, or for the establishment of any religion or imposing any

---

89 See HT Gibbs, 'Section 116 of the Constitution and the Territories of the Commonwealth' (1947) 20 *Australian Law Journal* 375.

90 Pannam, above n 3, 42–43. In 1944 and 1988 Australia has held referendums to amend Section 116 in an attempt to extend the operation of Section 116 to the States, both were unsuccessful. See Andrew Byrnes, Hilary Charlesworth and Gabrielle McKinnon, *Bills of Rights in Australia History, Politics and Law*, (The University of New South Wales Press, 2009) 26–27; Frank Brennan, 'The 1988 Referendum – A Lost Opportunity for an Australian Declaration on Religious Freedom' (1992) 69(2) *Australasian Catholic Record* 205.

91 *Attorney General (vic); ex rel Black v The Commonwealth* (1981) 146 CLR 559, 579 (Barwick CJ), 698, 603–604 (Gibbs J), 613 (Mason J), 652–654 (Wilson J); the different histories of America and Australia was also an important consideration.

religious observance and no religious test shall ever be required as a qualification for any office or public trust under the Commonwealth

It is interesting to consider how Section 116 might have been interpreted had
the drafting committee not made this small but significant change. [92]

The word 'for' has consistently been interpreted as requiring that a law must
have the purpose of establishing religion, imposing a religious observance or prohibit the free exercise of religion before it will infringe Section 116. The issue was
first raised in *Adelaide Company of Jehovah's Witnesses v Commonwealth*. Latham
CJ considered that '[t]he word "for" shows that the purpose of the legislation
in question may properly be taken into account in determining whether or not
it is a law of the prohibited character.'[93] In the *DOGS* case the majority came
to the same conclusion in relation the establishment clause. [94] Wilson J characterised this as requiring that a particular law must be in order to establish a
religion before it will be unconstitutional as opposed to the American respecting
which has a much broader meaning.[95] The issue was taken up again in *Kruger v
Commonwealth*. Chief Justices Brennan, Toohey, Gummow and Gaudron JJ all
considered the issue, again concluding that the use of the word 'for' meant that
it was the purpose of the law which must be taken into account in determining
whether or not a law infringed Section 116.[96] While a law may have multiple
purposes[97] ultimately

> [t]he use of the word 'for' indicates that the purpose is the criterion and the
> sole criterion selected by Section 116 for validity. Thus, purpose must be
> taken into account. Further, it is the only matter to be taken into account in
> determining whether a law infringes Section 116.[98]

... *establishing any religion* ...

The meaning of the 'establishment clause' of Section 116 was considered by
the High Court in *Attorney General (Vic); ex rel Black v The Commonwealth*[99]

---

92 Blackshield, above n 3, 85.
93 *The Adelaide Company of Jehovah's Witnesses Inc v The Commonwealth* (1943) 67 CLR
    116, 132.
94 *Attorney General (vic); ex rel Black v The Commonwealth* (1981) 146 CLR 559, 579 (Bar-
    wick CJ), 609 (Stephen J), 653 (Wilson J). While not discussing the meaning of 'for' in
    detail, Gibbs J also seems to assume that the purpose of the legislation must be to establish
    a religion, see *Attorney General (vic); ex rel Black v The Commonwealth* (1981) 146 CLR
    559, 604 (Gibbs J).
95 *Attorney General (vic); ex rel Black v The Commonwealth* (1981) 146 CLR 559, 653 (Wilson J).
96 See *Kruger v Commonwealth* (1997) 190 CLR 1, 160 (Brennan CJ, Toohey and Gummow
    JJ), 132–134 (Gaudron J).
97 *Kruger v Commonwealth* (1997) 190 CLR 1, 133 (Gaudron J).
98 *Kruger v Commonwealth* (1997) 190 CLR 1, 132 (Gaudron J).
99 (1981) 146 CLR 559.

(*DOGS Case*).[100] The Court found, in a 6:1 majority judgment, that the Commonwealth government's funding programme for religious schools did not violate Section 116.[101] All of the majority judges[102] came up with their own, slightly different, definition of 'establishing.' All five of the definitions had two things in common. First the judges asserted that their definition was the 'natural' meaning of the word and that there was no ambiguity to be resolved,[103] second, all five determined that the word 'establish' meant the setting up of a State church or religion.

Chief Justice Barwick adopted the narrowest interpretation defining establishing a religion as requiring that the religion be adopted as part of the Commonwealth establishment before Section 116 would be infringed. [104] Justice Gibbs agreed with Barwick CJ's approach but was willing to concede that the process from not being an established religion to being one may be a matter of degree.[105] Justices Stephen, Mason and Wilson were prepared to go further finding that the granting of favours or privileges in a discriminatory way to one religion over another may amount to establishing that church or religion. While they varied in how special that treatment or favour needed to be, they all set the bar very high.[106]

Justice Murphy, in dissent, rejected the majority's narrow definition of the word 'establishing.' In his opinion all constitutional provisions should be read widely. He reiterated a statement he had made in *Attorney-General (Cth); Ex rel McKinlay v Commonwealth*;[107] '[g]reat rights are often expressed in simple phrases.'[108] Given this, Murphy J determined that the prohibition against 'establishing any religion' included a prohibition against providing any sponsorship or support for religion.[109]

Recently, doubt has been expressed as to the correctness of the narrow interpretation of establishing adopted by the majority in the *DOGS case*.[110] Questions have been raised as to whether such a narrow interpretation would be adopted

---

100 For a detailed discussion of the background see Chapter 8.
101 For a discussion of these programmes see Chapter 8.
102 With the exception of Aickin J who simply agreed with Gibbs and Mason JJ.
103 *Attorney General (Vic); ex rel Black v The Commonwealth* (1981) 146 CLR 559, 579 (Barwick CJ), 597 (Gibbs J), 606 (Stephen J), 653 (Wilson J).
104 Ibid. 582 (Barwick CJ).
105 Ibid. 603–604 (Gibbs J).
106 Ibid. 610 (Stephen J), 612 (Mason J) and 653 (Wilson J).
107 (1975) 135 CLR 1, 65 (Murphy J).
108 *Attorney General (vic); ex rel Black v The Commonwealth* (1981) 146 CLR 559, 623 (Murphy J).
109 Ibid. 622–623 (Murphy J).
110 *Hoxton Park Residents Action Group Inc v Liverpool City Council (No 2)* (2011) 256 FLR 156, 165 (Basten JA); Luke Beck, 'Dead DOGS? Towards a less Restrictive Interpretation of the Establishment Clause; Hoxton park Residents Action Group Inc v Liverpool City Council (No 2)' (2014) 37(2) *University of Western Australia Law Review* 59; Luke Bek, 'The Establishment Clause of the Australian Constitution: Three Propositions and a Case Study' (2014) 35(2) *Adelaide Law Review* 226.

by the present High Court in light of the fact that the High Court has revised its stance on the use of both American precedent and the Constitutional Convention debates in interpreting the *Australian Constitution*.[111] Whether or not these doubts are well founded require a fresh High Court consideration of the issues.[112]

. . . imposing any religious observance . . .

There have been no cases which have directly considered the meaning of the no religious observance clause. In *R v Winneke; Ex parte Gallagher*[113] Murphy J considered the clause in *obiter*. He found that a law compelling a person to state that they object to taking an oath before being permitted to make an affidavit would infringe Section 116 because it imposed a religious observance.[114] It is important to note that, in the other Section 116 case in which Murphy J participated, he was in dissent.[115] Caution must therefore be exercised in attributing Murphy J's opinions on the meaning of Section 116 to the High Court in general. On the matter of oaths and Section 116, Quick and Garran wrote in 1901 that 'the Federal Parliament will have to provide for the administration of oaths in legal proceedings, and there is nothing to prevent it from enabling an oath to be taken . . . on the sanctity of the Holy Gospel.'[116]

Additional guidance on the meaning of the clause can also be found in the Constitutional Convention debates.[117] During the debate much was made of Sunday observance laws – which could be described as a 'religious observance.' As discussed above, Higgins relied heavily on the American experience with Sunday observance and the World Fair. Sunday observance laws were also raised by other delegates to the convention as the practice in the colonies varied. For example, New South Wales allowed the publication of newspapers on Sundays while Victoria did not. The opinion of the delegates was that issues such as this should be left to the States.[118] The plight of groups like the Seventh-day Adventists and Jews whose day of rest was Saturday rather than Sunday was also raised. There was concern that without a 'freedom of religion style' clause the Commonwealth

---

111 Luke Beck, 'Dead DOGS? Towards a less Restrictive Interpretation of the Establishment Clause; Hoxton park Residents Action Group Inc v Liverpool City Council (No 2)' (2014) 37(2) *University of Western Australia Law Review* 59, 65.

112 Ibid. 73.

113 (1982) 152 CLR 211.

114 *R v Winneke; Ex parte Gallagher* (1982) 152 CLR 211, 229 (Murphy J).

115 Murphy J gave a dissenting judgment in *Attorney General (Vic); ex rel Black v The Commonwealth* (1981) 146 CLR 559, 619–635.

116 John Quick and Robert Randolph Garran, *The Annotated Consiution of the Australian Commonwealth* (The Australian Book Company, 1901), 952.

117 In *Municipal Council of Sydney v The Commonwealth* (1904) 1 CLR 108 the High Court held that it could not use Constitutional Convention debates in interpreting the *Australian Constitution*. This rule was overturned in *Cole v Whitfield* (1988) 165 CLR 360.

118 Blackshield, above n 3, 84.

might impose Sunday observance laws, preventing individuals from these two groups from working on Sunday.[119]

On its face the Constitutional Convention debates would seem to support the view that Commonwealth Sunday observance laws would violate the religious observance clause of Section 116. The answer may not be this simple. As Higgins himself pointed out Section 116 would not prohibit Sunday closing laws – as long as the purpose for which they were enacted was not the imposition of a religious observance.[120]

Another potential observance of religion which may infringe Section 116 is the recitation of prayers at the beginning of each session of Federal Parliament. Order 38 of the Federal House of Representatives Standing Orders and Order 50 of the Federal Senate standing Orders provide for the recitation by the Chair or President of a Christian prayer along with the Lord's Prayer. This is followed by an acknowledgment of country.[121] Luke Beck has opined that the requirement to recite a prayer of any form may amount to imposition of a religious observance on Members of Parliament and Senators.[122] While the majority of MPs[123] and Senators[124] in 1901 supported the introduction of prayers at the beginning of each sitting support was not unanimous. Senator Gregory McGregor, in reference to the religious observance clause of Section 116, commented that:

What did the framers of the Constitution mean? Did they mean that the Parliament was not to impose religious observances in the streets or in the schools? Did they mean that Parliament was not to impose religious observances anywhere else but here?[125]

It is important to note that McGregor's reasons for opposing prayers in Parliament were religious, rather than secular. In his short speech he quoted scripture about praying in private rather than in public[126] and concluded by saying:

---

119 Ibid. 83–84; *Official Record of the Debates of the Australasian Federal Convention*, Melbourne, 7 February 1898, 656 (Henry Higgins).
120 Blackshield, above n 3, 86.
121 *House of Representatives Practice, 6th Ed – 8 – Order of business and the sitting day* (30 April 2015) Parliament of Australia <www.aph.gov.au/About_Parliament/House_of_ Representatives/Powers_practice_and_procedure/Practice6/Practice6HTML?file=Ch apter8&section=03>; *Chapter 8 – Sittings, Quorum and Adjournment of the Senate* (17 December 2013) Parliament of Australia www.aph.gov.au/About_Parliament/Senate/ Powers_practice_n_procedures/aso/so050.
122 Luke Beck, 'Clear and Emphatic: The Separation of Church and State under the Australian Constitution' (2008) 27(2) *University of Tasmania Law Review* 161, 182–184; Beck also expresses the view that the requirement to recite Christian prayers may amount to an establishment of religion, see 179–182.
123 See Commonwealth, *Parliamentary Debates*, House of Representatives, 7 June 1901, 815–821.
124 See Commonwealth, *Parliamentary Debates*, Senate, 14 June 1901, 1136–1140.
125 Commonwealth, *Parliamentary Debates*, Senate, 14 June 1901, 1138 (Gregory McGregor).
126 See Matthew 6: 5–6.

I believe in the religion that is in the heart, and not in the religion that is on the coat-sleeve. I believe in the religion that makes senators as well other individuals behave as brothers to each other and as Christians in all thing and not in the religion that requires to be paraded either in the Parliament House, the theatre, or at the street corners.[127]

While the constitutionality of federal parliamentary prayers has not yet been officially challenged with the increasing religious diversity of Australia's population and Parliament it is an issue which may well need to be examined in more detail.[128]

... *prohibiting the free exercise of any religion* ...

The free exercise limb of Section 116 has received the most judicial attention of the four Section 116 clauses. Three of the five reported High Court cases consider this clause,[129] along with a number of Federal and Family Court decisions.[130] The most extensive analysis of the clause was given by Latham CJ in *Adelaide Company of Jehovah's Witnesses v Commonwealth*, the following is based primarily on that judgment.[131]

The free exercise clause prevents the Commonwealth from making any laws prohibiting the free exercise of any religion. The Section operates not only to protect the free exercise of religion in the traditional sense, but also to protect the right to have no religion.[132] The Section has particular poignancy for minority religions, as Latham CJ put it '[t]he religion of the majority can look after itself.'[133] The extent of this protection is not unlimited. In part, this narrow interpretation is due to the need for the law to have the purpose of prohibiting the free exercise of religion. It is also due, in part, to the way in which 'freedom' has been interpreted.

127 Commonwealth, *Parliamentary Debates*, Senate, 14 June 1901, 1138 (Gregory McGregor).
128 In 2013 Ed Husic became the first Muslim frontbencher, taking his oath on a Qur'an. This was inspired by Prime Minister Julia Gillard, who was open about her atheistic beliefs and became the first Australian Prime Minister to take an Affirmation rather than an Oath of office. See also Helen Davidson, 'Swearing in for the Australian parliament – explained,' *The Guardian* (2 July 2013) <www.theguardian.com/world/2013/jul/02/swearing-in-australian-parliament-explained.>
129 *Krygger v Williams* (1912) 15 CLR 366; *Adelaide Company of Jehovah's Witnesses v Commonwealth* (1943) 67 CLR 366; *Kruger v Commonwealth* (1997) 190 CLR 1.
130 See, for example, *Minister for Immigration and Ethnic Affairs v Lebanese Moslem Association* (1987) 17 FCR 373; *Nelson v Fish* (1990) 21 FCR 430; *Halliday v Commonwealth* (2000) 45 ATR 458; *In the Marriage of Paisio* (1978) 36 FLR 1; *In the Marriage of Abbott* (1995) 123 FLR 424.
131 For a discussion of the background of this case see Chapter 7.
132 *The Adelaide Company of Jehovah's Witnesses Inc v The Commonwealth* (1943) 67 CLR 116, 123.
133 Ibid. 124.

As Lathan CJ emphasised in *Adelaide Company of Jehovah's Witnesses v Commonwealth* free does not mean license. Rather it means free within the confines of a free society.[134] 'It is consistent with the maintenance of religious liberty for the State to restrain actions and courses of conduct which are inconsistent with the maintenance of civil government or prejudicial to the continued existence of the community.'[135] A law of the Commonwealth will not infringe Section 116 merely because it prohibits the free exercise of religion if it does so in the furtherance of maintenance of the 'civil government.' Religious practices which are inconsistent with the ordinary civil or criminal law will not be protected from prosecution by operation of Section 116.[136] This is not to say that Section 116 only protects the right to believe and not to act on those beliefs. The wording of the Section itself denies such an interpretation. Rather the High Court has been prepared to impose limits on free exercise of religion in the interests of protecting a free society. It is left 'to the court to determine whether a particular law is an undue infringement of religious freedom.'[137]

The interpretation of the 'free exercise clause' raises the question of when the Court will determine that there has been an 'undue infringement.' The three reported High Court decisions determined the question in the negative. Requiring a pacifist to undertake compulsory military training did not infringe freedom of religion,[138] nor did declaring the Jehovah's Witnesses an unlawful association and seizing their property during World War II,[139] or the removal of Indigenous children from their parents as part of the Stolen Generations.[140] Federal Court decisions have reached similar conclusions. In *Judd v McKeon*[141] Higgins J suggested that requiring people to vote, whose religious beliefs and practices provided otherwise, might infringe Section 116. However his comments were in *obiter* and religion was not an issue in the case.[142]

. . . *no religious test* . . .

Prior to 2012 no case had considered the 'no religious test clause' in any detail. In *Crittenden v Anderson*,[143] Fullagar J had considered the issue in *obiter*. He found that prohibiting a Roman Catholic from sitting in Parliament would violate

134 *The Adelaide Company of Jehovah's Witnesses Inc v The Commonwealth* (1943) 67 CLR 116, 126–127, 131 (Latham CJ), 149 (Rich J), 154–155 (Stark J), 157 (McTiernan J), 159–160 (Williams J).
135 Ibid. 131 (Latham CJ).
136 Ibid. 129–131 (Latham CJ), 155 (Stark J).
137 Ibid. 131 (Latham CJ).
138 *Krygger v Williams* (1912) 15 CLR 366.
139 *The Adelaide Company of Jehovah's Witnesses Inc v The Commonwealth* (1943) 67 CLR 116.
140 *Kruger v Commonwealth* (1997) 190 CLR 1.
141 (1926) CLR 380.
142 *Judd v McKeon* (1926) CLR 380, 387.
143 (1950) 51 ALJ 171.

Section 116.[144] In *Woodward*, Aickins J found that the provision of information by the Australian Security Intelligence Organisation (ASIO) to Commonwealth ministers about the religious beliefs of the employees did not constitute a religious test.[145] As Luke Beck has observed, '[n]either proposition takes the analysis very far.'[146] This deficit was partially remedied in 2012 when the High Court handed down its decision in *Williams v The Commonwealth*.[147] Despite specifically considering the provision the case's analysis of the clause is only partial as the judges in that case only considered the first half of the clause.[148]

The 'no religious test clause' has two elements. First, there must be 'no religious test' and second that these tests are for an 'office or public trust under the Commonwealth.' The judgments in *Williams v The Commonwealth* only considered the second of these two elements. Justice Heydon determined that '[a]n office' is a position under constituted authority to which duties are attached' and that this required a direct relationship with the Commonwealth.[149] In that case a chaplain employed by a service provider who had a contract with the Commonwealth was not in a close enough relationship with the Commonwealth to be an 'officer under the Commonwealth.'[150] No case has specifically considered what constituted a 'religious test.'[151]

What we don't know

While the above explains the meaning of Section 116 as enunciated by the High Court, it is important to acknowledge there is much we don't know. With only five reported High Court judgments which consider the provision in *ratio* there simply isn't much to go on.

To date there have been no successful challenges on the basis of Section 116. While the Plaintiffs in the *Jehovah's Witnesses Case* and *Williams* were ultimately successful, the High Court dismissed their Section 116 arguments. As a result, we don't know what would constitute the establishment of a religion, the imposition of a religious observance, a prohibition on the free exercise of religion or the

---

144 *Crittenden v Anderson* (150) 51 ALJ 171, 171 (Fullagar J).
145 *Church of Scientology Inc v Woodward* (1979) 154 CLR 79, 83 (Aickins J).
146 Luke Beck, 'The Constitutional Prohibition on Religious Tests' (2011) 35(2) *Melbourne University Law Review* 323, 338.
147 (2012) 248 CLR 156.
148 For a detailed discussion of the background to *Williams* and a more detailed analysis of the judgments relating to Section 116 see Chapter 8.
149 *Williams v the Commonwealth* (2012) 248 CLR 156, [444] (Heydon J); see also more generally [107]–[110] (Gummow and Bell JJ), [305]–[307], [442]–[448] (Heydon J).
150 Ibid. [110], [447] (Heydon J); for a more in-depth analysis of this aspect of the judgment see Renae Barker, 'A Critical Analysis of Religious Aspects of the Australian Chaplaincy Cases' (2015) 4(1) *Oxford Journal of Law and Religion* 26, 41–45.
151 For a discussion of the 'no religious test clause' and what might constitute a religious test see also Luke Beck, 'The Constitutional Prohibition on Religious Tests' (2011) 35(2) *Melbourne University Law Review* 323.

imposition of a religious test. We can only speculate based on what we know it isn't and *obiter* in the decided cases.

Another mystery is the placement of Section 116 in 'Chapter VI – The States' of the *Constitution*. Given the Section only applies to the Commonwealth, its placement in a chapter which otherwise deals with issues relating to State powers and law-making ability seems odd. Quick and Garran certainly felt so commenting that:

> The appearance of this section in a chapter purporting to deal with the States is somewhat anomalous: it can only be accounted for by the fact that it took the place of clause 15 of Ch V. in the Draft Bill of 1891, which declared that a State should not prohibit the free exercise of any religion.[152]

Similarly, in *The Making of the Australian Constitution* Le Nauze suggested that Section 116 found its way into Chapter V as a result of apathy on the part of Sir Edmund Barton:

> As a final irony a ban referring exclusively to the Commonwealth legislation was left as a puzzling anomaly in a Chapter on the Constitution headed 'the States.' Barton must have noticed it during his final revision, but perhaps he was too fed up to care.[153]

This suggestion seems to rely on the fact that Barton had consistently opposed the inclusion of the clause and the fact that Barton was a member of the final drafting committee and therefore in a position to move the clause to a more appropriate chapter of the *Constitution*. However, we know that the clause was amended by the drafting committee as it was re-arranged.[154] So the committee did not ignore it altogether – they must have noted that a clause about the Commonwealth was in a chapter on the States.

Another possibility is that although Section 116 refers specifically to the Commonwealth it is in fact about State rights. As Dawson J observed in *Kruger:*

> The appearance of s.116 in a chapter headed 'The States' has often been regarded as anomalous, but in fact the section deals with the division of legislative power between the Commonwealth and the States within the federation.[155]

---

152 John Quick and Robert Randolph Garran, *The Annotated Constitution of the Australian Commonwealth* (The Australian Book Company, 1901), 952–953.

153 John La Nauze, *The Making of the Australian Constitution* (Melbourne University Press, 1972), 229.

154 Blackshield, above n 3, 85.

155 *Kruger v Commonwealth* (1997) 190 CLR 1, 60 (Dawson J).

As discussed above, crucial to the inclusion of Section 116 was that it left decisions about religion to the States. As Higgins himself observed:

> I feel that honorable members who value state rights reserved to the states, who value the preservation of the individuality of the states for state purposes, will agree with me that it is with the state we ought to leave this power, and that we ought not to intrust it to the Commonwealth.[156]

Section 116 Federation and the State–religion relationship in Australia

On 1 January 1901, Australia transitioned from six separate colonies to a Federation with a federal government and six State governments.[157] It can be argued either that this had a profound or a very limited impact on the relationship between the State and religion depending on how you look at it. On the one hand, Federation and Australia's new *Constitution* introduced a new formalised relationship between the State and religion as set out in Section 116 and added a new tier of government to the concept of State. On the other hand, the formal separation set up by Section 116 was already effectively in place prior to Federation and Section 116 has been interpreted narrowly in any event. In addition, a significant number of issues of importance to religion remain in the hands of the States; the creation of the new federal tier of government therefore had only a limited impact on the relationship between the State and religion in relation to these matters.

The profound effect of Federation

In many ways the Federation of Australia in 1901 had a profound effect on the interaction between the State and religion.

As was discussed above it is not entirely clear when the Church of England ceased to be the established church of the Australian colonies, if it ever was.[158] It is clearer that plural establishment ended with the removal of direct grants to the major Christian churches.[159] However, at Federation the position of the churches and religion more generally was less clear. The State no longer provided direct funding nor did the State fund religious schools. However, there was no formal separation. The colonial governments could have, at any time, chosen to establish any one of the churches or to prohibit the free exercise of any faith.

---

156 *Official Record of the Debates of the Australasian Federal Convention*, Melbourne, 2 March 1898, 1735–1736 (Henry Higgins).
157 *Commonwealth of Australia Constitution Act 1901* (Imp).
158 See Chapter 3.
159 Renae Barker, 'Under Most Peculiar Circumstances': The Church Acts in the Australian Colonies as a Study of Plural Establishment' (2016) 3 *Law & History* 28.

The exercise of Federation and its potential to formalise the future relationship between the State and religion did not pass the churches by. Many took an active part in the Federation debates.[160] The churches actively participated in petitioning the colonial governments and delegates to the Constitutional conventions.[161] There were in essence two sides to the debate. On the one hand, groups like the Council of Churches petitioned to have God recognised in the Constitution.[162] On the other side were the Seventh-day Adventists and secularists who petitioned strongly for the separation of church and State.[163] What the outcome would be was far from inevitable.

In the end, Section 116 found its way into the *Australian Constitution* as a formal statement of the relationship between the State and religion. To the extent that this provided certainty and formalised the existing situation was a significant moment in the relationship between the State and religion.

Federation was also a significant event in the relationship between the State and religion in Australia because it introduced a new tier of government to the State side of the equation. How religion would interact with the State now needed to be negotiated both at a local State and territory level and at the new national level.

The limited impact of Federation

While in some ways Federation had a profound impact on the relationship between the State and religion it can also be argued that in practical terms the impact on the relationship was minimal. While there may have been symbolic important in formalising the relationship and in the creation of a new tier of government, the day to day relationship between the State and religion changed very little on 1 January 1901.

In many ways the formal separation of religion and State established in Section 116 was already the *de facto* reality of the colonies. All colonies had already removed direct State funding to religion and State funding to religious education. All that Section 116 and Federation did was to formalise that relationship at the new federal level. At the State level the relationship remained much as it was prior to Federation. The States continued to maintain a *de facto* separation from religion but were not formally prohibited from either establishing their own State religion or prohibiting the free exercise of religion.[164]

---

160 Ely, above n 2.
161 Ibid. 21–22, 24–30, 32–33, 37–38, 43–44.
162 Ibid. 21–22, 32–33, 37–38.
163 Ibid. 24–30, 43–44.
164 Tasmania included a freedom of religion provision in its Constitution in 1934 see *Constitution Act 1934* (Tas) s. 46. While this Act was intended to consolidate existing legislation the inclusion of s. 46 is something of a puzzle see Museum of Australian Democracy, *Constitution Act 1934 (Tas)*, Documenting Democracy <http://foundingdocs.gov.au/item-sdid-32.html.>

The division of powers under the new *Australian Constitution* also contributed to the limited impact of Federation on the relationship between the State and religion. Under Australia's federal system, power to legislate on particular matters are divided between the States and the Commonwealth. Section 52 of the *Constitution* lists powers which are exclusive to the Commonwealth, while Section 51 lists powers which are held by both the States and the Commonwealth concurrently, with the Commonwealth prevailing in the event of an inconsistency.[165] Any areas of responsibility not listed in the *Constitution*, such as health and education, remained the exclusive province of the States. The power to legislate with respect of religious matters is not listed in the *Constitution*. It therefore remained the province of the States. As discussed above during the constitutional conventions Edmund Barton[166] expressed the view that Section 116 was not necessary because the Commonwealth had no power to legislate with respect to religion.[167] An argument can be mounted that Section 116 was as much about makings sure that religion remained the exclusive province of the States as it was about religion itself.[168]

In addition to the fact that religion remained a State concern many of the areas in which religion operated, such as education and welfare also remained State powers. The federal government has increased its areas of influence in relation to religion since Federation. This is most noticeable in the field of education, where the Commonwealth is the primary funding provider to religious schools. This was achieved via the use of State grants under Section 96 of the *Constitution*. Education itself remains the province of the States; the Commonwealth merely provides the funds with significant strings attached.[169]

While there is a significant interaction between religion and the federal government most of these interactions are in the latter half of the twentieth century into the twenty-first century. Federation itself did not precipitate an immediate change in the relationship. There was not an immediate and significant engagement between the federal level of government and religion. Rather it has been how Federation has played out in the 100 plus years since 1901 that has brought about the change.

Conclusion

Section 116 of Australia's *Constitution* is both the bedrock of the State–religion relationship and largely irrelevant to the day to day interaction between the two.

---

165 *Commonwealth of Australia Constitution Act 1901* (Imp) s 109.
166 Edmund Barton was Australia's first Prime Minister and later a justice of the High Court of Australia.
167 *Official Report of the Debates of the Australasian Federal Convention*, Melbourne, 8 February 1898, 661 (Edmund Barton).
168 Renae Barker, 'A Question to the Founding Father: Why Don't We Have a Freedom of Religion?' (Paper presented at RUSSLR Conference, Canberra, 14 August 2009).
169 See Chapter 8.

On the one hand, you could argue that Barton was correct to assert that it was in effect impossible to breach Section 116 as the federal government has no power to legislate with respect to religion.[170] As such it is nothing more than a symbolic reminder of the compromises necessary to achieve Federation.

On the other hand, you could argue that it has been remarkably successful in setting the tone of the State–religion relationship in Australia. The federal government has never breached Section 116, not because the provision cannot be reached but because the limit is there and has been respected by the State. The federal government has not attempted to set up a State church, impose unduly upon freedom of religion, impose a religious observance or require a religious test for public office. In each case where the actions of the government have been challenged, the High Court has found that they have stayed within the scope of Section 116.

Whether you accept the argument that Section 116 is largely symbolic or that it has been remarkably effective in setting the parameters of the State–religion relationship in Australia as a constitutional provision, it is an important component of the matrix of the Australian State–religion relationship. That matrix is, however, particularly in the context of a Federation, far more complex than a single constitutional provision. For example, Section 116 may not permit the federal government to establish a State church, but it has not prevented a significant amount of interaction from taking place between the State and religion at both a federal and State level. The remainder of this book considers many of the other interactions which help make up the matrix of the State–religion relationship in Australia.

170 *Official Record of the Debates of the Australasian Federal Convention*, Melbourne, 8 February 1898, 661 (Edmund Barton).

5 Comparison with other jurisdictions

Introduction

Across Australia's history there have been numerous recommendations and attempts to introduce a national Bill or Charter of Rights.[1] Most recently, the 2009 National Human Rights Consultation Report recommended the introduction of a federal Human Rights Act.[2] However, today Australia is (in)famous as the last western democracy not to have a statutory or constitutional Bill or Charter of Rights. As a result, the way in which freedom of religion, along with other human rights, are protected in Australia differs from other comparable common law countries.

As a secular western democracy Australia has much in common with other predominantly English speaking common law countries. This is perhaps unsurprising given Australia's colonial history as a former British colony. Like the Unites States, Canada, New Zealand and South Africa, Australia inherited many of its legal and political structures from the United Kingdom. While these legal and political structures have been adapted in each country to suit local conditions, many similarities remain. In the context of the relationship between the State and religion, there are also significant similarities in terms of both the formal State–religion relationships and the religious demographics of Australia, the United Kingdom, the United States, Canada, New Zealand and South Africa. As a result, law and policy makers along with religious and community leaders in these countries, are able to look to the experiences of the other five when formulating new laws and policy settings. However, the lack of a national bill or charter of rights in Australia means that the way in which debates about freedom of religion are carried out are necessarily different from these other countries.

Without a national Bill or Charter of Rights those claiming a violation of their rights must look to other avenues in order to protect their human rights, including

1 Andrew Byrnes, Hilary Charlesworth and Gabrielle McKinnon, *Bills of Rights in Australia: History, Politics and Law* (University of New South Wales Press, 2009) 24–34; Frank Brennan et al., *National Human Rights Consultation: Report* (Commonwealth of Australia Attorney General's Department, 2009) 229–240.
2 Frank Brennan et al., above n 1, recommendation 18.

freedom of religion. A common mechanism is to use administrative law or statutory interpretation-based arguments. The drawback of this approach, however, is that it does not involve an explicit balancing of rights nor does it allow for discussion and debate about human rights issues. Instead human rights issues tend to be subsumed into technical legal arguments.

Similarities with other jurisdictions

While there are many differences between Australia, the United States, the United Kingdom, Canada, New Zealand and South Africa, they also have much in common. All six are western, English-speaking democracies with a common law tradition. The United States, Canada, New Zealand, South Africa and Australia are all former colonies of the British Empire, now the United Kingdom, and as such inherited much of the legal tradition of the British Empire, including the common law. There are of course some variations. Canada also includes Quebec, a former French colony which today has a mixed legal system, incorporating elements of both civil and common law.[3] Unlike the other five former colonies South Africa has a majority indigenous population and like Canada was also in part subject to a different colonial power, in this case the Dutch. Further, the South African legal system incorporates elements of customary law in addition to the common law.[4]

In terms of the religious demographics there are significant similarities. All six countries have majority Christian populations with a significant percentage of the population self-identifying as having no religion.

All of the countries compared in this chapter experience relatively high levels of religious freedom. In terms of human rights and freedoms generally, New Zealand, Canada, the United Kingdom and Australia all rank in the top 10 of the 2016 Human Freedom Index.[5] South Africa ranks 74th and the United States of America ranks 23rd. Canada, the United Kingdom, Australia and the United States all received a score of 10/10 in relation to religious freedom specifically. The index rates both the freedom to establish religious organisations

---

3 See Michael McAuley, 'Quebec' in Vernon Palmer (ed), *Mixed Jurisdictions Worldwide: The Third Legal family* (Cambridge University Press, 2nd ed, 2012) 354; Vernon Palmer, 'Quebec and Her Sisters in the Third Legal Family' (2009) 54(2) *McGill Law Journal* 321; several American States also began as colonies of other colonial powers such as Spain and France.

4 For a very brief outline of the complex history of South Africa and therefore complex legal history see John Faris, 'African Customary Law and Common Law in South Africa: Reconciling Contending Legal Systems' (2015) 10(2) *International Journal of African Renaissance Studies – Multi-, Inter- and Transdisciplinarity* 171; see also C. G. Van Der Merwe et al., 'The Republic of South Africa' in Vernon Palmer (ed), *Mixed Jurisdictions Worldwide: The Third Legal family* (Cambridge University Press, 2nd ed 2012) 95.

5 Ian Vásquez and Tanja Por nik, *The Human Freedom Index 2016 – A Global Measurement of Personal, Civil and Economic Freedom* (Cato Institute, 2016) 5 also available at <https://object.cato.org/sites/cato.org/files/human-freedom-index-files/human-freedom-index-2016-update-3.pdf>.

Table 5.1 Religious affiliation in common law countries

Country	Data year	Christian	No-Religion	Islam	Judaism
United States[1]	2014	70.6%	22.8%	0.9%	1.9%
United Kingdom[2]	2011	59.3%	25.1%	4.8%	0.5%
Canada[3]	2011	67.3%	23.9%	3.2%	1.0%
New Zealand[4]	2013	47.7%	41.9%	1.2%	0.2%
South Africa[5]	2001[6]	79.8%	15.1%	1.5%	0.2%
Australia[7]	2016	52.1%	30.1%	2.6%	0.4%

1 Pew Research Centre – Religion and Public Life, *America's Changing Religious Landscape* (12 May 2015) <http://www.pewforum.org/2015/05/12/americas-changing-religious-landscape/>.
2 Office for National Statistics, *Religion Data from the 2011 Census* (16 December 2014) <http://webarchive.nationalarchives.gov.uk/20160105213246/http://www.ons.gov.uk/ons/rel/census/2011-census/key-statistics-for-local-authorities-in-england-and-wales/sty-what-is-your-religion.html>.
3 Statistics Canada, *Immigration and Ethnocultural Diversity in Canada* (15 September 2016) <http://www12.statcan.gc.ca/nhs-enm/2011/as-sa/99-010-x/99-010-x2011001-eng.cfm#a6>.
4 Stats NZ – Tatauranga Aotearoa, 2013 Census, *Profile and Summary Reports – Quickstats Culture Identity Tables* <https://web.archive.org/web/20140524102811/http://www.stats.govt.nz/~/media/Statistics/Census/2013%20Census/profile-and-summary-reports/quickstats-culture-identity/tables.xls>.
5 Statistics South Africa, *Census 2001: Primary tables South Africa - Census '96 and 2001 compared* (Statistics South Africa, 2004) available at <http://www.webcitation.org/6UxL3wQW4?url=http://www.statssa.gov.za/census01/html/RSAPrimary.pdf>.
6 The 2011 census did not ask participants about their religion.
7 Australian Bureau of Statistics, Religion in Australia – 2016 Census Data Summary (19 October 2017) <http://www.abs.gov.au/ausstats/abs@.nsf/Lookup/by%20Subject/2071.0~2016~Main%20Features~Religion%20Data%20Summary~70>.

and the autonomy of those organisations.[6] While this does not cover all aspects of religious freedom, it does give a good indication of how these countries fair as compared with other nations.[7]

All six jurisdictions could also broadly be described as secular. As discussed in Chapter 2, a range of State–religion relationships can be described as secular. There are several different definitions of what constitutes a secular State and it largely depends upon the arguments you wish to make. The relationships represented by the countries considered in this chapter span the full spectrum of the range of relationships which could be considered secular. At one end is the United Kingdom. Here the picture is complex.

6 Ibid. 13.
7 It does not for example cover freedom to engage in individual religious practice.

Table 5.2 Freedom of religion index in common law countries

Country	Rank (out of 159)	Overall Score (out of 10)	Freedom of Religion score (out of 10)
New Zealand	3	8.35	7.50
Canada	6	8.61	10
United Kingdom	6	8.61	10
Australia	6	8.61	10
Units States of America	23	8.27	10
South Africa	74	6.92	8.75

Data source: Ian Vásquez and Tanja Porčnik, *The Human Freedom Index 2016 A Global Measurement of Personal, Civil, and Economic Freedom* (Cato Institute, The Fraser Institute and the Friedrich Naumann Foundation for Freedom)

Each of the constituent countries has defined its own approach: England and Scotland have an established and national church respectively; whereas in Northern Ireland and Wales the (Anglican) Church of Ireland and the (Anglican) Church in Wales have been disestablished since 1871 and 1920 respectively.[8]

However, the United Kingdom could also be defined as secular. Society is certainly much more secular in its outlook in the United Kingdom than it once was.[9] However, religion, and in particular established religion, still plays an important role in government and other institutions in the United Kingdom.[10] Interestingly, as Bronney notes in the United Kingdom at least:

Secularisation of personal behaviour appears to be a continuing process, but society has not become completely secular. The significance of the theory of secularisation may, then, only relate to the sphere of private and personal behaviour without having major consequences for the public sphere – a complete reversal of the situation proposed by secularisation theory whereby religion is seen as becoming an exclusively private matter and not an issue of public concern.[11]

At the other end of the spectrum is the United States of America with strict separation of church and State.[12] The First Amendment provides that 'Congress shall

8 Jeroen Temperman, *State–religion Relationships and Human Rights Law: Towards a Right to Religiously Neutral Governance* (Brill, 2010) 47.
9 Norman Bonney, *Monarchy, Religion and the State: Civil Religion in the United Kingdom, Canada, Australia and the Commonwealth* (Manchester University Press, 2013) 2–4.
10 Ibid. 5–7.
11 Ibid. 7.
12 Temperman, above n 15, 116–118.

make no law respecting an establishment of religion.' In the words of Justice Black of the United States Supreme Court decision in *Everson v Board of Education*:

> The 'establishment of religion' clause of the First Amendment means at least this: Neither a state nor the Federal Government can set up a church. Neither can pass laws which aid one religion, aid all religions or prefer one religion over another. Neither can force nor influence a person to go to or to remain away from church against his will or force him to profess a belief or disbelief in any religion. No person can be punished for entertaining or professing religious beliefs or disbeliefs, for church attendance or non-attendance. No tax in any amount, large or small, can be levied to support any religious activities or institutions, whatever they may be called, or whatever form they may adopt to teach or practice religion. Neither a state nor the Federal Government can, openly or secretly, participate in the affairs of any religious organizations or groups and vice versa. In the words of Jefferson, the clause against establishment of religion by law was intended to erect 'a wall of separation between Church and State.'[13]

The remaining four fall somewhere in the middle of these two extremes. None have established churches; however, each allows for a certain amount of interaction between the State and religion.[14]

Like Australia, the preamble of the Canadian and South African Constitutions recognises God. Canada's *Constitution* begins with the words 'Whereas Canada is founded upon principles that recognize the supremacy of God and the rule of law.'[15] While the preamble to South Africa's Conisations contains both the words 'May God protect our people' and 'God bless South Africa'.[16] Even the United States, whose *Constitution* formally enshrines a 'wall of separation' between church and State has 'In God we Trust' inscribed on its currency.[17] However, these symbolic references to God have little practical implications. As discussed below, the Constitutions of all three Countries go onto guarantee freedom of religion in their Bills or Charters of rights.

New Zealand's Constitutional documents are silent on the issue of the place of religion, although freedom of religion is guaranteed under its Bill of Rights. However, religion is not completely absent from the State. For example, the New Zealand parliament, like the Australian parliament, opens proceedings with a prayer.[18]

---

13 *Everson v Board of Education*, 330 US 1, 15–16 (Black J) (1947).
14 Temperman, above n 15, 105–107.
15 *Canada Act 1892* (UK) c 11, sch B pt 1 (*'Canadian Charter of Rights and Freedoms'*).
16 *Constitution of the Republic of South Africa Act 1996* (South Africa) preamble.
17 See *An Act to provide that all United States Currency shall bear the inscription In God We Trust* 36 USC § 186 (1956); 31 USC §§ 5112(d)(1), 5114(b).
18 In 2007 MPs voted to keep the prayer see 'MPs vote to retain Prayer' (Press Release, 15 June 2007) <www.parliament.nz/en/visit-and-learn/how-parliament-works/office-of-the-speaker/press-releases-pre-2015/document/48Speakpress150620071/mps-vote-to-retain-prayer>;

As a result of these legal and religious similarities it is relatively easy to draw comparisons between Australia and the other five countries. Australian policy and law makers draw from the experience of other common law, secular democracies when considering changes in law or government policy. However, Australia differs in one important respect from all other western democracies: it does not have a national Bill or Charter of Rights. This has important consequences for the way in which human rights, including freedom of religion, are protected in Australia.

Bills and Charters of Rights

Australia is (in)famous for being the last western democracy not to have a Bill or Charter of Rights.[19] While a number of attempts have been made to introduce a Bill or Charter of Rights at a federal level, none have enjoyed any success.[20] A small number of rights are protected by the *Australian Constitution*; voting (Section 41), acquisition of property only on just terms (Section 51), trial by jury (Section 80), religion (Section 116), no discrimination as between residence of different States on the basis of residence (Section 117). However, all these rights have been consistently interpreted narrowly by the High Court.[21] As a result they are far from a comprehensive Bill or Charter of Rights.

At a State and territory level Victoria and the Australian Capital Territory both have legislative Charters of Rights.[22] However these have limited application. As State and territory-based legislation the charters only apply in their respective jurisdictions and, as ordinary acts of parliament, can easily be repealed or derogated from. All States and territories, along with the Commonwealth, also prohibit discrimination in their various anti-discrimination legislation.[23]

In relation to religion specifically, the *Australian Constitution* contains Section 116, which, as discussed in Chapter 4, on its face would appear to protect

in 2014 a proposed new prayer was rejected see Audrey Young, 'MPs' New Prayer Rejected', *NZ Herald* (online), 9 December 2014 <www.nzherald.co.nz/nz/news/article.cfm?c_id=1&objectid=11371418>; in 2017 MPs were again consulted on a new form of parliamentary prayer. The proposed new prayer would omit references to both the Queen and Jesus Christ see Derek Cheng, 'Politicians Look at Dropping God from Parliament's Opening Prayer', *NZ Herald* (online), 10 November 2017 <www.nzherald.co.nz/nz/news/article.cfm?c_id=1&objectid=11942504>.

19 Louise Chappell, John Chesterman and Lisa Hill, *The Politics of Human Rights in Australia* (Cambridge University Press, 2009) 27–29.
20 See Byrnes, Charlesworth and McKinnon, above n 1.
21 Chappell, Chesterman and Hill, above n 26, 28–29.
22 *Charter of Human Rights and responsibilities Act 2006* (Vic), *Human Rights Act 2004* (ACT).
23 See *Discrimination Act 1991* (ACT); *Age Discrimination Act 2004* (Cth); *Australian Human Rights Commission Act 1986* (Cth); *Disability Discrimination Act 1992* (Cth); *Racial Discrimination Act 1975* (Cth); *Sex Discrimination Act 1984* (Cth); *Anti-Discrimination Act 1977* (NSW); *Anti-Discrimination Act 1992* (NT); *Anti-Discrimination Act 1991* (Qld); *Equal Opportunity Act 1984* (SA); *Anti-Discrimination Act 1998* (Tas); *Equal Opportunity Act 2010* (Vic); *Equal Opportunity Act 1984* (WA).

freedom of religion. However, it has been interpreted narrowly by the High Court. Despite linguistic similarities with the United States First Amendment, it is its differences which have been most dominant in its interpretation. In *Attorney General (Vic); ex rel Black v The Commonwealth*[24] the High Court explicitly rejected an American style separation of church and State based on this difference.[25] While the Court has not addressed the question directly, it is likely it would similarly reject an American style interpretation of the freedom of religion clause of Section 116. Instead the Court has favoured a narrow interpretation of the provision as a limit on Commonwealth legislative power.

In 1998 the *Human Rights and Equal Opportunity Commission*[26] recommended the creation of a Federal Freedom of Religion Act.[27] The Commonwealth government did not act on this recommendation. At the time of writing, two inquiries into freedom of religion are underway. The Commonwealth Joint Standing Committee on Foreign Affairs, Defence and Trade handed down its Interim Report into the *Legal Foundations of Religious Freedom in Australia* in November 2017.[28] Further, in the wake of the same-sex marriage postal survey and concerns about freedom of religion following the legalisation of same-sex marriage, Prime Minister Malcom Turnbull announced that Philip Ruddock had been appointed the head of an expert panel to 'examine whether Australian law adequately protects the human right to religious freedom.'[29] The panel is due to report by 31 March 2018.[30]

Freedom of religion is also protected by anti-discrimination legislation, first by prohibitions on discrimination on the basis of religion and second by providing exemptions for religious organisations. All States and territories, except New

---

24 (1981) 146 CLR 559.
25 *Attorney General (Vic); ex rel Black v The Commonwealth* (1981) 146 CLR 559, 578–579 (Barwick CJ); 598–603 (Gibbs J); 609–610 (Stephen J); 613–614 (Mason J); 652–653 (Wilson J).
26 Now known as the Australian Human Rights Commission.
27 Human Rights and Equal Opportunity Commission, *Article 18 – Freedom of Religion and Belief* (Commonwealth of Australia, 1998) 24–25 also available at <www.humanrights. gov.au/sites/default/files/content/pdf/human_rights/religion/article_18_religious_ freedom.pdf>. See also the 2011 report, Australian Human Rights Commission, *2011 - Freedom of Religion and Belief in 21st century Australia* (Australian Human Rights Commission, 2011) also available at www.humanrights.gov.au/sites/default/files/content/frb/ Report_2011.pdf.
28 Joint Standing Committee on Foreign Affairs, Defence and Trade, *Interim Report Legal Foundations of Religious Freedom in Australia* (Commonwealth of Australia, 2017) also available at <http://parlinfo.aph.gov.au/parlInfo/download/committees/reportjnt/024110/ toc_pdf/InterimReport.pdf;fileType=application%2Fpdf>.
29 Prime Minister Malcolm Turnbull, 'Ruddock to examine religious freedom protection in Australia' (Media Release, 22 November 2017) <www.pm.gov.au/media/ruddock-examine-religious-freedom-protection-australia;> the Expert Panel comprises, Hon Philip Ruddock, Emeritus Professor Rosalind Croucher AM, Hon Dr Annabelle Bennett AO SC, Father Frank Brennan SJ AO and Professor Nicholas Aroney.
30 Prime Minister Malcolm Turnbull, above n 36.

South Wales, provides some form of prohibition on discrimination on the basis of religion in their anti-discrimination legislation.[31] South Australia however only prohibits discrimination on the basis of 'religious appearance or dress, rather than religion or belief generally.[32] Discrimination on the basis of religion is also prohibited in relation to employment by the Commonwealth's *Australian Human Rights Commission Act 1986.*[33]

Anti-discrimination legislation also contains exemptions from some of the provisions of the relevant laws for religious organisations. For example, the Commonwealth *Sex Discrimination Act* provides an exemption for, *inter alia,* 'any . . . act or practice of a body established for religious purposes, being an act or practice that conforms to the doctrines, tenets or beliefs of that religion or is necessary to avoid injury to the religious susceptibilities of adherents of that religion.'[34] This exemption does not however apply in relation to residents of Commonwealth-funded aged care.[35] State and territory anti-discrimination legislation also contain similar exemptions in relation to discrimination on the grounds of characteristics such as gender, marital status and sexual orientation.[36] Exemptions are also provided to religious schools.[37] Finally, Victoria, Queensland and Tasmania prohibit

31 *Discrimination Act 1991* (ACT) s 7; *Anti-Discrimination Act 1992* (NT) s 19(1); *Anti-Discrimination Act 1991* (Qld) s 7; *Equal Opportunity Act 1984* (SA) s 85T; *Anti-Discrimination Act 1998* (Tas) ss 14, 15, 16(o); *Equal Opportunity Act 2010* (Vic) s 6(n); *Equal Opportunity Act 1984* (WA) s 53.

32 *Equal Opportunity Act 1984* (SA) s 85T; see also Anne Hewitt, 'It's not because you wear Hijab, it's because you're Muslim – Inconsistencies in South Australia's Discrimination Laws' (2012) 7(1) *QUT Law Review* 57.

33 *Australian Human Rights Commission Act 1986* (Cth) ss 30–35.

34 *Sex Discrimination Act 1984* (Cth) s 37 (1)(d). The act also exempts religious organisations in relation to the 'ordination or appointment of priests, ministers of religion or member of any religious order, the training or education of persons seeking ordination or appointment as priests, ministers of religion or members of a religious order and he selection or appointment of persons to perform duties or functions for the purposes of or in connection with, or otherwise to participate in, any religious observance or practice' see *Sex Discrimination Act 1984* (Cth) sa 37 (1)(a)–(c).

35 *Sex Discrimination Act 1984* (Cth) s 37(2).

36 Anti-*Discrimination Act* 1977 (NSW) s 56(d); *Anti-Discrimination Act 1992* (NT) s 51(d); *Equal opportunity Act 1984* (SA) s 50(1)(c); *Anti-Discrimination Act* 1998 (Tas) s 52(d); *Equal Opportunity Act 2010* (Vic) s 82(2); *Equal opportunity Act 1984* (WA) s 72(d); The exact formulation of these grounds and the religious exemption provisions varies between the different jurisdictions, see, for example, Liam Elphick, 'Sexual Orientation and 'Gay Wedding Cake' Cases Under Australian Anti-Discrimination Legislation: A Fuller Approach to Religious Exemptions' (2017) 38(1) *Adelaide Law Review* 149, 156–161.

37 *Discrimination Act 1991* (ACT) s 33; *Sex Discrimination Act 1984* (Cth) s 38; *Anti-Discrimination Act 1977* (NSW) ss 4, 49ZO(3); *Anti-Discrimination Act 1992* (NT) s 37A; *Equal Opportunity Act 1984* (SA) s 34(3); *Equal Opportunity Act 2010* (Vic) s 83(1); *Equal Opportunity Act 1984* (WA) s 73; see Carolyn Evans and Beth Gaze, 'Discrimination by Religious Schools: Views from the Coal Face' (2010) 34(2) *Melbourne University Law Review* 392.

religious vilification.[38] During the same-sex marriage postal survey, the Common-wealth government also temporarily prohibited vilification on the basis of, *inter alia*, religious conviction.[39]

Despite this patchwork of protections, the absence of an Australian Bill or Charter of Rights is notable when you consider that all other western democra-cies, including comparable common law jurisdictions, have a Bill or Charter of Rights. Perhaps the most famous is the United States of America's Bill of Rights. Freedom of Religion is protected under the First Amendment:

> Congress shall make no law respecting an establishment of religion or pro-hibiting the free exercise thereof.

This protection has been extended to apply to the legislatures of all American states courtesy of the Fourteenth Amendment, also known as the equal protec-tion clause.[40]

Canada and South Africa also protect freedom of religion in Constitutional Bills of Rights. The *Canadian Charter of Rights and Freedoms* contained in the *Constitution Act 1982* includes 'freedom of Conscience and Religion' at the top of its list of Fundamental Freedoms.[41] Freedom of religion and belief is protected in both Section 15 of the 1996 *Constitution of the Republic of South Africa*[42] and the *South African Charter of Religious Rights and Freedoms.*[43]

Like Australia, New Zealand and the United Kingdom take a non-Constitutional approach to protecting human rights generally and freedom of religion specifically. However, unlike Australia, the courts of both countries have a Bill or Charter of Rights and a role for the courts in enforcing those rights, albeit in a more limited way than in the United States, Canada and South Africa.

Freedom of religion is protected in Sections 13 of the New Zealand *Bill of Rights 1990* and the United Kingdom *Human Rights Act 1998*. However, unlike the United States, Canada and South Africa, courts in New Zealand and the United Kingdom do not have the power to strike down legislation which the

---

38 *Racial and Religious Tolerance Act 2001* (Vic); *Anti-Discrimination Act 1991* (Qld) s 124A(1); *Anti-Discrimination Act 1998* (Tas) s 19(d).

39 See *Marriage Law Survey (Additional safeguards) Act 2017* (Cth) s 15(1)(c). The Act auto-matically lapsed at the end of the postal survey on 15 November 2017, see *Marriage Law Survey (Additional safeguards) Act 2017 (Cth)* s 27.

40 Clifford Pannam, 'Traveling Section 116 with a U.S. Road Map' (1963) 4 *Melbourne University Law Review* 41, 42–43.

41 See *Canada Act 1982* (UK) c 11, sch B (*'Constitution Act 1982'*) s 2(a).

42 *Constitution of the Republic of South Africa Act 1996* (South Africa) s 15.

43 The Council for the Protection and Promotion of Religious Rights and Freedoms, *The South African Charter Of Religious Rights And Freedoms* and *The South African Council For The Protection And Promotion Of Religious Rights And Freedoms* (11 September 2013) <www.strasbourgconsortium.org/content/blurb/files/South%20African%20Char-ter.pdf>.

court finds to be in breach of the relevant human rights instrument.[44] Instead the courts must, where possible, interpret legation in such a way as to be consistent with the rights included in the relevant Bill of Rights.[45] Where this is not possible, the court may make a finding of inconsistency, but this does not render the relevant law invalid.[46]

A lack of a Bill or Charter of Rights does not in and of itself mean that Australians enjoy any less freedom of religion than those living in the United States, Canada, South Africa, New Zealand or the United Kingdom. In fact, as outlined at the beginning of this chapter, these countries all have much in common with Australia in terms of the relationship between the State and religion. This includes a relatively high level of freedom of religion.[47]

The consequence for Australia

One of the consequences of a lack of a Bill or Charter of Rights generally, and a broad freedom of religion provision specifically, is that issues relating to freedom of religion are not argued before the courts on a human rights basis. Instead, issues relating to freedom of religion tend to be argued in the political arena. When issues relating to freedom of religion do find their way before the courts the cases tended to be argued on the basis of other Constitutional or administrative or legislative provisions, with the religious aspects of the case being little more than a side note to the other legal issues, even if they may be the main focus of the media commentary.

This trend, of using administrative and technical mechanism to address human rights issue can be seen in a number of cases in recent years. The facts of these cases ostensibly raise human rights issues. However, without a Bill or Charter of Rights these cases have been decided via other mechanisms. For example, Australia is well known for its tough stance on asylum seekers arriving via boat. The Australian government has implemented a number of 'solutions' aimed at discouraging people making the journey to Australia via boat. Many of these 'solutions' have been challenged in the High Court, with some success. Perhaps the most (in)famous is these is *M70/2011 v Minister for Immigration and Citizenship*[48] in which the High Court struck down the federal government's Malaysian Solution which saw asylum seekers who had arrived in Australia transferred

---

44 Rex Ahdar and Ian Leigh, *Religious Freedom in the Liberal State* (Oxford University Press, 2nd ed, 2013) 132.

45 *New Zealand Bill of Rights Act 1990* (NZ) s 6; *Human Rights Act 1998* (UK) s 3.

46 Ahdar and Leigh, above n 51, 132.

47 Kevin Boyle and Juliet Sheen (eds), *Freedom of Religion and Belief: A World Report* (Routledge, 1997) 166–175.

48 (2011) 244 CLR 144; for a summary of the decision see Tamara Wood and Jane McAdam, 'Australian Asylum Policy All at Sea: An Analysis of Plaintiff M70/2011 v Minister for Immigration and Citizenship and the Australia – Malaysia Arrangement' (2012) 61(1) *International and Comparative Law Quarterly* 274.

to Malaysia in return for Australia accepting certified refugees from Malaysia.[49] The central issue for the court however was not one of human rights, nor Australia's obligations under international refugee or human rights treaties. Instead, the central issue was one of statutory interpretation, namely what was the correct interpretation of Section 198A(3)(i)–(iv) of the *Migration Act*.[50] The majority found that the correct interpretation of the Section was that access to the protections set out in the relevant Section must be legal obligations in the receiving country and as this was not the case in Malaysia, removal of asylum seekers to Malaysia was unlawful.[51] One of the problems with the approach to human rights is that ordinary legislation can often be amended relatively easily to remedy any defects identified by the courts. In the case of the Malaysian Solution the federal government explored amending the *Migration Act* to remedy the defects identified by the High Court, but ultimately abandoned their plans to do so.[52]

Cases involving issues relating to the interaction of the State and religion, including freedom of religion, have been no different. In *Monis v the Queen*[53] the appellant was charged under Section 471.12 of the *Criminal Code* (Cth) with using a postal service 'in a way . . . that reasonable persons would regard as being, in all the circumstances . . . offensive.'[54] Monis had sent letters to the families of deceased soldiers which included 'assertions that they were murderers and inferior in moral merit to Adolf Hitler.'[55] The letters included statements such as 'May God grant you patience and guide us all to the right path' and compared the deceased soldier to a pig, referring to his body as 'the dirty body of a pig'.[56] While the case makes little mention of it, Monis' motivations are likely to have been, in part, religious. He was a self-styled Muslim cleric known to be politically active in protesting Australian government actions in the Middle East and to have issued '*fatwas*' via his web site on a range of topics.[57] The reference to pigs in the letter may be a reference to the Islamic prohibition on the consumption

---

49 Wood and McAdam, above n 55, 274, 276–282.

50 Ibid. 283.

51 *M70/2011 v Minister for Immigration and Citizenship* (2011) 244 CLR 144, 198–199 (Gummow, Hayne, Crennan and Bell JJ), 201–202 (Gummow, Hayne, Crennan and Bell JJ).

52 Sasha Lowes, 'The Legality of Extraterritorial Processing of Asylum Claims: The Judgement of the High Court of Australia in the Malaysian Solution Case' (2012) 12(1) *Human Rights Law Review* 168, 180–182.

53 (2013) 249 CLR 92; for a summary of the case see Madeleine Figg, 'The Implied Freedom of Political Communication in *Monis v The Queen*: 'A Noble and Idealistic Enterprise which has Failed, is Failing, and Will Go on Failing?'' (2013) 32(1) *University of Tasmania Law Review* 125.

54 The appellant, Man Monis, was later responsible for the Lint Café siege in Martin Place Sydney, see Chapter 6.

55 Figg, above n 60, 126.

56 *Monis v The Queen* (2013) 249 CLR 92, 179.

57 State Coroner of New South Wales, *Inquests into the deaths arising from the Lindt Café siege* (New South Wales Department of Justice, 2017) 64–69 also available at www.lindtinquest. justice.nsw.gov.au/Documents/findings-and-recommendations.pdf.

of pig products. Despite this, there is no reference in the case to his possible religious motivation nor is freedom to express religious views raised in the case. The case did consider the constitutionally implied freedom of political communication as laid down in *Lange v Australian Broadcasting Corporation*.[58] However, this implied freedom is far from being the equivalent to a freedom of speech.[59]

Attorney-General (SA) v Corporation of the City of Adelaide[60] has an even more explicit connection to religion, yet again religious freedom plays little role in the judgment. In that case the High Court upheld a local council by-law which has been used to prevent street preachers from operating in the City of Adelaide without permission from the city Council. Like *Monis*, the High Court considered the implied freedom of political communication. The Court also considered a statutory interpretation question relating to the by-law making power of the relevant local authority. The connection to religion is explicit in this case as the relevant Act made specific reference to religion and religious activities. Section 239(1) of the *Local Government Act 1999* (SA) empowered local governments to make by-laws for the use of roads for a number of purposes including 'soliciting for religious or charitable purposes.'[61] Further, the relevant by-law made under that provision prohibited a person from 'Preaching and Canvassing' without permission on any road.[62] While 'preach' was not defined '[t]here was, however, little controversy about [its] ordinary meaning. The term "preach" means to advocate or inculcate asserted religious or moral truth and right conduct in speech or in writing.'[63] The respondents in this case were street preachers and members of an incorporated association known as 'Street Church.' While French CJ did make reference to the fact that 'some "religious" speech may also be characterised as "political" communication for the purposes of the freedom [of political communication]'.[64] References to the religious aspect of the case were otherwise few and far between. Religious freedom was not raised at all as an independent issue.

58 (1997) 189 CLR 520.
59 *Monis v The Queen* is interesting for a number of reasons. First, it was a split 3–3 decision owing to the retirement of Justice William Gummow. As a result, the decision of the Supreme Court of New South Wales (Court of Criminal Appeal in *Monis v The Queen* (2011) 215 A Crim R 64) was affirmed and the relevant section of the *Criminal Code 1995* (Cth) was declared valid. Second, the split was along gender lines with all three male judges finding in favour of the appellant while all three female judges finding in favour of the respondent, see Gabrielle Appleby and Ngaire Naffine, 'Civility, Gender and the Law: Critical Reflections on the Judgements in *Monis v The Queen*' (2015) 24(4) *Griffith Law Review* 616.
60 (2013) 249 CLR 1; for a summary of the case see Adrienne Stone, '*Freedom to Preach in Rundle Mall: Attorney-General (SA) v Corporation of the City of Adelaide ('Corneloup's Case')*' (14 October 2013) Opinions on High <http://blogs.unimelb.edu.au/opinionsonhigh/2013/10/14/stone-corneloup.>
61 See *Attorney-General (SA) v Corporation of the City of Adelaide* (2013) 249 CLR 1, 20.
62 Ibid. 23.
63 Ibid. 32 (French CJ).
64 Ibid. 44 (French CJ).

Even *Williams v The Commonwealth*,[65] which did in fact consider Section 116 of the *Constitution*, was decided on the basis of the Commonwealth government's spending powers rather than as an issue of religious freedom.[66] Further, the clause of Section 116, which was considered, was the 'religious test clause', arguably the most formal or administrative of the four limbs of Section 116. As discussed in Chapter 4, the High Court has interpreted Section 116 so narrowly that there was little prospect of success in arguing the case on a freedom of religion or separation of religion and State basis.[67] Following the High Court's decision the federal government was able to remedy the defects identified by the High Court by implementing a new funding model for the National School Chaplaincy Programme.[68]

Going further back, the plaintiffs in *Adelaide Company of Jehovah's Witnesses v Commonwealth*[69] were successful, not on the basis of their Section 116 arguments, but in relation to their argument that the legislation was beyond the power of the Commonwealth. While Section 116 was discussed extensively in that case, the Court ultimately found that Section 116 had not been breached. Instead the Jehovah's Witnesses' 'freedom of religion' was protected in a similar way as in *Williams*, this time via a finding that the relevant legislation, as opposed to spending, was beyond power.[70]

What all of these cases, with the possible exception of *Adelaide Company of Jehovah's Witnesses*, lack despite the religious freedom implications of their facts, is any discussion of balancing the freedom of religion against other human rights. Other than the very limited freedom of political communication, which like the so called freedom of religion in Section 116 of the *Australian Constitution* acts as a limit on legislative power rather than as a personal right,[71] there is little reference to human rights in any of these cases. Instead these cases tend to be decided on technical or administrative issues such as statutory interpretation, legislative power and spending power. This is in stark contrast to the way in which cases whose facts reveal a freedom of religion or more generally a human rights issue are dealt with in other justifications. The very existence of a Bill or Charter of Rights compels courts to consider freedom of religion when raised and where relevant balance that against other human rights.

There are many examples of the courts using other mechanisms to deal with issues relating to freedom of religion and the relationship between the State and

---

65 (2012) 248 CLR 156.
66 Renae Barker, 'A Critical Analysis of Religious Aspects of the Australian Chaplaincy Cases' (2015) 4(1) *Oxford Journal of Law and Religion* 26, 45–47.
67 See also Barker, 'A Critical Analysis of Religious Aspects of the Australian Chaplaincy Cases', above n 73, 41–45.
68 See Chapter 8.
69 (1943) 67 CLR 116.
70 For a discussion of *Williams v the Commonwealth* see Chapter Eight, for a discussion of *Adelaide Company of Jehovah's Witnesses v Commonwealth* see Chapter 7.
71 *Attorney-General (SA) v Corporation of the City of Adelaide* (2013) 249 CLR 1, 73 (Crennan and Kiefel JJ).

religion more generally. The remainder of this chapter has identified two which have contemporary significance. First, the legalisation of same sex marriage in Australia has largely been a matter of political debate rather than one of fundamental human rights mediated through a Bill or Charter of Rights. Second, unlike other jurisdictions, cases concerning the wearing of the Islamic face veil in Australia have not needed to balance freedom of religion with other fundamental rights and freedoms. It is important to note that in both cases the final outcome in Australia and comparable jurisdictions is often the same or similar – however the process of getting there is different.

Same-sex marriage

A very contemporary example of the impact a lack of a Bill of Rights has had on freedom of religion debates can be seen in the current Australian debate surrounding the legalisation of same-sex marriage in Australia. As will be discussed in more detail in Chapter 6, marriage between two persons regardless of their gender was legalised in Australia on 9 December 2017. Prior to the passage of the *Marriage Amendment (Definition and Religious Freedoms) Act 2017* (Cth) amending the *Marriage Act 1986* (Cth), marriage in Australia had been defined as being between one man and one woman.[72]

There have been two important consequences in the way the debate has been carried out flowing from the lack of a Bill or Charter of Rights. First, the legalisation of same-sex marriage has been almost entirely the province of the federal legislature with only a minimal role for the courts. Second, issues relating to exemptions from anti-discrimination laws and freedom of religion more broadly have remained predominantly a political and legislative issue rather than being fought in the arena of the courts. The following section focuses on the first of these consequences, touching only briefly upon the second.

In *Commonwealth v Australian Capital Territory*[73] the High Court held that Australian Capital Territory legislation which purported to legalise same-sex marriage was invalid and that the Commonwealth had in effect covered the field in relation to marriage.[74] As a result, no State or territory could unilaterally legalise same-sex marriage. With no federal Bill or Charter of Rights, this left the issue firmly within the purview of the federal legislature. The court, in its unanimous joint judgment, began its judgment with the clear and emphatic statement that 'The only issue which this Court can decide is a legal issue.'[75] In beginning the judgment in this way the Court clearly signalled that it was not called upon to answer the broader human rights issue of whether or not same-sex marriage should be legalised. The only issue the Court could and did decide upon was

---

72 For a discussion of the legalisation of same-sex marriage in Australia see Chapter Six.
73 (2013) 250 CLR 441.
74 Ibid. 467 (French CJ, Hayne, Crennan, Kiefel. Bell and Keane JJ).
75 Ibid. 452 (French CJ, Hayne, Crennan, Kiefel. Bell and Keane JJ).

whether: 'the *Marriage Equality (Same Sex) Act 2013* (ACT), enacted by the Legislative Assembly for the Australian Capital Territory, inconsistent with either or both of two Acts of the Federal Parliament: the *Marriage Act 1961* (Cth) and the *Family Law Act 1975* (Cth)?.'[76] While the Court did find that the *Australian Constitution* gave the federal legislature the power to legislate with respect to same-sex marriage,[77] it did not find that their failure to do so breached the *Constitution* or a Bill or Charter of Rights. They could not do so as Australia has no such constitutional charter.

The Australian High Court's very legal and technical approach to the same-sex marriage issue can be contrasted with that of Superior Courts in jurisdictions which have a Bill or Charter of Rights. For example, in the Ontario Court of Appeal judgment the Court states in the second paragraph of its judgment:

> This appeal raises significant constitutional issues that require serious legal analysis. That said, this case is ultimately about the recognition and protection of human dignity and equality in the context of the social structures available to conjugal couples in Canada.[78]

Similarly, the joint majority judgment in the United States Supreme Court judgment in *Obergefell v Hodges* (*Obergefell*)[79] opens with:

> The Constitution promises liberty to all within its reach, a liberty that includes certain specific rights that allow persons, within a lawful realm, to define and express their identity. The petitioners in these cases seek to find that liberty by marrying someone of the same sex and having their marriages deemed lawful on the same terms and conditions as marriages between persons of the opposite sex.[80]

In the South African Constitutional Court decision in *Minister for Home Affairs v Fourie and others; Lesbian and Gay Equality Project and Others v Minister of Home Affairs and Other*[81] (*Fourie*), Sachs J emphasises the human element of the case, as opposed to the legal one, by giving a very brief outline of the applicant's story:

> Finding themselves strongly attracted to each other, two people went out regularly and eventually decided to set up home together. After being acknowledged by their friends as a couple for more than a decade, they decided that the time had come to get public recognition and registration of their

76 Ibid.
77 Ibid. 452 (French CJ, Hayne, Crennan, Kiefel. Bell and Keane JJ), 461 (French CJ, Hayne, Crennan, Kiefel. Bell and Keane JJ).
78 *Halpern v Canada (Attorney General)* (2003) CanLII 26403 (Ontario Court of Appeal).
79 135 S Ct 2584 (2015).
80 Ibid. 2593.
81 [2006] 1 SA 524 (Constitutional Court).

relationship, and formally to embrace the rights and responsibilities they felt should flow from and attach to it. Like many persons in their situation, they wanted to get married. There was one impediment. They are both women.[82]

In each of the paragraphs outlined above it is the human (and human rights) element of the case which is emphasised. That is not to say technical legal arguments are not important, as the Ontario Court of Appeal emphasised they are, but unlike Australia the cases have another primary consideration: human rights.

In 2005 Canada became just the fourth country in the world to legalise same-sex marriage throughout its territory.[83] The process through which it achieved this was initiated via court challenges to Provincial and national laws which limited marriage and the rights and privileges that go with marriage to opposite sex couples. The process arguably began with the Canadian Supreme Court decision in *M v H*[84] in which the Court held that same-sex couples were entitled to the same recognition of common-law marriages (*de facto* relationships) as opposite sex couples. However, the decision did not go as far as to allow same-sex couples access to civil marriage ceremonies.[85] A series of Provincial Court decisions followed, which legalised same sex marriage at the provincial level.[86] In 2002 and 2003, superior courts in Quebec,[87] Ontario[88] and British Columbia[89] held that the equal protection clause in the *Canadian Charter of Rights and Freedoms* was violated by the continued use of the common law definition of marriage as being between one man and one woman, effectively legalising same-sex marriage in these provinces.

Section 15(1) of the *Canadian Charter of Rights and Freedoms* provides that:

> Every individual is equal before and under the law and has the right to the equal protection and equal benefit of the law without discrimination and, in particular, without discrimination based on race, national or ethnic origin, colour, religion, sex, age or mental or physical disability.[90]

82 Ibid. [1] (Sachs J).
83 See Peter W. Hogg, 'Canada: The Constitution and Same-Sex marriage' (2006) 4(4) *International Journal of Constitutional law* 712, 712; The Netherlands, Belgium and Spain had already legalised same-sex marriage.
84 [1999] 2 SCR 3.
85 L. Marvin Overby, Christopher Raymond and Zeynep Taydas, 'Free Votes, MPs, and Constituents: The Case of Same-Sex Marriage in Canada' (2011) 41(4) *American Review of Canadian Studies* 465, 466; J. Scott Matthews, 'The Political Foundations of Support for Same-Sex Marriage in Canada' (2005) 38(4) *Canadian Journal of Political Science* 841, 849; R. Douglas Elliott and Mary Bonauto, 'Sexual Orientation and Gender Identity in North America' (2005) 48 (3–4) *Journal of Homosexuality* 91, 99.
86 For an overview of these cases see Elliott and Bonauto, above n 92, 102–103.
87 *Hendricks v Quebec (Attorney General)* [2002] RJQ 2506.
88 *Halpern v Canada (Attorney General)* (2003) CanLII 26403 (Ontario Court of Appeal).
89 *Eagle Canada Inc v Canada (Attorney General)* (2003) 225 DLR (4th) 472, this case overturned an early ruling which had found that there was no violation of the Charter see *Eagle Canada Inc v Canada Attorney General)* [2001] BCSC 1365.
90 *Canadian Charter of Rights and Freedoms* s 15(1).

An interesting aspect of the Ontario case was the involvement of the Metropolitan Community Church of Toronto (MCCT). The Church conduced two same-sex marriages in 2000 and 2001 following the 'ancient Christian tradition of publishing the banns of marriage' which the Church had discovered was 'a lawful alternative under the laws of Ontario to a marriage licence issued by municipal authorities.'[91] However, when the Church came to submit the required documentation to the Office of the Register General the registrar refuse to accept the documents.[92]

In the subsequent Ontario Court of Appeal case the Church argued, in addition to the arguments based on Section 15(1), that a refusal to allow them to solemnise same sex marriages constituted an infringement on their right to freedom of religion. They argued that:

> the common law definition of marriage is rooted in Christian values, as propounded by the Anglican Church of England, which has never recognized same-sex marriages. MCCT contends that this definition, therefore, has the unconstitutional purpose of enforcing a particular religious view of marriage and excluding other religious views of marriage. MCCT also contends that the common law definition of marriage, which provides legal recognition and legitimacy to marriage ceremonies that accord with one religious view of marriage, has the effect of diminishing the status of other religious marriages.[93]

The Court however rejected this argument drawing a distinction between religious and civil marriages.

> In our view, this case does not engage religious rights and freedoms. Marriage is a legal institution, as well as a religious and a social institution. This case is solely about the legal institution of marriage. It is not about the religious validity or invalidity of various forms of marriage. We do not view this case as, in any way, dealing or interfering with the religious institution of marriage.[94]

A number of subsequent provincial and territorial level decisions followed to the same effect.[95] While the federal and provincial governments initially opposed these rulings, they eventually abandoned this stance.[96]

In 2004 the federal government of Canada referred its *Proposal for an Act respecting certain aspects of legal capacity for marriage for civil purposes* to the

---

91 *Halpern v Canada (Attorney General)* (2003) CanLII 26403 (Ontario Court of Appeal) [11].
92 Ibid. [14].
93 Ibid. [51] (McMurtry CJO, MacPherson and Gillese JJ.A).
94 Ibid. [53] (McMurtry CJO, MacPherson and Gillese JJA).
95 See, for example, *Dunbar & Edge v Yokon Territory (Attorney General)* [2004] YKSC 54 (Supreme Court of Yukon Territory); *Vogel v Canada (Attorney General)* [2004] MJ No 418 (QL); *Boutilier v Nova Scotia (Attorney General)* [2004] NSJ No 357 (QL); *N.W v Canada (Attorney General)* [2004] SJ No 669 (QL).
96 Overby, Raymond and Taydas, above n 92, 466.

Canadian Supreme Court under Section 53(1) of the *Supreme Court Act*, RSC 1985, c. S-26.[97] The relevant sections of the proposed act were:

1   Marriage, for civil purposes, is the lawful union of two persons to the exclusion of all others.
2   Nothing in this Act affects the freedom of officials of religious groups to refuse to perform marriages that are not in accordance with their religious beliefs.

The government asked the Court to answer four questions in relation to these provisions[98]:

1   Is the annexed *Proposal for an Act respecting certain aspects of legal capacity for marriage for civil purposes* within the exclusive legislative authority of the Parliament of Canada? If not, in what particular or particulars, and to what extent?
2   If the answer to question 1 is yes, is Section 1 of the proposal, which extends capacity to marry persons of the same sex, consistent with the *Canadian Charter of Rights and Freedoms*? If not, in what particular or particulars, and to what extent?
3   Does the freedom of religion guaranteed by paragraph 2(*a*) of the *Canadian Charter of Rights and Freedoms* protect religious officials from being compelled to perform a marriage between two persons of the same sex that is contrary to their religious beliefs?
4   Is the opposite-sex requirement for marriage for civil purposes, as established by the common law and set out for Quebec in Section 5 of the *Federal Law-Civil Law Harmonization Act, No. 1*, consistent with the *Canadian Charter of Rights and Freedoms*? If not, in what particular or particulars and to what extent?

The Court held that under the *Canadian Constitution* marriage was not confined to being between one man and one woman and as such Section 1 of the proposed act was within the legislative competence of the federal government.[99] However, the Court held that Section 2 of the proposed act was *ultra vires*. While the Court acknowledged that '[t]he provision might be seen as an attempt to reassure the provinces and to assuage the concerns of religious officials who perform marriages' they concluded that '[h]owever worthy of attention these concerns are, only the provinces may legislate exemptions to existing solemnization requirements, as any such exemption necessarily relates to the solemnization

---

97 *Reference re Same-Sex Marriage* [2004] SCC 79; for a summary of the decision see Hogg, above n 90, 716–721.
98 *Reference re Same Sex Marriage* [2004] SCC 79, [2]–[3].
99 Ibid. [21]–[30].

of marriage under s. 92(12). Section 2 of the *Proposed Act* is therefore *ultra vires* Parliament.'[100]

The Court considered the issue of religion under its answer to both questions two and three. In relation to question two they commented that:

> The first allegation of infringement says in essence that equality of access to a civil institution like marriage may not only conflict with the views of those who are in disagreement, but may also violate their legal rights. This amounts to saying that the mere conferral of rights upon one group can constitute a violation of the rights of another. This argument was discussed above . . . and was rejected.[101]

They further commented that:

> The right to same-sex marriage conferred by the *Proposed Act* may conflict with the right to freedom of religion if the Act becomes law, as suggested by the hypothetical scenarios presented by several interveners. However, the jurisprudence confirms that many if not all such conflicts will be resolved *within* the *Charter*, by the delineation of rights prescribed by the cases relating to s. 2(*a*). Conflicts of rights do not imply conflict with the *Charter*; rather the resolution of such conflicts generally occurs within the ambit of the *Charter* itself by way of internal balancing and delineation.[102]

In relation to question three the Court concluded that:

> It therefore seems clear that state compulsion on religious officials to perform same-sex marriages contrary to their religious beliefs would violate the guarantee of freedom of religion under s. 2(*a*) of the *Charter*. It also seems apparent that, absent exceptional circumstances which we cannot at present foresee, such a violation could not be justified under s. 1 of the *Charter*.
>
> The question we are asked to answer is confined to the performance of same-sex marriages by religious officials. However, concerns were raised about the compulsory use of sacred places for the celebration of such marriages and about being compelled to otherwise assist in the celebration of same-sex marriages. The reasoning that leads us to conclude that the guarantee of freedom of religion protects against the compulsory celebration of same-sex marriages, suggests that the same would hold for these concerns.[103]

100 Ibid. [37].
101 Ibid. [48].
102 Ibid. [52].
103 Ibid. [58]–[59].

On 10 July 2005 the Canadian Parliament enacted the *Civil Marriage Act*.[104] Section 2 of the Act provided that 'Marriage, for civil purposes, is the lawful union of two persons to the exclusion of all others.'

Some of the issues around same sex marriage and freedom of religion were recognised in Section 3 and 3.1 of the Act. Section 3 states 'It is recognized that officials of religious groups are free to refuse to perform marriages that are not in accordance with their religious beliefs.' While 3.1 states:

> For greater certainty, no person or organization shall be deprived of any benefit, or be subject to any obligation or sanction, under any law of the Parliament of Canada solely by reason of their exercise, in respect of marriage between persons of the same sex, of the freedom of conscience and religion guaranteed under the Canadian Charter of Rights and Freedoms or the expression of their beliefs in respect of marriage as the union of a man and woman to the exclusion of all others based on that guaranteed freedom.[105]

The existence of the *Canadian Charter of Rights and Freedoms* was essential in the legalisation of same-sex marriage in Canada. Without it the Provincial level decisions would not have been possible. Further, its existence prompted both the legislature and courts to explicitly consider the need to balance competing human rights, in this case the right to freedom of religion and the right to equality.

The South African Constitutional Court followed the Supreme Court of Canada's lead when in 2006 they found that laws which limited marriage to persons of the opposite sex violated the right to equality found in Section 9(1) of the *South African Constitution*[106]:

> Everyone is equal before the law and has the right to equal protection and benefit of the law.[107]

While Section 9(3) explicitly prohibits discrimination on the grounds of, *inter alia*, sexual orientation:

> The state may not unfairly discriminate directly or indirectly against anyone on one or more grounds, including race, gender, sex, pregnancy, marital status, ethnic or social origin, colour, *sexual orientation*, age, disability, religion, conscience, belief, culture, language and birth.[108] (emphasis added)

It also prohibits discrimination on the grounds of religion, conscience and belief.

---

104 SC 2005, c 33.
105 Ibid. s 3.1.
106 *Minister for Home Affairs v Fourie and others; Lesbian and Gay Equality Project and Others v Minister of Home Affairs and Other* [2006] 1 SA 524 (Constitutional Court), [114].
107 *Constitution of the Republic of South Africa Act 1996* (South Africa) s 9(1).
108 Ibid. s 9(3).

The Court considered a number of arguments against the legalisation of same-sex marriage, including respect for the religious view of marriage namely that 'by its origins and nature, the institution of marriage simply cannot sustain the intrusion of same-sex unions' and therefore 'such unions can never be regarded as marriages, or even marriage-like or equivalent to Marriages.'[109] And that to find otherwise would 'disrupt and radically alter an institution of centuries-old significance to many religions, would accordingly infringe the *Constitution* by violating religious freedom in a most substantial way.'[110]

The Court acknowledged the significant place of religion in the lives of many South Africans stating:

> For believers, then, what is at stake is not merely a question of convenience or comfort, but an intensely held sense about what constitutes the good and proper life and their place in creation.[111]

However the Court went on to state that:

> It is one thing for the Court to acknowledge the important role that religion plays in our public life. It is quite another to use religious doctrine as a source for interpreting the Constitution.[112]

According to the Constitutional Court, the proper role of the Court in balancing the rights of same-sex couples and the right to freedom of religion was:

> [f]rom a constitutional point of view, what matters is for the Court to ensure that he be protected in his right to regard his marriage as sacramental, to belong to a religious community that celebrates its marriages according to its own doctrinal tenets, and to be free to express his views in an appropriate manner both in public and in Court. Further than that the Court could not be expected to go.

Ultimately the Constitutional Court concluded that:

> acknowledgement by the state of the right of same sex couples to enjoy the same status, entitlements and responsibilities as marriage law accords to

---

109 *Minister for Home Affairs v Fourie and others; Lesbian and Gay Equality Project and Others v Minister of Home Affairs and Other* [2006] 1 SA 524 (Constitutional Court), [88].
110 Ibid. [88].
111 Ibid. [89].
112 Ibid. [92]; on this point in relation to the *South African Constitution* and the balancing of the rights of same-sex couples and freedom of religion, see also *National Coalition for Gay and Lesbian Equality v Minister of Justice* [1999] 1 SA 6 (Constitutional Court); (1998) 12 BCLR 1517 (Constitutional Court), [38].

heterosexual couples is in no way inconsistent with the rights of religious organisations to continue to refuse to celebrate same-sex marriages. The constitutional claims of same-sex couples can accordingly not be negated by invoking the rights of believers to have their religious freedom respected. The two sets of interests involved do not collide, they co-exist in a constitutional realm based on accommodation of diversity.[113]

More recently, the United States Court in in *Obergefell v Hodges* found that a fundamental right to marry, including for same sex couples, was guaranteed by both the due process and equal protection[114] clauses of the *United States Constitution*.[115]

Section 1 of the 14th Amendment (which contains both the due process and equal protection clauses) provides that

> All persons born or naturalized in the United States, and subject to the jurisdiction thereof, are citizens of the United States and of the state wherein they reside. No state shall make or enforce any law which shall abridge the privileges or immunities of citizens of the United States; nor shall any state deprive any person of life, liberty, or property, without due process of law; nor deny to any person within its jurisdiction the equal protection of the laws.[116]

As with the cases in Canada and South Africa, the question of freedom of religion, which is protected in the first amendment of the *American Constitution*, was considered by the court. As with the South African decision the Court recognised the sincerity of religious beliefs that object to same-sex marriage:

> Many who deem same-sex marriage to be wrong reach that conclusion based on decent and honorable religious or philosophical premises, and neither they nor their beliefs are disparaged here.[117]

It then went on to explain that the Court and the State more generally cannot enact laws on the basis of religious belief and doctrine:

> But when that sincere, personal opposition becomes enacted law and public policy, the necessary consequence is to put the imprimatur of the State itself on an exclusion that soon demeans or stigmatizes those whose own liberty is then denied. Under the Constitution, same-sex couples seek in marriage the

---

113 *Minister for Home Affairs v Fourie and others; Lesbian and Gay Equality Project and Others v Minister of Home Affairs and Other* [2006] 1 SA 524 (Constitutional Court), [98].
114 *Obergefell v Hodges,* 135 S Ct 2584 (2015), 2604–2605.
115 *United States Constitution.*
116 *United States Constitution* amend XIV(1).
117 *Obergefell v Hodges,* 135 S Ct 2584 (2015), 2602.

same legal treatment as opposite-sex couples, and it would disparage their choices and diminish their personhood to deny them this right.[118]

The Court however emphasised that in legalising same-sex marriage they were not overruling the freedom of religion of those who continued to oppose same-sex marriage to advocate for their position and express their religious beliefs in this matter.

> Finally, it must be emphasized that religions, and those who adhere to religious doctrines, may continue to advocate with utmost, sincere conviction that, by divine precepts, same-sex marriage should not be condoned. The First Amendment ensures that religious organizations and persons are given proper protection as they seek to teach the principles that are so fulfilling and so central to their lives and faiths, and to their own deep aspirations to continue the family structure they have long revered. The same is true of those who oppose same-sex marriage for other reasons. In turn, those who believe allowing same-sex marriage is proper or indeed essential, whether as a matter of religious conviction or secular belief, may engage those who disagree with their view in an open and searching debate. The Constitution, however, does not permit the State to bar same-sex couples from marriage on the same terms as accorded to couples of the opposite sex.[119]

The courts in Canada, South Africa and the United States of America all addressed concerns regarding freedom of religion post the legalisation of same-sex marriage of religion in their judgments. In each case the Court appears to have been confident that such concerns were either unfounded or that the right to freedom of religion, protected in the respective Bills or Charters of Rights, could be adequately balanced with the rights of same-sex couples seeking marriage. This has not stopped, however, a suite of so called 'marriage industry cases' from making their way before the courts. In these cases the courts have been asked to balance the rights of religious individuals, business or organisations against same-sex couples seeking their services.

At the time of writing, superior courts in both the United States and the United Kingdom are considering appeals from 'wedding industry' type cases – both involve cakes. In *Lee v McArthur, McArthur & Ashers Baking Co Ltd*[120] (Asher's Bakery Case) the Northern Ireland Court of Appeal upheld the decision of District Court Judge Brownlie, finding that the appellants had discriminated against the respondents on the grounds of sexual orientation in refusing to supply a cake with the image of Burt and Ernie and the words 'Support Gay

---

118 Ibid. 2602.
119 Ibid. 2607.
120 [2016] NICA 39 (24 October 2016).

Marriage.'[121] While not strictly a wedding case, many of the same issues as would arise in the case of a wedding cake for a same sex marriage arose in this case. The United Kingdom Supreme Court is due to consider an appeal from the Northern Ireland Court of Appeal decision in early 2018.[122]

On 5 December 2018, the Supreme Court of the United States heard an appeal[123] from the Colorado Court of Appeal Decision in *Masterpiece Cakeshop v Colorado Civil Rights Commission*.[124] In 2015 the Colorado Court of Appeal upheld an appeal from an administrative decision by the Colorado Civil Rights Commission. The Court found that Masterpiece Cakeshop's refusal to make a cake for a same-sex wedding because of the owner's religious beliefs breached the *Colorado Anti-Discrimination Act*[125] which, *inter alia*, prohibits discrimination on the basis of sexual orientation.[126] Further, as a neutral law of general application, the *Colorado Anti-Discrimination Act* did not 'offend the Free Exercise Clause of the First Amendment.'[127]

It will be interesting to see how the United Kingdom Supreme Court and Supreme Court of the United States will balance the competing human rights in these cases. What is inevitable is that the respective courts will need to undertake some form of balancing exercise. By contrast, should similar cases arise in Australia, they are likely to be determined on the basis of State-based anti-discriminations legislation alone, which provide few if any exemptions for individuals and business.

Australia has had a small number of cases where the courts have been asked to consider whether ostensibly religious organisations can claim an exemption to anti-discrimination legislation prohibitions on discriminating on the grounds of sexuality. The results have been mixed. In *Christian Youth Camps Ltd v Cobaw Community Health Services Ltd*[128] the Victorian Court of Appeal in a split 2–1

---

121 Ibid. [1]–[6].
122 The Supreme Court, *Lee (Respondent) v Ashers Baking Company Ltd and others (Appellants) (Northern Ireland)* (2018) www.supremecourt.uk/cases/uksc-2017-0020.html.
123 Transcript of Proceedings, *Masterpiece Cakeshop Ltd. et al. v Colorado Civil Rights Commission, et al.* (Supreme Court of the United States, No 16–111, Roberts CJ, Sotomayor, Ginsburg, Kennedy, Kagan, Thomas, Breyer, Gorsuch and Alito JJ, 5 December 2015).
124 *Mullins v Masterpiece Cakeshop, Inc*, 2015 COA 115 (2015).
125 Colo Rev Stat §§ 24–34–301–308 (2014).
126 Transcript of Proceedings, *Masterpiece Cakeshop Ltd. et al. v Colorado Civil Rights Commission, et al.* (Supreme Court of the United States, No 16–111, Roberts CJ, Sotomayor, Ginsburg, Kennedy, Kagan, Thomas, Breyer, Gorsuch and Alito JJ, 5 December 2015) [30]–[43].
127 Ibid. [81]–[95].
128 (2014) 308 ALR 615; for a discussion of this case see Bobbi Murphy, 'Balancing Religious Freedom and Anti-Discrimination: Christian Youth Camps Ltd v Cobaw Community Health Services' (2017) 40(2) *Melbourne University Law Review* 594; Elphick, above n 43, 162–164; Neil Foster, 'Freedom of Religion and Balancing Clauses in Discrimination Legislation' (Paper presented at Magna Carta and Freedom of Religion or Belief Conference, St Hugh's College Oxford, 21–24 June 2015) 11–13 available at <https://works.bepress.com/neil_foster/95/.>

judgment found, *inter alia*, that a camping facility run by the Christian Brethren Church was not a body established for religious purposes as required by the Victorian *Equal Opportunity Act 1995* (Vic) and therefore not entitled to the religious exemptions under that Act.[129] While in *OV and OW v Members of the Board of Wesley Mission Council*[130] a foster care agency connected with the Uniting Church were able to take advantage of the religious exemptions under the New South Wales *Anti-Discrimination Act 1977*. These cases are however significantly different to 'wedding industry' cases in jurisdictions that have legalised same-sex marriage. First they involve organisations rather than individuals and business and second they were determined under anti-discrimination legalisation and concerned religious exemptions rather than under a Charter or Bill of Rights where the right to freedom of religion and the right not to be discriminated against on the basis of a person's sexuality would both be protected and therefore need to be balanced in the case of a conflict.

Islamic face veils in court

Another contemporary example of divergence in the Australian approach and that adopted by courts in jurisdictions with a Bill or Charter of Rights is the question of whether a witness can wear a face veil while giving evidence.[131] Australia

---

129 *Christian Youth Camps Ltd v Cobaw Community Health Services Ltd* (2014) 308 ALR 615, 666–669.

130 (2010) 79 NSWLR 606; see also *OV and OW v Members of the Board of Wesley Mission Council* [2010] NSWADT 293 (10 December 2010).

131 For a discussion of these cases more generally see Natasha Bakht, 'What's in a Face? Demeanour Evidence in the Sexual Assault Context' in Elizabeth Sheehy (ed), *Sexual Assault in Canada: Law, Legal Practice and Women's Activism* (University of Ottawa Press, 2012) 591; Natasha Bakht, 'Objection, Your Honour! Accommodating Niqab-Wearing Women in Courtrooms' in Ralph Grillo et al. (eds), *Legal Practice and Cultural Diversity* (Ashgate, 2009) 123; Jessica Walker, 'I Will Not Take off My Clothes: The Application of International Obligations and the Wearing of the Niqab in Australian Courts' (Paper presented at London Human Rights Congress, 22 November 2011) 11; Gareth Morley, 'Veils of Ignorance: How the Supreme Court of Canada Came to Render Muslim Women Outlaws (Sometimes) and What it Should Have Done Instead' (2013) 33 *Inroads* 119; David Griffiths, 'There's No Art to Find the Mind's Construction in the Face: Some Thoughts on the Burqa Case in New Zealand' (2005) 1(2) *NZ Postgraduate Law E-Journal* 1; Paul Morris, 'Covering Islam—Burqa and Hijab: Limits to the Human Right to Religion' (2004) 2 *Human Rights Research Journal* 1; Jane Foster, 'Is it a Breach of Religious Rights?' (2006) 4 *Human Rights Research Journal* 1; Rex J Ahdar, 'Religious Liberty in a Temperate Zone: A Report from New Zealand' (2007) 21(1) *Emory Int'l L Rev* 205; Rex J Ahdar, 'Reflections on the Path of Religion-State Relations in New Zealand' (2006) 3 *Brigham Young University Law Review* 619; Faisal Bhabha, 'R v NS: What's a Fair Trial? The Supreme Court of Canada's Divided Opinion on the Niqab in the Courtroom' (2013) 50(4) *Alberta L Rev* 871; Karl Laird, 'Confronting Religion: Veiled Witnesses, the Right to a Fair Trial and the Supreme Court of Canada's Judgement in R v NS' (2014) 77(1) *Modern Law Review* 123; Ranjan K. Agarwal and Carlo di Carlo, 'The Re-emergence of a Clash of Rights: A Critical Analysis of the Supreme Court of Canada's Decision in R v S(N)' (2013)

has had two such cases *R v Sayed*[132] and *Elzahed and Anors v Commonwealth of Australia and State of New South Wales.*[133] In neither case does the judge make reference to the need to balance rights under a Bill or Charter of Rights as there is no such Bill or Charter for them to consider. This does not mean, however, that considerations of religious freedom are completely absent from the decisions. For example, in *R v Sayed* Judge Deane comments:

> one returns to the exercise of balancing what might be described as the competing interests of the right of an accused person to have a fair trial in every sense that that concept is understood, with what in this case is a strongly held view and long-term practice of a witness who puts forward genuine reasons as to why she should be permitted to give her evidence in a particular way.[134]

Judge Deane also makes reference to Article 18 of the International Convention on Civil and Political Rights (ICCPR).[135] However, while she accepts the sentiments in Article 18 she also notes that, despite the fact Australia is a signatory to the convention it does not have the force of law at the domestic level in Australia.[136]

> I do not think one could sensibly or properly argue against the sentiments expressed in the material referred to by council for the Crown and contained in the ICCPR. It seems to me, however, the immediate question is not the view or opinion of the court as to the respect and/or tolerance of the wearing of a particular item of clothing based on religious or cultural beliefs or reasons or a combination of such matters.[137]

63 *Supreme Court Law Review* 143; Renae Barker, 'Burqas and Niqabs in the Courtroom: Finding Practical Solutions' (2017) 91(2) *Australian Law Journal* 225; Renae Barker, 'Of Burqas (and Niqabs) in Courtrooms: The Neglected Women's Voice' in Rex Ahdar (ed) *Research Handbook on Law and Religion* (Edward Elgar Publishing, 2018) (forthcoming).

132 Transcript of Proceedings, *The Queen v Anwar Shah Wafiq Sayed* (District Court of Western Australia, 164 of 2010, Dean DCJ, 19 August 2010); for a discussion of this case see Renae Barker, 'The Full Face Covering Debate: An Australian Perspective' (2012) 36(1) *University of Western Australia Law Review* 143, 148–150; Barker, 'Burqas and Niqabs in the Courtroom: Finding Practical Solutions', above n 138, 229; Barker, 'Of Burqas (and Niqabs) in Courtrooms: The Neglected Women's Voice', above n 138, (forthcoming).

133 [2016] NSWDC 327; for a discussion of this case see Renae Barker, 'Burqas and Niqabs in the Courtroom: Finding Practical Solutions', above n 138, 230–231; Renae Barker, 'Of Burqas (and Niqabs) in Courtrooms: The Neglected Women's Voice', above n 138, (forthcoming).

134 Transcript of Proceedings, *The Queen v Anwar Shah Wafiq Sayed* (District Court of Western Australia, 164 of 2010, Dean DCJ, 19 August 2010) 1051.

135 Ibid. 1057.

136 Ibid. 1057–1058.

137 Ibid. 1058.

She also made reference to both the New Zealand decision in *Police v Razam-joo*[138] and the Canadian Ontario Superior Court of Justice decision in *R v NS*.[139] However, Judge Deane acknowledged that the decisions were peculiar to the legal systems of New Zealand and Canada respectively and in particular the existence of Bill or Charters of Rights in both cases.[140] Ultimately, Judge Deane determined the case on the basis of the needs of the jury and in particular whether the jury 'will be impeded in their ability to fully assess the reliability and credibility of the evidence of a particular witness.'[141] She ordered that the witness remove her face veil while giving evidence but left the arrangement as to how this was to occur to the parties.[142] Despite references to balancing of rights in the judgment, there is no explicit balancing of rights, as would occur if there had been a Charter or Bill of Rights.

The absence of a discussion around balancing of rights under a Charter or Bill of Rights in *R v Sayed* can be contrasted with the New Zealand, Canadian and United Kingdom judgments on the issue.

In *Police v Razamjoo*[143] Judge Moore identified a number of rights in the New Zealand *Bill of Rights Act 1990* which were relevant to determining whether the two witnesses in that case would be permitted to give evidence while wearing a face veil.[144] These included the right not to be subject to torture or cruel treatment,[145] freedom of thought, conscience, and religion,[146] Manifestation of religion and belief,[147] Freedom from discrimination,[148] Rights of minorities,[149] Minimum standards of criminal procedure[150] and the Right to justice.[151] He also recognised that limits can only be placed on rights enumerated in the New Zealand *Bill of Rights Act 1990* where they are 'prescribed by law as can be demonstrably justified in a free and democratic society.'[152] In addition to the rights of the parties, Judge Moore also considered the interests of the public, particularly

---

138 [2005] DCR 408 (New Zealand District Court).
139 (2009) 95 OR (3d) 735 (Ontario Supreme Court of Justice). This case was subsequently appealed to the Ontario Court of appeal in *R v N* [2010] ONCA 670 (Ontario Court of Appeal) before making its way to the Canadian Supreme Court in *R v NS* [2012] 3 SCR 726 (Supreme Court of Canada).
140 Transcript of Proceedings, *The Queen v Anwar Shah Wafiq Sayed* (District Court of Western Australia, 164 of 2010, Dean DCJ, 19 August 2010) 1054, 1056.
141 Ibid. 1058.
142 Ibid. 1061.
143 [2005] DCR 408 (New Zealand District Court).
144 Ibid. [39].
145 *Bill of Rights Act 1990* (NZ) s 9.
146 Ibid. s 13.
147 Ibid. s 15.
148 Ibid. s 19.
149 Ibid. s 20.
150 Ibid. s 25.
151 Ibid. s 27.
152 Ibid. s 5.

the public interest in 'maintain[ing] public confidence in the criminal justice system.'[153] Judge Moore concluded that:

> Mr Razamjoo (and indeed the public) has a legitimate expectation of trial by the normal processes of the Court except to the extent that departure from those processes is merited in the interests of justice. Mrs Salim has the right to manifest her religious beliefs by wearing her burqa in public, but (as she herself recognised) there can be situations in which that manifestation has to yield to other needs. She also has the right, as a witness, of equality with others in terms of how her evidence is evaluated. The public have rights and legitimate expectations in the context of the public nature of the criminal process. The Court has an obligation to the community it serves to recognise and uphold the values of a free and democratic society

Consequently, he rules that although the witnesses would be required to remove their face veils while giving evidence, 'screens may be used to ensure that only Judge, counsel, and Court staff (the latter being females) are able to observe the witness's face.

Similarly, in Canadian Supreme Court case *R v NS*,[154] it was identified that both the freedom of religion[155] and the right to a fair trial[156] was relevant to the issue at hand:[157]

> What is required is an approach that balances the vital rights protecting freedom of religion and trial fairness when they conflict. The long-standing practice in Canadian courts is to respect and accommodate the religious convictions of witnesses, unless they pose a significant or serious risk to a fair trial. The *Canadian Charter of Rights and Freedoms*, which protects both freedom of religion and trial fairness, demands no less.[158]

In order to balance these rights the Court sought to answer four questions:

1   Would requiring the witness to remove the niqab while testifying interfere with her religious freedom?
2   Would permitting the witness to wear the niqab while testifying create a serious risk to trial fairness?
3   Is there a way to accommodate both rights and avoid the conflict between them?

---

153 *Police v Razamjoo* [2005] DCR 408 (New Zealand District Court) [100].
154 [2012] 3 SCR 726 (Supreme Court of Canada).
155 *Constitution Act 1982* s 2.
156 Ibid. ss 7, 11(d).
157 *R v NS* [2012] 3 SCR 726 [7].
158 Ibid. [2].

4   If no accommodation is possible, do the salutary effects of requiring the witness to remove the niqab outweigh the deleterious effects of doing so?[159]

Ultimately the Court concluded that given both the freedom of religion and right to a fair trial were engaged 'the preliminary inquiry judge must consider the possibility of accommodation based on the evidence presented by the parties.'[160] But that ultimately if no accommodation was possible 'the [preliminary inquiry] judge must assess all [the relevant] factors and determine whether, in the case at hand, the salutary effects of requiring the witness to remove the niqab outweigh the deleterious effects of doing so.'[161] However, the Supreme Court was of the view that 'where the liberty of the accused is at stake, the witness's evidence is central to the case and her credibility vital, the possibility of a wrongful conviction must weigh heavily in the balance, favouring removal of the niqab.'[162]

Again in the United Kingdom case of *The Queen v D(R)* the Court undertook a balancing exercise in relation to rights contained in the *Human Rights Act 1998* incorporating the *European Convention on Human Rights* into domestic UK law. In particular, Judge Murphy noted that determining whether or not a witness would be permitted to wear a face veil while giving evidence in court was more than an issue of 'judge craft' or court room procedure. It was a matter of law, in this case a law which included a Charter or Bill of Rights:

> The issue of whether a defendant before the Crown Court may wear the niqaab during some or all the proceedings is not one of 'judge craft', or even one for 'general guidance'. It is a question of law. The defendant has the qualified right to manifest her religion or belief pursuant to art. 9 of the European Convention on Human Rights ('the Convention'). By virtue of the Human Rights Act 1998, that right is cognisable as a matter of domestic law in the Crown Court. By virtue of s.6(1) and (3) of that Act, the Court is a public authority and may not act in a way incompatible with a Convention right. At the same time, the Court may be entitled to place restrictions on a qualified Convention right, such as that under art. 9.[163]

In this case the right to freedom of religion needed to be balanced against fundamental principles of justice such as the rule of law,[164] open justice[165] and the adversarial trial process.[166] Judge Moore also recognised that it was necessary not only to consider the rights of the defendant, but also those of the victims,

159 Ibid. [9].
160 Ibid. [33].
161 Ibid. [45].
162 Ibid. [44].
163 *The Queen v D(R)* (Unreported, Blackfriars Crown Court, Murphy J, 16 September 2013) [11].
164 Ibid. [27].
165 Ibid. [28].
166 Ibid. [29].

jury and the public in a democratic society.[167] Ultimately, he concluded that the defendant in this case would be permitted to wear her face veil during the trial but would be required to remove it if she chose to give evidence.[168]

While all of the judgments came to the same or similar conclusions, that a witness must remove her face veil in order to give evidence, there is a marked difference in the reasoning in those jurisdictions where a Bill or Charter of Rights exists. There is an explicit and deliberate balancing of specific rights as opposed to the more general discussion which took place in *R v Sayed*.

Conclusion

The opening lines of *Commonwealth v Australian Capital Territory*[169] sums up Australia's approach to human rights questions: 'The only issue which this Court can decide is a legal issue.'[170] Without a Bill or Charter of Rights, the courts, and litigants, have little choice but to take a legalistic, rather than human rights, approach. Freedom of religion and issues related to the State–religion relationship are no exception. Just as with other human rights issues, those who are concerned that their freedom of religion has been violated have limited recourse for raising this as a human rights issue. Unlike many other human rights, freedom of religion is given some limited protect via Section 116 of the *Australian Constitution*. However, as outlined in Chapter 4, Section 116 has been interpreted narrowly by the High Court and only applies to the purpose of laws passed by the Federal Parliament. As a result, where litigants have had success in the High Court in protecting their freedom of religion, it has not been as a result of a violation of Section 116 or a freedom of religion clause in a national Bill or Charter of Rights. Instead they have relied on other technical legal arguments. In both *Williams v The Commonwealth*[171] and *Adelaide Company of Jehovah's Witnesses v Commonwealth*[172] the plaintiffs were successful on the basis of their technical arguments relating to the spending and legislative powers of the Commonwealth. The outcomes would have been the same without the religious dimension of their cases.[173]

This does not necessarily mean that the ultimate outcome will be different from those countries with a Bill or Charter of Rights. As highlighted in the examples given above, the ultimate outcome for Australia and the related religious issues have been the same, or similar, in both Australia and comparable

---

167 Ibid. [57]–[59]
168 Ibid. [82]–[83].
169 (2013) 250 CLR 441.
170 Ibid. 452 (French CJ, Hayne, Crennan, Kiefel, Bell and Keane JJ).
171 (2012) 248 CLR 156.
172 (1943) 67 CLR 116.
173 For example, had William challenged another federally funded programme which was funded in the same way as the National School Chaplaincy Programme, such as the Roads for Regions Scheme, he would still have been successful.

jurisdictions. Australia has now legalised same-sex marriage and witnesses in Australia are unlikely to be permitted to wear a face covering while giving evidence in court. What is different is the process by which these questions are decided. In many cases, as with same-sex marriage, the larger question must be decided via the legislative process and public debate. The role of the courts is necessarily restricted. Where the courts do have a role, as with the wearing of face coverings, Australian courts are limited in their use of human rights techniques such as balancing of competing rights. Given that the outcomes are the often the same or similar it may well be that Australia's lack of a national Bill or Charter of Rights is not a problem that needs remedying. Australians, like their counterparts in the United Kingdom, the United States, Canada, New Zealand and to a less extent South Africa, enjoy a relatively high level of human rights, including freedom of religion. What Australia's lack of a Bill or Charter of Rights does mean is that law and policy makers need to be cautious in their use of comparisons with other countries in relation to human rights, including freedom of religion, issues.

Part II

Australian case studies

6 Contemporary issues

Introduction

The relationship between the State and religion is inherently dynamic. As religious demographics and society more broadly evolve so too does the relationship between the State and religion. Over Australia's relatively short history since colonisation it has gone from a penal colony made up predominantly of white Protestant Christians to a multi-cultural, and therefore multi-faith, democracy. While the majority of Australia's population continue to self-identify as Christian (52.1%), the margin between those who self-identify as having a religion and those who do not is narrowing. The majority Christian faith is no longer the Church of England or Anglican and is instead Roman Catholic (22.6%). Those who self-identify as having no religion now make up a significant, and growing, proportion of Australia's population (30.1%). While those who come from other, non-Christian, faiths (8.2%) also make up a significant proportion of Australia's population.[1]

More important than the percentages, in terms of the dynamic nature of the State and religion relationship, is the changes that have occurred over the last few decades. Just a decade ago Christians made up 63.9% of the population, two decades ago 70.9% and 50 years ago 88.2%. At the time of Federation Christians made up 96.1% of the Australian population. By comparison, at Federation those self-identifying as having no religion comprised just 0.2% of the population. Fifty years ago, they made up just 0.8%, two decades ago 16.6% and a decade ago 18.7%.[2] This dramatic shift, both in terms of the decline of Christianity and the increase in those identifying as having no religion, has inevitably lead to new challenges for the State, religious organisations and individuals in navigating the relationship between the State and religion in Australia.

---

1 Australian Bureau of Statistics, *Religion in Australia, 2016* (23 October 2017) <>www.abs.gov.au/ausstats/abs@.nsf/Lookup/by%20Subject/2071.0~2016~Main%20Features~Religion%20Article~80>; see also Chapter 1.
2 Australian Bureau of Statistics, *Losing My Religion?* (17 March 2014) <>www.abs.gov.au/ausstats/abs@.nsf/Lookup/4102.0Main+Features30Nov+2013>; Tom Frame, *Losing My Religion: Unbelief in Australia* (University of New South Wales Press, 2009) ch. 5.

Many features of the State and religion relationship have come into existence only relatively recently. For example, the Australian Charities and Not for Profit Commission (ACNC) has only been in existence since 2012.[3] While the National School Chaplaincy Programme (NSCP) has been around a little longer it is only a decade old having commenced in 2007.[4] Similarly important issues such as where and when it is in/appropriate to wear a full face covering, commonly referred to as a burqa or niqab, for religious reasons along with the role of religious principles such as the sharia have become staples of discussion when considering the Australian State–religion relationship despite being relative none issues just a decade or so ago.[5]

This chapter deals specifically with three emerging issues in the dynamic State and religion relationship in Australia: terrorism, same-sex marriage and institutional responses to child sexual abuse.[6] Australia's response to terrorism is the longest standing of the three issues. However, it was not until the wake of the 2001 terrorist attacks in the United States that Australia legislated for a criminal offence of terrorism. Since then Australia has enacted numerous new criminal offences related to terrorism in response to terrorist incidents and organisations overseas.

The most recent legal change is in relation to same-sex marriage which was legalised in Australia in December 2017. While the law has been changed to permit same-sex marriage how this will impact on those whose religious and conscientious beliefs conflict with this legal change are yet to be fully worked through. It is yet to be seen if Australia will have a series of marriage cases as has occurred in the United States and the United Kingdom with those who continue to oppose same sex marriage coming into conflict with couples seeking to purchase their goods and services as part of their wedding plans. As a result, it may be sometime before all the legal changes in the State–religion relationship that have occurred as a result of the legalisation of same-sex marriage are fully known and appreciated.

Finally, the Royal Commission into Institutional Responses to Child Sexual Abuse handed its final report to the federal government in December 2017. At the time of writing both the State and religious organisations are still digesting the recommendations and findings in the report. While a national redress scheme has been announced, the laws necessary to make this new scheme a feature of the

---

3 David Bradbury and Mark Butler, 'New Era for Charities Sector Begins' (Joint Media Release, No 163, 10 December 2012) <>http://ministers.treasury.gov.au/DisplayDocs. aspx?doc=pressreleases/2012/163.htm&pageID=003&min=djba&Year=&DocType=0>; see Chapter 9.
4 Australian Government, *National School 2011 Chaplaincy Program* (Commonwealth of Australian, 2011) 3; See Chapter 8.
5 See Chapter 7.
6 The law in these areas is in a state of transition. As a result, while every effort has been made to reflect the current state of the law more changes may not be included. The law and Government policies discussed in this chapter are correct as of January 2018.

State–religion relationship have yet to pass parliament. When it does pass it will put in place an ongoing interaction between the federal government and those religious organisations that opt-in which is likely to last for at least 10 years.[7]

Terrorism

Background

Terrorism and its dramatic consequences was thrust onto the world stage in 2001 with the 9/11 terrorist attacks in the United States of America. While terrorism was not a new[8] phenomenon, the unprecedented scale and publicity of the attack prompted political, legal and military action around the world. The United Nation's Security Council, in resolution 1373, *inter alia,* called on:

> all states to work together urgently to prevent and suppress terrorist acts, including through increased cooperation and full implementation of the relevant international conventions relating to terrorism.[9]

At the time Australia had no laws specifically criminalising terrorist activities. In response to both the United Nation Security Council declaration, and the September 11 terrorist attack more broadly, the Commonwealth government passed its first wave of anti-terrorism legislation including a legislative definition of terrorism on which all other offences are based.[10] Australia has since enacted a host of anti-terrorism laws in what Kent Roach has described as 'hyper-legislation.'[11]

Today, Australia's anti-terrorism laws are found in Part 5.3 of the *Criminal Code Act 1995* (Cth) while offences dealing with foreign incursion and recruitment are found in Part 5.5.[12] Offences include, *inter alia,* committing a terrorist act,[13] being a

---

7 Commonwealth, *Parliamentary Debates,* House of Representatives, 26 October 2017, 12130–12131 (Christian Porter).

8 See, for example, David Rapoport, 'The Four Waves of Modern Terrorism' in Audrey Cronin and James Ludes (eds), *Attacking Terrorism: Elements of a Grand Strategy* (Georgetown University Press, 2004).

9 SC Res 1373, UN SCOR, 56th sess, 4385 mtg, UN Doc S/RES/1373 (28 September 2001) available at <www.un.org/en/sc/ctc/specialmeetings/2012/docs/United%20Nations%20Security%20Council%20Resolution%201373%20(2001).pdf>.

10 Andrew Lynch, Nicola McGarrity and George Williams, *Inside Australia's Anti-Terrorism Laws and Trials* (NewSouth, 2015) 1–2; Keiran Hardy and George Williams, 'What is Terrorism? Assessing Domestic Legal Definitions' (2011) 16 *UCLA Journal of International and Foreign Affairs* 77, 130.

11 Kent Roach, *The 9/11 Effect: Comparative Counter Terrorism* (Cambridge University Press, 2011) 310.

12 A detailed analysis of Australia's Anti-terrorism regime is beyond the scope of this chapter. For an analysis of Australia's anti-terrorism laws see Lynch, McGarrity and Williams, above n 10.

13 S 101.1.

member of a terrorist organisation,[14] providing support for a terrorist organisation,[15] financing terrorism and financing a terrorist.[16] The Act also permits the making of Control Orders to 'allow obligations, prohibitions and restrictions to be imposed on a person' to prevent them carrying out activities related to terrorism,[17] preventative detention orders to 'allow a person to be taken into custody and detained for a short period of time' to prevent a terrorist act or preserve evidence[18] and continuing detention orders to 'providing for the continuing detention of terrorist offenders who pose an unacceptable risk of committing serious [terrorism] offences if released into the community.'[19]

Since 2001 Australia has been impacted by very few terrorist attacks on its own soil. The most well-known has been the Lindt café siege carried out by Man Monis. On 15 December 2014 Monis took 18 people (eight staff and 20 customers) hostage in the Lindt Café in Martin Place Sydney. The siege ended 16.5 hours later with the deaths of hostages Tori Johnson and Katrina Dawson along with Monis himself.[20] There is some doubt as to whether the Lindt café siege constituted terrorism under the Australian legal definition of an 'act of terrorism.' The question can never be tested in a court of law due to Monis' death.[21] A terrorist act is distinguished from an ordinary criminal act (in this case hostage taking and murder) by both the intent and motivation of the perpetrator/s. In order to classify as a terrorist act, for the purposes of prosecution under Australian law, the perpetrators must intend to intimidate 'the public or a section of the public' and be motivated by a 'political, religious or ideological cause.'[22] While on the surface Monis's actions would appear to fit this description, doubt may be cast on both his intention and motivation. As Lynch, McGarrity and Williams identify:

> at the time, Monis appears to have had no actual connection to the Islamic State organisation.... There were also numerous personal circumstances which appear to have driven the timing of, if not the motivation behind, the siege.[23]

However, the New South Wales Coronial Inquest into the siege concluded that:

> Even with the benefit of expert evidence, it remains unclear whether Monis was motivated by IS to prosecute its bloodthirsty agenda or whether he used

---

14 S 102.3.
15 S 102.7.
16 Ss 103.1, 103.2.
17 Div 104.
18 Div 105.
19 Div 105A.
20 State Coroner of New South Wales, *Inquests into the deaths arising from the Lindt Café siege* (New South Wales Department of Justice, 2017) 3 also available at www.lindtinquest.justice. nsw.gov.au/Documents/findings-and-recommendations.pdf>.
21 Lynch, McGarrity and Williams, above n 10, 23.
22 *Criminal Code Act 1995* (Cth) s 100.1.
23 Lynch, McGarrity and Williams, above n 10, 23.

that organisation's fearsome reputation to bolster his impact. Either way, he adopted extreme violence with a view to influencing government action and/ or public opinion concerning Australia's involvement in armed conflict in the Middle East. That clearly brings his crimes within the accepted definition of terrorism.[24]

Commonwealth Treasurer, Joe Hockey, declared the Lindt Café Siege to be a terrorist incident for the purposes of the *Terrorism Insurance Act 2003* on 15 January 2015.[25]

While there have been relatively few terrorist incidents on Australian soil, Australians have been caught up in terrorist incidents overseas. Many of Australia's anti-terrorism laws have been passed in response to these incidents.[26] Ten Australian were killed in the 2001 9/11 Terrorist attacks.[27] Closer to home, 202 people including 88 Australians were killed in Bali, Indonesia in two bombings of popular night clubs on 12 October 2002.[28] In 2004 Australia's embassy in the Indonesian capital of Jakarta was bombed, killing nine people.[29] A further four Australians were killed in 2005 in another series of bombings in Bali.[30]

Defining terrorism

Unlike many of the other interactions between the State and religion discussed in this book, the legal connection between terrorism and religion is made explicit in the definition of terrorism in Section 100.1 of the *Criminal Code Act 1995* (Cth). In order for an action to constitute a terrorist act it must be 'done or the threat is made with the intention of advancing a political, *religious* or ideological cause'[31] [emphasis added]. This is commonly understood to require that the motivation

24 State Coroner of New South Wales, above n 20, 17. See also State Coroner of New South Wales, above n 20, 231–240.
25 Joe Hockey, *Terrorism Insurance Act 2003, Declaration of Terrorist Incident* (15 January 2015) Federal Register of Legislation www.legislation.gov.au/Details/F2015L00053>; Joe Hockey, 'Declaration of a terrorist incident: Government acts to ensure payment of insurance claims for Lindt Café Incident' (Media Release, 15 January 2015) http://jbh.ministers.treasury.gov.au/media-release/001-2015/>.
26 George Williams, 'A Decade of Australian Anti-Terror Laws' (2011) 35 *Melbourne University Law Review* 1136, 1170.
27 SBS News, *September 11: The Australian stories* (3 September 2013) www.sbs.com.au/news/article/2011/09/08/september-11-australian-stories>.
28 Edward F. Mickolus and Susan L. Simmons, *The 50 Worst Terrorist Attacks* (Praeger Publishing, 2014) 133.
29 Simon Jeffries and Mark Oliver, 'Australian embassy bomb kills nine', *The Guardian* (online), 10 September 2004 www.theguardian.com/world/2004/sep/09/indonesia.australia1>.
30 ABC News, *Ceremonies mark 2005 Bali bombing* (1 October 2006) www.abc.net.au/news/2006-10-01/ceremonies-mark-2005-bali-bombing/1275408>.
31 Criminal Code Act 1995 (Cth) s 100.1.

of the perpetrators be political, religious or ideological.[32] This is distinct from the intent of the perpetrators which, according to the Australian definition, must be to coerce or influence 'by intimidation, the government of the Commonwealth or a State, Territory or foreign country, or of part of a State, Territory or foreign country; or intimidating the public or a section of the public.'[33] While intent is a common element of criminal offences, the motivation of an accused is usually considered to be irrelevant.[34] That is not to say that motive is entirely absent from ordinary criminal law. It may be relevant at the sentencing stage or as part of circumstances of aggravation. For example, the Western Australian *Criminal Code* includes increased penalties where an offence is committed in circumstances of 'racial aggravation.'[35] Circumstances of racial aggravation can include 'the offence [being] motivated, in whole or part, by hostility towards persons as members of a racial group.'[36]

In his second reading speech on the Security Legislation Amendment (Terrorism) Bill (No 2) 2002 (Cth), which amended to *Criminal Code* to insert, *inter alia*, a definition of terrorism and related terrorism offences, the Attorney General gave no explanation for the inclusion of a motive element generally or of religious motivation specifically.[37] During debate on the Bill, relatively little mention was made of the inclusion of religion in the motive element of the definition of terrorism by government members or senators. One exception was the member for Wentworth Peter King. In his somewhat rambling speech he referred to the United States Department of State definition of terrorism, which refers to political motivation only:

> Premeditated, politically motivated violence perpetrated against non-combatant targets by subnational or clandestine agents, usually intended to influence an audience.[38]

---

32 Ben Saul, 'The Curious Element of Motive in Definitions of Terrorism: Essential Ingredient or Criminalising Thought?' in Andrew Lynch, Edwina MacDonald and George Williams (eds), *Law and Liberty in the War on Terror* (Federation Press, 2007) 28, 28.

33 Criminal Code Act 1995 (Cth) s 100.1.

34 Nadirsyah Hosen, 'Religion and Security What's your Motive?' in Nadirsyah Hosen and Richard Mohr (eds), *Law and Religion in Public Life: The Contemporary Debate* (Routledge, 2011) 137, 146; Keiran Hardy, 'Hijacking Public Discourse: Religious Motive in the Australian Definition of a Terrorist Act' (2011) 34(1) *University of New South Wales Law Journal* 333, 337; Saul, above n 32, 28.

35 See *Criminal Code Act Compilation Act 1913* (WA) ss 313, 317, 317A, 338B, 444.

36 Ibid. s 80I(b).

37 Commonwealth, *Parliamentary Debates,* House of Representatives, 12 March 2002, 1040–1043 (Daryl Williams). See also Commonwealth, *Parliamentary Debates,* House of Representatives, 13 March 2002, 1139–1142 (Peter Slipper); Commonwealth, *Parliamentary Debates,* Senate, 14 March 2002, 744–747.

38 Commonwealth, *Parliamentary Debates,* House of Representatives, 13 March 2002, 1156 (Peter King).

Before going on to refer to a speech by United States President George Bush which referred to the terrorist threat posed by al-Qaeda which he described as practicing a 'fringe form of religious extremism' and linked to the Islamic religion.[39]

By contrast a small number of opposition and minority senators expressed concern about the impact of the inclusion of a 'religious motivation' element on Australian Muslims.[40] As Senator Brian Grieg explained

> Regrettably, this stereotyping has caused all people of Middle Eastern background and Islamic faith to become the target of suspicion, mistrust and occasional abuse. As a nation, we need to take great care not to equate Islam with terrorism or Islam with religious extremism.[41]

Senator Chris Schacht drew attention to the complexity of the issue of how to define terrorism, as well as the involvement of multiple religions with reference to conflicts in Northern Ireland, Burma, East Timor, South Africa, Israel and Palestine. In particular, Senator Schacht highlighted that while the actions of many of the groups involved in these conflicts may be described as terrorist they may also be seen as legitimate struggles for independence and an end to oppression. It all depends on your point of view.[42] As he put it:

> the terrorist act is in the eye of the beholder. Unfortunately, various people at various times feel very strongly that their views are not being properly received and that they are suffering oppression, and they are willing to carry out outright terrorist acts to advance their political cause.[43]

In relation to Northern Ireland, he commented that

> you do not apportion blame to one side or the other in that sectarian dispute. It is ironic that both sides claim to be Christian and are willing to cheerfully murder each other – and have been doing so for several decades – and thousands of innocent people have been killed. Both sides have committed terrorist acts. Both sides claim they are defending and protecting the rights of their people, including the right to have their view or particular position adopted.[44]

---

39 Ibid.
40 Commonwealth, *Parliamentary Debates*, Senate, 20 June 2002, 2356–3257 (Brian Grieg), 2369 (Steve Hutchins); Commonwealth, *Parliamentary Debates*, Senate, 24 June 2002, 2455 (Barney Cooney).
41 Commonwealth, *Parliamentary Debates*, Senate, 20 June 2002, 2355 (Brian Grieg).
42 Commonwealth, *Parliamentary Debates*, Senate, 20 June 2002, 2373–2374 (Chris Schacht).
43 Commonwealth, *Parliamentary Debates*, Senate, 20 June 2002, 2373 (Chris Schacht).
44 Ibid.

The inclusion of a motive element, including religious motivation, in Australia's' anti-terrorism laws can be traced back to the United Kingdom's legislative definition of terrorism enacted some 14 months before the 9/11 terrorist attacks.[45] This definition, or slight variations on it, have since been copied into the anti-terrorism laws of New Zealand, Canada and South Africa and has been retained in the United Kingdom.[46]

Opinion is divided as to whether the motive element of terrorist act, including religious motivation, is necessary or whether it creates more problems than it solves.[47] Those who support its inclusion argue that it narrows the definition of terrorism by focusing on that which is truly different and objectionable about terrorist acts when compared with other criminal acts of violence.[48] By contrast, those who argue for the removal of the motive element claim that it is unnecessary as the intent element, namely an intent to coercing or 'by intimidation, the government of the Commonwealth or a State, Territory or foreign country, or of part of a State, Territory or foreign country; or intimidating the public or a section of the public'[49] is sufficient to distinguish terrorism from other criminal acts of violence.[50] They further argue that the inclusion of 'religious motivation', in particular, risks alienating, marginalising and stereotyping already vulnerable religious minorities, particularly unjustifiably linking Islam with terrorism.[51]

Religion and terrorism?

Determining whether there is a link between religion and terrorism is far from simple. As Nadirsyah Hosen points out:

> One can always find scriptural verses to legitimate both the slaughter and the acceptance of the Other. The same Torah that contains the commands to slaughter the idolatrous nations inhabiting the Land of Israel also contains the commitment 'Thou shalt not oppress a stranger: for ye know the heart of a stranger, seeing ye were strangers in the land of Egypt.' (Exodus 23:9). The same Gospel of Matthew that declares 'His blood be on us, and on our children' (27:25) also declares 'Love your enemies, bless them that curse you' (5:44). Similarly, the same Qur'an that states 'slay the idolaters

45 Hardy, above n 34, 229–342.
46 Ibid. 344.
47 Saul, above n 32, 29; see also Kent Roach, 'The Case for Defining Terrorism with Restraint and Without Reference to Political or Religious Motive' in Andrew Lynch, Edwina Mac-Donald and George Williams (eds), *Law and Liberty in the War on Terror* (Federation Press, 2007) 39.
48 Saul, above n 32, 28.
49 Criminal Code Act 1995 (Cth) s 101.1.
50 Roach, 'The Case for Defining Terrorism with Restraint and Without Reference to Political or Religious Motive', above n 47, 39.
51 Hardy, above n 34, 342; Saul, above n 32, 34–37.

wherever you find them' (9:5) also states 'Let there be no compulsion in religion' (2:256).[52]

In Australia a connection is almost inevitably drawn between Islam and terrorism. However as discussed above, the inclusion of religion in the United Kingdom definition of religion, and copied into the Australian definition, was not included in response to Islamic extremism but in response to the sarin gas attack carried out on a Tokyo subway by apocalyptic cult Aum Shinrikyo.[53] Further, when examined more closely, 'religiously motivated terrorists' often have other secular goals such as the release of religious leaders from State detention or the return of 'occupied' land. Far from being irrational fanatics 'religiously motivated' terrorists, may, like terrorists motivated by political or other ideology, have rational practical motivations.[54]

Despite this, modern terrorism appears to be unavoidably linked in the minds of the public and some political leaders with religion generally and Islamic extremism more specifically. It is this popular understanding of terrorism that is often cited as a justification for the continued inclusion of religion in the definition of terrorism.[55]

Examining Australia's list of declared terrorist organisations also gives the impression that modern terrorism is intrinsically linked to religion. Section 102 of the *Criminal Code Act 1995* (Cth) empowers the Governor General to make regulations specifying that certain organisations are terrorist organisations. Before doing so the Attorney General must be satisfied on reasonable grounds that the organisation 'is directly or indirectly engaged in, preparing, planning, assisting in or fostering the doing of a terrorist act' or 'advocates the doing of a terrorist act.'[56]

At the time of writing 25 organisations were listed as terrorist organisations under the Criminal Code. 24 of the 25 organisations (96%) listed are described as having some form of link with Islam by, for example, desiring to set up a caliphate or Sharia state or are described as undertaking jihad. Both Sunni and Shia groups are included on the list.[57] The only listed terrorist organisation which is not described as having some kind of link to Islam is the Kurdistan Workers' Party (PKK). Its current objective is 'for autonomy for Kurds within Turkey and seeks to promote the rights of Kurds living in Turkey, specifically the right to

52 Hosen, 'Religion and Security What's your Motive?', above n 34, 138.
53 Hardy, above n 34, 340–341.
54 Nadirsyah Hosen, 'Religion and Security What's your Motive?' in Nadirsyah Hosen and Richard Mohr (eds) *Law and Religion in Public Life: The Contemporary Debate* (Routledge, 2011), 137, 141–142.
55 Hardy, above n 34, 342–348.
56 S 102.1(2) *Criminal Code Act 1995* (Cth). Regulations made under this Section lapse after three years and can be renewed, see s 102.1(3).
57 Australian Government, Australian National Security, *Listed terrorist organisations* (2017) www.nationalsecurity.gov.au/listedterroristorganisations/pages/default.aspx>.

maintain a Kurdish ethnic identity.'[58] While the PKK 'has periodically sought to increase its popularity by exploiting the religious sentiment of the Kurdish community, but the organisation remains predominantly secular.'[59] By comparison, at the time of writing the United States Department of State listed 61 Foreign Terrorist Organisations.[60] Of these, 15 (24.6%) could be described as secular.[61] Of the remaining 46, two do not have a link to Islamic extremism; Aum Shinrikyo (AUM) and Kahane Chai (Kach). All of the organisations listed since July 2009 have been Islamic extremist organisations.[62]

Specific offences

While all terrorism related offences have the potential to impact upon the relationship between the law and religion given the inclusion of religion in the definition of terrorist act and the risk of religious profiling that this entails,[63] there are some offences where the interaction between law and religion is more acute. This section will look specifically at offences related to the financing of terrorism and visiting a declared area, both of which are of particular concern to Australian Muslims.

At the heart of Islam are the five pillars of Islam; Shahada, Salat, Sawm, Zakat and Hajj.[64] The last two, Zakat and Hajj, have the potential to interact negatively with laws relating to the financing of terrorism and declared area.

Financing terrorism

Australia's anti-terrorism laws contain several offences related to the financing of terrorism. These can be found in Section 102.6 and Division 103 of the *Criminal Code Act 1995* (Cth) along with Part 4 of the *Charter of the United Nations*

---

58 Australian Government, Australian National Security, *Kurdistan Workers' Party (PKK)* www.nationalsecurity.gov.au/Listedterroristorganisations/Pages/KurdistanWorkersPartyPKK.aspx>.

59 Ibid.

60 United States Department of State, *Foreign Terrorist Organizations* (2017) www.state.gov/j/ct/rls/other/des/123085.htm>.

61 Basque Fatherland and Liberty (ETA), Kurdistan Workers Party (PKK) (Kongra-Gel), Liberation Tigers of Tamil Eelam (LTTE), National Liberation Army (ELN), Palestine Liberation Front (PLF), Popular Front for the Liberation of Palestine (PFLP), PFLP-General Command (PFLP-GC), Revolutionary Armed Forces of Colombia (FARC), Revolutionary People's Liberation Party/Front (DHKP/C), Shining Path (SL), Real Irish Republican Army (RIRA), Al-Aqsa Martyrs Brigade (AAMB), Communist Party of the Philippines/New People's Army (CPP/NPA), Continuity Irish Republican Army (CIRA) and Revolutionary Struggle (RS).

62 United States Department of State, above n 60.

63 Saul, above n 32, 34–37.

64 Declaration that there is no God but God and that Muhammad is the Messenger of God, Daily Prayers, Fasting, Giving Charity and Pilgrimage to Mecca; see Abdullah Saeed, *Islam in Australia* (Allen & Unwin, 2003) 52–63.

Act 1945 (Cth). The main interaction between these offences and religious obligation occur in relation to the fault element and the Islamic obligation of zakat or charitable giving. Of particular concern is the mental element of some offences which only requires that a person be 'reckless' as to how the funds will be used or the nature of the organisation receiving them.

Section 102.6 (2) makes it an offence for a person to, *inter alia*, make funds available to or collect funds on behalf of a terrorist organisation where the person 'is *reckless* as to whether the organisation is a terrorist organisation' (emphasis added). Similarly, Section 103.1 makes it an offence to provide or collect funds where the person is '*reckless* as to whether the funds will be used to facilitate or engage in a terrorist act' (emphasis added) while Section 103.2 makes it an offence to make funds available to another person or collect funds for or on behalf of another person where the person collecting or providing the funds 'is *reckless* as to whether the other person will use the funds to facilitate or engage in a terrorist act' (emphasis added).[65] 'Recklessness' is defined in Section 5.4 of the *Criminal Code Act 1995* (Cth) and requires that a person be aware of a substantial risk that a circumstance exists or will exists or result will occur and it is unjustifiable to take the risk.

Giving to charity is an important element of Islam.[66] This is highlighted by the inclusion of zakat (charitable giving) in the five pillars of Islam. Zakat requires all adult Muslims to give 2.5% of their saved wealth for charitable purposes annually.[67] Muslims are also encouraged to be generous and make voluntary donations to charity, also known as sadaqa.[68] Terrorist organisations have been known to take advantage of this generosity and religious obligation by creating fake charitable organisations and soliciting funds from well-meaning Muslims.[69] The challenge for Australian Muslims therefore is in knowing whether or not a charity to which they want to direct their giving may have a link to terrorism and that their funds may therefore be directed towards either a terrorist organisation or terrorist act. As Lynch, McGarrity and Williams observe:

> What this means, in practice is that a person wishing to donate to a foreign charitable organisation must conduct a rigorous investigation into the purpose for which any funds will be used. Even then, especially where we are talking about organisations in regions wracked by civil war … it may be difficult to get definitive answers.[70]

---

65 For a more detailed discussion of these provisions see Lynch, McGarrity and Williams, above n 10, 66–71.
66 Waleed Aly, 'Muslim Communities: Their Voice in Australia's Anti-Terrorism Law and Policy' in Andrew Lynch, Edwina MacDonald and George Williams (eds), *Law and Liberty in the War on Terror* (The Federation Press, 2007) 198, 200.
67 For a more detailed explanation of zakat see Saeed, above n 64, 59–60.
68 Saeed, above n 64, 60.
69 Aly, above n 66, 201.
70 Lynch, McGarrity and Williams, above n 10, 69.

Waleed Aly has argued that the definition of 'reckless' in the *Criminal Code Act* is inherently political suggesting that:

> If one is inclined to regard terrorism as the definitive existential threat of our age, then it is arguably 'unjustifiable' to take any risk whatsoever – which may mean the end of charity. Alternatively, if one considers terrorism to be no significantly more threatening than any other crime, a greater degree of risk may be justifiable.[71]

Given that the question of whether a particular action will be 'reckless' is a matter of fact and that each case is likely to be unique it is therefore very difficult for an Australian Muslim to know whether or not they are being reckless in providing funds to their chosen charity. Add to this the inherent difficulty in getting accurate information about many charities operating in some parts of the Muslim world as a result of war and other destabilising factors and Australian Muslims are placed in a precarious position.

While the risk of being 'accidently' caught up in financing terrorism is very real for Australian Muslims, it is important to note that at the time of writing no one has been charged under Section 103.1 or 103.2. While a number of people have been charged under Section 102.6, these charges have so far had a very low conviction rate and none of the convictions have related to what might be termed 'accidental' financing of terrorism.[72]

Declared area

While terrorism financing offences were part of the initial wave of anti-terrorism laws in the wake of the September 11 terrorist attacks, offences relating to declared areas were not introduced until 2014. Section 119.3 of the *Criminal Code Act 1995* (Cth) gives the Foreign Affairs Minister the power to declare an area in a foreign country if they are satisfied that 'a listed terrorist organisation is engaging in a hostile activity in that area of the foreign country.' Once declared it is an offence under s 119.2 to 'enter or remain in' a declared area. There is no requirement in the offence that the person either entered the area with the intent of engaging in a terrorist act or related activity or that they did in fact engage in a terrorist act. All they need to do is enter or remain in the area.

It is a defence to a charge under s. 119.2 if the person enters or remains in a declared area for a legitimate reason. These are listed in s. 119.2 (3):

(a) providing aid of a humanitarian nature;
(b) satisfying an obligation to appear before a court or other body exercising judicial power;

---

71 Aly, above n 66, 200.
72 See Lynch, McGarrity and Williams, above n 10, 73–77.

(c) performing an official duty for the Commonwealth, a State or a Territory;

(d) performing an official duty for the government of a foreign country or the government of part of a foreign country (including service in the armed forces of the government of a foreign country), where that performance would not be a violation of the law of the Commonwealth, a State or a Territory;

(e) performing an official duty for the United Nations or an agency of the United Nations;

(f) making a news report of events in the area, where the person is working in a professional capacity as a journalist or is assisting another person working in a professional capacity as a journalist;

(g) making a bona fide visit to a family member;

(h) any other purpose prescribed by the regulations.

Performing a religious obligation or making a religious pilgrimage is not included on the list.

At the time of writing there is one declared area: Mosul district, Ninewa providence in Iraq.[73] The Al-Raqqa province in Syria was also previously a declared area but was no longer in force at the time of writing.[74] While neither of these areas are of particular religious significance there is nothing in the legislation preventing the Minister from making a declaration over an area containing a site of religious significance such as Jerusalem, Mecca or even Rome.

Should the Minister ever make a declaration over an area containing Mecca this would pose a significant problem for Australian Muslims. Undertaking a pilgrimage to Mecca, known as Hajj, is one of the five pillars of Islam and therefore obligatory for all Muslims. All Muslims who are physically and financially able are required to make a pilgrimage to Mecca at least once in their lifetime.[75] While it may be possible for a Muslim to delay their Hajj until such time when a declared area declaration is no longer in force, there is unlikely to be any guarantee as to when this may be forcing the individual to put their religious obligations on hold for an indefinite period of time.[76]

While Hajj is obligatory the performance of other voluntary religious rituals at a variety of places of significance is part of many religious traditions. Declared area offences therefore have the potential to impact upon the ability of people of many faiths to freely exercise their religion.

---

73 Australian Government, Australian National Security, *Declared area offence - Mosul District* <*www.nationalsecurity.gov.au/whataustraliaisdoing/pages/declaredareaoffence.aspx#Mosul District*>.

74 Australian Government, Australian National Security, *Declared area offence – Al Raqqa Province* <www.nationalsecurity.gov.au/whataustraliaisdoing/pages/declaredareaoffence.aspx#AlRaqqaProvince>.

75 For a more detailed explanation of Hajj see Saeed, above n 64, 61–63.

76 A declaration of a declared area last for 3 years unless renewed.

Same-sex marriage

Background

Prior to 1961 each Australian State and territory had its own laws relating to marriage. This produced differences across Australia in areas such as the age at which a person could marry and the permitted degree of co-sanguination.[77] The introduction of the *Matrimonial Causes Act 1959* (Cth)[78] and the *Marriage Act 1961* (Cth)[79] together brought unity to the laws relating to marriage across Australia.[80] However, as Sir Garfield Barwick stated:

> To bring unity to the marriage law of Australia was not, however, the main task of the architects of the Marriage act. Their main task was to produce a marriage code suitable to present day Australian needs, a code which, on the one hand, paid proper regard to the antiquity and foundations of marriage as an institution, but which, on the other hand, resolved modern problems in a modern way.[81]

The *Marriage Act* as passed in 1961 did not contain a definition of marriage and instead relied on the common law definition.[82] In *Hyde v Hyde*[83] Lord Penzance stated that 'marriage, as understood in Christendom, may for this purpose be defined as the voluntary union for life of one man and one woman, to the exclusion of all others.'[84] Similarly, Quick and Garran in *The Annotated Constitution of the Australian Commonwealth* defined Marriage for the purpose of Sections 51 (xxi) of the *Australian Constitution* ('the marriages power')[85] as "(1) a voluntary union (2) for life, (3) of one man and one woman, (4) to the exclusion of all others."[86]

---

77 Garfield Barwick, 'The Commonwealth Marriage Act 1961' (1962) 3(3) *Melbourne University Law Review* 277, 277, 282–288.
78 The *Matrimonial Causes Act 1959* (Cth) commenced on 1 February 1961 and was repealed by the *Family Law Act 1975* (Cth) s 3(1).
79 Sections 1–3, Subsection 5(1), Section 9, Parts III and VIII and Section 120 came into effect on 6 May 1961. The remainder of the act commended on 1 September 1963.
80 Barwick, above n 77, 277; see also Commonwealth, *Parliamentary Debates*, House of Representatives, 19 May 1960, 2000–2001 (Garfield Barkwick).
81 Barwick, above n 77, 277.
82 Michael Quinlan, 'Marriage, Tradition, Multiculturalism and the Accommodation of Difference in Australia' (2016) 18 *University of Notre Dame Australia Law Review* 71, 78–79.
83 (1866) LR 1 P&D 130.
84 Ibid. 133 (Lord Penzance).
85 Section 51 (xxii) gives the Commonwealth power over Divorce and Matrimonial Causes and was therefore the basis for the *Matrimonial Causes Act 1959* (Cth) and for today's *Family Law Act 1975* (Cth).
86 John Quick and Robert Randolph Garran, *The Annotated Constitution of the Australian Commonwealth* (Angus and Robertson, 1901), 608.

During the committee stage Senator George Hannan proposed to include a definition of marriage to the effect that:

> Marriage means the union of one man with one woman for life to the exclusion of all others, such union being contracted in the manner provided in this Act.[87]

His reasoning for including such a definition was that he

> [believed] a matter so important as marriage, which affects the status of well over 90 per cent, of the adults in our community, should be specifically defined and regulated by statute, not left to common law decisions by the courts of the land based on precedent or case law, in the case of the Privy Council, possibly based on the opinions of its personnel of the Judicial Committee from time to time, since that distinguished tribunal is not bound by its own decisions. I believe that this most important status should be defined by legislation.[88]

However, in formulating his definition he felt bound by the meaning of marriage at the time of Federation and therefore felt bound by common law decisions such as that in *Hyde v Hyde* as well as more recent decisions such as the New Zealand case of *Wong v Wong*.[89] The majority of senators did not agree, preferring to rely on the common law definition.[90] While not part of the debate on Senator Hannon's proposed definition, the sentiments expressed by Kim Edward Beazley in the House of Representatives reflect some of the reasoning behind the rejection of Senator Hannan's amendment:

> I do not think it is necessary to have such a definition, and the fact that it is not necessary is also an indication that the marriage customs of the people of this country are not going to be radically changed by transferring the authority which makes the legislation with regard to marriage from the State to the Commonwealth. The marriage customs of the community are, in fact, customs and they have not been framed around law. Perhaps to a considerable extent they have been framed around religion.[91]

While the *Marriage Act* as passed in 1961 did not contain a specific definition of marriage it did make reference to the meaning of marriage. Section 46

---

87 Commonwealth, *Parliamentary Debates*, Senate, 18 April 1961, 542 (George Hannan).
88 Ibid.
89 [1948] NZLR 348; see Commonwealth, *Parliamentary Debates*, Senate, 18 April 1961, 542–543 (George Hannan).
90 Commonwealth, *Parliamentary Debates*, Senate, 18 April 1961, 555.
91 Commonwealth, *Parliamentary Debates*, House of Representatives, 18 August 1960, 229 (Kim Beazley).

of the Act required authorised celebrants, who are no ministers of religion of a recognised denomination, to state, *inter alia*, that: "Marriage, according to law in Australia, is the union of a man and a woman to the exclusion of all others, voluntarily entered into for life." This requirement was not removed until 2017 with the passage of the *Marriage Amendment (Definition and Religious Freedoms) Act 2017* (Cth). Authorised celebrants are now required to state that: Marriage, according to law in Australia, is the union of two people to the exclusion of all others, voluntarily entered into for life.[92]

In 2004, in response to the legalisation of same-sex marriages oversee the Commonwealth inserted a definition of marriage into the *Marriage Act*.[93] The new definition defined marriage as 'the union of a man and a woman to the exclusion of all others, voluntarily entered into for life.'[94] The 2004 Act also made it clear that a marriage solemnised in another country between two people of the same sex would not be recognised as a marriage in Australia for the purposes of the *Marriage Act*.[95]

Since 2004 there have been a number of attempts to reverse the changes made to the Act and therefore legalise marriage between two people regardless of their sex.[96] A total of 22 bills have been introduced to the Federal Parliament. Some such as the Same-Sex Marriage Bill 2006 (Cth) were relatively simply and sought to do little more than reverse the changes made in 2004.[97] Others such as the Marriage Amendment Bill 2012 (Cth) were a little more complex in that they also included specific provisions making it clear that ministers of religion would not be obliged to perform same-sex marriages.[98] Others contained even more complex provision relating to the rights of religious and none-religious marriage

---

92 *Marriage Act 1961* (Cth) s 46(1).
93 *Marriage Amendment Act 2004* (Cth).
94 Ibid. sch 1, s 1.
95 Ibid. sch 1, s 3.
96 Deirdre McKeown, *Chronology of same-sex marriage bills introduced into the federal parliament: A quick guide* (1 December 2017) Parliament of Australia <>www.aph.gov.au/About_Parliament/Parliamentary_Departments/Parliamentary_Library/pubs/rp/rp1718/Quick_Guides/SSMarriageBills>.
97 The Same-Sex Marriage Bill 2006 (Cth) also sought to remove gendered references to husband and wife and replace these with gender neutral terms such as 'spouse' or 'two people'. Other similar Bills include Marriage (Relationships Equality) Amendment Bill 2007, Marriage (Relationships Equality) Amendment Bill 2008, Same-Sex marriage Bill 2008, Marriage Equality Amendment Bill 2009, Marriage Equality Amendment Bill 2010 and Marriage Legislation Amendment Bill 2015; the Marriage Act Amendment (Recognition of Foreign Marriages for Same-Sex Couples) Bill 2013 and Recognition of Foreign Marriages Bill 2014 only sought to repeal the provisions in the *Marriage Act 1961* (Cth) relating to the recognition of foreign marriages between people of the same sex.
98 See also Marriage Equality Amendment Bill 2012, Marriage Amendment Bill (No. 2) 2012, Marriage Equality Amendment Bill 2013, Marriage Equality Amendment Bill 2013, Marriage Amendment (Marriage Equality) Bill 2015, Marriage Amendment (Marriage Equality) Bill 2016, Marriage Legislation Amendment Bill 2016 and Marriage Legislation Amendment Bill 2016 [No. 2].

celebrants in relation to marriages between people of the same sex.[99] None of the Bills proposed between 2004 and 2016 provided any exemptions to anti-discrimination laws for individuals and business engaged in providing services to weddings nor dealt with matters relating to freedom of religion or LGBTIQ+ rights beyond the marriage ceremony itself. Of the 22 bills introduced in this period only four came to a vote, all of which were lost at the second reading stage.[100]

A number of States and territories have also explored the possibility of passing State or territory based same-sex marriage legislation.[101] In 2013 the Australian Capital Territory (ACT) passed the *Marriage Equality (Same Sex) Act 2013* (ACT). The Act purported to provide for marriages of people of the same sex in the ACT, but did not make provision for marriages between people of the opposite sex. A month later in *Commonwealth v Australian Capital Territory*[102] the High Court unanimously found that the ACT legislation was inconsistent with the Commonwealth *Marriage Act* and therefore invalid under Section 28(1) of the *Australian Capital Territory (Self Government) Act 1988* (Cth).[103] While not directly relevant to similar State-based legislation, Section 109 of the *Australian Constitution* states that:

> When a law of a State is inconsistent with a law of the Commonwealth, the latter shall prevail, and the former shall, to the extent of the inconsistency, be invalid.

It is therefore likely that similar State-based legislation would, similarly, be found to be invalid.

The High Court also considered the Constitutional definition of marriage. The Court found that:

> 'marriage' is to be understood in s 51(xxi) of the *Constitution* as referring to a consensual union formed between natural persons in accordance with

---

99 See Freedom to Marry Bill 2014 and Freedom to Marry Bill 2016.

100 See Marriage Equality Amendment Bill 2009, Marriage Amendment Bill 2012, Marriage Amendment Bill (No. 2) 2012, Marriage Act Amendment (Recognition of Foreign Marriages for Same-Sex Couples) Bill 2013.

101 See Same-Sex Marriage Bill 2012 (Tas), Legislative Council Standing Committee on Social Issues, *Same-sex Marriage law in New South Wales*, No 47 of 2013, 26 July 2013 available at <>www.parliament.nsw.gov.au/committees/DBAssets/InquiryReport/ReportAcrobat/5549/Report%20-%2047%20-%20Same-sex%20marriage%20law%20in%20New%20South%20W.pdf>; Tasmania Law Reform Institute, *The Legal Issues Relating to Same Sex Marriage*, No 3 of 2013, October 2013 available at www.utas.edu.au/__data/assets/pdf_file/0004/424525/SSM_FinalB5_05.pdf>.

102 (2013) 250 CLR 441.

103 Ibid. 467 (French CJ, Hayne, Crennan, Kiefel, Bell and Keane JJ); a detailed discussion of this case and its wider implications is beyond the scope of this section. For further discussion of the case see Shipra Chordia, 'The High Court, Same-Sex Marriage and Federalism' (2014) 39(2) *Alternative Law Journal* 84.

legally prescribed requirements which is not only a union the law recognises as intended to endure and be terminable only in accordance with law but also a union to which the law accords a status affecting and defining mutual rights and obligations.[104]

The Court went on to state that 'When used in s 51(xxi), "marriage" is a term which includes a marriage between persons of the same sex.'[105] While these comments are *obiter* and the High Court is always free to overturn its previous decisions, they give a strong indication of the High Court's likely finding should the amendments introduced by the *Marriage Amendment (Definition and Religious Freedoms) Act 2017* (Cth) be challenged on the grounds that marriages between persons of the same-sex are not with in the definition of marriage in the *Australian Constitution*.[106]

In August 2015, then Prime Minister Tony Abbott announced that the Coalition's policy[107] for the remaining term of government was to retain the definition of marriage in the *Marriage Act* as being between one man and one woman but to take the issue to a plebiscite should the coalition win the next federal election.[108] In explaining his party's position he commented that:

> I think I can say arising out of today is that if you support the existing definition of marriage between a man and a woman, the Coalition is absolutely on your side but if you would like to see change at some time in the future, the Coalition is prepared to make that potentially possible.[109]

Following this announcement Greens Senator Janet Rice introduced a private member's bill to provide for a national plebiscite to be held alongside the

---

104 *Commonwealth v Australian Capital Territory* (2013) 250 CLR 441, 461 (French CJ, Hayne, Crennan, Kiefel, Bell and Keane JJ).

105 Ibid. 463 (French CJ, Hayne, Crennan, Kiefel, Bell and Keane JJ).

106 For the arguments relating to the Constitutional validity of same-sex marriage laws in Australia see Neville Rochow, '... Speak Now or Forever Hold Your Peace... – The Influence of Constitutional Arguments on Same-Sex Marriage Legislation Debates in Australia' (2013) *Brigham Young University Law Review* 521, 530–542; James McLean, 'The Constitutionality of Same-Sex Marriage' (2013) 15 *University of Notre Dame Australia Law Review* 1, 2–12; Dan Meagher, 'The times are they a-changin'? – Can Commonwealth Parliament Legislate for Same Sex marriage?' (2003) 17(2) *Australian Journal of Family Law* 134; Margaret Brock and Dan Meagher, 'The Legal Recognition of Same-Sex Unions in Australia: A Constitutional Analysis' (2011) 22(4) *Public Law Review* 266.

107 The Coalition consists of the Liberal Party and the National Party.

108 Judith Ireland, 'Tony Abbott flags plebiscite on same-sex marriage in bid to defuse anger', *Sydney Morning Herald* (online), 12 August 2015 <>www.smh.com.au/federal-politics/political-news/tony-abbott-flags-plebiscite-on-samesex-marriage-in-bid-to-defuse-anger-20150811-giwyg1.html>.

109 Ibid.

upcoming federal election.[110] The Bill lapsed with the prorogation of the 44th Parliament.

Despite a change in leadership in the lead up to the 2016 federal election to the more progressive Malcom Turnbull, the Liberal Party maintained the policy of taking the issue of same-sex marriage to a plebiscite should they win the election.[111] By contrast, the Labor Party promised to legalise same-sex marriage within 100 days of the new parliament.[112] Following their election win, Prime Minister Malcom Turnbull, on behalf of the Coalition government, introduced the Plebiscite (Same Sex Marriage) Bill 2016 (Cth).[113] During his second reading speech Turnbull acknowledged the diversity of views on same-sex marriage throughout the community and in particular that those who opposed same-sex marriage often did so out of a deeply held religious conviction:

> We have to respect there are sincerely held views on this issue. They are views very often informed by deeply felt conscience; informed by religious commitment, very often; informed by faith. We have to respect, we must respect – and I can say the government respects – the diversity of views on this issue.[114]

He went on to outline his personal view that same-sex marriage should be legalised:

> As it happens, as honourable members are aware, my view and that of my wife, Lucy, is that the law should be changed to allow same-sex couples to marry. We have been married for over 36 years and we do not believe that if same-sex couples are allowed to have their union recognised as marriage that will undermine our relationship of long standing.... David Cameron summed it up very well some years ago when he said, 'I support same-sex

---

110 Marriage Equality Plebiscite Bill 2015 (Cth); the leader for the Greens, Senator Richard Di Natale, announced on 13 August of the Greens' intention to introduce a Bill to this effect, see Richard Di Natale and Janet Rice, 'Greens Propose Way Forward on Marriage Equality' (Media Release, 13 August 2015) < >http://parlinfo.aph.gov.au/parlInfo/download/media/pressrel/4010076/upload_binary/4010076.pdf;fileType=application%2Fpdf#search=%22media/pressrel/4010076%22>.

111 Election Watch, University of Melbourne, *P-TECH announcement with the Minister for Education and Training, Emu Plains, NSW* (30 May 2016) <>http://electionwatch.unimelb.edu.au/__data/assets/pdf_file/0006/1994244/Doorstop-with-PM-marriage-equality.pdf>.

112 Election Watch, University of Melbourne, *Positive Policy – Marriage* Equality, http://electionwatch.unimelb.edu.au/__data/assets/pdf_file/0011/1994222/Labor-Marriage-Equality.pdf>.

113 See Commonwealth, *Parliamentary Debates*, House of Representatives, 14 September 2016, 845–849 (Prime Minister Malcolm Turnbull).

114 Ibid. 846 (Prime Minister Malcolm Turnbull).

marriage not despite being a conservative but because I am a conservative, because we value commitment.'[115]

The Labor Party,[116] Greens[117] and several independent Senators[118] opposed the proposed plebiscite. Despite passing the House of Representatives the Bill was blocked in the Senate.

With any future proposals for a compulsory plebiscite on same sex marriage unlikely to pass the Senate, the Coalition instead instructed the Australian Bureau of Statistics (ABS) to conduct a voluntary postal survey to determine, *inter alia*, 'the proportion of participating electors who are in favour of the law being changed to allow same-sex couples to marry.'[119] The High Court confirmed the validity of the government's actions following a challenge by Andrew Wilkie and Austrian Marriage Equability Ltd in September 2017 enabling the postal survey to go ahead.[120]

On 15 November the Australian Statistician announced that 61.6% of those who participated had voted in support of changing the law to allow same-sex couples to marry.[121] In response Senator Dean Smith introduced to the Senate a private members Bill to legalise same-sex marriage – the Marriage Amendment (Definition and Religious Freedoms) Bill 2017 (Cth) – on 15 November 2015. The Bill passed the third reading in the Senate on the 29 November 2018 and the House of Representatives on 7 December 2018. It received Royal Assent on 8 December 2017.

Section 42 of the *Marriage Act 1961* (Cth) requires all people intending to marry to give not less than one months' written notice. However a prescribed authority may give permission for a shorter notice period if certain conditions are

115 Ibid.
116 Mark Dreyfus and Terri Butler, 'Time for Turnbull to Allow a Free Vote on marriage Equality' (Media Release, 28 September 2016) <>http://parlinfo.aph.gov.au/parlInfo/download/media/pressrel/4844115/upload_binary/4844115.pdf;fileType=application%2Fpdf#search=%22media/pressrel/4844115%22>.
117 Richard Di Natale and Janet Rice, 'Greens will vote against plebiscite legislation' (Media Release, 26 August 2016) <>http://parlinfo.aph.gov.au/parlInfo/download/media/pressrel/4778971/upload_binary/4778971.pdf;fileType=application%2Fpdf#search=%22media/pressrel/4778971%22>.
118 Parliament of Australia, *Plebiscite (Same-Sex Marriage) Bill 2016* (October 2016) <>www.aph.gov.au/Parliamentary_Business/Bills_Legislation/bd/bd1617a/17bd022#_ftnref34>.
119 Federal Register of Legislation, *Census and Statistics (Statistical Information) Direction 2017* (9 August 2017) https://web.archive.org/web/20170810014829/www.legislation.gov.au/Details/F2017L01006>.
120 *Wilkie v The Commonwealth; Australian Marriage Equality Ltd v Cormann* [2017] HCA 40.
121 Australian Bureau of Statistics, *Survey Process* (11 December 2017) https://marriage-survey.abs.gov.au/results/>; the question on the postal survey was "Should the law be changed to allow same-sex couples to marry?"

met.[122] These include employment-related or other travel commitments, binding nature of existing wedding arrangements or religious considerations, medical reasons, legal proceedings or errors in giving notice by the celebrant.[123] The first same-sex weddings took place just a week after the passage of the *Marriage Amendment (Definition and Religious Freedoms) Act 2017* (Cth) as a result of waivers to the one month notice period granted on the basis of travel commitments, existing wedding arrangements[124] and medical grounds.[125] Same-sex couples who had married overseas prior to the passage of the *Marriage Amendment (Definition and Religious Freedoms) Act 2017* (Cth) had their marriages recognised immediately.[126]

Marriage and religion in Australia

In 1834 the Governor and council of New South Wales passed the *Marriages Act 1834.*[127] The purpose of the *Act* was, *inter alia*, 'to remove doubts as to the validity of certain Marriages' that has been solemnized in the colony.[128] The *Act* provided that marriages solemnized in the colony by minsters of the Church of Scotland or priests of the Roman Catholic Church according to the rituals of those faiths were valid as if they have been conducted by a clergyman of the Church of England.[129] The *Act* further provided that ministers of the Church of Scotland and priests of the Roman Catholic Church could continue to solemnize marriages in the colony.[130] Religion continues to play a role in Australian marriage law today. While the majority of couples opt for a civil celebrant (76.4% in

---

122 *Marriage Act 1961* (Cth) s 5; prescribed authorities include, in relation to a marriage proposed to be solemnised in Australia, a person, being an officer or employee of the Commonwealth, a state or a territory, appointed by the Minister to be a prescribed authority or, in relation to a marriage proposed to be solemnised in accordance with Division 3 of Part V of the *Act*, a chaplain or an officer (within the meaning of the Defence Act 1903), other than a chaplain, authorised by the Chief of the Defence Force under Section 71A of the *Act* to solemnise marriages under that Division.
123 *Marriage Regulations 2017* (Cth) sch 3.
124 One couple had already planned a commitment ceremony prior to the legalisation of same-sex marriage and applied to convert this to a wedding ceremony with a waiver of the one month notice period.
125 ABC News, *Same-sex marriage: First weddings take place in Melbourne, Sydney* (16 December 2017) www.abc.net.au/news/2017-12-16/same-sex-marriage-first-weddings-take-placein-australia/9265598>; see also ABC News, *Same-sex marriage: How Australia's first wedding can happen within a month* (13 December 2017) www.abc.net.au/news/2017-12-13/why-the-first-ssm-wedding-will-happen-in-under-a-month/9256610>.
126 *Marriage Amendment (Definition and Religious Freedoms) Act 2017* (Cth) ss 70–71.
127 Barwick, above n 77, 280.
128 *Marriages Act 1834* (NSW) s 1; see also the long title of the Act: *An Act to remove Doubts as to the Validity of certain Marriages had and solemnized within the Colony of New South Wales and to regulate the registration of certain Marriages Baptisms and Burials.*
129 *Marriages Act 1834* (NSW) s 1.
130 *Marriages Act 1834* (NSW) s 2.

2016[131]), couples may still choose to be married according to the rituals of their chosen faith.

Marriage by a religious minister

Under the *Marriage Act 1961* (Cth) there are four main types of marriage celebrants: Marriage Celebrants,[132] state and territory Officers,[133] Ministers of Religion[134] and Religious Marriage Celebrants.[135] Under Section 26 of the *Marriage Act 1961* (Cth), the Governor-General may declare religious bodies or organisation to be a recognised denomination. Ministers of Religion from recognised denominations may register as a marriage celebrant as a Minister of Religion under Part IV Division 1 Subdivision A of the *Marriage Act 1961* (Cth). At the time of writing there are 141 recognised denominations.[136] These cover a wide range of religious denominations from A2A Ltd to the Worship Centre Christian Churches Worldwide (Australia) Ltd. Well known religious organisations such as the Roman Catholic Church, the Anglican Church of Australia and the Uniting Church in Australia are listed along with more controversial religious organisations such as the Brethren, the Jehovah's Witnesses and the Church of Scientology Incorporated and less well-known groups such as the Church of Tonga in Australia and Spirit of the Earth Medicine Society. While the list of recognised denominations covers a wide spectrum, not all religions operating in Australia are included.[137] However, individuals who are ministers of religion but do not belong to one of the 141 recognised denominations may still celebrate marriages if they register as a civil marriage celebrant.[138] As will be discussed in more detail below, they may also register as a religious marriage celebrant which entitled them to certain exemptions from the law not available to other marriage celebrants or State and territory officials.

The primary difference between a Minister of Religion of recognised denominations, Minister of Religion from other denominations and all other marriage celebrants is the form of service and other statements which must be made during the marriage ceremony. Where a marriage is solemnised by a Minister of Religion, being from either a recognised or other denomination, it 'may be solemnised according to any form and ceremony recognised as sufficient for the purpose by

131 Australian Bureau of Statistics, *Marriages and Divorces, Australia* (28 November 2017) www.abs.gov.au/ausstats/abs@.nsf/mf/3310.0>; since 1999 marriages have been conducted by civil celebrants each year than religious ones.
132 *Marriages Act 1961* (Cth) ss 39A–39D.
133 Ibid. s 39.
134 Ibid. ss 25–38.
135 Ibid. ss 39DA–39DE.
136 *Marriage (Recognised Denominations) Proclamation 2007* (Cth) sch 1.
137 In *Nelson v Fisher* (1990) 21 FCR 430 the Federal Court found that a failure to recognise a particular denomination as a recognised denomination under the *Marriage Act 1961* (Cth) did not breach Section 116 of the *Australian Constitution*.
138 *Nelson v Fisher* (1990) 21 FCR 430, 435.

the religious body or organisation of which he or she is a minister.'[139] By contrast, all other marriage celebrants must use words to the effect 'I call upon the persons here present to witness that I, A.B. (*or* C.D.), take thee, C.D. (*or* A.B.), to be my lawful wedded wife (*or* husband, *or* spouse).'[140] As a result there is potential for significant variation in terms of the form of marriage ceremony conducted by religious ministers.

In addition to the form of words outlined above, Marriage Celebrants, State and territory Officials and Religious Marriage Celebrants are required to explain the nature of marriage using words to the effect that:

> I am duly authorised by law to solemnise marriages according to law.
>
> Before you are joined in marriage in my presence and in the presence of these witnesses, I am to remind you of the solemn and binding nature of the relationship into which you are now about to enter.
>
> Marriage, according to law in Australia, is the union of 2 people to the exclusion of all others, voluntarily entered into for life.[141]

Ministers of religion of recognised denominations are exempt from this requirement.[142]

Prior to the passage of the *Marriage Amendment (Definition and Religious Freedoms) Act 2017* (Cth) Ministers of Religion from recognised denominations already had the ability refuse to solemnise a marriage and/or to require couples who wished to be married to comply with additional requirements, including a longer notice provision. With the legalisation of same-sex marriage the ability of ministers of religion of recognised denominations was further clarified and expanded. While Ministers of Religion could stipulate additional requirements, the act did not explicitly state that they could refuse to conduct the ceremony if the requirements were not met, this was added by the *Marriage Amendment (Definition and Religious Freedoms) Act 2017* (Cth).[143] The amendments also added a provision which permitted ministers of religion of a recognised denomination to refuse to solemnise a marriage if

> the refusal conforms to the doctrines, tenets or beliefs of the religion of the minister's religious body or religious organisation, the refusal is necessary to avoid injury to the religious susceptibilities of adherents of that religion,

139 *Marriages Act 1961* (Cth) s 45(1).
140 Ibid. s 45(2).
141 Ibid. s 46(1).
142 State and territory officials may also be exempted from this requirement see *Marriages Act 1961* (Cth) s 46(2).
143 *Marriages Act 1961* (Cth) ss 47(1)–(2) see also *Marriage Amendment (Definition and Religious Freedoms) Act 2017* (Cth) sch 1, cl 20.

or the minister's religious beliefs do not allow the minister to solemnise the marriage.[144]

Ministers of Religion of recognised denominations are also provided with exemptions in relation to marriages in the *Sex Discrimination Act* 1984 (Cth).[145]

Religious Marriage Celebrants

In addition to legalising same sex marriage, the *Marriage Amendment (Definition and Religious Freedoms) Act 2017* (Cth) created a new type of marriage celebrant: Religious Marriage Celebrants. From 9 December 2017 celebrants registered as Religious Marriage Celebrants will have an annotation on their registration to that effect.[146] There are two types of Religious Marriage Celebrants: religious ministers from religious groups which are not recognised denominations and civil celebrants who wish to be registered as a religious marriage celebrant due to their personal religious beliefs.

As outlined above, ministers of religion who did not belong to a recognised denomination can register as a Civil Marriage Celebrant. Following the passage of the *Marriage Amendment (Definition and Religious Freedoms) Act 2017* (Cth) they can now also apply to register as a Religious Marriage Celebrant.[147] In addition, Civil Marriage Celebrants who are not also ministers of religion who were registered as marriage celebrants on the 8 December 2017 may choose to be registered as a Religious Marriage Celebrant on the basis of their religious belief.[148] They have until 9 March 2018 to elect to become religious marriage celebrants. After this date only Civil Marriage Celebrants who are also Ministers of Religion will be able to register as a Religious Marriage Celebrant.

Like Ministers of Religion, discussed above, Religious Marriage Celebrants may refuse to conduct a marriage 'if the celebrant's religious beliefs do not allow the celebrant to solemnise the marriage.'[149] This section was deliberately created not only to permit Religious Marriage Celebrants to refuse to conduct same-sex marriage but any marriage where the reason for refusal was the Religious Marriage Celebrant's religious beliefs as not to single out same-sex couples.[150] Religious Marriage Celebrants are also given exemptions under the *Sex Discrimination Act* 1984 (Cth). Under that Act they may refuse to solemnise a marriage on the basis of a party to the marriage's sexual orientation, gender identity, intersex status, or marital or relationship status if the Religious Marriage Celebrant's

---

144 *Marriages Act 1961* (Cth) s 47(3).
145 *Sex Discrimination Act 1984* (Cth) s 40(2A).
146 *Marriage Amendment (Definition and Religious Freedoms) Act 2017* (Cth) sch 1, cl 8.
147 *Marriages Act 1961* (Cth) s 39DA.
148 Ibid. s 39DD.
149 Ibid. s 47A(1).
150 Commonwealth, *Parliamentary Debates,* Senate, 15 November 2017, 8562–8563 (Dean Smith).

'religious beliefs do not allow the celebrant to solemnise the marriage.'[151] While this exemption is more targeted it is not limited to same-sex couples. For example, a religious marriage celebrant may refuse to solemnise a marriage on the basis of a person's marital status as a divorcee.

Bodies established for religious purposes

The *Marriage Amendment (Definition and Religious Freedoms) Act 2017* (Cth) also introduced exemptions in relation to the use of their premises for marriage ceremonies for bodies established for a religious purpose.

Under the *Marriage Act 1961* (Cth) bodies established for religious purposes may refuse to allow their premises to be used for the solmisation of a marriage or purposes reasonably incidental to it if the refusal 'conforms to the doctrines, tenets or beliefs of the religion of the body; or is necessary to avoid injury to the religious susceptibilities of adherents of that religion.'[152] A similar exemption already existed in the *Sex Discrimination Act 1984* (Cth).[153] The inclusion of this new exemption in the *Marriage Act 1961* (Cth) was intended to make clear that the exemption to normal anti-discrimination law applies in relation to the solmisation of marriages and purposes reasonably incidental to the solmisation of marriage.[154]

The *Marriage Act 1961* (Cth) defines 'body established for a religious purpose' as having the same meaning as that used in Section 37 of the *Sex Discrimination Act 1984* (Cth). However, that Act does not explicitly define 'body established for religious purposes.' Instead it relies on the common law definition of the phrase. Unfortunately, there continues to be some inconsistency and doubt as to the breadth of the phrase. While a church, temple or mosque would most likely be covered, more doubt exists as to bodies owned and operated by a religious organisation who may not have an explicit religious purpose. For example, in *Christian Youth Camps Ltd v Cobaw Community Health Services Ltd*[155] the Victorian Court of Appeal in a split 2–1 judgment found, *inter alia*, that a camping facility run by the Christian Brethren Church was not a body established for

---

151 *Sex Discrimination Act 1984* (Cth) s 40(2AA).
152 *Marriage Act 1961* (Cth) s 47B(1); the exemption applies to facilities made available, and goods and services provided, whether for payment or not see *Marriage Act 1961* (Cth) s 47B(2).
153 *Sex Discrimination Act 1984* (Cth) s 37(1)(d).
154 Commonwealth, *Parliamentary Debates,* Senate, 15 November 2017, 8561 (Dean Smith).
155 (2014) ALR 615; for a discussion of this case see Bobbi Murphy, 'Balancing Religious Freedom and Anti-Discrimination: Christian Youth Camps Ltd v Cobaw Community Health services' (2016) 40(2) *Melbourne University Law Review* 594; Liam Elphick, 'Sexual Orientation and 'Gay Wedding Cake' Cases Under Australian Anti-Discrimination Legislation: A Fuller Approach to Religious Exemptions' (2017) 38(1) *Adelaide Law Review* 149, 162–164; Neil Foster, 'Freedom of Religion and Balancing Clauses in Discrimination Legislation' (Paper presented at Magna Carta and Freedom of Religion or Belief Conference, St Hugh's College Oxford, 21–24 June 2015) 11–13 available at https://works.bepress.com/neil_foster/95/>.

religious purposes.[156] Inconsistencies in the meaning of the phrase 'body established for religious purposes' exists across jurisdictions leaving some doubt as to the exact breadth of this exemption.[157]

Unsuccessful amendments

During debate on the Marriage Amendment (Definition and Religious Freedoms) Bill 2017 (Cth) a number of amendments were proposed in both the Senate and House of Representatives. These related broadly to freedom of religion issues, many of which were raised during the public debate which took place alongside the same-sex marriage postal survey. With the exception of primarily mechanical and consequential amendments moved by Senator Brandis,[158] all of the proposed amendments were rejected by both the Senate and House of Representatives. The unsuccessful amendments included issues such as:

- extending the right to refuse to conduct a wedding on conscientious grounds to civil celebrants as well as Ministers of Religion and Religious Marriage Celebrants, [159]
- removing the transitional provisions in relation to civil celebrants which allow existing celebrants to elect to be identified as Religious Marriage Celebrants,[160]
- only allowing Religious Marriage Celebrants to refuse to conduct a wedding on the basis of the religious beliefs of their religion rather than their own personal religious beliefs,[161]
- retaining the pre-existing definition of marriage alongside the new definition of marriage,[162]

---

156 *Christian Youth Camps Ltd v Cobaw Community Health Services Ltd* (2014) ALR 615, 666–669.
157 Elphick, above n 155, 166–167.
158 See Commonwealth, *Parliamentary Debates,* Senate, 28 November 2017, 8949–8959 (George Brandis).
159 See Commonwealth, *Parliamentary Debates,* Senate, 28 November 2017, 8964–8965 (David Fawcett); 8966–8967 (James Paterson); 9137–9138 (Brandis); Commonwealth, *Parliamentary Debates,* Senate, 29 November 2017, 9146–9148 (Pauline Hanson); 9165–9166 (David Leyonhjelm); Commonwealth, *Parliamentary Debates,* House of Representatives, 7 December 2017, 13009 (Michael Sukkar); 13130–13131 (Sarah Henderson)
160 Commonwealth, *Parliamentary Debates,* Senate, 29 November 2017, 9176 (Janet Rice); Commonwealth, *Parliamentary Debates,* House of Representatives, 7 December 2017, 12999–13000 (Adam Bandt).
161 Commonwealth, *Parliamentary Debates,* Senate, 29 November 2017, 9176–9177 (Janet Rice).
162 See Commonwealth, *Parliamentary Debates,* Senate, 28 November 2017, 8965–8966 (David Fawcett), 8967 (James Paterson); Commonwealth, *Parliamentary Debates,* House of Representatives, 7 December 2017, 13008–13009 (Michael Sukkar).

- the freedom to hold, express or act on a belief about marriage,[163]
- preventing detrimental actions being taken against those who continue to hold a 'tradition' view of marriage particularly in relation to public authorities and agents or public authorities,[164]
- the right of parents who have a 'traditional' view of marriage or sexuality to remove their children from classes which teach something inconsistent with their values,[165]
- allowing an office in the Australian Defence Force overseas to refuse appointment as a person able to solemnise marriages,[166]
- ensuring charities can retain their registration with the Australian Charities and Not-for-profit Commission (ACNC) and tax free status with the Australian Taxation Office (ATO) despite continuing to hold a 'traditional' view of marriage after the legalisation of same-sex marriage,[167]
- the definition of religious bodies,[168]
- inserting an explicit guarantee of freedom of religion,[169]
- widening the exemptions relating to marriage in the *Sex Discrimination Act 1984* (Cth),[170]
- removing exemptions for religious organisations from the *Marriage Act*,[171] and
- inserting an objects clause to clarify how the *Marriage Act* interacts with State and territory legislation.[172]

163 See Commonwealth, *Parliamentary Debates*, Senate, 28 November 2017, 9058–9060 (James Paterson); Commonwealth, *Parliamentary Debates*, House of Representatives, 7 December 2017, 13038–13039 (Andrew Hastie).
164 See Commonwealth, *Parliamentary Debates*, Senate, 28 November 2017, 9060–9061 (James Paterson).
165 See Commonwealth, *Parliamentary Debates*, Senate, 28 November 2017, 9061 (James Paterson).
166 See Commonwealth, *Parliamentary Debates*, Senate, 28 November 2017, 9090–9091 (David Fawcett); Commonwealth, *Parliamentary Debates*, House of Representatives, 7 December 2017, 13056–13058 (Alex Hawke).
167 See Commonwealth, *Parliamentary Debates*, Senate, 28 November 2017, 9099–9101 (James Paterson), 9101 (David Fawcett); Commonwealth, *Parliamentary Debates*, House of Representatives, 7 December 2017, 13067–13068 (Scott Morrison), 13124–13125 (Andrew Broad).
168 See Commonwealth, *Parliamentary Debates*, Senate, 28 November 2017, 9117–9118 (David Fawcett).
169 See Commonwealth, *Parliamentary Debates*, Senate, 28 November 2017, 9125–9127 (George Brandis); Commonwealth, *Parliamentary Debates*, House of Representatives, 7 December 2017, 13130 (Sarah Henderson).
170 See Commonwealth, *Parliamentary Debates*, Senate, 29 November 2017, 9169–9170 (David Leyonhjelm).
171 See Commonwealth, *Parliamentary Debates*, Senate, 29 November 2017, 9188 (Rice); Commonwealth, *Parliamentary Debates*, House of Representatives, 7 December 2017, 13000–13001 (Adam Brandt).
172 See Commonwealth, *Parliamentary Debates*, Senate, 29 November 2017, 9178 (Janet Rice); Commonwealth, *Parliamentary Debates*, House of Representatives, 7 December 2017, 13000 (Adam Brandt).

While these amendments were rejected by both the House of Representatives and the Senate, many of the issues which they sought to address are likely to be raised during the inquiry into Freedom of Religion announcement by Prime Minister Malcom Turnbull on 22 November 2017.[173] The inquiry, chaired by Hon Philip Ruddock will 'examine whether Australian law adequately protects the human right to religious freedom.'[174] The inquiry is due to report by 31 March 2018.[175]

Child sexual abuse by religious institutions

Background

On 12 November 2012, Prime Minister Julia Gillard announced the establishment of a Royal Commission into institutional responses to instances and allegations of child sexual abuse in Australia.[176] The Letters Patent and Terms of Reference for the Royal Commission into Institutional Responses to Child Sexual Abuse (the Royal Commission) were issued on 11 January 2013[177] with the commission holding its first hearing on 3 April 2013.[178] The catalyst for Gillard's announcement was the explosive media reports about apparent cover ups by the Catholic Church.[179] This included claims by serving police officer Detective Chief Inspector Peter Fox that the Catholic Church was actively involved in protecting and covering up the abuses committed by paedophile priests.[180] These were not the first reports of such abuse or cover ups nor the first calls for a public inquiry or Royal Commission.[181]

---

173 Prime Minister Malcolm Turnbull, 'Ruddock to examine religious freedom protection in Australia' (Media Release, 22 November 2017) www.pm.gov.au/media/ruddock-examine-religious-freedom-protection-australia>;

174 Ibid; The Expert Panel comprises, Hon Philip Ruddock, Emeritus Professor Rosalind Croucher AM, Hon Dr Annabelle Bennett AO SC, Father Frank Brennan SJ AO and Professor Nicholas Aroney.

175 Prime Minister Malcolm Turnbull, above n 173.

176 Former Prime Minister Julia Guillard, 'Establishment of Royal Commission into Child Sexual Abuse' (Media Release, 12 November 2012) <>http://resources.news.com.au/files/2012/11/14/1226516/790280-aus-na-royal-commission-media-release.pdf>.

177 Royal Commission into Institutional Responses to Child Sexual Abuse, *Terms of Reference – Letters Patent* (13 November 2014) www.childabuseroyalcommission.gov.au/about-us/terms-of-reference>.

178 Commonwealth, Royal Commission into Institutional Responses to Child Sexual Abuse, *Formal Opening of The Inquiry – Transcript* (2013) available at www.childabuseroyalcommission.gov.au/documents/transcript-3-april-2013.pdf>.

179 William Budiselik, Frances Crawford and Donna Chung, 'The Australian Royal Commission into Institutional Responses to Child Sexual Abuse: Dreaming of Child Safe Organisations?' (2014) 3 *Social Sciences* 565, 567–568; Luke Beck, 'Institutional Responses to Child Sexual Abuse: The Constitutionality of a Royal Commission' (2013) 38(1) *Alternative Law Journal* 14, 14.

180 Budiselik, Crawford and Chung, above n 179, 567.

181 See, for example, Hetty Johnston and Carol Ronken, *The Need for a Royal Commission of Inquiry into the Sexual Assault of Children in Australia* (Bravehearts, 2012) available at

Inquiries into the abuse of children in institutional contexts are not new. In its early research the Royal Commission identified 83 inquires of various types conducted between 1852 and 2013 into institutions providing out-of-home care for children. The research identified three categories of inquiries. Those conducted between 1852 and the 1860s were 'concerned with establishing and refining child welfare systems,'[182] while inquiries conducted between the 1860s and 1990s were generally 'convened in response to allegations of abuse'[183] and are dubbed in the report as being about 'Damage Control.'[184] It is not until the 1990s and beyond that inquires turned their attention to 'Listening to Victims.'[185] While the majority of these inquiries do not specifically deal with the sexual abuse of children and are often limited to certain types of institutions, the vast number of such inquiries indicates the scale of the problem and the failure of previous inquires to produce meaningful results.[186]

In the period immediately preceding the establishment of the Roya Commissions several State-based inquiries were conducted into child abuse in institutional contexts including the New South Wales *Special Commission of Inquiry into Matters Relating to the Police Investigation of Certain Child Sexual Abuse Allegations in the Catholic Diocese of Maitland-Newcastle*[187] the Victorian *Inquiry*

---

https://bravehearts.org.au/wp-content/uploads/2016/06/Royal-Commission_2012. pdf>.

182 Shurlee Swain, *History of Australian Inquires Reviewing Institutions Providing Care for Children* (Royal Commission into Institutional Responses to Child Sexual Abuse, 2014) 3 also available at <>www.childabuseroyalcommission.gov.au/getattachment/76f437c1-1100-4620-a09b-32a29c538fb5/History-of-inquiries-reviewing-institutions-provid>.

183 Ibid.

184 Ibid. 7–9.

185 Ibid. 9–11.

186 See also Commonwealth, Royal Commission into Institutional Responses to Child Sexual Abuse, *Final Report – Religious Institutions Volume 16 Book 1* (2017) 227–273 also available at <>www.childabuseroyalcommission.gov.au/sites/default/files/final_report_-_volume_16_religious_institutions_book_1.pdf>.

187 Margaret Cunneen, *Special Commission of Inquiry into Matters Relating to the Police Investigation of Certain Child Sexual Abuse Allegations in the Catholic Diocese of Maitland – Newcastle Volume 1* (State of New South Wales through the Special Commission of Inquiry into Matters Relating to the Police Investigation of Certain Child Sexual Abuse Allegations in the Catholic Diocese of Maitland – Newcastle, 2014); Margaret Cunneen, *Special Commission of Inquiry into Matters Relating to the Police Investigation of Certain Child Sexual Abuse Allegations in the Catholic Diocese of Maitland – Newcastle Volume 2* (State of New South Wales through the Special Commission of Inquiry into Matters Relating to the Police Investigation of Certain Child Sexual Abuse Allegations in the Catholic Diocese of Maitland – Newcastle, 2014); Margaret Cunneen, *Special Commission of Inquiry into Matters Relating to the Police Investigation of Certain Child Sexual Abuse Allegations in the Catholic Diocese of Maitland – Newcastle Volume 3* (State of New South Wales through the Special Commission of Inquiry into Matters Relating to the Police Investigation of Certain Child Sexual Abuse Allegations in the Catholic Diocese of Maitland – Newcastle, 2014). These documents can be accessed at New South Wales – Premier & Cabinet, *Special Commission of Inquiry concerning the investigation of certain child*

into the Handling of Child Sexual Abuse by Religious and Other Organisations[188] and the Western Australian inquiry into the St Andrew's Hostel.[189]

A number of international inquiries have also been conducted into Institutional abuse of children by religious organisations. In Ireland the Ryan Commission took nine years to conduct its inquiry into the abuse of children in Irish institutions.[190] At the time of writing the United Kingdom is also conducting an *Independent Inquiry into Child Sexual Abuse*.[191] In its *Second Periodic Report on the Holy See* the United National Committee on the Rights of the Child commented that:

> The Committee is particularly concerned that in dealing with allegations of child sexual abuse, the Holy See has consistently placed the preservation of the reputation of the Church and the protection of the perpetrators above the child's best interests, as observed by several national commissions of inquiry.[192]

The Committee also

> express[ed] deep concern about child sexual abuse committed by members of the Catholic Church operating under the authority of the Holy See, wherby clerics have been involved in the sexual abuse of tens of thousands of children worldwide. The Committee is gravely concerned that the Holy See has not acknowledged the extent of the crimes committed, nor taken the necessary measures to address cases of child sexual abuse and to protect children, and has adopted policies and practices which have enabled the continuation of sexual abuse by clerics and impunity for the perpetrators.[193]

    sexual abuse allegations in the Hunter region (4 September 2017) www.dpc.nsw.gov.au/announcements/scoi_child_sexual_abuse_allegations_in_the_hunter_region>.
188 Family and Community Development Committee, *Betrayal of Trust Volume 1 – Inquiry into The Handling Of Child Abuse By Religious And Other Non-Government Organisations* (Parliament of Victoria, 2013); Family and Community Development Committee, *Betrayal of Trust Volume 2 – Inquiry into The Handling Of Child Abuse By Religious And Other Non-Government Organisations* (Parliament of Victoria, 2013). These documents can be downloaded at Parliament of Victoria, *Report and Response* (8 May 2014) www.parliament.vic.gov.au/fcdc/article/1788>.
189 Peter Blaxell, *St Andrew's Hostel Katanning: How the System and Society Failed our Children* (Government of Western Australia, 2012) available at <>https://publicsector.wa.gov.au/sites/default/files/documents/st_andrews_hostel_katanning_-_2012_report.pdf>.
190 Commission to Inquire into Child Abuse, *Pdfs* www.childabusecommission.ie/rpt/pdfs/>.
191 Independent Inquiry into Child Sexual Abuse, *Home Page* www.iicsa.org.uk/>.
192 United Nations Convention on the Rights of the Child, *Concluding Observations on the Second Periodic Report of the Holy See*, CRC/C/VAT/CO/2 (28 February 2014) 5.
193 Ibid. 9.

Terms of reference

The terms of reference for the Royal Commission were extremely wide. They did not limit the inquiry to abuse occurring within a specific time frame nor did they limit the type of institutions the Royal Commission was tasked with inquiring into. Despite the emphasis on religious organisations, and the Roman Catholic Church in particular, in the lead up to the announcement of the Royal Commission in the previous State-based inquiries, the Royal Commission was not limited to these organisations. Institution was defined widely to mean:

> any public or private body, agency, association, club, institution, organisation or other entity or group of entities of any kind (whether incorporated or unincorporated), and however described, and:
>
> includes, for example, an entity or group of entities (including an entity or group of entities that no longer exists) that provides, or has at any time provided, activities, facilities, programs or services of any kind that provide the means through which adults have contact with children, including through their families; and
>
> does not include the family.

In his opening address during the first sitting of the Royal Commission the Chair of the Royal Commission, Justice Peter McClellan, made reference to the wide definition of institution saying:

> The Royal Commission's terms of Reference are broad-ranging. They are not confined as to the time at which a person says he or she was abused and the definition of institution is broad. It extends from the organised Churches through schools, childcare centres and recreational bodies. It also includes any state run institution providing residential care for children and each of the state departments and non-government organisations responsible for organising and supervising foster care arrangements.[194]

The only specific reference to religion or the churches in the terms of reference are in terms of the benefit public and private institutions, including religious intuitions, provide to children and their families.[195]

---

194 Commonwealth, Royal Commission into Institutional Responses to Child Sexual Abuse, *Formal Opening of The Inquiry – Transcript*, above n 178.

195 Royal Commission into Institutional Responses to Child Sexual Abuse, *Terms of Reference – Letters Patent*, above n 177.

The work of the Royal Commission

The Royal Commission conducted its work via three principle methods: private sessions with survivors, public hearings and research and policy work.[196] The Royal Commission conducted 8,013 private session hearings from 7,981 survivors of child sexual abuse and received an additional 1,344 written accounts.[197] They conducted 57 public hearings and 67 private hearings relating to 57 case studies which examined 134 institutions as well as more general topic such as case study 57 which examined the nature, cases and impacts of Child sexual abuse.[198] As at 31 August 2017, 35 case study reports had been published.[199] Three were published with redactions so as not to "prejudice current or future criminal or civil proceedings."[200] A further two have not been published as the Commissioners were of the opinion that 'redactions would not have been sufficient to address potential prejudice to relevant criminal proceedings.'[201] Finally, the Royal Commission engaged in extensive research and policy work on issues relating to child sexual abuse in institutions. This included the release of issues and consultation papers, conducting roundtables and forums, consulting experts and conducting public and private hearings on policy issues.[202] In addition, the Royal Commission both commissioned and conducted its own research on a range of issues. A total of 59 research reports were published as a result of Royal Commission's research agenda.[203]

Religion and the Royal Commission

As outlined above, the Royal Commission looked at institutional responses to child sexual abuse from a range of different types of institutions. This included religious institutions such as churches and schools. Volume 16 of the Royal Commission's final report deals specifically with sexual abuse and institutional

---

196 Commonwealth, Royal Commission into Institutional Responses to Child Sexual Abuse, *Final Report – Our Inquiry Volume 1* (2017) 23 also available at www.childabuseroyalcommission.gov.au/sites/default/files/final_report_-_volume_1_our_inquiry.pdf>; the Royal commission also received written accounts from survivors where they were unable or did not wish to attend a private session see Commonwealth, Royal Commission into Institutional Responses to Child Sexual Abuse, *Final Report – Our Inquiry Volume 1* (2017) 33.

197 Commonwealth, Royal Commission into Institutional Responses to Child Sexual Abuse, *Final information update* www.childabuseroyalcommission.gov.au/sites/default/files/final_information_update.pdf>.

198 Royal Commission into Institutional Responses to Child Sexual Abuse, *Case Study 57: Nature, cause and impact of child sexual abuse* <>www.childabuseroyalcommission.gov.au/case-studies/case-study-57-nature-cause-and-impact-child-sexual-abuse>.

199 Commonwealth, Royal Commission into Institutional Responses to Child Sexual Abuse, *Final Report – Our Inquiry Volume 1*, above n 196, 41.

200 Ibid. 41.

201 Ibid. 41.

202 Ibid. 42.

203 Ibid. 45.

responses to that abuse in religious institutions.[204] One way to try and gain a sense of the extent to which the work of the Royal Commission was about religious institutions is to look at the statistics generated by the work of the Royal Commission. However, despite the extensive work of the Royal Commission, it is difficult to evaluate both the prevalence and incidents of child sexual abuse across both the Australian population and more specifically in religious institutions.[205] As a result the Royal Commission recommended that:

> The Australian Government should conduct and publish a nationally representative prevalence study on a regular basis to establish the extent of child maltreatment in institutional and non-institutional contexts in Australia.[206]

The following therefore does not attempt to analyse or comment upon either the prevalence or incident of child sexual abuse in religious institutions. Instead it aims to provide an overview of the work of the Royal Commission in order to evaluate the extent to which the work of the Royal Commission involved religious institutions.

In its final report the Royal Commission looked at six types of institutions: children's residential institutions prior to 1990;[207] institutions providing contemporary out-of-home care;[208] schools;[209] sport and recreation institutions;[210]

204 Royal Commission into Institutional Responses to Child Sexual Abuse, *Religious institutions* www.childabuseroyalcommission.gov.au/religious-institutions>.

205 Commonwealth, Royal Commission into Institutional Responses to Child Sexual Abuse, *Final Report –Religious Institutions Volume 16 Book 1*, above n 186, 302–303.

206 Commonwealth, Royal Commission into Institutional Responses to Child Sexual Abuse, *Final Report – Nature and Cause Volume 2* (2017) 16, Recommendation 2.1 also available at <>www.childabuseroyalcommission.gov.au/sites/default/files/final_report_-_volume_2_nature_and_cause.pdf>.

207 Commonwealth, Royal Commission into Institutional Responses to Child Sexual Abuse, *Final Report –Historical and Residential Institutions Volume 11* (2017) also available at <>www.childabuseroyalcommission.gov.au/sites/default/files/final_report_-_volume_11_historical_residential_institutions.pdf>.

208 Commonwealth, Royal Commission into Institutional Responses to Child Sexual Abuse, *Final Report – Contemporary Out-of-Home Care Volume 12* (2017) also available at <>www.childabuseroyalcommission.gov.au/sites/default/files/final_report_-_volume_12_contemporary_out-of-home_care.pdf>.

209 Commonwealth, Royal Commission into Institutional Responses to Child Sexual Abuse, *Final Report – Schools Volume 13* (2017) also available at www.childabuseroyalcommission.gov.au/sites/default/files/final_report_-_volume_13_schools.pdf>.

210 Commonwealth, Royal Commission into Institutional Responses to Child Sexual Abuse, *Final Report – Sport, recreation, arts, culture, community and hobby groups Volume 14* (2017) available at <>www.childabuseroyalcommission.gov.au/sites/default/files/final_report_-_volume_14_sport_recreation_arts_culture_community_and_hobby_groups.pdf>.

contemporary detention environments;[211] and religious institutions.[212] The inclusion of religious institutions as one of those to receive particular attention in the final report was influenced by a number of factors including, *inter alia*, that the Royal Commission 'received more allegations of child sexual abuse in relation to institutions managed by religious organisations than any other management type.'[213] 58.1% of survivors who spoke to the Royal Commission during a private session or who provided a written account said that their abuse occurred in an institution managed by a religious organisation.[214] Of those, 61.4% were abused in an institution managed by the Catholic Church, 14.8% by the Anglican Church and 7.2% by the Salvation Army.[215]

As the Royal Commission acknowledge, 'The relative size of a religious organisation in Australia, including the extent to which it has provided services to children, may have affected the number of allegations of child sexual abuse made in relation to that organisation.'[216]

Another statistic to look at in evaluating the extent to which the work of the Royal Commission involved religion is the number of case studies which looked at specific religious institutions. The Royal Commission identified 30 of the 57 case studies (53%) as examining child sexual abuse in religious institutions.[217] These included 15 Catholic institutions,[218] seven Anglican

---

211 Commonwealth, Royal Commission into Institutional Responses to Child Sexual Abuse, *Final Report – Contemporary detention environments Volume 15* (2017) <>www.childabuseroyalcommission.gov.au/sites/default/files/final_report_-_volume_15_contemporary_detention_environments.pdf>.

212 Commonwealth, Royal Commission into Institutional Responses to Child Sexual Abuse, *Final Report –Religious Institutions Volume 16 Book 1*, above n 186; Commonwealth, Royal Commission into Institutional Responses to Child Sexual Abuse, *Final Report –Religious Institutions Volume 16 Book 2* (2017) also available at <>www.childabuseroyalcommission.gov.au/sites/default/files/final_report_-_volume_16_religious_institutions_book_2.pdf>; Commonwealth, Royal Commission into Institutional Responses to Child Sexual Abuse, *Final Report –Religious Institutions Volume 16 Book 3* (2017) also available at <>www.childabuseroyalcommission.gov.au/sites/default/files/final_report_-_volume_16_religious_institutions_book_3_0.pdf>.

213 Commonwealth, Royal Commission into Institutional Responses to Child Sexual Abuse, *Final Report –Religious Institutions Volume 16 Book 1*, above n 186, 84.

214 Commonwealth, Royal Commission into Institutional Responses to Child Sexual Abuse, *Final information update*, above n 197.

215 Ibid.

216 Commonwealth, Royal Commission into Institutional Responses to Child Sexual Abuse, *Final Report –Religious Institutions Volume 16 Book 1*, above n 186, 302.

217 Ibid. 94.

218 Ibid. 103; Commonwealth, Royal Commission into Institutional Responses to Child Sexual Abuse, *Report of Case Study No. 4 – The experiences of four survivors with the Towards Healing process* (2015) also available at <>www.childabuseroyalcommission.gov.au/sites/default/files/file-list/Case%20Study%204%20-%20Findings%20Report%20-%20The%20experiences%20of%20four%20survivors%20with%20the%20Towards%20Healing%20process.pdf>; Commonwealth, Royal Commission into Institutional Responses to Child Sexual Abuse, *Report of Case Study No. 6 – The response of a primary school and the Toowoomba*

Catholic Education Office to the conduct of Gerard Byrnes (2015) also available at <>www. childabuseroyalcommission.gov.au/sites/default/files/file-list/Case%20Study%206%20 -%20Findings%20Report%20-%20Toowoomba%20Catholic%20school%20and%20Catholic%20Education%20Office.pdf>; Commonwealth, Royal Commission into Institutional Responses to Child Sexual Abuse, *Report of Case Study No. 8 – Mr John Ellis's experience of the Towards Healing process and civil litigation* (2015) also available at <>www. childabuseroyalcommission.gov.au/sites/default/files/file-list/Case%20Study%208%20 -%20Findings%20Report%20-%20Mr%20John%20Ellis%2C%20Towards%20Healing%20 and%20civil%20litigation.pdf>; Commonwealth, Royal Commission into Institutional Responses to Child Sexual Abuse, *Report of Case Study No. 9 – The responses of the Catholic Archdiocese of Adelaide, and the South Australian Police, to allegations of child sexual abuse at St Ann's Special School* (2015) also available at <>www.childabuseroyalcommission. gov.au/sites/default/files/file-list/Case%20Study%209%20-%20Findings%20Report%20 -%20St%20Anns%20Special%20School.pdf>; >; Commonwealth, Royal Commission into Institutional Responses to Child Sexual Abuse, *Report of Case Study No. 11 – Congregation of Christian Brothers in Western Australia response to child sexual abuse at Castledare Junior Orphanage, St Vincent's Orphanage Clontarf, St Mary's Agricultural School Tardun and Bindoon Farm School* (2014) also available at <>www.childabuseroyalcommission. gov.au/sites/default/files/file-list/Case%20Study%2011%20-%20Findings%20Report%20 -%20Christian%20Brothers.pdf>; Commonwealth, Royal Commission into Institutional Responses to Child Sexual Abuse, *Report of Case Study No. 13 – The response of the Marist Brothers to allegations of child sexual abuse against Brothers Kostka Chute and Gregory Sutton* (2015) also available at <>www.childabuseroyalcommission.gov.au/sites/default/files/ file-list/Case%20Study%2013%20-%20Findings%20Report%20-%20Marist%20Brothers. pdf>; Commonwealth, Royal Commission into Institutional Responses to Child Sexual Abuse, *Report of Case Study No. 14 – The response of the Catholic Diocese of Wollongong to allegations of child sexual abuse, and related criminal proceedings, against John Gerard Nestor, a priest of the Diocese* (2014) also available at <>www.childabuseroyalcommission. gov.au/sites/default/files/file-list/Case%20Study%2014%20-%20Findings%20Report%20 -%20Catholic%20Diocese%20of%20Wollongong.pdf>; Commonwealth, Royal Commission into Institutional Responses to Child Sexual Abuse, *Report of Case Study No. 16 – The Melbourne Response* (2015) also available at <>www.childabuseroyalcommission.gov.au/ sites/default/files/file-list/Case%20Study%2016%20-%20Findings%20Report%20-%20 Melbourne%20Response.pdf>; Commonwealth, Royal Commission into Institutional Responses to Child Sexual Abuse, *Report of Case Study No. 26 – The response of the Sisters of Mercy, the Catholic Diocese of Rockhampton and the Queensland Government to allegations of child sexual abuse at St Joseph's Orphanage, Neerkol* (2016) also available at <>www. childabuseroyalcommission.gov.au/sites/default/files/file-list/Case%20Study%2026%20 -%20Findings%20Report%20-%20St%20Josephs%20Orphanage%2C%20Neerkol.pdf>; Commonwealth, Royal Commission into Institutional Responses to Child Sexual Abuse, *Report of Case Study No. 28 - Catholic Church authorities in Ballarat* (2017) also available at <>www.childabuseroyalcommission.gov.au/sites/default/files/case_study_28_-_findings_report_-_catholic_church_authorities_in_ballarat_catholic_church_authorities_in_ ballarat2.pdf>; Royal Commission into Institutional Responses to Child Sexual Abuse, *Case Study 31: Retired Catholic Bishop Geoffrey Robinson* <>www.childabuseroyalcommission.gov.au/case-studies/case-study-31-retired-catholic-bishop-geoffrey-robinson>; Commonwealth, Royal Commission into Institutional Responses to Child Sexual Abuse, *Report of Case Study No. 35 - Catholic Archdiocese of Melbourne* (2017) also available at <>www.childabuseroyalcommission.gov.au/sites/default/files/case_study_35_-_findings_report_-_catholic_archdiocese_of_melbourne_catholic_archdiocese_of_melbourne. pdf>; Commonwealth, Royal Commission into Institutional Responses to Child Sexual

institutions[219] and three Salvation Army institutions.[220] Case studies also considered

Abuse, *Report of Case Study No. 41 – Institutional responses to allegations of the sexual abuse of children with disability* (2017) also available at <>www.childabuseroyalcommission.gov.au/sites/default/files/file-list/Case%20Study%2041%20-%20Findings%20Report%20-%20Disability%20service%20providers.pdf>; Royal Commission into Institutional Responses to Child Sexual Abuse, *Case Study 43: Catholic Church authorities in Maitland-Newcastle* <>www.childabuseroyalcommission.gov.au/case-studies/case-study-43-catholic-church-authorities-maitland-newcastle>; Royal Commission into Institutional Responses to Child Sexual Abuse, *Case Study 44: Catholic Church authorities in Armidale and Parramatta* <>www.childabuseroyalcommission.gov.au/case-studies/case-study-44-catholic-church-authorities-armidale-and-parramatta>.

219 Commonwealth, Royal Commission into Institutional Responses to Child Sexual Abuse, *Final Report –Religious Institutions Volume 16 Book 1*, above n 186, 104; The majority of case studies involving Anglican institutions involved schools; Commonwealth, Royal Commission into Institutional Responses to Child Sexual Abuse, *Report of Case Study No. 3* (2014) also available at <>www.childabuseroyalcommission.gov.au/sites/default/files/file-list/Case%20Study%203%20-%20Findings%20Report%20-%20North%20Coast%20Childrens%20Home.pdf>; Commonwealth, Royal Commission into Institutional Responses to Child Sexual Abuse, *Report of Case Study No. 12 – The response of an independent school in Perth to concerns raised about the conduct of a teacher between 1999 and 2009* (2015) also available at <>www.childabuseroyalcommission.gov.au/sites/default/files/file-list/Case%20Study%2012%20-%20Findings%20Report%20-%20Perth%20Independent%20School.pdf>; >; Commonwealth, Royal Commission into Institutional Responses to Child Sexual Abuse, *Report of Case Study No. 20 – The response of The Hutchins School and the Anglican Diocese of Tasmania to allegations of child sexual abuse at the school* (2015) also available at <>www.childabuseroyalcommission.gov.au/sites/default/files/file-list/Case%20Study%2020%20-%20Findings%20Report%20-%20The%20Hutchins%20School.pdf>; Commonwealth, Royal Commission into Institutional Responses to Child Sexual Abuse, *Report of Case Study No. 32 – The response of Geelong Grammar School to allegations of child sexual abuse of former students* (2016) also available at <>www.childabuseroyalcommission.gov.au/sites/default/files/file-list/Case%20Study%2032%20-%20Findings%20Report%20-%20Geelong%20Grammar%20School.pdf>; Commonwealth, Royal Commission into Institutional Responses to Child Sexual Abuse, *Report of Case Study No. 34 – The response of Brisbane Grammar School and St Paul's School to allegations of child sexual abuse* (2017) also available at <>www.childabuseroyalcommission.gov.au/sites/default/files/file-list/Case%20Study%2034%20-%20Findings%20Report%20-%20Brisbane%20Grammar%20School%20and%20St%20Pauls%20School.pdf>; >; Commonwealth, Royal Commission into Institutional Responses to Child Sexual Abuse, *Report of Case Study No. 36 – The response of the Church of England Boys' Society and the Anglican Dioceses of Tasmania, Adelaide, Brisbane and Sydney to allegations of child sexual abuse* (2017) also available at <>www.childabuseroyalcommission.gov.au/sites/default/files/file-list/Case%20Study%2036%20-%20Findings%20Report%20-%20Church%20of%20England%20Boys%20Society.pdf>; Commonwealth, Royal Commission into Institutional Responses to Child Sexual Abuse, *Report of Case Study No. 42 – The responses of the Anglican Diocese of Newcastle to instances and allegations of child sexual abuse* (2017) also available at <>www.childabuseroyalcommission.gov.au/sites/default/files/case_study_42_-_findings_report_-_the_responses_of_the_anglican_diocese_of_newcastle_to_instances_and_allegations_of_child_sexual_abuse.pdf>.

220 Commonwealth, Royal Commission into Institutional Responses to Child Sexual Abuse, *Final Report –Religious Institutions Volume 16 Book 1*, above n 186, 105; see also Commonwealth, Royal Commission into Institutional Responses to Child Sexual Abuse, *Report*

The Uniting Church,[221] Jehovah's Witnesses,[222] Australian Christian Churches and affiliated Pentecostal Churches,[223] Yeshiva Bondi and Yeshiva Melbourne[224] and the Australian Indigenous Ministries.[225] In addition, Case Study 21 considered the Satyananda Yoga Ashram.[226]

of *Case Study No. 5 – Response of The Salvation Army to child sexual abuse at its boys homes in New South Wales and Queensland* (2015) also available at <>www.childabuseroyalcommission.gov.au/sites/default/files/file-list/Case%20Study%205%20-%20Findings%20Report%20-%20The%20Salvation%20Army%20boys%20homes%2C%20Australia%20Eastern%20Territory.pdf>; Commonwealth, Royal Commission into Institutional Responses to Child Sexual Abuse, *Report of Case Study No. 10 – The Salvation Army's handling of claims of child sexual abuse 1989 to 2014* (2015) also available at <>www.childabuseroyalcommission.gov.au/sites/default/files/file-list/Case%20Study%2010%20-%20Findings%20Report%20-%20The%20Salvation%20Army%20claims%20handling%2C%20Australia%20Eastern%20Territory.pdf>; Commonwealth, Royal Commission into Institutional Responses to Child Sexual Abuse, *Report of Case Study No. 33 – The response of The Salvation Army (Southern Territory) to allegations of child sexual abuse at children's homes that it operated* (2016) also available at <>www.childabuseroyalcommission.gov.au/sites/default/files/file-list/case_study_33_-_findings_report_-_the_salvation_army_childrens_homes_australia_southern_territory.pdf>.

221 Commonwealth, Royal Commission into Institutional Responses to Child Sexual Abuse, *Report of Case Study No. 23 – The response of Knox Grammar School and the Uniting Church in Australia to allegations of child sexual abuse at Knox Grammar School in Wahroonga, New South Wales* (2016) also available at <>www.childabuseroyalcommission.gov.au/sites/default/files/file-list/Case%20Study%2023%20-%20Findings%20Report%20-%20Knox%20Grammar%20School.pdf>.
222 Commonwealth, Royal Commission into Institutional Responses to Child Sexual Abuse, *Report of Case Study No. 29 – The response of the Jehovah's Witnesses and Watchtower Bible and Tract Society of Australia Ltd to allegations of child sexual abuse* (2016) also available at <>www.childabuseroyalcommission.gov.au/sites/default/files/file-list/Case%20Study%2029%20-%20Findings%20Report%20-%20Jehovahs%20Witnesses.pdf>.
223 Commonwealth, Royal Commission into Institutional Responses to Child Sexual Abuse, *Report of Case Study No. 18 – The response of the Australian Christian Churches and affiliated Pentecostal churches to allegations of child sexual abuse* (2015) also available at <>www.childabuseroyalcommission.gov.au/sites/default/files/file-list/Case%20Study%2018%20-%20Findings%20Report%20-%20Australian%20Christian%20Churches.pdf>.
224 Commonwealth, Royal Commission into Institutional Responses to Child Sexual Abuse, *Report of Case Study No. 22 – The response of Yeshiva Bondi and Yeshivah Melbourne to allegations of child sexual abuse made against people associated with those institutions* (2016) also available at <>www.childabuseroyalcommission.gov.au/sites/default/files/file-list/Case%20Study%2022%20-%20Findings%20Report%20-%20Yeshiva%20Bondi%20and%20Yeshivah%20Melbourne.pdf>.
225 Commonwealth, Royal Commission into Institutional Responses to Child Sexual Abuse, *Report of Case Study No. 17 – The response of the Australian Indigenous Ministries, the Australian and Northern Territory governments and the Northern Territory police force and prosecuting authorities to allegations of child sexual abuse which occurred at the Retta Dixon Home* (2015) also available at <>www.childabuseroyalcommission.gov.au/sites/default/files/file-list/Case%20Study%2017%20-%20Findings%20Report%20-%20Retta%20Dixon%20Home.pdf>.
226 Commonwealth, Royal Commission into Institutional Responses to Child Sexual Abuse, *Report of Case Study No. 21 – The response of the Satyananda Yoga Ashram at Mangrove*

Religious institutions were also examined as part of other policy-based case studies. For example, the Catholic Church and Uniting Church was considered during Case Study 45 *Harmful Sexual Behaviours of Children in Schools.*[227] The Royal Commission identified a further six case studies as being relevant to the sexual abuse of children in religious institutions.[228] Finally, the Royal Commission conducted a number of review hearings at the end of its public hearing schedule. Seven of these were about religious institutions previously covered by a case study.[229]

At least 44 of the 57 case studies (77%) conducted by the Royal Commission involved, considered or is relevant to religious institutions.

Another measure of the extent that the Royal Commission's work involved religious institution is the number of referrals to police. As at 31 July 2017, the Royal Commission had made 2,252 referrals to police of which 1,129 (50%) related to sexual abuse in religious institutions. Referrals were made where the perpetrator was known to be alive or could have been alive and where the survivor wished the matter to be reported. Where there was an ongoing risk to children the matter was reported irrespective of the survivor's wishes.[230]

Recommendations of the Royal Commission

Another way in which to assess the extent of the Royal Commission's work which involved religious institutions is to look at the Royal Commissions' recommendations. In its Final Report, the Royal Commission made 189 recommendations.[231] These are in addition to the recommendations already made by the Royal

Mountain to allegations of child sexual abuse by the ashram's former spiritual leader in the 1970s and 1980s (2016) also available at <>www.childabuseroyalcommission.gov.au/sites/default/files/file-list/Case%20Study%2021%20-%20Findings%20Report%20-%20Satyananda%20Yoga%20Ashram.pdf>.

227 Commonwealth, Royal Commission into Institutional Responses to Child Sexual Abuse, *Report of Case Study No. 45 – Problematic and harmful sexual behaviours of children in schools* (2017) also available at <>www.childabuseroyalcommission.gov.au/sites/default/files/case_study_45_findings_report_problematic_and_harmful_sexual_behaviours_of_children_in_schools.pdf>.

228 Case study 24: *Preventing and Responding to allegations of child sexual abuse occurring in out-of-home care*; Case study 25: *Redress and Civil Litigation*; Case study 38: *Criminal justice issues relating to child sexual abuse in an institutional context*; Case study 41: *Institutional responses to allegations of the sexual abuse of children with a disability*; Case study 45: *Problematic and harmful sexual behaviours of children in schools*; Case study 46: *Criminal justice*.

229 Commonwealth, Royal Commission into Institutional Responses to Child Sexual Abuse, *Final Report –Religious Institutions Volume 16 Book 1*, above n 186, 109.

230 Commonwealth, Royal Commission into Institutional Responses to Child Sexual Abuse, *Final Report – Our Inquiry Volume 1*, above n 196, 25.

231 Commonwealth, Royal Commission into Institutional Responses to Child Sexual Abuse, *Final Report Recommendations* (2017) 3–62 also available at www.childabuseroyalcommission.gov.au/sites/default/files/final_report_-_recommendations.pdf>.

Commission in it *Working With Children Checks* Report (36),[232] *Redress and Civil Litigation* report (99),[233] *Criminal Justice* report (85).[234] In relation to religious institutions specifically, the Royal Commission made 58 recommendations.[235] Of these five related specifically to the Anglican Church,[236] 21 to the Catholic Church,[237] three to the Jehovah's Witnesses[238] and one to Jewish institutions. The remaining 28 recommendations were made in relation to all religious institutions in Australia,[239] as the Royal Commission acknowledge there is some overlap between the general recommendations to religious institutions and those made to specific religious institutions.[240] For example, Recommendation 16.48, which is made in respect of all religious institutions, recommends that:

> Religious institutions which have a rite of religious confession for children should implement a policy that requires the rite only be conducted in an open space within the clear line of sight of another adult. The policy should specify that, if another adult is not available, the rite of religious confession for the child should not be performed.[241]

Recommendation 16.26, which was made specifically in relation to the Catholic Church, recommends:

> The Australian Catholic Bishops Conference should consult with the Holy See, and make public any advice received, in order to clarify whether:

232 Ibid. 63–72; Commonwealth, Royal Commission into Institutional Responses to Child Sexual Abuse, *Working with Children Checks Report* (2015) also available at <>www.childabuseroyalcommission.gov.au/sites/default/files/final_report_-_working_with_children_checks_report.pdf>.

233 Commonwealth, Royal Commission into Institutional Responses to Child Sexual Abuse, *Final Report Recommendations*, above n 231, 73–90; Commonwealth, Royal Commission into Institutional Responses to Child Sexual Abuse, *Redress and Civil Litigation Report* (2015) also available at <>www.childabuseroyalcommission.gov.au/sites/default/files/file-list/final_report_-_redress_and_civil_litigation.pdf>.

234 Commonwealth, Royal Commission into Institutional Responses to Child Sexual Abuse, *Final Report Recommendations*, above n 231, 91–114; Commonwealth, Royal Commission into Institutional Responses to Child Sexual Abuse, *Criminal Justice Report – Parts III – VI* (2017) also available at <>www.childabuseroyalcommission.gov.au/sites/default/files/file-list/final_report_-_criminal_justice_report_-_parts_iii_to_vi.pdf>; Commonwealth, Royal Commission into Institutional Responses to Child Sexual Abuse, *Criminal Justice Report – Parts VII – X* (2017) also available at <>www.childabuseroyalcommission.gov.au/sites/default/files/file-list/final_report_-_criminal_justice_report_-_parts_vii_to_x_and_appendices.pdf>.

235 Commonwealth, Royal Commission into Institutional Responses to Child Sexual Abuse, *Final Report –Religious Institutions Volume 16 Book 1*, above n 186, 71–82.

236 Ibid. 72.

237 Ibid. 73–77.

238 Ibid. 77.

239 Ibid. 78–82.

240 Ibid. 78.

241 Ibid. 81.

information received from a child during the sacrament of reconciliation that they have been sexually abused is covered by the seal of confession

if a person confesses during the sacrament of reconciliation to perpetrating child sexual abuse, absolution can and should be withheld until they report themselves to civil authorities.[242]

A number of the recommendations in the *Working with Children Checks, Redress and Civil Litigation* and *Criminal Justice* reports also relate specifically to religious institutions. For example, the Royal Commission states in Recommendation 35 of the *Criminal Justice* report that:

Each state and territory government should ensure that the legislation it introduces to create the criminal offence of failure to report recommended in Recommendation 33 addresses religious confessions as follows:

a   The criminal offence of failure to report should apply in relation to knowledge gained or suspicions that are or should have been formed, in whole or in part, on the basis of information disclosed in or in connection with a religious confession.

b   The legislation should exclude any existing excuse, protection or privilege in relation to religious confessions to the extent necessary to achieve this objective.

c   Religious confession should be defined to include a confession about the conduct of a person associated with the institution made by a person to a second person who is in religious ministry in that second person's professional capacity according to the ritual of the church or religious denomination concerned.[243]

In addition, many of the more general recommendations throughout both the Final Report and earlier reports are relevant to all institutions that care for children and many of the recommendations for changes to federal and States laws will impact upon religious institutions both directly and indirectly. Of particular note is the recommendation in the *Redress and Civil Litigation* report to establish a national redress scheme for survivors of childhood sexual abuse.[244] The Commonwealth Redress Scheme for Institutional Child Sexual Abuse Bill 2017 (Cth) was introduced to the federal Parliament by the minister for Social Services,

242 Ibid. 77.
243 Commonwealth, Royal Commission into Institutional Responses to Child Sexual Abuse, *Criminal Justice Report–Executive Summary and Parts I–II* (2017) 54 also available at <www.child-abuseroyalcommission.gov.au/sites/default/files/file-list/final_report_-_criminal_justice_report_-_executive_summary_and_parts_i_to_ii.pdf>
244 Commonwealth, Royal Commission into Institutional Responses to Child Sexual Abuse, *Redress and Civil Litigation Report*, above n 233, 26, 322.

Christian Porter, on 26 October 2017.[245] It is intended that the scheme will commence in July 2018 and run for 10 years.[246] Survivors will be eligible to apply for compensation under the scheme if they were abused in a participating institution while a child prior to the commencement of the scheme.[247]

As recommended by the Royal Commission, the scheme will operate on the basis that 'the responsible entity pays.'[248] However, the scheme relies for its success on institutions responsible for the past sexual abuse of children opting in. While mechanisms are built into the scheme to encourage participation,[249] at the time of writing it is unclear how many of Australia's religious and other institutions will opt into the scheme. Given the number of survivors who were abused in religious institutions the scheme's success may largely rely on institutions such as the Catholic Church, Anglican Church and Salvation Army along with the States and territories opting in. At the time of writing the Bill is before the Senate Community Affairs Legislation Committee. Their report is due in March 2018.

The majority of the recommendations directed at religious institutions deal with issues such as the selection and training of clergy, the handling of complaints and the adoption of appropriate standards and procedures for the care of children. However, a small number deal directly with religious belief, practice or doctrine. For example, Recommendation 16.30, which was directed towards at Jewish institutions states:

All Jewish institutions in Australia should ensure that their complaint handling policies explicitly state that the halachic concepts of mesirah, moser and loshon horo do not apply to the communication and reporting of allegations of child sexual abuse to police and other civil authorities.[250]

In their Report Case Study 22: *The Response of Satyanada Yeshiva Bondi and Yeshivah Melbourne to allegations of Child sexual abuse made against people associated with those institutions* the Royal Commission identified the application of the Jewish law concepts of *mesirah, moser* and *loshon horo* in relation to the communication about and reporting of child sexual abuse to authorities as having 'caused significant concern, controversy and confusion amongst members of the

245 Commonwealth, *Parliamentary Debates*, House of Representatives, 26 October 2017, 12128 (Christian Porter).
246 Ibid. 12130–12131 (Christian Porter).
247 Ibid. 12131 (Christian Porter).
248 Ibid. 12130 (Christian Porter), 12133 (Christian Porter); Commonwealth, Royal Commission into Institutional Responses to Child Sexual Abuse, *Redress and Civil Litigation Report*, above n 233, 30–32, recommendations 34 and 35.
249 Commonwealth, *Parliamentary Debates*, House of Representatives, 26 October 2017, 12132–12133 (Christian Porter).
250 Commonwealth, Royal Commission into Institutional Responses to Child Sexual Abuse, *Final Report –Religious Institutions Volume 16 Book 1*, above n 186, 77.

Chabad-Lubavitch communities.'[251] In particular 'because of the way those concepts were applied, some members of those communities were discouraged from reporting child sexual abuse.'[252] *Mesirah* is 'a prohibition upon a Jew informing upon, or handing over another Jew to, a secular Authority.' *Moser* is 'a term of contempt applied to a Jew who has committed mesirah.' *Loshon horo* is 'the act of gossiping (or speaking negatively) of another Jew or a Jewish institution or place. *Loshon horo* is discouraged under Jewish law, even if what is said about a person, institution or place is objectively true.'[253]

Recommendations by the Royal Commission which relate to religious belief, practice or doctrine have implications for freedom of religion should the government attempt to force religious institutions to comply with the Recommendations of the Royal Commission. Two such recommendations are considered below in relation to the Jehovah's Witnesses and Catholic Church.

The Jehovah's Witnesses two-witness rule

In its final report the Royal Commission made three recommendations in relation to the Jehovah's Witnesses. These relate to the scripturally based two-witness rule, the exclusion of women from certain roles including in relation to the investigation of allegations of child-sexual abuse and shunning of individuals who leave the Jehovah's Witnesses.[254] All three are matters of religious belief, practice or doctrine.[255] This section will consider the two-witness rule which is based on specific scriptural passages and is fundamental in determining how the Jehovah's Witness organisation responds to an allegation of child sexual abuse.

The Jehovah's Witnesses interpret the bible literally and base their policies and procedures, including in relation to child sexual abuse, on their interpretation of scriptural passages.[256] The two-witness rule requires that, in the absence of a confession from the accused,[257] the testimony of two or three credible witnesses

---

251 Commonwealth, Royal Commission into Institutional Responses to Child Sexual Abuse, *Report of Case Study No. 22 – The response of Yeshiva Bondi and Yeshivah Melbourne to allegations of child sexual abuse made against people associated with those institutions*, above n 224, 16–17.

252 Ibid. 17.

253 Ibid. 9.

254 Commonwealth, Royal Commission into Institutional Responses to Child Sexual Abuse, *Final Report –Religious Institutions Volume 16 Book 1*, above n 186, 77.

255 Commonwealth, Royal Commission into Institutional Responses to Child Sexual Abuse, *Final Report –Religious Institutions Volume 16 Book 3*, above n 212, 100.

256 Ibid. 76; the Jehovah's Witnesses use the New World Translation of the Holy Scriptures (NWT) see Commonwealth, Royal Commission into Institutional Responses to Child Sexual Abuse, *Report of Case Study No. 29 – The response of the Jehovah's Witnesses and Watchtower Bible and Tract Society of Australia Ltd to allegations of child sexual abuse*, above n 222, 21; for a more detailed discussion of the beliefs and practices of the Jehovah's Witnesses see Chapter 7.

257 See Josh 7:19 NWT which reads "Then Joshua said to A'chan: "My son, please, honor Jehovah the God of Israel and make confession to him. Tell me, please, what you have done. Do not hide it from me."

to the same incident is required before a finding of wrong doing can be made.[258] This is primarily based on two biblical verses[259] – Deuteronomy 19:15:

> No single witness may convict another for any error or any sin that he may commit. On the testimony of two witnesses or on the testimony of three witnesses the matter should be established.[260]

And John 8:17:

> Also, in your own Law it is written: 'The witness of two men is true.[261]

In the absence of two credible witnesses 'the congregation will continue to view the one accused as an innocent person' and the matter will be left 'in Jehovah's hands.'[262] Despite finding that the two-witness rule was scripturally based, and therefore a matter of religious belief, the Royal Commission found that:

> the application of inflexible, scripture-based policies and practices, which are, by and large, inappropriate and unsuitable for application in cases of child sexual abuse, is a central contributor to the inadequate institutional responses to allegations of child sexual abuse by the Jehovah's Witness organisation.[263]

And that:

> Regardless of the biblical origins of the two-witness rule, the Jehovah's Witness organisation's continued application of the rule to complaints of child sexual abuse is wrong.[264]

Throughout Case Study 29 members of the Jehovah's Witnesses defended their use of the two-witness rule, even where the elders involved agreed that the rule produced an 'unfair' outcome.[265] The rule was applied even where the elders believed the alleged abuse had in fact taken place.[266] The leaders of the Jehovah's Witnesses do not believe they are free to change or depart from the rule given

---

258 Commonwealth, Royal Commission into Institutional Responses to Child Sexual Abuse, *Report of Case Study No. 29 – The response of the Jehovah's Witnesses and Watchtower Bible and Tract Society of Australia Ltd to allegations of child sexual abuse*, above n 222, 25.

259 Ibid. 25.

260 Deuteronomy 19:15 NWT.

261 John 8:17 NWT.

262 Commonwealth, Royal Commission into Institutional Responses to Child Sexual Abuse, *Report of Case Study No. 29 – The response of the Jehovah's Witnesses and Watchtower Bible and Tract Society of Australia Ltd to allegations of child sexual abuse*, above n 222, 25–26.

263 Commonwealth, Royal Commission into Institutional Responses to Child Sexual Abuse, *Final Report –Religious Institutions Volume 16 Book 3*, above n 212, 100.

264 Ibid. 101.

265 Ibid.

266 Ibid.

its scriptural basis. As Rodney Spinks, a senior elder in the Jehovah's Witnesses origination in Australia,[267] explained:

> So if the question is are Jehovah's Witnesses likely or open to changing what we see as a scriptural requirement, repeated by Christ Jesus himself, that before you could take judicial action, in the absence of other evidence or confession, that that aspect of the process would need to be held in abeyance. Do I think there is flexibility to change that? I don't see how, because it's a clear scriptural injection.[268]

During the public hearing into Case Study 29, Angus Stewart, Council Assisting the Royal Commission, took Geoffrey Jackson, a member of the Governing body of the Jehovah's Witnesses in New York,[269] through the rules in Deuteronomy relating to sexual abuse and the relevant penalties. The thrust of the questioning is an attempt to question the scriptural basis for the two-witness rule. For example, Stewart asked:

> Is it not the case that had Jesus been asked about a case of sexual abuse, he may have referred back to this part of Deuteronomy and said that it's not required to have two witnesses?[270]

To which Jackson responded:

> I certainly would like to ask Jesus that, and I can't at the moment, I hope to in the future. But that's a hypothetical question which, if we had the answer, then we could support what you said.[271]

---

267 Commonwealth, Royal Commission into Institutional Responses to Child Sexual Abuse, *Report of Case Study No. 29 – The response of the Jehovah's Witnesses and Watchtower Bible and Tract Society of Australia Ltd to allegations of child sexual abuse*, above n 222, 17.

268 Commonwealth, Royal Commission into Institutional Responses to Child Sexual Abuse, *Public Hearing – Case Study 29 (Day 152) – Transcript* (2015) 15705 also available at <>www.childabuseroyalcommission.gov.au/sites/default/files/file-list/Case%20 Study%2029%20-%20Transcript%20-%20Jehovahs%20Witnesses%20-%20Day%20152%20 -%2004082015.pdf>; see also Commonwealth, Royal Commission into Institutional Responses to Child Sexual Abuse, *Public Hearing – Case Study 29 (Day 153) - Transcript* (2015) 15833 also available at <>www.childabuseroyalcommission.gov.au/sites/default/ files/file-list/Case%20Study%2029%20-%20Transcript%20-%20Jehovahs%20Witnesses%20 -%20Day%20153%20-%2005082015.pdf>.

269 Commonwealth, Royal Commission into Institutional Responses to Child Sexual Abuse, *Public Hearing – Case Study 29 (Day 155) – Transcript* (2015) 15930–15933 also available at <>www.childabuseroyalcommission.gov.au/sites/default/files/file-list/Case%20 Study%2029%20-%20Transcript%20-%20Jehovahs%20Witnesses%20-%20Day%20155%20 -%2014082015.pdf>.

270 Ibid. 15971.

271 Ibid. 15971.

In effect the questioner is attempting to tell a believer that they have got their scriptural interpretation wrong and should therefore amend their religious practice in line with an external opinion of what the religion should believe. However, religious belief is not a matter of logic. As outlined by Murphy J in *Church of the New Faith v Commissioner of Pay Roll Tax (Vic)* (the *Scientology Case*):[272]

> Administrators and judges must resist the temptation to hold that groups or institutions are not religious because claimed religious beliefs or practices seem absurd, fraudulent, evil or novel; or because the group or institution is new, the numbers of adherents small, the leaders hypocrites.[273]

Equally, administrators and judges must resist the temptation to find that a particular religious belief or practice is incorrect because it appears, to an outside observer, to be inconsistent with other beliefs or practices of the faith. As Lord Bingham of Cornhill explained in *R v Secretary of State Education and Employment; Ex Parte Williamson*[274]

> it is not for the court to embark on an inquiry into the asserted belief and judge its 'validity' by some objective standard such as the source material upon which the claimant founds his belief.[275]

It is one thing to be critical of a particular religious belief or practice. It is however another to suggest that a religious institution or individual believer has gotten their own religion wrong.[276]

The two-witness rule by its very nature 'will more often than not operate in favour of a perpetrator of child sexual abuse' who will as a result of its application 'not only avoid sanction but will also remain in the congregation and the community with their rights intact and with the capacity to interact with their victim.'[277] On this basis it is open to criticism. However, suggesting that the Jehovah's Witnesses have got their own beliefs wrong is taking that criticism too far.

While the State is unlikely to legislate to require the Jehovah's Witnesses to specifically abandon the two-witness rule, other recommended amendments to the criminal law may impact upon the Jehovah's Witnesses if they continue to apply the two-witness rule. For example, in their report into Criminal Justice, the Royal

---

272 (1983) 154 CLR 120.

273 Ibid. 150 (Murphy J).

274 [2005] UKHL 15 (24 February 2005).

275 Ibid. [24].

276 Renae Barker, 'Rebutting the Ban the Burqa Rhetoric: A Critical Analysis of the Arguments for a Ban on the Islamic Face Veil in Australia' (2016) 37(1) *Adelaide Law Review* 191, 199–201.

277 Commonwealth, Royal Commission into Institutional Responses to Child Sexual Abuse, *Report of Case Study No. 29 – The response of the Jehovah's Witnesses and Watchtower Bible and Tract Society of Australia Ltd to allegations of child sexual abuse*, above n 222, 65.

Commission recommended the creation of 'a criminal offence of failure to report targeted at child sexual abuse in an institutional context.'[278] The Royal Commission recommended that such an offence apply 'if the person fails to report to police in circumstances where they know, suspect, or should have suspected ... that an adult associated with the institution was sexually abusing or had sexually abused a child.'[279] An elder of the Jehovah's Witness to whom child sexual abuse was reported and who failed to act by reporting the allegation to police on the basis of the two witness rule would arguably fall foul of such an offence. Of the at least 1,006 perpetrators of child sexual abuse recorded in the Jehovah's Witnesses own case files since the 1950s, none were reported to the police.[280]

Seal of the confession and mandatory reporters

The Royal Commission considered the issue of the religious ritual of confession – also referred to as penance, forgiveness and reconciliation – in three separate contexts. In their report on *Criminal Justice*, the Commission considered whether or not information about child sexual abuse received during the sacrament of confession should be exempt from criminal failure to report offences.[281] Similarly in Volume 7 of the Final Report: *Improving Institutional Responding and Reporting*, the Commission considered the Royal Commission consider the sacrament of confession and whether it should be exempt from laws relating to mandatory reporting of child sexual abuse to protection authorities.[282] Finally in Book 16 of the Final Report: *Religious Institutions*, the Royal Commission considered the sacrament of confession as a contributing factor to the Catholic Church's poor response to allegations of child sexual abuse.[283] While the Catholic Church is not the only church to practice a ritual or sacrament of confession, the focus of this section will be on the beliefs and practices of the Catholic Church.[284]

---

278 Commonwealth, Royal Commission into Institutional Responses to Child Sexual Abuse, *Criminal Justice Report – Executive Summary and Parts I – II*, above n 243, 123 (Recommendation 33).

279 Ibid.

280 Commonwealth, Royal Commission into Institutional Responses to Child Sexual Abuse, *Final Report –Religious Institutions Volume 16 Book 3*, above n 212, 88.

281 Commonwealth, Royal Commission into Institutional Responses to Child Sexual Abuse, *Criminal Justice Report – Parts III – VI*, above n 234, 216–224.

282 Commonwealth, Royal Commission into Institutional Responses to Child Sexual Abuse, *Final Report – Improving institutional responding and reporting – Volume 7* (2017) 97–100 also available at <>www.childabuseroyalcommission.gov.au/sites/default/files/final_report_-_volume_7_improving_institutional_responding_and_reporting.pdf>.

283 Commonwealth, Royal Commission into Institutional Responses to Child Sexual Abuse, *Final Report –Religious Institutions Volume 16 Book 2*, above n 212, 849–872.

284 The Anglican, Orthodox and Lutheran Churches also have a rite of confession see Commonwealth, Royal Commission into Institutional Responses to Child Sexual Abuse, *Final Report –Religious Institutions Volume 16 Book 2*, above n 212, 850. For a discussion of the contribution of the Anglican rite of confession to their poor response to allegations of child sexual abuse see Commonwealth, Royal Commission into Institutional Responses to Child Sexual Abuse, *Final Report – Religious Institutions Volume 16 Book 1*, above n 186, 739–748.

A number of recommendations in both the *Criminal Justice* report and Final Report specifically deal with the issue of religious confessions.[285] As outlined above, in its *Criminal Justice* report the Royal Commission recommended the creation of 'a criminal offence of failure to report targeted at child sexual abuse in an institutional context.'[286] They further recommended that:

> The criminal offence of failure to report should apply in relation to knowledge gained or suspicions that are or should have been formed, in whole or in part, on the basis of information disclosed in or in connection with a religious confession.[287]

In Volume 7 of their Final Report the Royal Commission recommended that:

> State and territory governments should amend laws concerning mandatory reporting to child protection authorities to achieve national consistency in reporter groups.
>
> At a minimum, state and territory governments should also include the following groups of individuals as mandatory reporters in every jurisdiction:
>
> a   out-of-home care workers (excluding foster and kinship/relative carers)
> b   youth justice workers
> c   early childhood workers
> d   registered psychologists and school counsellors
> e   people in religious ministry.[288]

They further recommended that:

> Laws concerning mandatory reporting to child protection authorities should not exempt persons in religious ministry from being required to report knowledge or suspicions formed, in whole or in part, on the basis of information disclosed in or in connection with a religious confession.[289]

---

285 See Commonwealth, Royal Commission into Institutional Responses to Child Sexual Abuse, *Final Report – Religious Institutions Volume 16 Book 1*, above n 186, 77, 81 (Recommendation 16.48); Commonwealth, Royal Commission into Institutional Responses to Child Sexual Abuse, *Final Report – Improving institutional responding and reporting – Volume 7*, above n 282, 100 (Recommendation 7.4); Commonwealth, Royal Commission into Institutional Responses to Child Sexual Abuse, *Criminal Justice Report – Parts III – VI*, above n 234, 224 (Recommendation 35).

286 Ibid. 213–214 (Recommendation 33).

287 Ibid. 224 (Recommendation 35).

288 Commonwealth, Royal Commission into Institutional Responses to Child Sexual Abuse, *Final Report – Improving institutional responding and reporting – Volume 7*, above n 282, 100 (Recommendation 7.3).

289 Ibid 100 (Recommendation 7.4).

'The concept of confession and forgiveness is at the very heart of Christianity.'[290] However, the Royal Commission identified the practice of both the Catholic and Anglican Churches to view child sexual abuse as a sin which could be repented from and therefore forgiven, as opposed to a crime for which punishment attached, as a contributing factor to both Churches' poor institutional response to child sexual abuse.[291]

Catholics over the age of seven are required by Canon Law to make a confession at least once per year.[292] Priests who hear a confession are bound, under Canon 983, not to reveal anything which they hear in confession:

> The *sacramental seal* is inviolable; therefore it is *absolutely forbidden* for a *confessor* to *betray* in any *way* a *penitent* in *words* or in any *manner* and for any *reason*.[293]

Violation of this Canon results in automatic excommunication which can only be lifted by the Pope.[294] While attendance at ritual confession has declined significantly in Australia in recent years[295] it is still an important religious practice. However, children attending Catholic schools continue to take part in ritual confession.[296] It is considered to be a sacrament, one of seven recognised by the Catholic Church, and as such is an important part of Catholic belief and practice.[297]

While the Royal Commission outlined many compelling reasons why information received via ritual confession should not be exempt from either form of mandatory reporting laws, this does not dispel the fact that requiring priest who hear a confession about child sexual abuse to report that information to the police or

---

290 Renae Mabey, 'The Priest-Penitent Privilege in Australia and Its Consequences (2006) 13(2) *ELaw* 51, 63.

291 Commonwealth, Royal Commission into Institutional Responses to Child Sexual Abuse, *Final Report –Religious Institutions Volume 16 Book 2*, above n 212, 856–862; Commonwealth, Royal Commission into Institutional Responses to Child Sexual Abuse, *Final Report –Religious Institutions Volume 16 Book 1*, above n 186, 739–743.

292 Gerard Sheehy, The Canon Law Society of Great Britain and Ireland and Canadian Canon Law Society, *The Canon Law Letter and Spirit* (Geoffrey Chapman, 1995) 539.

293 Ibid. 535–536.

294 Commonwealth, Royal Commission into Institutional Responses to Child Sexual Abuse, *Final Report –Religious Institutions Volume 16 Book 2*, above n 212, 854.

295 Commonwealth, Royal Commission into Institutional Responses to Child Sexual Abuse, *Criminal Justice Report – Parts III – VI*, above n 234, 220–221.

296 Ibid. 220.

297 Commonwealth, Royal Commission into Institutional Responses to Child Sexual Abuse, *Final Report –Religious Institutions Volume 16 Book 2*, above n 212, 850.

other authorities abrogates their freedom of religion. The Royal Commission acknowledged the impact of their recommendations stating:

> We acknowledge the submissions and evidence we received that a civil law duty on clergy to report information learned in religious confessions, even of child sexual offending, would constitute an intrusion into the religious practice and that complying with that obligation would raise serious issues of conscience for Catholic clergy. We accept this would be the case for any faith in which clergy are required by that faith's teachings or particular laws to keep religious confessions confidential.[298]

In concluding that an exemption to mandatory reporting laws should not be given for information received via ritual confession, the Royal Commission balanced the freedom of religion of priests against the right of children to be protected from sexual abuse.[299] In particular, they noted that the right to freedom of religion is not absolute and that 'the right to practise one's religious beliefs must accommodate civil society's obligation to provide for the safety of all.'[300] In particular:

> Institutions directed to caring for and providing services for children, including religious institutions, must provide an environment where children are safe from sexual abuse. Reporting information relevant to child sexual abuse to the police is critical to ensuring the safety of children.[301]

The response from the Catholic Church to these, and the other 20 recommendations, made in relation to the Catholic Church has been mixed. Archbishops Denis Hart and Anthony Fisher have both stated that they could not support any recommendations which would require priests to break the seal of confession.[302] By contrast, Pope Frances stated that:

> The final report of the Royal Commission into Institutional Responses to Child Sex Abuse in Australia is the result of the accurate efforts made by the Commission in recent years and deserves to be studied in depth.[303]

---

298 Commonwealth, Royal Commission into Institutional Responses to Child Sexual Abuse, *Criminal Justice Report – Parts III – VI*, above n 234, 218.
299 Ibid. 218–219.
300 Ibid. 219.
301 Ibid.
302 Riley Stuart, *Royal commission: Celibacy and confessional overhaul proposed in child sex abuse findings* (18 December 2017) ABC News <>www.abc.net.au/news/2017-12-15/royal-commission-into-child-abuse-makes-almost-200-new-findings/9261286>; Riley Stuart, *Pope Francis says sex abuse royal commission findings should be 'studied in depth'* (17 December 2017) ABC News www.abc.net.au/news/2017-12-16/pope-francis-responds-to-royal-commission-report/9265466>.
303 Riley Stuart, *Pope Francis says sex abuse royal commission findings should be 'studied in depth'*, above n 302.

Although he did not go as far as to suggest any changes the Church may make in response to the Royal Commission's recommendations.

Conclusion

The relationship between the State and religion in Australia in relation to terrorism, same-sex marriage and institutional responses to child sexual abuse will continue to evolve as the religious demographics and societal expectations about the role and place of religion continue to change. While these issues have only been at the forefront of the State–religion relationship for a relatively short period of time they have already had a significant influence on that relationship. Australia's response to terrorism, and particular terrorism inspired by religious extremism, has had and will continue to have a profound influence on both Australia's own Muslim population along with Australia's relationship with Muslim majority nations. The debate around same-sex marriage and its legalisation have brought to the fore issues relating to freedom of religion and have forced both the State and religious organisations to confront these issues directly. The Royal Commission into Institutional responses to Child Sexual Abuse has shone a light on the poor past practice of some of Australia's most respected religious institutions. As a result, the State has been forced to face its own responsibilities in setting the legal matrix in which religious and other institutions will continue to care for children into the future. As a result, all three issues are likely to continue to have a profound effect on the State–religion relationship in Australia into the future.

7 Restricting religion

Introduction

Freedom of religion and belief is protected in numerous international and domestic human rights instruments. For example, Article 18(1) of the *International Covenant on Civil and Political Rights* states that:

> Everyone shall have the right to freedom of thought, conscience and religion. This right shall include freedom to have or to adopt a religion or belief of his choice, and freedom, either individually or in community with others and in public or private, to manifest his religion or belief in worship, observance, practice and teaching.[1]

Despite the fact that Australia is (in)famous as being the last western democracy without a Charter or Bill of Rights, there is a limited protection for freedom of religion in Section 116 of the *Australian Constitution*. However, as identified in Chapter 4, Section 116 operates primarily as a restriction on State power rather than as an individual freedom.

Throughout Australia's history there are numerous examples of the State restricting religious practice. Section 116 has been of little utility in providing protection against these restrictions. In many cases Section 116 did not apply either because the restriction took place before Federation in 1901 or because it was carried out at a State or territory level. However, even where the restriction was implemented by the federal government, and Section 116 therefore applied, it offered no protection.

This chapter examines a number of well-known examples of State restrictions on religious practice across Australia's history: restrictions on Roman Catholics in the early colony, the banning of the Jehovah's Witnesses during World War Two, the banning of Scientology, the provision of blood transfusions to the children of Jehovah's Witnesses and restriction of the wearing of face coverings. These examples

---

1 *International Covenant on Civil and Political Rights*, opened for signature 16 December 1966, 999 UNTS 171 (entered into force 23 March 1976) art 18(1).

have been selected as representative of the array of restrictions imposed by the State in Australia. They cover a wide time span, stretching from prior to the arrival of the first fleet in 1788 through to the federal parliamentary 'burqa ban' in 2014.

The examples covered in this chapter are by no means the only examples of State restrictions on religious practice in Australia. Other current and historical examples include the impact of Sabbath laws on Jews and seventh day Adventist prior to Federation,[2] restrictions on FGM,[3] Polygamy,[4] Paganism and witchcraft,[5] the exclusion of unvaccinated children from childcare in some States[6] and the requirement for Sikh men to wear a helmet while riding a motor bike.[7]

As discussed in Chapters 2 and 4, both international law and Australia's High Court affirm that freedom of religion in not absolute. Article 18(3) of the *International Covenant on Civil and Political Rights* states that:

> Freedom to manifest one's religion or beliefs may be subject only to such limitations as are prescribed by law and are necessary to protect public safety, order, health or morals or the fundamental rights and freedoms of others.[8]

While in the *Jehovah's Witness Case* Latham CJ affirmed that 'free,' in the context of Section 116, did not mean license. Rather, it meant free within the confines of the maintenance of the community and civil government.[9]

---

2 Tony Blackshield, 'Religion and Australian Constitutional Law' in Peter Radan, Denis Meyerson and Rosalind F Croucher (eds), *Law and Religion: God, the State and the Common Law* (Routledge, 2nd ed, 2005) 83–84.

3 *Crimes Act 1900* (ACT) s 73–77; *Crimes Act 1900* (NSW) s 45; *Criminal Code Act* (NT) s 186A–186D; *Criminal Code 1899* (Qld) s 323A–323B; *Criminal Law Consolidation Act 1935* (SA) s 33–33B; *Criminal Code Act 1924* (Tas) s 178A, s389; *Crimes Act 1958* (Vic) s 32–34A; *The Criminal Code* (WA) s 306; see also Australian Government, *Review of Australia's Female Genital Mutilation Legal Framework* (March 2013) Attorney-General's Department <www.ag.gov.au/Publications/Documents/ReviewofAustraliasfemalegenitalmutilationlegalframework/Review%20of%20Australias%20female%20genital%20mutilation%20legal%20framework.pdf>.

4 Human Rights and Equal Opportunities Commission, *Article 18 Freedom of Religion and Belief* (Commonwealth of Australia, 1998), 41–43.

5 Human Rights and Equal Opportunities Commission, *Article 18 Freedom of Religion and Belief* (Commonwealth of Australia, 1998), 60–65; *Criminal Code 1899* (Qld) (as passed) s 432, which previously criminalised witchcraft, was omitted by the *Justice and Other Legislation (Miscellaneous Provisions) Act 2000* (Qld).

6 Renae Barker, 'No Jab-No pay, No Jab-No Play, No Exceptions; The Removal of Conscientious and Religious Exemptions from Australia's Childhood Vaccination Policies' (2017) (2) *Quaderni di diritto e politica ecclesiastica* 513

7 Currently only South Australia and Western Australia provide exemptions, see *Road Traffic (Road Rules – Ancillary and Miscellaneous Provisions) Regulations 2014* (SA) reg 34; *Road Traffic Act* 1961 (SA) s 162C(4)(a); *Road Traffic Code* 2000 (WA) s 222(3)(a).

8 *International Covenant on Civil and Political Rights*, opened for signature 16 December 1966, 999 UNTS 171 (entered into force 23 March 1976).

9 *The Adelaide Company of Jehovah's Witnesses Inc v The Commonwealth* (1943) 67 CLR 116, 131 (Latham CJ).

It is therefore not the aim of this chapter to determine the desirability of any of the restrictions discussed. Many are arguably based on good public policy considerations. Instead, the chapter demonstrates that restrictions on religious practice have existed across Australia's history, they are not unique to any one time period and therefore cannot be attributed to features unique to certain time periods of Australia's history such as increased National security concerns during the world wars or during the current 'war on terror.' Further, it illustrates the limited utility of Section 116 of Australia's *Constitution* in protecting against State restrictions on religious practice.

While restrictions on religious practice can be seen throughout Australia's history, they are not uniform in character. Restrictions on Roman Catholics in the early Australian colony, Jehovah's Witnesses during World War Two and the Church of Scientology in the 1960s were overt in nature, targeting the religion as a whole. By contrast, the imposition of blood transfusions on minors against their religious beliefs and the restrictions on facial coverings target specific religious practices. In these cases, the restrictions are couched in neutral, non-religious, language. It is only when the history, background, the practical effect and impact of these laws are examined closely that their restrictive and religious nature becomes clear.

Restrictions on Roman Catholics

Although Roman Catholics today make up the largest single Christian denomination, this has not always been the case.[10] Until 1986 the Anglican Church (Church of England) was the dominant Christian denomination in Australia.[11] Roman Catholics were the first religious group in Australia to face discrimination and restrictions on their ability to practice their faith. These began before the arrival of the first fleet and arguably continued well into the twentieth century. This section will focus on the restrictions face by Roman Catholics in the very early Australian colony. The examples covered bellow demonstrates that restrictions on religious practice have been present in Australia from its very foundations. In the early colony, the State, via the autocratic governors, had ultimate power over all things temporal and spiritual.

Restrictions on Roman Catholics in the early colony took two main forms: first, the State prevented Roman Catholic priests from travelling to and ministering in the new colony; second, when Roman Catholic priests were permitted to officially minister, strict regulations were imposed upon how and when they could practise their religion.

---

10 *Religion in Australia – 2016 Census Data Summary* (28 June 2017) Australian Bureau of Statistics <www.abs.gov.au/ausstats/abs@.nsf/Lookup/by%20Subject/2071.0~2016~Main%20Features~Religion%20Data%20Summary~70>.

11 Ian Castles, *Religion: Census of Population and Housing 30 June 1986* (3 October 2008) Australian Bureau of Statistics <www.ausstats.abs.gov.au/ausstats/free.nsf/0/804F27A83754B481CA2574D500165929/$File/25100_1986_Religion_in_Australia.pdf> 1–2.

Early restrictions on Roman Catholics

While there is some dispute as to whether requests for Roman Catholic priests to be sent to the colony were actually denied, or simply overlooked or ignored, the failure to provide Roman Catholic priests for the Roman Catholic convicts, emancipists, and later settlers would have acted as a significant restriction on the practice of religion by Roman Catholics in the colony. A number of Roman Catholic religious ceremonies can only be performed by ordained priests, such as the celebration of the Eucharist and confession.[12] As a result, the denial of a priest to Roman Catholics in the colony acted as a restriction on their ability to practise these aspects of their religion.

The first example of the State denying permission for Roman Catholic priests to travel to and minister to Roman Catholics in the colony may have occurred prior to the first fleet leaving England. In his authoritative work on Australian History *A History of Australia,* Manning Clark asserts that the colonial secretary Lord Sydney refused the request of two Roman Catholic priests to accompany the first fleet in order to minister to the Roman Catholic convicts.[13] Clark refers to an undated letter from the Rev Thomas Walshe to Lord Sydney in which he expresses the 'desire of two clergymen of the Catholick [sic] persuasion which they have to instruct the convicts who are of their faith who are destined for Botony Bay [sic].'[14] As the letter is undated, it is impossible to be certain if the letter was written prior to the sailing of the first fleet. Cardinal Moran in his book *The History of the Catholic Church in Australasia* suggested that the letter was written in 1791.[15] Whether the letter was written before 1788 or in 1791 is immaterial. The reference to Botany Bay rather than Sydney Cove suggests that, at the very least, it was written very early in the Australian colony's history.

There is also some doubt as to whether or not Lord Sydney in fact refused the request. No response has survived, and it is possible that in the rush to get the Australian colony established the matter was simply forgotten or put to one side.[16] What the letter does show is a desire by at least two English Roman Catholic priests to minister to the convicts. The fact that no Roman Catholic priests arrived at Sydney Cove until the arrival of the convict priests suggests that at the very best the spiritual needs of the Catholic convicts were ignored, and at worst Clark may be right in asserting that they were discriminated against in favour of Protestant ascendancy.

---

12 Holy See, *Code of Canon Law: Canon* 900 (8 January 2015) Holy See <www.vatican.va/ archive/ENG1104/__P38.HTM> ; Holy See, *Code of Canon Law: Canon 965* (8 January 2015) Holy See www.vatican.va/archive/ENG1104/__P3G.HTM>.

13 Manning Clark, *AHistory of Australia* (Melbourne University Press, 1962) vol 1, 78.

14 James Cook (author), Britton Alexander and Frank Murcott Bladen (eds), *Historical Records of New South Wales* (Government Printer, 1892–1901) vol 1, pt 1, 119.

15 Patrick Francis Cardinal Moran, *History of the Catholic Church in Australasia From Authentic Sources* (The Oceanic Publishing Company, 1896), 5–6; James Waldersee, *Catholic Society in New South Wales 1788–1860* (Sydney University Press, 1974), 2–3.

16 Waldersee, above n 15, 3.

Another example of the State restricting the practice of Roman Catholicism is a petition in 1872 by five settlers and emancipists requesting a Roman Catholic priest be sent to the colony to minister to their needs.[17] As with the previous petition by Rev Walshe, no Roman Catholic priest was appointed in response. However, given the struggling nature of the colony, and the fact that the Church of England clergyman Rev Richard Johnson had not been provided with much support, it is perhaps understandable that the request was at best ignored and at worst denied.[18]

There is also evidence of the State restricting the religious practice of Roman Catholic convicts by regulating their religious practice. In the early days of the colony all convicts, regardless of religious persuasion, were required to attend religious services run by the Church of England clergyman Rev Richard Johnson. Failure to attend could result in punishment, including flogging.[19] While attendance at the religious ceremonies of another faith does not prevent a person from carrying out the ceremonies of their own religion, it is an example of the power of the State over religion. By requiring all convicts to attend Church of England services, the State is imposing a particular religious observance on the convicts, and by implication endorsing those religious beliefs and practices over others.

While all three of these examples could be used to support an assertion that the State restricted religious practice of Roman Catholics in the early colony, it is important to note that the same conditions applied to other convicts who were not adherents of the Church of England. No Non-conformists priests accompanied the first fleet, and convicts who adhered to the Non-conformist sects were also required to attend the Church of England services.[20] Rather than the State restricting the practice of Roman Catholics specifically, it may be more accurate to say that the State restricted the religious practices of anyone who was not an adherent of the Church of England.

Governor King and Roman Catholics

While the restrictions faced by Roman Catholics in the first few years after the arrival of the first fleet at Sydney Cove were also shared by others whose religious affiliation was not Church of England, specific examples of the State restricting the religious practices of Roman Catholics began to occur with the arrival of the first Roman Catholic priests. While it might be expected that the arrival of the first Roman Catholic priests would demonstrate a lifting of State restrictions, the surrounding facts and conditions under which they arrived and ministered, instead demonstrates another instance of the State's power over religion. This time the

---

17 Jean Woolmington (ed), *Religion in Early Australia The Problem of Church and State* (Cassell Australia, 1976), 30–31.
18 Waldersee, above n 15, 3–4.
19 Tom Luscombe, *Builders and Crusaders* (Lansdowne Press, 1st ed, 1967) 3.
20 Waldersee, above n 15, 4–5.

restrictions were not shared by all who were not adherents of the Church of England, instead the State's restrictions were specifically aimed at Roman Catholics and their priests.

The first Roman Catholic priests to arrive at Sydney Cove were Rev James Harold, Rev James Dixon and Rev Peter O'Neil. [21] They did not arrive as free men with the intention of ministering to Roman Catholic convicts. Instead, they arrived as convicts themselves, accused of crimes related to the Vinegar Hill uprising in Ireland in 1789.[22] While Rev James Harold and Rev Peter O'Neil had little interaction with the State beyond their status as convicts, Rev James Dixon was eventually permitted to minister under strict conditions before having this permission withdrawn as punishment for Australia's own 'Vinegar Hill' uprising. Rev Dixon's whole interaction with the State was defined by the State restricting Roman Catholics' practice of religion, even when it did permit them to worship.

Permission is given – but with restrictions attached

Rev James Dixon arrived on the *Friendship* on 16 February 1800. He had been transported to New South Wales because of his relationship to active United Irishmen including his two cousins and brother.[23] Lord Sydney recommended that Rev Dixon, along with Rev Harold and Rev O'Neil, should be considered for conditional emancipation. Unlike the other two,[24] Governor King felt that Rev Dixon's behaviour since arriving in the colony had been 'exemplary,' allowing

21 Also known as O'Neal.
22 Luscombe, above n 19, 7. A number of protestant clergy were also transported for their involvement in the vinegar Hill uprising. See Lynette Ramsay Silver, *The Battle of Vinegar Hill: Australia's Irish Rebellion, 1804* (Doubleday, 1st ed, 1989) 21.
23 Silver, above n 22, 25; Vivienne Parsons, *Dixon, James (1758–1840)* (30 December 2017) Australian Dictionary of Biography http://adb.anu.edu.au/biography/dixon-james-1980>.
24 Governor King refused to pardon Rev Harold, as in his opinion Rev Harold's behaviour had been far from exemplary and he had been removed to Norfolk Island. In August 1800, Rev Harold had been implicated in an attempted Irish uprising in the colony. Although he reported the conspiracy, he refused to reveal the names of those involved leading to his exile to Norfolk Island. Rev Harold was eventually allowed to exercise private ministry in Parramatta from 1808, but left the colony just two year later when he was pardoned by Governor Macquarie. See Governor King, 'Despatch from Governor King to Lord Hobart, 9 May 1803' in Frederick Watson (ed), *Historical Records of Australia Series 1* (Library Committee of the Commonwealth Parliament, 1914–1925) vol 4, 82; Silver, above n 22, 28, 30–31; Patrick O'Farrell, *The Catholic Church and Community: An Australian History* (New South Wales University Press, 1st ed, 1985) 5; Rev O'Neil had already left the colony when Lord Sydney's recommendation reached Governor King. Prior to his transportation he was imprisoned for three days without trial, given 275 lashes, threatened with further flogging and decapitation, and finally given a drugged drink, all in an attempt to compel him to confess. The drugging resulted in him writing to his brother, which was taken to be a confession; however, the drugging was discovered before he could be hanged. He was ordered to be released, but the order did not reach him before the *Luz StAnn* sailed. The release order caught up with him two years later leading him to leave the colony. See Luscombe, above n 19, 6–8; Silver, above n 22, 19.

him not only to pardon him but also to follow Lord Sydney's other suggestion and permit him to officially minister to the Roman Catholic convicts.[25]

While Governor King permitted Rev Dixon to minister, it was with some reluctance, as can be seen from comments in his despatch to Lord Hobart informing him of his decision.

> Your Lordship's suggestion respecting the exercise of their clerical functions I have most maturely considered, and weighed the certain advantages with the possible disadvantages. I believe it will be admitted that no description of people are so bigoted [sic] to their religion and priests as the lower order of the Irish; grid such their credulous ignorance that an artful priest may lead them to every action that is either good or bad. The number of this description now in the colony is more than a fourth of the inhabitants.[26]

The permission came with a string of conditions published in the *Proclamation Respecting the Toleration of the Roman Catholic Religion* on 19 April 1803.[27] They included when Roman Catholic services could take place, where they could take place, the requirement of police attendance at the services, and an injunction against sedition talk during worship. While Roman Catholics might have been permitted to practise their religion they could not do so freely at a time and place of their choosing.[28]

The permission is removed

Initially Governor King's fears seemed to be unfounded and his hope of some good coming of his indulging Roman Catholics seemed to be bearing fruit. In a letter to Lord Hobart dated 1 March 1804, he praised the effect Rev Dixon's ministry was having on the Irish Catholics:

> the Rev'd Mr Dixon performing the functions of his clerical office as a Roman Catholic . . . has had the most salutary effect on the number of Irish Catholics

25 Governor King, 'Despatch from Governor King to Lord Hobart, 9 May 1803' in Frederick Watson (ed), *Historical Records of Australia Series 1* (Library Committee of the Commonwealth Parliament, 1914–1925) vol 4, 82; Lord Hobart, 'Despatch from Lord Hobart to Governor King, 29 August 1802' in Frederick Watson (ed), *Historical Records of Australia Series 1* (Library Committee of the Commonwealth Parliament, 1914–1925) vol 3, 564; Waldersee, above n 15, 10.

26 Governor King, 'Despatch from Governor King to Lord Hobart, 9 May 1803' in Frederick Watson (ed), *Historical Records of Australia Series 1* (Library Committee of the Commonwealth Parliament, 1914–1925) vol 4, 83.

27 Luscombe, above n 19, 8–10; James Cook (author), Britton Alexander and Frank Murcott Bladen (eds), *Historical Records of New South Wales* (Government Printer, 1892–1901) vol 5, 97–98.

28 James Cook (author), Britton Alexander and Frank Murcott Bladen (eds), *Historical Records of New South Wales* (Government Printer, 1892–1901) vol 5, 98.

we have, and since its toleration there has not been the most distant cause for complaint amount that description, who regularly attend divine service.[29]

Governor King's optimism was premature. On 4 March, only days after Governor King wrote his letter, the Irish Catholics, along with their English supporters, began a revolt at the government farm at Castle Hill. The uprising finished the next day with Australia's 'battle of Vinegar Hill.'[30] The result was 15 convicts killed as part of the uprising,[31] 10 hung,[32] seven sentenced to flogging,[33] and 34 exiled to Coal River.[34]

Governor King's response was to re-assert the State's absolute control over religion by re-imposing all previous restriction; by removing Rev Dixon's right to minister to the Catholics in the colony.

While the permission granted to Rev Dixon stands as an example of the State restricting the religious practice of Roman Catholics, for the Roman Catholic convicts it was arguably better than nothing. What few restrictions had been lifted were now re-imposed. Rev Dixon's authority to perform Mass was revoked and his salary withheld.[35] He was also ordered to watch the flogging of five of the convicts and was forced to place his hand upon their back at the conclusion.[36]

The restrictions imposed upon Roman Catholics as a result of the uprising did not end with Rev Dixon. As part of the punishment of the 34 convicts exiled to Coal River, Governor King ordered that they have Church of England prayers read to them every Sunday.[37] This punishment is arguably worse than simply being refused permission to practise their own religion. The forced attendance at Church of England prayers went a step further forcing them to participate in the practices of a religion not their own.

Macquarie and Roman Catholics

For the decade following the departure of Rev Harold in 1810, the New South Wales Roman Catholics were left without either an official or unofficial priest.

---

29 Ibid. 324.
30 For a detailed account, see Silver, above n 22.
31 Ibid. 344, 108.
32 Ibid. 110–112.
33 Ibid. 113.
34 Ibid.
35 Clark, above n 13, 173; Waldersee, above n 15, 8.
36 Silver, above n 22, 113. Following the removal of his official commission Rev Dixon continued to minister privately to the Roman Catholics in the colony. With his departure in 1808 this ministry was taken over by Rev Harold. With Rev Harold's departure in 1810 the colony was again left with no Roman Catholic priests. Vivienne Parsons, *Dixon, James (1758–1840)* (30 December 2017) Australian Dictionary of Biography http://adb.anu.edu.au/biography/dixon-james-1980>; Harold Perkins, *Harold, James (1744–1830)* (30 December 2017) Australian Dictionary of Biography http://adb.anu.edu.au/biography/harold-james-2156>; Luscombe, above n 19, 11.
37 Silver, above n 22, 114.

Governor Macquarie's Governorship saw the arrival of both an unofficial Roman Catholic priest and finally the arrival of two free and officially sanctioned Roman Catholic priests. However, the State continued to restrict the religious practices of Roman Catholics. In the first instance by removing the priest and in the second by imposing restrictions similar to those imposed on Rev Dixon.

Governor Macquarie and the Rev O'Flynn affair

The Rev O'Flynn[38] affair is a stark example of the power of the State over religion in the early Australian colony. As referred to above, Roman Catholics had been without a priest for nearly a decade, and as a result would have been unable to practise many of their religious ceremonies. This restriction on their religious practice appeared to have been removed with the arrival of Rev O'Flynn.[39] However, his arrival was unofficial and unsanctioned and he was soon deported, leaving Roman Catholics without a priest and again effectively restricting their religious practice.

Rev O'Flynn arrived in New South Wales on 8 November 1817.[40] Rome had appointed Rev O'Flynn as Prefect Apostolic of New Hold, the same title give to Rev Dixon.[41] However, the Colonial Secretary, Lord Bathurst, refused to sanction him as the official Roman Catholic chaplain for the colony.[42] Assuming the official status would eventually be forthcoming O'Flynn travelled to New South Wales and presented himself to Governor Macquarie.[43] On his arrival in Sydney O 'Flynn represented to Governor Macquarie that Lord Bathurst had sanctioned his arrival, although he could not produce any paperwork, instead indicating that the paperwork would be on the next ship from England. Although Governor Macquarie was suspicious, he initially allowed O'Flynn to remain in the colony on the condition that he not minister publically while they waited to see if O'Flynn's credentials would arrive. When no authorisation arrived and O'Flynn began to minister publically, performing marriages, baptisms and Mass, Governor Macquarie ordered him to leave the colony. [44] Instead of complying, O'Flynn disappeared

---

38 Also known as Flinn and Flynn.

39 Governor Macquarie, 'Dispatch, Governor Macquarie to Lord Bathurst, 12 December 1817' in Frederick Watson (ed), *Historical Records of Australia Series 1* (Library Committee of the Commonwealth Parliament, 1914–1925) vol 9, 710; Luscombe, above n 19, 13.

40 Governor Macquarie, 'Dispatch, Governor Macquarie to Lord Bathurst, 12 December 1817' in Frederick Watson (ed), *Historical Records of Australia Series 1* (Library Committee of the Commonwealth Parliament, 1914–1925) vol 9, 710; Luscombe, above n 19, 13.

41 Luscombe, above n 19, 12.

42 Frederick Watson (ed), *Historical Records of Australia Series 1* (Library Committee of the Commonwealth Parliament, 1914–1925) vol 9, 881.

43 Luscombe, above n 19, 13.

44 Governor Macquarie, 'Dispatch, Governor Macquarie to Lord Bathurst, 12 December 1817' in Frederick Watson (ed), *Historical Records of Australia Series 1* (Library Committee of the Commonwealth Parliament, 1914–1925) vol 9, 710; Governor Macquarie, 'Dispatch, Governor Macquarie to Lord Bathurst, 18 May 1818' in in Frederick Watson (ed),

into the country, returning a short time later and apologising to Governor Macquarie.[45] Again, Governor Macquarie ordered him to leave the colony, which Rev O'Flynn agreed to do on the next available ship. Months went by and several ships departed for England without Rev O'Flynn aboard. Governor Macquarie again ordered Rev O'Flynn to leave and suspecting that he would again disappear into the countryside ordered his arrest.[46] Rev O'Flynn was arrested on the 15 May 1818 and deported five days later on the *Davis Shaw*.[47]

While it is arguable that O'Flynn was deported, not because he was a Roman Catholic priest, but because he was a 'meddling, ignorant; dangerous character,'[48] other comments by Macquarie would suggest that Rev O'Flynn's deportation was at least in part because of his position as a Roman Catholic priest. In the same dispatch, in which he described Rev O'Flynn, he also commented that:

> Convinced, from the experience I have had of this Country, that nothing can possibly promote or preserve its internal peace and tranquillity so much as uniformity of religion, I beg leave most earnestly to recommend that no sectarian Preacher or Teacher be permitted to come hither.[49]

This would seem to indicate that Governor Macquarie would have preferred that no Roman Catholic priests be permitted in the colony, preferring instead that the colony have a single Protestant religion. This indicates an intention by the State, embodied in the autocratic Governor, to restrict the religious practices of Roman Catholics in favour of Protestantism. This is further evidenced by the

---

Historical Records of Australia Series 1 (Library Committee of the Commonwealth Parliament, 1914–1925) vol 9, 799–801; O'Farrell, above n 24, 13.

45 Governor Macquarie, 'Dispatch, Governor Macquarie to Lord Bathurst, 18 May 1818' in Frederick Watson (ed), *Historical Records of Australia Series 1* (Library Committee of the Commonwealth Parliament, 1914–1925) vol 9, 799–801.

46 Ibid. 800; Frederick Watson (ed), *Historical Records of Australia Series 1* (Library Committee of the Commonwealth Parliament, 1914–1925) vol 9, 804.

47 Luscombe, above n 19, 16; Clark, above n 13, 320; Frederick Watson (ed), *Historical Records of Australia Series 1* (Library Committee of the Commonwealth Parliament, 1914–1925) vol 8, 799–801. On receiving Governor Macquarie's dispatch regarding Rev O'Flynn, Lord Bathurst indicated his approval of Governor Macquarie's handling of the matter. See Lord Bathurst, 'Lord Bathurst to Governor Macquarie, 24 August 1818' in Frederick Watson (ed), *Historical Records of Australia Series 1* (Library Committee of the Commonwealth Parliament, 1914–1925) vol 9, 833.

48 Governor Macquarie, 'Dispatch, Governor Macquarie to Lord Bathurst, 18 May 1818' in Frederick Watson (ed), *Historical Records of Australia Series 1* (Library Committee of the Commonwealth Parliament, 1914–1925) vol 9, 800. See also Waldersee, above n 15, 10–15.

49 Governor Macquarie, 'Dispatch, Governor Macquarie to Lord Bathurst, 18 May 1818' in Frederick Watson (ed), *Historical Records of Australia Series 1* (Library Committee of the Commonwealth Parliament, 1914–1925) vol 9, 801.

fact that Governor Macquarie, as with his predecessors, also saw no difficulty in Roman Catholic convicts being forced to attend Church of England services.[50]

While it is perhaps debatable whether Rev O'Flynn was deported because he was a Roman Catholic priest, because of his poor character, or because of a combination of the two, the incident does demonstrate the power of the State over religion. First, Governor Macquarie attempted to ban O'Flynn from ministering to Roman Catholics in the colony. While this exercise of the State's power was unsuccessful, with O'Flynn ministering to Roman Catholics despite the injunction not to, it demonstrates the power of the State to restrict religious practice. While Roman Catholics in the colony had a priest, he was not permitted to minister to them in effect restricting the practice of their religion. When this restriction failed, the State used a second method of restricting the practices of Roman Catholics by deporting Rev O'Flynn.

The first official Roman Catholic chaplains are appointed

With the deportation of Rev O'Flynn, Roman Catholics in the colony were again left without a priest as a result of State action, and therefore were again restricted in how they could practise their religion. This time the restriction imposed by the absence of a Roman Catholic priest did no last as long as in previous instances. However, as with the arrival and ministry of Rev Dixon, the arrival of the first officially sanctioned Roman Catholic priest is not an example of the State lifting restrictions, but an example of the State imposing restrictions via another method. While Roman Catholics could now practice all those aspects of their religion that required a priest, restrictions were imposed on the priests curtailing this freedom.

The first two officially sanctioned Roman Catholic priests, Rev Joseph Therry and Rev Philip Conolly,[51] arrived in the colony on the 3 May 1820.[52] The newly arrived priests were presented with a list of conditions under which they were to exercise their ministry. They were only permitted to minister to Roman Catholics and could only conduct marriages between two people of the Roman Catholic faith. More importantly, they were both prevented from ministering to children in the government run Orphan schools.[53]

50 Governor Macquarie, 'Dispatch, Governor Macquarie to Lord Bathurst, 12 December 1817' in Frederick Watson (ed), *Historical Records of Australia Series 1* (Library Committee of the Commonwealth Parliament, 1914–1925) vol 9, 710.

51 Luscombe, above n 19, 28–29.

52 Luscombe, above n 19, 19. Governor Macquarie had been informed of their appointment in a letter from the Colonial Secretary Lord Bathurst on 24 August 1818. See Lord Bathurst, 'Despatch, Lord Bathurst to Governor Macquarie, 24 August 1818' in Frederick Watson (ed), Historical Records of Australia Series 1 (Library Committee of the Commonwealth Parliament, 1914–1925) vol 9, 833; Acknowledged by Governor Macquarie on 24 March 1819 see Frederick Watson (ed), *Historical Records of Australia Series 1* (Library Committee of the Commonwealth Parliament, 1914–1925) vol 9, 833 and vol 10, 84–100.

53 Luscombe, above n 19, 27–28; O'Farrell, above n 24, 21–22.

Many of the children in the government run Orphan school were not, as the name suggests, orphans in the traditional sense. Rather they were the 'neglected' children of the poor and of unofficial liaisons.[54] The education of children at the Orphan schools was to be the exclusive purview of the Church of England clergy.[55] This was a situation Rev Therry could not accept, as he put it:

> The lambs are allured abroad, and forcibly prevented from returning to the fold of the only Good Shepherd, Christ Jesus, our Lord and must his humble watchman hold his peace?[56]

While it is arguable that many of the restrictions placed on the Roman Catholic clergy, especially those relating to marriage were understandable,[57] this does not make them any less restrictive. In relation to the Orphan school, the State restriction did not only prevent the Roman Catholic priests from carrying out their ministry as they saw fit, it also restricted the religious practice of the Roman Catholic children who, as a result of circumstances outside their control, found themselves at the Orphan school.

In his book *Catholic Society in New South Wales 1788–1860,* James Waldersee disputes some of the claims of persecution levelled against the State in relation to Roman Catholics in the early Australian colony.[58] While he may be right that the restrictions faced by Roman Catholics were understandable, and even justifiable, in the circumstances faced by the infant colony, this does not make it any less restrictive.

While restrictions on Roman Catholics were lifted in the mid-1800s[59] the tension between Roman Catholics and Protestants/Anglicans continued into the 1900s. As late as 1950, the High Court was asked to consider in *Crittenden v Anderson*[60] whether a Roman Catholic was disqualified from 'being chosen or

---

54 See Alan Barcan, *A History of Australian Education* (Oxford University Press, 1980), 12–13; O'Farrell, above n 24, 26.

55 O'Farrell, above n 24, 22, 25.

56 Ibid. 25.

57 See Waldersee, above n 15, 15–20.

58 Ibid. 1–41.

59 The passage of the *Roman Catholic Relief Act 1829* (UK) and subsequently the *Roman Catholic Relief Act 1830* (Qld) and *Roman Catholic Relief Act 1830* (Vic) saw the repeal of the *Test Act 1672* (UK) and the remaining Irish Penal Laws. Although the Queensland Act adopted the British Act, the Victorian Act went as far as to state that 'all His Majesty's Subjects professing the Roman Catholic Religion, are relieved from all civil and military disabilities, [however still] with certain specified exceptions.' Among many other things, this had the effect of allowing Roman Catholics to sit in Parliament as Ministers of Parliament and hold most forms of public office. To read more about Catholic Emancipation in the mid-1800s, see Marjie Bloy, *Catholic Emancipation* (7 August 2002) The Victorian Web www.victorianweb.org/history/emancipation2.html>.

60 *Crittenden v Anderson* (Unreported, High Court of Australia, Fullagar J, 23 August 1950), extracted in 'An Unpublished Judgment on s 116 of the Constitution' (1977) 51 Australian Law Journal 171.

sitting as a Member of the House of Representatives he being under acknowledgment of adherence, obedience and/or allegiance to a foreign power.'[61] Crittenden alleged that as a Roman Catholic, Anderson was under 'acknowledgment of adherence, Obedience or allegiance' to the Papal State. Fuller J rejected this argument stating:

> it is, in my opinion, s 116, and not s 44(i) of our *Constitution* which is relevant when the right of a member of any religious body . . . is challenged on the ground of his religion. Effect could not be given to the petitioner's contention without the imposition of a 'religious test.'[62]

While Section 116 may have been of assistance to Anderson, it was of no assistance to the Jehovah's Witnesses, in what is perhaps the most overt restriction on religious practice by the federal government in Australia's history.

The Jehovah's Witnesses' World War Two ban

Unlike Roman Catholics in the early Australian colony, who did not have recourse to any form of freedom of religion protections, the passage of the *Australian Constitution* and in particular Section 116 should have provided at least some protection against restrictions on religious practice for minority faiths. However, as discussed in Chapter 4 and as this section will demonstrate, Section 116 has been of little assistance to those whose religious beliefs and practices have been restricted by the State. The section was of no assistance to the Jehovah's Witnesses following the attempt by the federal government to ban them during World War Two. Instead, the Jehovah's Witnesses had to rely on other provisions of the *Australian Constitution*, not ostensibly about religion, to protect their rights.

During World War Two Jehovah's Witnesses were the subjects of significant State restrictions, both as individuals and as a religious group. The restrictions culminated in the group and its associated organisations being declared unlawful in January 1941. As a result of the declaration, the Jehovah's Witnesses were subject to the most severe form of State restrictions; it became unlawful for them to practice their religion. While it was not illegal to be a Jehovah's Witness, the ban effectively made it unlawful to practice the Jehovah's Witness faith. The

---

61 *Crittenden v Anderson* (Unreported, High Court of Australia, Fullagar J, 23 August 1950), extracted in 'An Unpublished Judgment on s 116 of the Constitution' (1977) 51 Australian Law Journal 171, 171; *Australian Constitution* s 44(i) which states "Any person who is under any acknowledgement of allegiance, obedience, or adherence to a foreign power, or is a subject or a citizen or entitled to the rights or privileges of a subject or citizen of a foreign power . . . shall be incapable of being chosen or of sitting as a senator or a member of the House of Representatives."
62 *Crittenden v Anderson* (Unreported, High Court of Australia, Fullagar J, 23 August 1950), extracted in 'An Unpublished Judgment on s 116 of the Constitution' (1977) 51 Australian Law Journal 171, 171.

subsequent High Court case *Adelaide Company of Jehovah's Witnesses Incorporated v The Commonwealth*[63] held that the regulations under which the ban was put in place were unconstitutional. However, this finding was not based on the fact that Jehovah's Witnesses were a religious organisation. As a result, the ban on the Jehovah's Witnesses stands as perhaps one of the starkest examples of the State, lawfully, restricting the religious practices of an entire religion.

The laws

On 3 September 1939, Prime Minister Robert Menzies announced that Australia was at war with Germany, three days later, on 9 September, Parliament passed the *National Security Act 1939* (Cth).[64] *Inter alia*, the Act granted the Governor General the power to 'make regulations to secure public safety and for the defence of the Commonwealth.'[65] Nine months later the Governor General enacted the *National Security (Subversive Associations) Regulations 1940* (Cth) under this provision. Nothing in either the *Regulations* or the *Act* pointed to their application to religious groups such as the Jehovah's Witnesses. They were, on their face, neutral language laws of general application. The original purpose of the regulations was not to ban the Jehovah's Witnesses, but to give the Governor General the power to ban the Communist Party.[66] However, the provisions of the regulations were couched in a way that meant that they could potentially apply to many other organisations that also opposed the War. For example, Regulation 3 stated that 'ANY body corporate or unincorporated the existence of which the Governor General, by order published in the *Gazette,* declares to be in his opinion, prejudicial to the defence of the Commonwealth or the efficient prosecution of the war, is hereby declared to be unlawful' (emphasis added).[67] These words are so wide that they could potentially apply to almost any group. Given the Jehovah's Witnesses beliefs about the War, it could be seen as inevitable that the regulations would be used to ban them.

Application to the Jehovah's Witnesses

The Jehovah's Witnesses were vulnerable to being declared unlawful under the *National Security (Subversive Associations) Regulations 1940* (Cth) because of their particular religious beliefs about the State and the war more generally. They

---

63 (1943) 67 CLR 116.
64 Roger Douglas, 'Law, War and Liberty: The World War II Subversion Prosecutions' (2003) 27 *Melbourne University Law Review* 65, 74.
65 *National Security Act 1939* (Cth) s 5, as repealed by *Statute Law Revision Act 1950* (Cth) sch 3.
66 Douglas, above n 64, 79.
67 *Adelaide Company of Jehovah's Witnesses Incorporated v The Commonwealth* (1943) 67 CLR 116; 134. For a discussion of the various provision of the Regulations, see Douglas, above n 64, 74–79.

believed that in 1914 Jesus Christ had returned to earth invisibly and established God's Kingdom on earth, a Kingdom of which all Witnesses were citizens. As a result, they were not able to be citizens of any country and would not vote, salute national flags or serve in the army.[68] In particular, they believed that all worldly governments were 'organs of Satan, unrighteously governed and identifiable with the Beast in the 13th chapter of the Book of Revelation.'[69] These beliefs led both the Allies and Nazi Germany to persecute the Jehovah's Witnesses during World War Two. Canada,[70] New Zealand,[71] and Australia all banned the Jehovah's Witnesses, while Nazi Germany interned them in concentration camps.[72]

In Australia, during the early years of World War Two, there were consistent calls for the Jehovah's Witnesses to be banned by community groups such as the Returned Servicemen's League (RSL), State and federal politicians, religious leaders, such as Catholic Archbishop Mannix, the media, and the general community.[73] The Australian Attorney General, Thomas Hughes, initially ruled out a ban on the Jehovah's Witnesses on the basis that they were doing nothing illegal.[74] Instead, the State focused on individual Witnesses who refused to participate in compulsory military service,[75] and eventually on four radio stations[76] associated with the Jehovah's Witnesses, radio 5KA in particular.[77]

Radio Station 5KA

In 1941, prior to the complete banning of the Jehovah's Witnesses, the State shut down radio station 5KA and three other associated stations controlled by the Witnesses. While the closure of radio station 5KA did not restrict any religious practices, it is an important aspect of the overall picture of the State's interaction with the Jehovah's Witnesses during this period. The closure of these radio stations demonstrates the level of concern in Australia during World War Two about

---

68 William Kaplan, 'The World War Two Bans on the Jehovah's Witnesses in Canada and Australia: Do Constitutional Protections Really Work?' (1991) 9 *Australian Canadian Studies* 5, 5–6.

69 *Adelaide Company of Jehovah's Witnesses Incorporated v The Commonwealth* (1943) 67 CLR 116, 146.

70 Kaplan, above n 68.

71 Bobbie Oliver, 'Australia: Jehovah's Witnesses, Censorship During World War II' in Derek Jones (ed) *Censorship A World Encyclopaedia Vol I A–D* (Fitzroy Dearborn Publishers, 2001) 144.

72 Ibid.

73 Oliver, above n 71, 143–144; Peter Strawhan, 'The Closure of radio 5KA, January 1941' (1985) 21(85) *Historical Studies* 550, 555–556, 557; Jayne Persian, 'A National Nuisance: The Banning of Jehovah's Witnesses in Australia in 1941' (2008) 25 *Flinders Journal of History and Politics* 4, 5–6.

74 Oliver, above n 71, 144.

75 Ibid.

76 5AU (Port Augusta), 5KA (Adelaide), 2HD (Newcastle) and 4AT (Atherton Tablelands).

77 For a detailed discussion of the treatment of radio 5KA see Strawhan, above n 73; Oliver, above n 71, 145–146.

the beliefs and activities of the Jehovah's Witnesses and is an important aspect of the State's eventual ban of the group.

The four radio stations had come under the influence of the Jehovah's Witness during the 1930s.[78] Even before World War Two, 5KA came under scrutiny after complaints by the Roman Catholic Church and the general public, in relation to its broadcasts of lectures by the leader of the Jehovah's Witnesses, Joseph Rutherford. There were also complaints about the station in relation to their refusal to play the national anthem at the close of transmission, which was the custom at the time. By 1939, 5KA was subject to restrictions that required that it submit all religious material for approval prior to broadcast.[79]

With the outbreak of World War Two, 5KA came under increased scrutiny. This included Naval Intelligence monitoring of all broadcasts by the station. As a result of this surveillance a small number of broadcasts were identified as possibly containing coded messages referring to merchant and troop ship movements.[80] On 8 January 1941, in reliance of these reports and on the recommendation of Admiral Sir Raynar Musgrave Colvin, Chief of Naval Staff, the Attorney General Thomas Hughes, approved the closure of all four radio stations under the control of the Jehovah's Witnesses.[81] Nine days later the Jehovah's Witnesses were declared an unlawful organisation.

The declaration

While the closure of radio station 5KA, and its associated stations, demonstrated the level of concern in Australia about the beliefs of the Jehovah's Witnesses, it did not directly restrict their religious practices. However, the next action by the State against the Witnesses – the declaration that they and their associated organisations were unlawful on 17 January 1941 – directly restricted the practice of their faith.[82] As Williams J noted, the declaration of unlawfulness and the resulting prohibition on the advocacy of the principles of the Jehovah's Witnesses was so wide that it, in effect, made 'every church service held by believers in the birth of Christ an unlawful assembly.'[83]

In the nine days between the cessation of broadcast and the declaration that the Jehovah's Witnesses were unlawful, the Attorney General had attempted to negotiate the re-opening of the stations. On 14 January he announced that,

---

78 Strawhan, above n 73, 550–551; Oliver, above n 71, 145.

79 Strawhan, above n 73, 551–555.

80 For details of these broadcasts see Strawhan, above n 73, 557–559.

81 Strawhan, above n 73, 560.

82 Douglas, above n 64, 79; *Commonwealth of Australia Gazette*, No 8, 17 January 1941, 123. The associations declared unlawful were the Jehovah's Witness, Watchtower Bible and Tract Society, International Bible Students' Association, Adelaide Company of Jehovah's Witnesses, and Consolation Publishing Co.

83 *Adelaide Company of Jehovah's Witnesses Incorporated v The Commonwealth* (1943) 67 CLR 116, 164.

subject to a series of conditions, the stations would be permitted to resume their broadcast.[84] On 16 January, the Federal Cabinet met in Sydney to discuss, *inter alia*, the problem of the Jehovah's Witnesses. Hughes was unable to attend as he was still in Canberra, despite a request from Hughes to move the meeting, Prime Minister Robert Menzies refused to do so.[85] The Cabinet determined that the Jehovah's Witnesses should be declared unlawful, despite Hughes' decision to re-open the radio stations. As a result, the stations remained closed and on 7 February Cabinet determined that their licenses should be revoked because they were held by an unlawful organisation.[86]

The declaration of unlawfulness made against the Jehovah's Witnesses specifically named both the Jehovah's Witnesses and their associated organisations.[87] There is no argument that can be made that the bans were neutral or of general application. Nor were the restrictions against specific practices or beliefs of the Jehovah's Witnesses. Rather, the declaration overtly targeted the Jehovah's Witnesses as a whole.

As a result of the declaration property of the Jehovah's Witnesses was seized, including Kingdom Hall in Adelaide, which was to become the subject of the High Court case.[88]

The High Court case

On 4 September 1941, in response to the declaration and the seizure of their property, the Adelaide Company of Jehovah's Witnesses commenced High Court proceedings against the Commonwealth.[89] The Court handed down its decision on 14 June 1943.[90] Each of the five judges gave their own judgment declaring various parts of the *National Security (Subversive Associations) Regulations 1940* (Cth) unlawful. Latham CJ and McTiernan J determined that only Regulation 6A, which concerned the seizure of property, was invalid.[91] Williams and Rich JJ determined that Regulations 3 to 6B were invalid.[92] Stark J went the furthest, declaring the entire *National Security (Subversive Associations) Regulations 1940* (Cth)

---

84 Persian, above n 73, 8.

85 Jayne Persian has suggested that the banning of the Jehovah's Witnesses may have been as much about a power play between Hughes and Menzies as about the Jehovah's Witnesses themselves. See Persian, above n 73.

86 Persian, above n 73, 8–13.

87 See 'Widespread Police Raids on Jehovah's Witnesses in Australia,' *Examiner* (Launceston) 18 January 1941, 1.

88 Persian, above n 73, 11. See *National Security (Subversive Associations) Regulations 1940* (Cth) reg 4–6B repealed by *Statute Law Revision Act 1950* (Cth).

89 *Adelaide Company of Jehovah's Witnesses Incorporated v The Commonwealth* (1943) 67 CLR 116, 118.

90 Oliver, above n 71, 144.

91 *Adelaide Company of Jehovah's Witnesses Incorporated v The Commonwealth* (1943) 67 CLR 116, 148 (Latham CJ), 157 (McTiernan J).

92 Ibid. 150 (Rich J), 168 (Williams J).

unlawful.[93] The result was that the Jehovah's Witnesses were successful in at least having the regulations relating to the seizure of their property declared unconstitutional. However, the reasoning behind the Court's decisions had nothing to do with freedom of religion, instead, the Court focused on the power granted to the Commonwealth under the defence power and the power of the Attorney General to make regulations under the *National Security Act 1939* (Cth).[94]

One of the Jehovah's Witnesses' main arguments was that the *National Security (Subversive Associations) Regulations 1940* (Cth) were unlawful as a result of the operation of Section 116 of the *Australian Constitution*. They argued that the *Regulations* contravened the free exercise limb of Section 116, because the declaration effectively prohibited the free exercise of their religion. Despite the fact that the Jehovah's Witnesses were unsuccessful in this argument, *Adelaide Company of Jehovah's Witnesses Incorporated v The Commonwealth*[95] has become well known for Latham CJ's long exegesis on the meaning of freedom of religion.[96]

Despite finding that Section 116 'operates not only to protect the freedom of religion, but also to protect the right of a man to have no religion'[97] and

> that such a provision as Section 116 is not required for the protection of the religion of a majority. The religion of the majority of the people can look after itself. Section 116 is required to protect the religion (or absence of religion) of minorities, and, in particular unpopular minorities,[98]

Latham CJ ultimately concluded that the *National Security (Subversive Associations) Regulations 1940* (Cth) did not infringe Section 116 despite the effect the regulations had on the Jehovah's Witnesses, a religious organisation. It cannot be doubted, given the background outlined above, that the Jehovah's Witnesses were one of the 'unpopular minorities,' referred to by Latham CJ. So why did Latham CJ find that Section 116 did not protect them in this instance?

The answer can be found in the meaning of the word 'free.' Latham CJ devoted several pages to determining how 'free' should be interpreted in the context of Section 116. He ultimately concluded that 'it is consistent with the maintenance of religious liberty for the State to restrain actions and courses of conduct which are inconsistent with the maintenance of civil government or prejudicial to the continued existence of the community.'[99] In his opinion, it was entirely appropriate for the government to restrain activities that obstructed recruitment of

---

93 Ibid. 156 (Stark J).
94 Blackshield, above n 2, 93–95.
95 (1943) 67 CLR 116.
96 See *Adelaide Company of Jehovah's Witnesses Incorporated v The Commonwealth* (1943) 67 CLR 116, 122–134 (Latham CJ).
97 Ibid. 123 (Latham CJ).
98 Ibid. 124 (Latham CJ).
99 *Adelaide Company of Jehovah's Witnesses Incorporated v The Commonwealth* (1943) 67 CLR 116, 131 (Latham CJ).

soldiers and encouraged soldiers not to perform their duties.[100] In effect, there was no constitutional problem with the State restricting the religious practices of the Jehovah's Witnesses in this instance.

While the other judges did consider Section 116, they did so only briefly, and reached the same conclusion as Latham CJ, Section 116 was of no avail to the Witnesses.[101]

In a time of war, advocating that your own country, and those it is aligned with, is an organ of Satan is arguably prejudicial to the war effort.[102] However, these beliefs were also religious beliefs. Unlike the Communist Party, their reasons for advocating what they did were religious not political. Just as the Governors of the early Australian colony had restricted the religious practices of Roman Catholics, now the Commonwealth government restricted the religious practices of the Jehovah's Witnesses because their religious beliefs were inconvenient.

Today the Jehovah's Witnesses continue to face restrictions in the practice of their faith around the world. As will be discussed below, Australian laws in all States and territories permit Jehovah's Witness children to be given a blood transfusion against their religious beliefs without either their or their parent's consent. While no longer unlawful in Australia, the Jehovah's witnesses continue to face discrimination around the world. For example, in 2017 the Russian Supreme Court upheld a ban on the group.[103]

The State restrictions on the Jehovah's witnesses may be explainable as the result of wartime paranoia. However, they are not the only religion in Australia to be subject to State restrictions amounting to a ban in the twentieth century.

The State bans Scientology

The severe restriction and effective ban on the Church of Scientology during the 1960s and 1970s is another example of State restriction on an entire religion. In the 1960s, Victoria, Western Australia and South Australia all passed legislation effectively banning the practices of Scientology. While these bans were ineffective they demonstrate another episode where the State attempted to restrict the practices of a religious organisation, to the extent that the State was in effect trying to eliminate them completely.

This section will examine the bans that were put in place, along with the background and origins of the bans. It will begin by examining the inquiry into Scientology conducted by Kevin Anderson QC, which was used as the justification for the bans. A discussion of the Inquiry is included to provide an overall picture of the State's interaction with the Church of Scientology during this period. Following the

---

100 Ibid. 132–133 (Latham CJ).
101 Ibid. 148–149 (Rich J), 154–155 (Stark J), 158–160 (Williams J).
102 Ibid. 146 (Latham CJ).
103 Vladimir Soldatkin (author), Andrew Osborn and Ralph Boulton (eds), *Russian court bans Jehovah's Witnesses as extremist* (21 April 2017) Reuters www.reuters.com/article/us-russia-religion-jehovah-s-idUSKBN17M1ZT>.

discussion of the Anderson Report, this section will go on to examine the restrictions put in place in Victoria, Western Australia, and South Australia. Finally, the section will briefly examine the removal of the bans on the Church of Scientology.

The Anderson Report

The first step towards the State's restrictions on the Church of Scientology was The Board of Enquiry into Scientology, conducted by Kevin Anderson QC between 1963 and 1965. The finding of The Board of Enquiry into Scientology, also known as the Anderson Report, led the Victorian Government to pass the *Psychological Practices Act 1965* (Vic) which, *inter alia*, effectively banned the practice of Scientology in Victoria.

The inquiry was precipitated by complaints about the actions of Scientology by representatives of the medical profession and members of the public, prompting Labor Leader John Galbally to raise the issue in Parliament on 19 November 1963.[104] In his speech, he described Scientologists as,

> a group of charlatans who for monetary gain are exposing children of tender age, youths and adults to intimidation and blackmail, insanity and even suicide, family estrangement and bankruptcy.[105]

Galbally introduced the *Scientology Restriction Bill 1963* (Vic) on 26 November 1963,[106] in response, the government set up the Board of Enquiry into Scientology on 27 November 1963.[107]

Anderson's assessment of Scientology

The Anderson Report was devastating in its assessment of Scientology right from the first sentence of the report:

> There are some features of Scientology that are so ludicrous that there may be a tendency to regard scientology as silly and its practitioners as harmless cranks.[108]

104 Victoria, *Parliamentary Debates*, Legislative Council, 19 November 1963, 2127–2159 (John W. Galbally); J Devon Mills, 'The Victorian Psychological Practices Act 1965' (1966) 1(1) *Australian Psychologist* 30, 30.
105 Victoria, *Parliamentary Debates*, Legislative Council, 19 November 1963, 2127 (John W. Galbally).
106 Victoria, *Parliamentary Debates*, Legislative Council, 26 November 1963, 2386–2388 (John W. Galbally).
107 see Victoria, *Parliamentary Debates*, Legislative Assembly, 5 October 1965, 481 (William McDonald); Victoria, *Parliamentary Debates*, Legislative Council, 5 October 1965, 436.
108 Kevin Anderson, *Report of the Board of Enquiry into Scientology* (Government Printer, 1965) 1.

Later in the same paragraph, the Report states that

> Scientology is evil; its techniques evil; its practice a serious threat to the community, medically, morally and socially; and its adherents sadly deluded and often mentally ill.[109]

Despite acknowledging that Scientologists had the right to hold whatever beliefs they wished, the Board made it clear that they were not permitted to practices those beliefs if they were harmful, likening the practices of Scientology to human sacrifice.[110]

The report made three recommendations. First that the public be warned 'of the dangers to mental health of psychological techniques practices by unqualified persons,'[111] second the creation of a Psychologists Registration Board and the prohibition of the administration of hypnosis, IQ and personality tests, and the use of E-meters by unregistered persons,[112] and third the destruction of records held by the Scientology organisation of auditing sessions.[113] Interestingly, the report recommended against the banning of the use of the name Scientology as in the Board's opinion Scientologists would 'find ways of changing names of processes-even changing the name of scientology- and continuing to practise in much the same way under another guise.'[114] The report did not recommend the banning of Scientology.

Religion vs science

Scientology is one of only two religious belief systems in Australia to have their beliefs subject to a governmental inquiry of this scale.[115] Had the Enquiry restricted itself to investigating whether or not the practices of Scientology breached existing criminal law, or even into the desirability of the practices themselves, the setting up of the Enquiry may arguably be justifiable on public policy grounds.[116] The Enquiry did not so confine itself. Instead, it made comment on the veracity of the beliefs claimed by Scientologists, including declaring that it is not a religion.[117] The report describes adherents of Scientology as 'sadly deluded

---

109 Ibid.
110 Ibid. 147.
111 Ibid. 170.
112 Ibid. 170–172.
113 Ibid. 172.
114 Ibid. 169.
115 The spiritual beliefs of Australia's Indigenous people were subject to scrutiny in the Hind Marsh Island Royal Commission. See Neil Andrews, 'Dissenting in Paradise? The Hindmarsh Island Bridge Royal Commission' (1998) 5(1–2) *Canberra Law Review* 5.
116 The Inquiry found that the activities of Scientology in Victoria did not breach any existing criminal laws. Adam Possamai and Alphia Possamai–Inesdey, 'Scientology Down Under' in James Lewis (ed), *Scientology* (Oxford University Press, 2009) 351.
117 Anderson, above n 108, 147.

and often mentally ill,' a description which can only be justified after concluding that the beliefs cannot possibly be believable by any sane person. If similar comments were made about the adherents to more mainstream religions they would be considered unacceptable. However, belief in the tenants of these religions rests as much on faith as does belief in the tenants of Scientology, and not on the scientific veracity of the beliefs. As Murphy J put it in the *Scientology Case:*

> If each purported religion had to show that its doctrines were true, then all might fail. Administrators and judges must resist the temptation to hold that groups or institutions are not religious because claimed religious beliefs or practices seem absurd, fraudulent, evil or novel; or because the group or institution is new, the numbers of adherents small, the leaders hypocrites, or because they seek to obtain the financial and other privileges which come with religious status. In the eyes of the law, religions are equal.[118]

Throughout the report the Board emphasised the 'false' 'scientific' claims of Scientology, and the use of auditing via e-meters as being harmful to mental health.[119] Chapter 7 of the Report is devoted to outlining 'Hubbard's Scientific Deficiencies.' It would be unthinkable to include a similar chapter on the Pope's scientific deficiencies in a similar government enquiry on the beliefs and practices of the Roman Catholic Church, or Mohammad's scientific deficiencies in an enquiry into Islam. Both Roman Catholicism and Islam make claims that cannot be backed up scientifically.[120]

The focus of Anderson on the 'scientific' claims of Hubbard and Scientology also obscures the fact that just because something claims to be a science, rather than religion, does not necessarily make it so. For example, the fact that the Church of Christ, Scientist has the word 'science' in its name does not convert it from a religion to a science. Neither does the claims of the proponents of intelligent design to be a science, or that creationism should be taught in science classrooms make it a science rather than a religious belief.

As well as pointing out the scientific deficiencies of L Ron Hubbard and Scientology, the Board of Enquiry also rejected the religiosity of Scientology. While it may be understandable to reject scientific evidence for religious beliefs that are based on faith, to also reject the religiosity of the beliefs is a step further.

On the same page of the Report, the Board of Enquiry stated that theirs was not a theological enquiry into the veracity of Scientology beliefs, nor did their conclusions hang on whether or not Scientology was a religion, yet also stating that Scientology was not a religion.[121] If it was not a theological enquiry into the

---

118 *Church of the New Faith v The Commissioner for Payroll Tax (Victoria)* (1983) 154 CLR 120, 150 (Murphy J).
119 Anderson, above n 108, 12–15.
120 For example, the virgin birth of Jesus in Roman Catholicism.
121 Anderson, above n 108, 147.

veracity of beliefs, the Board should not have been able to conclude that Scientology was not a religion. In addition, if the Board's findings did not rely on a determination of whether or not Scientology was a religion, then there should have been no need to determine Scientology's religiosity.[122]

Victoria's Psychological Practices Act

In a direct response to the Anderson Report, the Victorian Government passed the *Psychological Practices Act 1965* (Vic). At first glance the *Psychological Practices Act 1965* (Vic) does not appear to be targeted at Scientology. Both its name and the majority of its provisions focus instead on the practice of psychology. As such, the majority of the provisions of the *Act* are couched in neutral language and appear to be of general application. However, the reasoning given by the government for these apparently general provisions relate back to the government's desire to restrict Scientology. The majority of the provisions in the *Act* focus on the perceived similarities between Scientology, psychology, and hypnosis.[123] The government believed that 'by establishing controls over these aspects, in addition to banning Scientology itself and the organizations practising it, much more effective restrictions will be imposed, and there will be less likelihood of its resurrection in some different form.'[124] Importantly, Section 39 of the *Act* made the practice of psychology by an unregistered person[125] for fee or reward an offence; the term psychology was defined widely with the intention of catching the practices of Scientology.[126]

The provisions relating to the Victorian Psychological Council and the registration of psychologists are consistent with the second recommendation of the Anderson Report. While the provisions were specifically designed to restrict Scientology, they were couched in neutral terms. They were similar in nature to the face covering legislation discussed below in their use of neutral language to catch the practices of a particular religious group. These provisions may even be seen as less restrictive, given the much wider application of the provisions than the face covering legislation. The non-discriminatory nature of these provisions is further strengthened by an exemption for 'any priest or minister of a recognised religion

---

122 Scientology was found to be a religion in *Church of the New Faith v The Commissioner for Payroll Tax (Victoria)* (1983) 154 CLR 120. The lower courts had found that Scientology was not a religion. See *Church of the New Faith v Commissioner for Payroll Tax* [1983] 1 VR 97. For a discussion of Scientology's claim to the status of a religion see Renae Barker, 'Scientology the Test Case Religion' (2015) 40(4) *Alternative Law Journal* 275.

123 Victoria, *Parliamentary Debates*, Legislative Assembly, 10 November 1965, 1342–1345 (Jim Manson).

124 Ibid. 1342–1343 (Jim Manson).

125 *Psychological Practices Act 1965* (Vic) s 16 repealed by *Psychologists Registration Act 1987* (Vic) s 47.

126 Victoria, *Parliamentary Debates*, Legislative Assembly, 10 November 1965, 1345 (Jim Manson).

in accordance with the usual practices of that religion.'[127] The term 'recognised religion' was defined as a religion whose priests or ministers are recognised under Commonwealth laws relating to marriage.[128] Scientology was recognised under the *Marriage Act* 1961(Cth) on 15 February 1973,[129] effectively nullifying the operation of Section 39.[130] Perhaps as a result of this, there has never been a successful prosecution of Scientologists under the *Psychological Practices Act 1965* (Vic).[131]

Had these been the only provisions of the *Psychological Practices Act 1965* (Vic), it would at least be arguable that the *Act* did not specifically restrict the practices of Scientology, and that any restrictions that did exist were only incidental. However, the *Act* went further with Sections 30 to 32 directly dealing with the practices of Scientology.[132] Section 30 is perhaps the most offensive of these provisions. Section 30 prohibited the use of the E-meter by any person unless they were a registered psychologist. Given the importance of the E-meter to Scientologist's Auditing, this provision could have potentially been very restrictive. The restrictive nature of this provision was heightened by the fact that Scientologists and their founder L Ron Hubbard do not believe in the use of traditional psychology or psychiatry.[133] As a result, Scientologists could not 'get around' this provision by simply 'getting in' sympathetic psychologist to help conduct auditing sessions using the E-meter.

Section 31 banned the teaching, practice, and application of Scientology for fee or reward. The provision was no doubt aimed at the perception that the teaching and practice of Scientology was a money-making scheme, and that Scientologists would not be prepared to teach or practice Scientology without receiving a fee.[134] For the purposes of this section, Scientology was defined very widely as:

> the system or purported system of study of knowledge and human behaviour advocated in the writings of Lafayette Ronald Hubbard and disseminated by the Hubbard Association of Scientologists International, a company incorporated in the State of Arizona in the United States of America, and includes

127 *Psychological Practices Act 1965* (Vic) s2(3) repealed by *Psychologists Registration Act 1987* (Vic) s 47.

128 Ibid. s2(4) repealed by *Psychologists Registration Act 1987* (Vic) s 47.

129 Ian Ellis-Jones, *Beyond the Scientology Case* (PhD Thesis, University of technology Sydney, 2007) 92 fn 61.

130 The registration of Scientology as a religion for the purposes of the *Marriage Act 1961*(Cth) was controversial. See Commonwealth of Australia, *Parliamentary Debates*, Senate, 13 March 1973, 343–344, 346–347, 349–353.

131 New South Wales Anti-Discrimination Board, *Discrimination and Religious Conviction* (New South Wales Anti-Discrimination Board, 1984) 212.

132 Victoria, *Parliamentary Debates*, Legislative Assembly, 10 November 1965, 1345 (Jim Manson); Victoria, Parliamentary Debates, Legislative Assembly, 16 March 1966, 2852 (John Rossiter).

133 David G Bromley, 'Making Sense of Scientology: Prophetic, Contractual Religion' in James R Lewis (ed) *Scientology* (Oxford University Press, 2009) 98.

134 Anderson, above n 108, 2, 22–39.

and system or purported system associated with or derived from the same and the system or purported system known as dianetics.[135]

The final section dealing specifically with Scientology, Section 32, required that all "'scientological records' be delivered to the Attorney General and destroyed. As with the term Scientology itself, 'scientological records' was widely defined as any document 'which relates to the practice of scientology on by or with respect to any particular person.'[136] This provision related to the third of the Anderson Report's recommendations, that records of Auditing sessions kept by Scientology should be destroyed. On the 21 December 1965, the police raided the Scientology centre in Melbourne, seizing around 4,000 personal files.[137]

While Scientology itself was not banned as such, these three provisions were designed to make it extremely difficult, if not impossible, for Scientology to continue operating in Victoria. Unlike the other provisions of the *Psychological Practices Act 1965* (Vic), Sections 30 to 32 could not be argued to be of general application or couched in neutral language. They were designed to specifically restrict the practices of the Church of Scientology.

Western Australia and South Australia

While the majority of the Victorian *Psychological Practices Act 1965* (Vic) was couched in neutral language, and was of general application, the laws restricting Scientology in Western Australia and South Australia were aimed entirely at Scientology.[138]

In Western Australia the relevant Act was the *Scientology Act* 1968 (WA), while in South Australia it was the *Scientology (Prohibition) Act 1968* (SA). These two *Acts* replicated the Victorian provisions dealing exclusively with Scientology. No argument can be made that the Western Australian or South Australian legislation was neutral in language or general in application. The entirety of the *Acts* passed in these States dealt only with one religion and its practices, the Church of Scientology.

The ineffectiveness and eventual removal of the ban on Scientology

Despite the legislation in Victoria, Western Australia and South Australia there were no successful prosecutions under any of the anti-Scientology legislation

---

135 *Psychological Practices Act 1965* (Vic) s 31(2) repealed by *Psychologists Registration Act 1987* (Vic) s 47.
136 Ibid. s 32(1) repealed by *Psychologists Registration Act 1987* (Vic) s 47.
137 'Scientology Files Seized in Raid,' *Sydney Morning Herald* (Sydney), 22 December 1965, 1.
138 *Scientology Act 1968* (WA); *Scientology (Prohibition) Act 1968* (SA) repealed by *Scientology (Prohibition) Act, 1968, Repeal Act, 1973–1974* (SA). For a comprehensive analysis of the Victorian and Western Australian legislation see E. K. Braybrooke, 'The Scientology Act 1968' (1968) 8(4) *University of Western Australia Law Review* 545.

during its existence.[139] As referred to above, this may be because of the exemptions relating to ministers of religion. Another possibility could be definitional problems revealed during the unsuccessful prosecution of the Hubbard Association of Scientologists International Ltd (HASI) in Western Australia.[140]

HASI was initially found guilty of breaching Section 3(1) *Scientology Act 1969* (WA) in the Court of Petty Sessions. Section 3(1) prohibited the 'practice' of Scientology. HASI appealed to the Full Court of the Supreme Court of Western Australia, where their appeal was upheld. The Court found that the prosecution had not provided evidence that HASI had in fact 'practiced' Scientology during the specified period.[141] The prosecution had relied heavily on a large number of documents found at a raid of a premises formally leased by HASI. These documents were provided to the Court but the prosecution did not specify how these documents were supposed to show the 'practice' of Scientology contrary to the *Act*.[142] The prosecution also ran into difficulty, as they did not attempt to demonstrate a single, or even multiple, acts of 'practicing' Scientology. Instead they attempted to show a course of business carried on by HASI that amounted to the 'practice' of Scientology. As Burt J pointed out, this method of trying to establish the 'practice' of scientology would be extremely difficult.[143]

Following the successful appeal by HASI, the Western Australian Crown Law Department reviewed the *Scientology Act 1969* (WA) and determined that it was so poorly drafted that it was essentially unenforceable.[144] As a result, they recommended that 15 charges before the Police Court be withdrawn, and that the documents seized under the *Act* be returned.[145] The documents were returned on 5 May 1970 and the charges were dropped on 10 March 1972.[146]

Following the advice of the Crown Law Department, and consideration of the Scientology issue over some 20 months, the Minister for Health, Ronald Davies, introduced the *Scientology Act Repeal Bill 1972* (WA) on 14 November 1972.[147] Along with the unenforceability of the *Act*, Davies was persuaded to repeal the *Scientology Act 1972* (WA) by the fact that since 1968, no other government had banned Scientology, despite inquiries in England, New Zealand and South Africa.[148] The English inquiry was heavily critical of the Australian legislation as

---

139 New South Wales Anti-Discrimination Board, above n 131, 212.
140 See *Hubbard Association of Scientologists International Ltd v Parker* (Unreported, Supreme Court of Western Australia, Virtue SPJ, Nevile J and Burt J, 18 November 1969).
141 Ibid. 8.
142 Ibid. 6–8.
143 Ibid. 3.
144 Western Australia, *Parliamentary Debate*, Legislative Assembly, 14 November 1972, 5104–5105 (Ronald Davies).
145 Ibid.
146 Ibid. 5105 (Ronald Davies).
147 Ibid. 5103 (Ronald Davies).
148 Ibid, 5106.

being 'discriminatory and contrary to all the best traditions of the Anglo-Saxon legal system.'[149]

South Australia repealed its *Scientology (Prohibition) Act 1969* (SA) the following year with the passage of the *Scientology (Prohibition) Act 1968, Repeal Act 1973–1974* (SA). Victoria did not repeal its anti-Scientology provisions until 1982.[150]

Despite the ineffectiveness of the anti-Scientology legislation, the existence of these *Acts* stands as one of the most overt instances of the State attempting to restrict the religious practices of a specific religion in Australia. Not only is Scientology singled out by name, as happened with both Roman Catholics in the early colony and the Jehovah's Witnesses during World War Two, but the State also banned the practice of Scientology 'for fee or reward,' effectively banned the religious practice of auditing, and seized the records of the Church of Scientology. Individually, each of these State actions would arguably amount to a restriction on the religious practices of Scientology, when taken together they effectively banned Scientology in Victoria, Western Australia and South Australia.

While the Jehovah's Witnesses at least had the option of challenging their ban in the High Court this option was not available to the Church of Scientology. As discussed in Chapter 4, Section 116 does not operate at the State level. At the time there was no freedom of religion provisions at the State level which they could have recourse to. Legislative Bills of Rights have since been introduced in Victoria, the Australian Capital Territory and Tasmania.[151] These however are relatively weak protections as, unlike Constitutional Bills of Rights, they can be relatively easily repealed or amended.[152]

While the Church of Scientology, Jehovah's Witnesses and Roman Catholics were all targeted by name in the relevant laws and orders more recent restriction on religious practice have been couched in neutral language and appear to be of general application. It is only when the effect and history of the relevant laws are considered, that the restrictive nature of the laws becomes apparent.

Child blood transfusion laws and Jehovah's Witnesses' beliefs

All Australian States and territories have laws that permit medical practitioners to administer blood transfusions to minors without the consent of the minor's

---

149 Ibid. 5107 (Ronald Davies); John G Foster, *Enquiry into the Practice and Effects of Scientology* (Her Majesty's Stationery Office, 1971) 181. While the United Kingdom was critical of Australia's approach they too imposed restrictions on members of the Church of Scientology. For example, until the late 1980s Scientologists were denied entry into the United Kingdom and were not recognised as a religion until 2014, see Renae Barker, 'Scientology the Test Case Religion' (2015) 40(4) *Alternative Law Journal* 275.

150 *Psychological Practices (Scientology) Act 1982* (Vic); Possamai and Possamai-Inesdey, above n 116, 351.

151 *Human Rights Act 2004* (ACT) s 14; *Constitution Act 1934* (Tas) s 46; *Charter of Human Rights and Responsibilities Act 2006* (Vic) s 14.

152 Although Tasmania's is found in their State Constitution, the Constitution is an ordinary act of Parliament and can be repealed and amended relatively easily.

parents or guardians (blood transfusion laws).[153] In all cases, the laws are couched in neutral terms, with no reference to religion, a particular religious group, religious belief, or practice. They appear on their face to be of general application. However, both the practical effect of the laws, and the background to their introduction, reveal that the laws deliberately restrict religious practice.

Content of the laws

The blood transfusion laws can be divided into two categories. First, those that specifically deal with blood transfusions to minors and second those that are more general in application, dealing with all lifesaving medical procedures carried out on a minor. The Australian Capital Territory, Queensland, Tasmania, Victoria, and Western Australia fall into this first category.[154] The Northern Territory, New South Wales, and South Australia fall into the second category.

Both categories operate by providing immunity from civil and criminal sanctions for medical practitioners who administer blood transfusions, or other medical procedures in the case of the second category, to a minor without or against parental consent. Without this legislation, a medical practitioner who carried out any medical procedure on a minor without their parent or guardian's consent may be charged with the criminal offence of assault, and be liable to civil action for battery. While the exact wording of the various *Acts* differ, they are broadly similar in that they all permit a medical practitioner to give a child a blood transfusion or lifesaving medical treatment without or against the consent of child's parent when the medical practitioner is satisfied that without it the child is likely to die. The *Acts* provide various safeguards such as the need for the medical practitioner to gain a second opinion, or have previous experience in administering blood transfusions.[155]

The blood transfusion laws do not provide any exceptions for minors whose religious beliefs do not permit blood transfusions or other medical procedures, nor do the laws refer to any religion or religious practice. As such, they appear on their face to be of general application as there is nothing in the laws themselves that suggests that they may have a restrictive effect on any religious belief or practice. However, when the specific religious beliefs of the Jehovah's Witnesses

---

153 See *Transplantation and Anatomy Act 1978* (ACT) s 23; *Children and Young Persons (Care and Protection) Act 1998* (NSW) s 174; *Emergency Medical Operations Act 1973* (NT) s 2–3; *Transplantation and Anatomy Act 1979* (Qld) s 20; *Consent to Medical Treatment and Palliative Care Act 1995* (SA) s 13(5); *Human Tissue Act 1985* (Tas) s 21; *Human Tissue Act 1982* (Vic) s 24; *Human Tissue and Transplant Act 1982* (WA) s 21.

154 When the blood transfusion laws were first introduced in 1960, New South Wales also fell into this category, but amended its laws in 1983. See New South Wales Anti-Discrimination Board, above n 131, 117.

155 See, eg, *Consent to Medical Treatment and Palliative Care Act 1995* (SA) s 13(1)(b); *Human Tissue Act 1982* (Vic) s 24(1)(b); *Human Tissue and Transplant Act 1982* (WA) ss 21(1)(a)–(b).

concerning blood transfusions are examined alongside the neutral wording of the blood laws, it becomes clear that the laws do restrict the practice of that belief by Jehovah's Witness children and their parents.

Jehovah's Witnesses' beliefs

The Jehovah's Witnesses do not believe in the use of blood transfusions. This is based on their interpretation of various biblical passages.[156] Passages such as Genesis 9: 3–4, Leviticus 17: 13–14, and Acts 15: 28–29 prohibit the consumption of blood. Jehovah's Witnesses interpret this to include consumption via medical procedures, including blood transfusions.[157] As a result, the administration of a blood transfusion to a minor of the Jehovah's Witness faith by a medical practitioner under the blood transfusion laws would conflict with this belief. Given that the laws can be used by medical practitioners against the parent and the child's wishes, the laws have the potential to restrict the religious practices of a Jehovah's Witness child by forcing them to take part in a procedure which conflicts with their religious beliefs.

The blood laws are couched in neutral language and on their face are of general application. In theory, they could be applied to any minor of any faith, or none. A parent or older child may refuse a blood transfusion for reasons other than religious belief. However, given the specific beliefs of the Jehovah's Witnesses the laws are likely to have a disproportionate impact on them, as they are the group most likely to object to a blood transfusion for a minor.

In determining the differential impacts of the laws, the two categories of blood transfusion laws should be distinguished. The laws that only deal with blood transfusions have a greater disproportionate effect on Jehovah's Witnesses than the second category, which permits any form of life saving medical treatment. In the case of the laws that only cover blood transfusions; the laws have a specific differential impact on Jehovah's Witnesses. There is a wide range of potentially lifesaving medical treatments that a parent may refuse to consent to for their child. However, the first category of blood transfusion laws do not allow for the administration of any lifesaving treatment a medical practitioner may wish to administer to save the life of a child. Instead, they deal specifically with blood transfusions. The creation of a law overriding parental consent for one specific medical treatment, to the exclusion of all others, that is rejected by one religious sect, specifically, suggests that the law may be targeted at that particular religious sect and their beliefs, rather than at a wider public policy of saving the life of children. The targeted nature of these laws becomes even clearer when considering

---

156 Watchtower Bible and Tract Society of Australia – Hospital Information Services, '*Family Care and Medical Management for Jehovah's Witnesses*' (Watchtower Bible and Tract Society of Australia, 1995) 3–4.
157 Ibid. 4.

that Jehovah's Witnesses will consent to almost any other medical treatment.[158] The only medical treatment objected to by Jehovah's Witnesses is blood transfusions, and the only medical procedure that can be administered without parental consent in the first category of laws is blood transfusions.

The second category of blood transfusion laws does not have as much of a disproportionate impact on the Jehovah's Witnesses. The second category permits medical practitioners to administer any lifesaving treatment; as such, it does not appear to target Jehovah's Witnesses and their beliefs regarding blood transfusions. While Jehovah's Witnesses' beliefs will still be captured by this category, theirs are not the only beliefs that will be affected by the more general laws in the Northern Territory, New South Wales, and South Australia.[159] Another group identified when the laws were introduced in 1960 are Christian Scientists, who reject all forms of modern medical intervention.[160] It is arguable that these laws are so neutral in their language, and so general in their application, that any differential effect is minimal. This is particularly the case when compared to blood transfusion specific legislation. This is not to say that these laws do not restrict the religious practices of Jehovah's Witnesses. Their children can still be forced to undergo a blood transfusion, without or against parental consent. Rather, the differential impact is lessened because there are more groups that will be affected. From a public policy point of view, this type of law may be more defensible as the practical effect of the legislation is not a specifically targeted at a particular religious belief.

The history of the laws

Given the neutral language and apparent general application of the various blood laws, it could be argued that any State restriction on Jehovah's Witnesses' religious beliefs were unintentional and merely incidental to other public policy concerns. The history of the blood laws does not support this interpretation. The background to the blood transfusion laws, along with the parliamentary debate when the laws were first introduced, reinforces the argument that the blood transfusion laws were designed to restrict the religious beliefs of Jehovah's Witnesses.

The potential need for laws regarding blood transfusions and minors was sparked by the death of two-day-old baby Stephen Jehu, who died in January

---

158 Ibid. 3–5.

159 New South Wales Anti-Discrimination Board, above n 131, 113–114.

160 New South Wales, *Parliamentary Debates*, Legislative Assembly, 9 March 1960, 2901 (William Sheahan); New South Wales, *Parliamentary Debates*, Legislative Assembly, 17 March 1960, 3138 (William Sheahan). The Church of Christ Scientists believe in a form of faith healing and are most well known for their objection to vaccination. See Renae Barker, 'No Jab-No pay, No Jab-No Play, No Exceptions; The Removal of Conscientious and Religious Exemptions from Australia's Childhood Vaccination Policies' (2017) (2) *Quaderni di diritto e politica ecclesiastica* 513.

1959 after his father, Alvin Leonard Jehu, refused to consent to a blood transfusion.[161] After a coronial inquest, Mr Jehu was charged with manslaughter.[162] He was found guilty by a jury on 30 March 1960, after a very public trial.[163] He was released on a £100 bond to be of 'good behaviour' for five years.[164] Mr Jehu's reason for refusing to allow a blood transfusion for his child was his religious beliefs as a Jehovah's Witness. He was prepared to try any other treatment to save his child's life, but in accordance with his faith, he could not permit Stephen to have a blood transfusion.[165] In the wake of baby Stephen's death, the coronial inquest, and the trial of Mr Jehu, all States and territories introduced laws permitting blood transfusions to be administered to minors without or against parental consent.[166]

An examination of the parliamentary debate shows that the beliefs of Jehovah's Witnesses concerning blood transfusions, and the Jehu case in particular, were a motivating factor behind the passage of the blood laws. While baby Stephen and his father were never referred to by name, the case was referred to several times.[167] The case was in the minds of the New South Wales parliamentarians as the trial of Mr Jehu was being conducted at the time of the debate on the New South Wales

---

161 'Transfusion for baby Refused; Father For trial,' *Sydney Morning Herald* (Sydney), 19 May 1959, 4.

162 Ibid.

163 'Guilty Verdict at Jehovah's Witness Transfusion Trial,' *Sydney Morning Herald* (Sydney), 30 May 1960, 4. See also 'Father let Baby Die, Court Told,' *Sydney Morning Herald* (Sydney), 24 March 1960, 18; 'Blood Kept From Baby, Court Told,' *Sydney Morning Herald* (Sydney), 25 March 1960, 5; 'Wanted His Baby to Live, Says Jehovah's Witness,' *Sydney Morning Herald* (Sydney), 29 March 1960, 11.

164 'Guilty Verdict at Jehovah's Witness Transfusion Trial,' above n 163, 4.

165 'Transfusion for Baby Refused,' above n 161, 4; 'Guilty Verdict at Jehovah's Witness Transfusion Trial,' above n 163, 4.

166 The first State to introduce blood transfusion laws was Queensland in December 1959. See *Health Act Amendment Act 1960* (Qld). See also Queensland, *Parliamentary Debates*, Legislative Assembly, 9 December 1959, 1981. New South Wales, South Australia and Victoria followed in 1960. See *Public Health (Amendment) Act 1960* (NSW); *Emergency Medical Treatment of Children Act 1960* (SA); *Medical (Blood Transfusion) Act 1960* (Vic). Tasmania, Western Australia, the Northern Territory, and the Australian Capital Territory introduced their laws in 1961, 1962, 1973, and 1978 respectively. See Watchtower Bible and Tract Society of Australia, '*Free to Believe? The Right of freedom of Religion and belief in Australia Submission to the Human Rights Commissioner* (Human Rights and Equal Opportunity Commission, 1997) 22–26.

167 See Queensland, *Parliamentary Debate*, Legislative Assembly, 8 December 1959, 1972 (Winston Noble); New South Wales, *Parliamentary Debates*, Legislative Assembly, 22 March 1960, 3208 (Vernon Treatt), 3212 (Ken McCaw), 3214–3215 (William Sheahan); New South Wales, *Parliamentary Debates*, Legislative Council, 24 March 1960, 3295–3296 (H. P. Fitzsimons); Victoria, *Parliamentary Debates*, Legislative Council, 18 October 1960, 614 (E. P. Cameron); Victoria, *Parliamentary Debates*, Legislative Council, 2 November 1960, 864–865 (William Oliver Fulton); Victoria, *Parliamentary Debates*, Legislative Assembly, 6 December 1960, 1824 (Sutton); South Australia, *Parliamentary Debates*, Legislative Council, 25 October 1960, 1497; South Australia, *Parliamentary Debates*, Legislative Assembly, 3 November 1960, 164, 1668.

Bill.[168] Further evidence can be found in the speech of Victorian MP Rupert Hamer. He made extensive reference to a medical condition suffered by infants where their blood and that of their mother is incompatible.[169] This condition was, at the time, treated by a blood transfusion to the infant after birth, and is the condition from which baby Stephen died.[170] There were also several references to the Jehovah's Witnesses either by name, or by reference to their beliefs concerning blood transfusions.[171] The targeted nature of these laws was made clear by a statement from the New South Wales Minister for Health, William Sheahan:

> when the Medical Practitioners Act was amended in 1956 to prohibit unregistered persons from treating cancer, tuberculosis, poliomyelitis, epilepsy and diabetes, the treatment of such diseases by a person in the bona fides practice of the religious tenants of any church was specially exempted. This action was taken at the request of one sect that is opposed to blood transfusions. It and another group have made representations that they should be given similar exemption in connection with the proposals for giving blood transfusions to minors, without parental consent. I do not consider, however, that the circumstances are parallel, because *these two sects are the main objectors to blood transfusions and if they are exempt from the provisions of the bill, its whole purpose would be defeated* [emphasis added].[172]

The parliamentarians debating the blood laws in 1959 and 1960 seem to have been well aware that the creation of these laws could impact upon religious beliefs. Almost all speakers mentioned the religious element of the proposed laws and expressed sympathy with people who hold strong religious beliefs. Ultimately, all concluded that the laws were not discriminatory, or that in any event the parent's religious views should be overridden in order to save the life of the child.[173]

---

168 New South Wales, *Parliamentary Debates*, Legislative Assembly, 22 March 1960, 3208 (Vernon Treatt).

169 Victoria, *Parliamentary Debates*, Legislative Council, 2 November 1960, 866 (Rupert Hamer); John Qurik in South Australia also referred to this condition. See South Australia, *Parliamentary Debates*, Legislative Council, 3 November 1960, 1669.

170 Victoria, *Parliamentary Debates*, Legislative Council, 2 November 1960, 866 (Rupert Hamer); 'Transfusion for baby Refused, above n 161, 4.

171 Victoria, *Parliamentary Debates*, Legislative Council, 2 November 1960, 867 (Rupert Hamer); New South Wales, *Parliamentary Debates*, Legislative Assembly, 17 March 1960, 3137–3138 (William Sheahan); South Australia, Legislative Assembly, 3 November 1960, 1663, 1664–1665.

172 New South Wales, *Parliamentary Debates*, Legislative Assembly, 17 March 1960, 3137–3138 (William Sheahan).

173 See for example Queensland, *Parliamentary Debates*, legislative Assembly, 8 December 1959, 1972, 1973; New South Wales, *Parliamentary Debates*, Legislative Assembly, 9 March 1960, 2901, 2902, 2904; New South Wales, *Parliamentary Debates*, Legislative Assembly, 17 March 1960, 3139 (William Sheahan); New South Wales, *Parliamentary Debates*, Legislative Assembly, 22 March 1960, 3211; New South Wales, *Parliamentary Debates*, Legislative Assembly, Legislative Council, 24 March 1960, 3293 (J. M. Carter);

When this history is combined with the effect of the blood transfusion laws, their restrictive nature becomes evident. Not only is the effect of the blood laws to restrict the religious practices of Jehovah's Witnesses children and their parents, the history also reveals that this was the original intention of the laws. While the restrictive nature of the blood transfusion laws may not be evidence on the face of the laws this does not make them any less restrictive. Arguably their apparent neutrality makes the restrictions they impose more concerning for those affected as the differential impact on the Jehovah's Witnesses is not drawn to the attention of those unfamiliar with the beliefs of the Jehovah's Witnesses and the history of the laws.

Another example of laws which appear neutral on their face but which in fact have a significant restrictive impact on a specific religion are those which restrict or limit the wearing of face veils in public. Like the blood laws, those which restrict the wearing of facial coverings do not refer specifically to religion and if read without knowledge of their historical context and religious significance appear to be laws of general application. However, when these things are examined it becomes clear that face covering laws restrict the religious practice of some Muslim women.

The wearing of the niqab and burqa

The wearing of the niqab and burqa[174] has provoked fierce debate worldwide.[175] Australia has been no exception.[176] While Australia has not followed the lead of countries like France, which have banned the wearing of face coverings in public, it has introduced laws which restrict the wearing of face coverings in some circumstances. In 2011, the New South Wales Government passed the *Identification Legislation Amendment Act 2011* (NSW) giving police the power to require a person wearing a full-face covering, such as a niqab, burqa or motorbike

Victoria, *Parliamentary Debates*, Legislative Council, 18 October 1960, 615 (E. P. Cameron); Victoria, *Parliamentary Debates*, Legislative Council, 2 November 1960, 863 (John W. Galbally), 865 (William Fulton), 867 (Rupert Hamer); Victoria, *Parliamentary Debates*, Legislative Assembly, 9 November 1960, 1068 (John Bloomfield); South Australia, *Parliamentary Debates*, Legislative Council, 20 October 1960, 1458–1459; South Australia, *Parliamentary Debates*, Legislative Council, 25 October 1960, 1496; South Australia, *Parliamentary Debates*, Legislative Council, 27 October 1960, 1561–1562, 1563; South Australia, *Parliamentary Debates*, Legislative Assembly, 3 November 1960, 1663, 1664, 1667, 1669.

174 A burqa (also burka) is a garment that completely covers the body including the head and face. A niqab also completely covers the body; however, a niqab has a slit in the material through which the wearer's eyes can be seen.

175 Renae Barker, 'Burqas and Niqabs in the Courtroom: Finding Practical Solutions' (2017) 91(3) *The Australian Law Journal* 225, 225.

176 See Renae Barker, 'The Full Face Covering Debate: An Australian Perspective' (2012) 36(1) *University of Western Australia Law Review* 143; Renae Barker, 'Rebutting the Ban the Burqa Rhetoric: A Critical Analysis of the Arguments for a Ban on the Islamic Face Veil in Australia' (2016) 37(1) *Adelaide Law Review* 191.

helmet, to remove their face covering for the purpose of identification. In 2014 the federal Parliament temporarily introduced a ban on people wearing a face covering entering the public viewing areas of parliament.[177]

While in both cases Muslims, burqas, niqabs and Islam were not referred to specifically in the relevant laws and orders, like the blood laws discussed above, their impact and background suggests that they are examples of the State restricting religious practice.

This section will first examine the content of the *Identification Legislation Amendment Act 2011* (NSW). As will be seen below, it is neutral in its language and would appear, without further information, not to restrict any particular religious practice. This section will then examine the actual effect of the legislation, which despite the neutral language with which the laws are written, does have a disproportionate impact on Muslim women. Finally, this section will examine the 2014 federal parliamentary ban on the wearing of face coverings in the public galleries. While the ban may have been short-lived, its impact on Muslim women and the message it sent to the Muslim community had the potential to alienate and exclude Muslim, and in particular Muslim women, from Australia's democratic processes.[178]

The Identification Legislation Amendment Act 2011 (NSW)

On 15 September 2011 the New South Wales Parliament passed the *Identification Legislation Amendment Act 2011* (NSW) (the *Act*) giving Police and other officials the power to require people to remove face coverings for the purposes of identification. The *Act* is very narrow in its application. It does not ban the wearing of full-face coverings in public, nor does it refer to the burqa, niqab, Muslims, Muslim women, Islam or religion more generally. Instead, designated public officers are given the power to request that face coverings be removed in certain circumstances and impose penalties if this request is not complied with. Instead of referring to the niqab or burqa specifically, the term 'face covering' is used, which is defined as 'an item of clothing, helmet, mask or any other thing that is worn by a person and prevents the person's face from being seen (whether wholly or partially).[179] While this definition would cover the niqab and burqa, it also covers a wide range of other types of face coverings.[180] As a result the law would appear, on its face, to be a law of general application.

---

177 Renae Barker, 'Rebutting the Ban the Burqa Rhetoric: A Critical Analysis of the Arguments for a Ban on the Islamic Face Veil in Australia' (2016) 37(1) *Adelaide Law Review* 191, 214–216.

178 There has also been a number of instances where the Australian Courts have been called on to determine whether a witness can wear a face covering while in court. A discussion of these instances is beyond the scope of this section. For a further discussion of them see Renae Barker, 'Burqas and Niqabs in the Courtroom: Finding Practical Solutions' (2017) 91(3) *The Australian Law Review* 225.

179 *Identification Legislation Amendment Act 2011* (NSW) sch 1[1].

180 New South Wales, *Parliamentary Debate*, Legislative Assembly, 12 September 2011, 5459 (Kevin Conolly); New South Wales, *Parliamentary Debate*, Legislative Assembly, 13 September 2011, 5510 (Bryan Doyle).

Despite appearing to be of general application, both the effect of the law and the reasoning given for the law demonstrate that the *Identification Legislation Amendment Act 2011* (NSW) has a disproportionate impact on and restricts the religious practice of some Muslim women.

The content of the Identification Legislation Amendment Act 2011 (NSW)

The *Identification Legislation Amendment Act 2011* (NSW) amended five existing statutes and two regulations.[181] It is divided into two schedules. The first schedule deals specifically with police officers, while the second schedule deals with juvenile justice officers, court security officers, officers authorised by Corrective Services, and people witnessing affidavits and statutory declarations. In the first schedule police offers are given the power to require a person to remove any face covering where that person has been requested to show photographic identification or provide their identity.[182] The second schedule gives juvenile justice officers, court security officers, and officers authorised by Corrective Services a similar power.[183] If a person fails to comply they can be removed from the relevant premises.[184]

The *Act* contains some safeguards to ensure that, where practical, the person who is required to uncover their face is afforded privacy and respect. For example, a police officer must, as far as reasonably practical, provide reasonable privacy and view the person's face as quickly as possible.[185] These requirements imply that once the person's identity has been confirmed they will be able to re-cover their face if they wish. New South Wales Attorney General, Greg Smith, acknowledged that this might not always be possible.

> A witness, who is required to remove a face covering, may request that they be taken back to a police station to afford some privacy. This may or may not be reasonably practicable, depending on the circumstances. The scene may not be contained and police may be required to remain at the scene.

---

181 *Amendment of Law Enforcement (Powers and Responsibilities) Act 2002* (NSW); *Children (Detention Centre) Act 1987* (NSW); *Court Security Act 2005* (NSW); *Crimes (Administration of Sentences) Act 1999* (NSW); *Oaths Act 1990 Children (Detention Centres) Regulation 2010* (NSW); *Crimes (Administration of sentences) Regulation 2008* (NSW) which has since been repealed by the *Subordinate Legislation Act 1989* (NSW) s 10(2) and replaced with the *Crimes (Administration of Sentences) Regulation 2014* (NSW).

182 *Identification Legislation Amendment Act 2011* (NSW) sch 1[5] (inserting s 19A into the *Law Enforcement (Powers and Responsibilities) Act 2002* (NSW)).

183 *Identification Legislation Amendment Act 2011* (NSW) sch 2 (inserting *Children (Detention Centres) Regulation 2010* (NSW) s 34A, *Court Security Act 2005 No 1* (NSW) s 13A; *Crimes (Administration of Sentences) Regulation 2008* (NSW) cls 89 2A–2D.

184 *Identification Legislation Amendment Act 2011* (NSW) sch 2 ss 2.2, 2.3[3], 2.5[1].

185 *Identification Legislation Amendment Act 2011* (NSW) sch 1[5] (inserting s 19A(3) *Amendment of Law Enforcement (Powers and Responsibilities) Act 2002* (NSW)).

[. . .] There may be times when officers at male correctional centres are unable to locate a female to assist with a visitor's request for a female to conduct the inspection, as there are few female staff working in those facilities. The inability of an officer to meet such a request does not invalidate the requirement to remove the face covering.[186]

The second schedule also amends the *Oaths Act 1990* (NSW). Under the amendment witnesses of statutory declarations or affidavits will be required to see the face of the person making the declaration or affidavit. Failure to do so will result in a maximum fine of $220 for the person who witnesses the statutory declaration or affidavit.[187]

None of these provisions appear to relate specifically to the niqab, burqa, Muslims, Muslim women, or Islam. Religious beliefs and practices are not referred to in any provision of the *Identification Legislation Amendment Act 2011* (NSW). Without knowledge of the surrounding circumstances of the introduction of this legislation, or the religious practices of some Muslim women to cover their face in public, the law appears on its face to be of general application and to have no special impact on any particular religious practice.

The disproportionate impact of the Identification Legislation Amendment Act 2011 *(NSW)*

In theory, the *Identification Legislation Amendment Act 2011* (NSW) can apply to several different types of face coverings such as balaclavas, masks, and even large pairs of sunglasses. However, it has been Muslim women who have been most affected. Of the eight occasions recorded in the New South Wales Ombudsman's review of the legislation, seven related to a female driver wearing an Islamic face covering. The one incident that did not comprised of a person wearing a t-shirt over their head.[188] Given that only 3.6% of the population of New South Wales is Islamic,[189] the fact that all bar one of the reported uses of the legislation related to this statistically small group of New South Wales residents, demonstrates the disproportionate impact of *Identification Legislation Amendment Act 2011* (NSW) on Muslim women.

---

186 New South Wales, *Parliamentary Debate*, Legislative Assembly, 25 August 2011, 4716, (Greg Smith).
187 *Identification Legislation Amendment Act 2011* (NSW) sch 2 s 2.6; New South Wales, *Parliamentary Debate*, Legislative Assembly, 25 August 2011, 4716, (Greg Smith).
188 New South Wales Ombudsman, *Issues Paper Law Enforcement (Powers and Responsibilities) Act 2002 Part 3, Division 4; Removal of Face Coverings for Identification Purposes* (New South Wales Ombudsman, 2012) 6; New South Wales Ombudsman, *Review of Division 4, Part 3 of the Law Enforcement (Powers and Responsibilities) Act 2002: Face Coverings and Identification* (New South Wales Ombudsman, August 2013) 15.
189 Australian Bureau of Statistics, *2016 Census QuickStats: New South Wales* (23 October 2017) Australian Bureau of Statistics <www.censusdata.abs.gov.au/census_services/getproduct/census/2016/quickstat/1?opendocument>.

Further face coverings are not worn habitually in Australia. As a result, any law targeting face coverings is going to have a disproportionate effect on any group that does cover their face in public. For most Australians the *Identification Legis-lation Amendment Act 2011* (NSW) will have little impact, as they do not cover their face in public. One, if not the largest, group in Australia who do habitually cover their face in public are Muslim women who follow that tradition. This means that the laws have a disproportionate effect on Muslim women.[190]

The reasoning for the Identification Legislation Amendment Act 2011 *(NSW)*

As referred to above, the *Identification Legislation Amendment Act 2011* (NSW) is couched in neutral language. This does not mean that the burqa, niqab and Islam were not in the minds of the parliamentarians when debating the legislation. New South Wales Attorney General, Greg Smith, referred to Islam towards the very end of his speech saying:

> The bill is not specific in its application to any particular group in the community and the provisions apply to any person wearing a face covering of any type that falls within the definition. However, the Government recognises that there are members of our community who wear face coverings for religious, cultural or personal reasons, and the Government is committed to working with these groups and the broader community to ensure that people understand not only their obligations but also the extent to which safeguards can reasonably be expected to apply.
>
> In this regard, the Government has consulted with members of the Islamic community on the content of this bill and is committed to ongoing work through the Community Relations Commission on the development of guidelines that will apply to government agencies.[191]

The New South Wales Shadow Attorney General, Paul Lynch, also specifically linked the Act to Islam and the wearing of the niqab and burqa. [192] The recognition of the effect of the legislation on Muslim women by both the Attorney General and the shadow Attorney General of the effect of the legislation on Muslim women demonstrates that despite the neutral language of the legislation, the laws are related to the wearing of the niqab and burqa by Muslim women. Despite all

---

190 The actual number of Muslim women in Australia who wear the full face covering regularly is unknown, see Samina Yasmeen, 'Australia and the Burqa and Niqab Debate: The Society, the State and Cautious Activism' (2013) 25(3) *Global Change, Peace& Security* 251, 258.

191 New South Wales, *Parliamentary Debate*, Legislative Assembly, 25 August 2011, 4716 (Greg Smith).

192 New South Wales, *Parliamentary Debate*, Legislative Assembly, 12 September 2011, 55 (Paul Lynch).

attempts at neutral language, these comments suggest that the laws are not about motorbike helmets and balaclavas – they are about burqas and niqabs.

On their own, these comments would suggest that the *Identification Legislation Amendment Act 2011* (NSW) was, at least partially, about the religious practices of some Muslim women; however an even more explicit recognition of the Act's connection with the wearing of the niqab and burqa can be found. The inclusion of the amendments to the *Oaths Act 1990* (NSW) and comments by the New South Wales Shadow Attorney General, Paul Lynch, explicitly linking the need for the Act to the case of Ms Carnita Matthews, demonstrate even more clearly the link between *Identification Legislation Amendment Act 2011* (NSW) Islam.[193]

Arguably, the catalyst for the *Identification Legislation Amendment Act 2011* (NSW) was the case of Carnita Matthews. Ms Matthews's case was referred to specifically during the parliamentary debate on the *Identification Legislation Amendment Act 2011* (NSW).[194] Further, the important role played by a statutory declaration purportedly signed by Ms Matthews while wearing a niqab was arguably the reason behind the inclusion of amendments to the *Oaths Act 1990* (NSW).

On 7 June 2010, Ms Matthews was stopped by New South Wales police for a random breath test. On 8 June, a woman made a statutory declaration in front of a Justice of the Peace relating to the random breath test on the previous day. The statement was signed Carnita Matthews, but the woman did not remove her face veil while making the declaration.[195] The statement accused the police officer involved of forcibly trying to remove Ms Matthews' face covering. The accusations were found to be inconsistent with footage taken by a video camera in the police car. Ms Matthews was charged with making a false statement, and was initially found guilty in the Magistrates Court and sentenced to six months in jail. Ms Matthews appealed that decision, and on 20 July 2011 her appeal was upheld in the New South Wales District Court by Judge Jeffreys.[196]

In giving his decision, Judge Jeffreys stated that he could not be certain that the woman who had made the complaint was Ms Matthews, because the woman who made the statement was wearing a full-face veil.[197] There was an attempt to identify the woman as Ms Matthews by comparing the signature on Ms Matthews driver's license with that on the statutory declaration, however Judge Jefferys said

193 Ibid.
194 Ibid.
195 Janet Fife-Yeomans, 'Uncovering the writing of this signature case,' *The Daily Telegraph* (Sydney), 1 July 2011.
196 Janet Fife-Yeomans and Paul Kent, 'Muslim woman Carnita Matthews escapes jail by remaining behind her burqa,' *The Daily Telegraph* (Online), 21 June 2011 <www.heraldsun.com.au/news/more-news/judge-could-not-be-sure-who-was-behind-the-veil/story-fn7x8me2–1226078801032>.
197 Anna Patty, 'Fingerprints Touted as way to Check Identity of Burqa Wearers,' *The Sydney Morning Herald (Sydney)*, 22 June 2011, 3.

that 'When I compare the signature on the statutory declaration and the signature (on the license) I am unable to conclude they appear to be the same.'[198]

Had the changes to the *Oaths Act 1990* (NSW) been in force at the time Ms Matthews made her statutory declaration, it is possible that she would not have been acquitted, if in fact it was Ms Matthews who made the statutory declaration. The amendments require people witnessing statutory declarations to see the face of the person making the declaration,[199] presumably, so that they can later positively identify them. If the amendments had been in place the person who took Ms Matthews' statutory declaration would have seen her face and would have been able to identify her as the person who made it, thus confirming the false statement to police. Had the witness not done so, they would have been subject to a fine.[200]

Other legislation

Since the introduction of the *Identification Legislation Amendment Act 2011* (NSW) the Australian Capital Territory (ACT) and Western Australia have both introduced similar legislation.[201]

In the ACT Section 58B of the *Road Transport (General) Act 1999* (ACT)[202] gives a police officer the authority to direct a driver to remove a face covering for the purposes of identification or administering a drug or alcohol test. In Western Australia Section 26(4A) of the *Criminal Investigation (Identifying People) Act 2002* (WA)[203] gives police the power to request people to remove all or part of their face covering for the purpose of identification.

While neither the New South Wales laws nor the Western Australian ones refer specifically to religion, the ACT law does. Section 58B(2) states that Subsection (3) applies if a thing a person is directed to remove is worn by the person for genuine religious or cultural reasons. Section 58B(3) provides:

> The directed person may ask the officer or authorised person to allow the person to remove the thing in either or both of the following ways:
> (a) in front of a police officer or an authorised person who is the same sex as the directed person;
> (b) at a place or in a way (or both) that gives the directed person reasonable privacy to remove the thing.

---

198 Janet Fife-Yeomans, above n 195, 2.
199 *Identification Legislation Amendment Act 2011* (NSW) sch 2, s 2.6; New South Wales, *Parliamentary Debate*, Legislative Assembly, 25 August 2011, 4716, (Greg Smith, Attorney General and Minister for Justice).
200 *Identification Legislation Amendment Act 2011* (NSW) sch 2, s 2.6.
201 See *Road Transport (General) Amendment Act 2012* (ACT); *Criminal Investigation (Identifying People) Amendment Act 2013* (WA).
202 Inserted by *Road Transport (General) Amendment Act 2012* (ACT).
203 Inserted by *Criminal Investigation (Identifying People) Amendment Act 2013* (WA).

On the surface, this seems to be a reasonable accommodation of the religious beliefs of some Muslim women. On the other hand, the very need to include such a provision indicates that there was an acknowledgment that these new laws would have a disproportionate impact on Muslim women.

There was also recognition of the disproportionate impact of the new laws on Muslim women in comments made during the passage of both the WA and ACT bills. In the ACT the Attorney General, Simon Corbell,[204] Jeremy Hanson on behalf of the opposition,[205] and Amanda Bresnan on behalf of the Greens,[206] all went to some lengths to point out that they were not targeting Muslims, the burqa or niqab, and that there had been consultation with the Muslim community. Rather than ameliorating the disproportionate impact on Muslim women of the legislation, this emphasis only highlights it. If the laws were not likely to have a disproportionate effect on the Muslim community there would be no need to emphasise that they were not being targeted.

In Western Australia the Minister for Police, Liza Harvey, made specific reference to the New South Wales laws and the Carnita Matthews case during the second reading.[207] Member for Gosnells, Chris Tallentire, also referred specifically to Muslim women and the wearing of the burqa, niqab and hijab in relation to the difference between headwear and face covering.[208] The original Bill used the term headwear, which was later amended to face covering in response to concern that the former was too wide.[209] The distinction between headwear and face covering also highlighted the intention to target niqabs and burqas, as opposed to hijabs and Sikh turbans. Senator Liz Behjat, for example, drew attention to the fact that the legislation was not intended to cover Sikhs.[210]

Federal Parliament ban on facial coverings

In 2014, in response to a rumour from journalists, the Federal Department of Parliamentary services effectively banned Muslim women wearing a burqa or niqab from the public viewing areas of parliament.[211] In the wake of the hysteria

---

204 Australian Capital Territory, *Parliamentary Debate*, Legislative Assembly, 8 December 2011, 5918–5919 (Simon Corbell).
205 Australian Capital Territory, *Parliamentary Debates*, Legislative Assembly, 20 March 2012, 860 (Jeremy Hanson).
206 Ibid. 861 (Amanda Bresnan).
207 Western Australia, *Parliamentary Debate*, Legislative Assembly, 20 June 2013, 1933 (Liza Harvey).
208 Western Australia, *Parliamentary Debate*, Legislative Assembly, 6 August 2013, 2631–2640, 2640–2641 (Chris Tallentire).
209 Western Australia, *Parliamentary Debate*, Legislative Council, 22 October 2013, 5239–5240 (Sue Ellery).
210 Western Australia, *Parliamentary Debate*, Legislative Council, 22 October 2013, 5242 (Liz Behjat).
211 Renae Barker, 'Rebutting the Ban the Burqa Rhetoric: A Critical Analysis of the Arguments for a Ban on the Islamic Face Veil in Australia' (2016) 37(1) *Adelaide Law Review* 191, 214–216.

over the Islamic face veil and an increased security threat level, the Department announced increased security measures at Parliament House. These included, 'that anyone entering the building covering themselves in such a way they cannot be clearly identified will be asked to be identified and to produce identification that matches their identity' and second, that 'people [who] do not wish to be readily identified in the galleries of each chamber . . . may use the galleries that are fully enclosed in glass.'[212]

On their face, these seemed to be proportionate responses. People wearing Islamic face veils would still be permitted within Parliament House and when it came to identifying people, '[i]f people [had] a cultural or religious sensitivity in relation to this, they [would] be given the privacy and sensitivity that is required in relation to that identification.'[213] This aspect of the new security arrangements is proportionate as it is minimally invasive and sensitive to an individual's religious and cultural needs. However, it was the second aspect that garnered public attention and was the most problematic.

While it is not entirely clear from the statement by the President of the Senate as to the effect of the security changes, the practical outcome was that people wearing an Islamic face veil who wished to continue to wear it while viewing sessions of Parliament were required to do so from behind a screen. These glassed areas are usually used by school children, who presumably cannot be trusted to contain their excitement at being in the nation's capital and remain silent. The explanation given for relegating these women to sit with the school children was that if there is an

> incident or if someone interjects from the gallery . . . they need to be identified quickly and easily so that they can be removed from that interjection. Or if they are asked to be removed from the gallery, we need to know who that person is so they cannot return to the gallery, disguised or otherwise.[214]

As referred to above, those most likely to be affected by these security measures are Muslim women who choose to wear a face veil. The irony is that the measure appears to have been put in place in order to prevent protests against Muslim women's right to wear face coverings in public.

After the ban had been lifted, the President of the Senate, Senator Stephen Parry, revealed that the measures had been put in place in response to advice that a group of people, some being male, were going to disrupt question time in the House of Representatives. The advice further indicated that this group would be wearing garments that would prevent recognition of their facial features and

212 Commonwealth, *Parliamentary Debates*, Senate, 2 October 2014, 7660 (Stephen Parry).
213 Ibid.
214 Ibid.

possibly their gender.[215] It also became apparent that the advice was based on the presence of a film crew who had arrived in anticipation of the rumoured protest:

> I was informed that there was a film crew at the front of Parliament House on the forecourt and that they were there in anticipation of a group of people wearing burqas attempting to enter Parliament House or something to that effect.[216]

The protest did not eventuate. Given the timing, the suggestion that some of the protesters were likely to be men and the later protest by the three men wearing the Islamic face veil, motorbike helmet and Ku Klux Klan outfit, it is likely the rumoured protest was going to be against the wearing of the Islamic face veil in Australia. In order to prevent a protest against Muslim women's freedom of religion, the speaker of the House and President of the Senate curtailed the freedom of these women – in effect doing the protestors' work for them.

On the face of it, the short-lived parliamentary face covering ban, along with the identification laws, appears to be neutral and of general application. It is only when their history and the religious significance of face covering is examined that it becomes clear that they are restrictive in nature. The use of neutral language does not make them any less restrictive. Arguably, like the blood laws discussed above, the use of neutral language risks the restrictive nature of the laws being missed and therefore not taken into account by law and policy makers in the future.

Conclusion

Across Australia's history, minority religious groups have faced restrictions on their religious practice. While many of these restrictions have arguably been based on good public policy considerations this does not make them any less restrictive for the religion and individuals directly affected. Today, Australia prides itself on being a multicultural tolerant society, what the persistence of these restrictions highlights is that this has not always been the case for those from unpopular religious groups. Even today the law continues to restrict the religious practice of Jehovah's Witness children and their parents by allowing doctors to give them blood transfusions without or against their wishes. Similarly, Muslim women who choose to wear a face covering may be required to unveil for the purpose of checking their identity. State imposed restrictions on religious practices is not a product of a by gone less tolerant era. Rather it is a live issue for many Australians.

One interesting aspect of the restrictions discussed in the chapter is their futility in the longer term. Roman Catholics, once the subject of suspicion and

---

215 Evidence to Senate Finance and Public Administration Legislation Committee, Parliament of Australia, Canberra, 20 October 2014, 8 (Stephen Parry).
216 Ibid. 15 (Stephen Parry).

therefore restrictions, are today the largest single religious group in Australia.[217] The Jehovah's Witnesses and Church of Scientology continue to operate despite the attempts to ban them, even at the time those attempts were largely futile. The blood transfusion laws have not lead to a wholesale re-evaluation of the beliefs and practices of the Jehovah's Witnesses. Even at an individual level these laws are often ineffective. In *X v Sydney Children's Hospital*[218] the Court dismissed an appeal from a boy, then aged 17 and eight months against the lower court decision that he undergo blood transfusions as part of his treatment for cancer. It did so on the basis that the 'interest of the State is in keeping him alive'[219] despite the fact that, as the Court itself acknowledges, on reaching his 18 birthday just five months later he '[would] be free to make his own decisions as to medical treatment.'[220] The condition from which he suffered was unlikely to be cured with in those five months. The utility in requiring him to undergo medical treatment which he opposed on the basis of his religious beliefs must, in the knowledge that such medical treatment was likely to be futile in the long run, therefore be questioned. Finally, while the laws giving permission for public officials to request to view the face of a person wearing a full-face cover for the purpose of checking their identify may have good public policy grounds, the parliamentary ban not only was short lived, it did the work of those who wish to further suppress Muslims for them by imposing an arguably unnecessary restriction in the name of 'security.'

Australians enjoy a comparatively high level of religious freedom,[221] however that does not mean that some Australian's are not subject to significant restrictions on their religious practice. These laws are often couched in apparently neutral language of general application and in many instances, may well be futile. Care must therefore be exercised both to make sure that the restrictive nature of these laws is acknowledged and that they in fact achieve the public policy goals they aim to.

---

217 Australian Bureau of Statistics, *Religion In Australia*, 2016 (23 October 2017) <www.abs.gov.au/ausstats/abs@.nsf/Lookup/by%20Subject/2071.0~2016~Main%20Features~Religion%20Article~80>; those who self-identify as having no religion make up a larger percentage of the population however they are arguably not accurately described as a 'religious group.'

218 *X v The Sydney Children's Hospitals Network* [2013] NSWCA 320.

219 *X v The Sydney Children's Hospitals Network* [2013] NSWCA 320, [74].

220 Ibid.

221 Kevin Boyle and Juliet Sheen (eds), *Freedom of Religion and Belief: A World Report* (Routledge, 1997) 166–175.

8 Religion and education

Introduction

Whether or not the statement attributed to Aristotle 'give me a child until the age of seven and I will show you the man'[1] is apocryphal or not, both the State and religious institutions place great importance on the education of the nation's young. The importance of education as an issue for both the State and religion is highlighted by the two Section 116 cases which consider federally funded education programmes. As discussed in Chapter 4, the High Court has only considered Section 116 on a handful of occasions. The fact that on two of these occasions the cases revolves around funding for education programmes is significant.

In 1981 the High Court held that federal funding of non-government religious schools via State grants under Section 96 of the *Australian Constitution* did not violate the establishment clause of Section 116.[2] Thirty-one years later the Court held that chaplains employed under the federally funded National School Chaplaincy Programme did not hold an 'office or public trust under the Commonwealth.' As a result, the programme did not breach the Section 116 prohibition on religious tests being required for such an office or public trust.[3]

The significance and contentious nature of the relationship between the State and education is also visible in the pre-Federation era. For example, it took 15 years and three Governors for a solution to be found after the dissolution of the Church and Schools Corporation in 1833. This was not for a lack of trying. Rather the Governors were unable to get agreement between the various Christian denominations as to the best method of instruction. Each fought passionately for their preferred method. Governor Fitzroy eventually broke the deadlock

---

1 Aristotle (author), J. L. Creed and A. E. Wardman (translators), *The Philosophy of Aristotle* (Mentor/Signet Books, 1963). This edition is a reproduction of Aristotles famous work, first thought to be produced and published in 322 BC.
2 *Attorney General (Vic); ex rel Black v The Commonwealth* (1981) 146 CLR 559.
3 *Williams v the Commonwealth* (2012) 248 CLR 156; the High Court however did find that the NSCP was invalid as the funding method was not constitutionally sound. The programme was challenged again in *Williams v the Commonwealth* (2014) 252 CLR 416 however Section 116 was not directly relevant to that case.

by introducing a new type of school – State-run schools. Another example of the importance and tension inherent in the relationship between the State and religion in relation to education can be seen with the removal of State funding to religious schools in the years leading up to Federation. While in some colonies this was a relatively painless process, this was not the case for New South Wales. Despite recommendations as early as 1855 to reform the education system in that colony, it took a further 11 years and 10 attempts before they were successful in establishing a single Board of Education. The cause – political instability. In such a climate no one was willing to risk upsetting the churches by curtailing their control and dominance over education.

This chapter traces the evolution of the relationship between the State and religion in Australia in relation to education from the arrival of the first fleet in 1788 through to the second High Court challenge to the federal government's National School Chaplaincy Programme (NSCP)[4] in 2014. The school systems which operated at the beginning of this period and the education system as it exists today are very different from one another. For example, today there are both government schools, which are wholly supported by State funding, and non-government schools, which also receive State funding. In effect, there is a dual system of education. It is a formal, organised system regulated by both State, territory and federal legislation.[5] In contrast, in the very early colonial period, the education system was, for most of the period, *de facto* rather than systematic.

The development of the education system across this period, in relation to the place of religion, can be envisaged as two halves of a journey. In the first half of the journey, the relationship between the State and religion decreased via a series of incremental steps until, by the turn of the century, the relationship was effectively severed with the creation of a wholly secular system of education in every colony. In the second half of the journey, the relationship between the State and religion gradually increased. The second half of the journey can be seen as a return journey. While the journey has not been completely reversed (which would require the collapse of government secular schools), the relationship has reversed a long way down the path it took towards secular education. While it is not argued that this final step will be taken, the creation of the NSCP is yet another step back towards religious education by introducing a federally-supported religious programme into otherwise secular schools.

Federation and Section 116 of the *Australian Constitution* played little part in shaping the journey. The shift from a religious to a wholly secular education system was already well underway at the time of Federation in 1901. During the

---

4 Also referred to as the National School Chaplaincy and Student Welfare Programme (NSCSWP).
5 See *Education Act 2004* (ACT); *School Assistance Act 2008* (Cth); *Education Act 1990* (NSW); *Education Act 1979* (NT); *Education (General Provisions) Act 2006* (Qld); *Education Act 1972* (SA); *Education and Training Reform Act 2006* (Vic) and *School Education Act 1999* (WA).

constitutional convention debates on what would become Section 116, George Reid asked 'I suppose that money could not be paid to any churches under the Constitution?' Edmund Barton replied 'No; you have only two powers of spending money, and a church could not receive the funds of the Commonwealth under either of them.'[6] While Reid and Barton were speaking of the future, the question also points to the recent past. At the time of Federation all colonies had abolished both State aid, discussed in Chapter Nine, and State funding for religious schools. At the time of Federation the delegates are unlikely to have foreseen its re-introduction.[7] However, as indicated above, State funding for religious schools has been re-introduced and is now an entrenched feature of the Australian education landscape.

However, Section 116 has not been completely absent from the changes that have taken place in the relationship between the State and religion since Federation. As identified above, there have been two High Court challenges to the funding of federal government programmes involving education and religion. However, in each case the High Court has rejected any suggestion that the programme has breached Section 116, despite the fact that the federal government now pays money to churches in the form of funding for religious schools and the National School Chaplaincy Programme (NSCP).

Attempts at a Church of England monopoly in education

In the early Australian colony there was little concern for education, which was essentially left to the clergy. However, as religious diversity increased, it brought with it an increase in religious diversity in education, the State responded by attempting to impose a system of education that was based on Church of England doctrines.[8] When this failed, a final attempt was made at creating a Church of England monopoly over education with the creation of the Church and Schools Corporation. While all attempts to create a Church of England monopoly failed, they demonstrate the State's attempts to impose a religious programme on education.

---

6 Tony Blackshield, 'Religion and Australian Constitutional Law' in Peter Radan, Denis Meyerson and Rosalind F. Croucher (eds), *Law and Religion: God, the State and the Common Law* (Routledge, 2005) 89.

7 The first colony to remove State funding for religious schools was Victoria in 1872 and the last was Western Australia in 1895. See Renae Barker, 'Under most peculiar circumstances: The Church Acts in the Australian Colonies as a study of Plural establishment' (2016) 3(3) *Law& History* 28, 48–50.

8 The Church of England changed its name in Australia to the Anglican Church of Australia on 24 August 1981. Anglican Church of Australia, *When did the Church of England become the Anglican Church of Australia?* (2012) <http://archive.is/sWmr>. The two names are often used interchangeably. For the purpose of this thesis, the name Church of England is used, as this is the name used during the period under consideration.

This section will begin with a brief explanation of the beginning of education in the very early colony before going on to examine in more detail the two attempts by the State to establish a Church of England monopoly over education.

Very early schools

In the very early colony the Church of England effectively had a monopoly over education because there was no-one else to provide it. The education of the colony's children does not appear to have initially been a major concern for those responsible for setting up the colony. The only concessions to education were the inclusion of land for a schoolmaster in the additional instructions to Governor Philip, and the inclusion of Rev Richard Johnson on the first fleet.[9] Although Governor Philip had been instructed to provide land for a schoolmaster, none was sent out from England with the first fleet or for many years after.[10] This left Rev Johnson as the only person in the colony available to give any consideration to education.

Rev Johnson set up the very first school in 1789 with a convict woman, Isabella Rosson, as the first schoolmistress.[11] The fact that the schools were established and run by the Church of England clergy did not make these early schools religious, denominational, or non-government schools in the same way modern non-government schools are. Rather, these schools were closer in nature to government or public schools despite their religious nature and control. This arose from two factors. First, the Chaplains were effectively members of the government. They were paid and controlled by the Governor, and as such could often be better described as government officials than as religious ones. This can be further demonstrated by the fact that Rev Johnson had to ask for permission from the Governor to set up his school, rather than being able to establish it at his own initiative.[12] Further, these schools, while organised by the chaplains, were usually at least partially funded by the State.[13]

The second factor was the purpose of education in the early Australian colony. The early Australian Governors and clergy saw education as a way to save the children of the poor from the sinful nature of their families.[14] Many of the senior officials in the colony, including but not limited to the clergy, felt that the adult convicts were beyond redemption, but that with education the children could

---

9 James Cook (author), Britton Alexander and Frank Murcott Bladen (eds), *Historical Records of New South Wales* (Government Printer, 1892–1901) vol 1, pt 2, 90.

10 See Bernard Keith Hyams and Bob Bessant, *Schools for the People? An Introduction to the History of State Education in Australia* (Longman, 1972) 3–4; John Cleverley, *The First Generation: School and Society in Early Australia* (Sydney University Press, 1971) 2.

11 Alan Barcan, *A History of Australian Education* (Oxford University Press, 1980) 9; for Isabella Rossen's background see Cleverley, above n 10, 24–25.

12 Cleverley, above n 10, 63.

13 Hyams and Bessant, above n 10, 6–7.

14 Hyams and Bessant, above n 10.

be saved, and the future of the colony secured.[15] Johnson expressed this popular belief in a letter to the Society for the Propagation of the Gospel in 1794:

> If any hope are [sic] to be formed of any Reformation being effected in this Colony, I believe it must be amongst those of the rising generation.[16]

This salvation was to be Christian, with bible reading seen as the means by which this end could be achieved.[17] There was little distinction between secular subjects and religious ones, with the Bible acting as the main reading material.[18] If the new colony was to survive then it would need honest decent citizens. Given the convict history of most adults, the only hope was seen to be the children, if they could be saved from their parents. This was an aim of the State, not just religion, and a view held by many State officials.

The default monopoly of the Church of England over education continued in place until the arrival of a group of missionaries from Tahiti in 1798. Their arrival heralded the beginning of religious diversity in the colony, as well as boosting the number of people capable and available to provide for the education of the colony's children.[19]

The first attempt at a Church of England monopoly

Until the arrival of the Tahiti missionaries, all schools were assumed to be conducted as Church of England schools under the supervision of the Church of England chaplains Rev Johnson, and later Rev Marsden, in effect a default monopoly. This began to change with the arrival of the missionaries.

The arrival of the missionaries brings religious pluralism and conflict

The missionaries who arrived in 1798 were members of the London Missionary Society, a non-denominational organisation. While the London Missionary Society included Church of England members, those who came to New South Wales were predominantly non-conformists and dissenters.[20]

---

15 Cleverley, above n 10, 8–12.
16 Ibid. 10.
17 Manning Clark, *A History of Australia* (Melbourne University Press, 1963) 324.
18 Hyams and Bessant, above n 10, 9; Cleverley, above n 10, 45–50.
19 The missionaries had originally been sent to Tahiti but had abandoned it after conflict with the native inhabitants. The missionaries were a driving force behind the founding of schools at Kissing Point, Toongabbie, and Green Hills. See Cleverley, above n 10, 73–77, 86.
20 Cleverley, above n 10, 73–79. The terms 'non-conformists' and 'dissenters' refer to those protestant groups and individuals who refused to conform to the doctrines and practices of the Church of England. Groups commonly referred to as non-conformists and dissenters include Presbyterians, Congregationalists, Quakers, Methodists and Baptists. See Frank Leslie Cross (ed), *The Oxford Dictionary of the Christian Church* (Oxford University Press, 1st ed, 1957) 963.

Initially the missionaries appear to have gotten on well with the Church of England clergy.[21] The London Missionary Society instructed the missionaries to 'pay special regard to the advice of the chaplain of the Church of England' and warned them against evangelising.[22] In the case of education, this instruction appears to have been heeded by at least some of the missionaries. Despite not being members of the Church of England, the schoolmasters at Kissing Point, Toongabbie and Green Hills all taught the Church of England catechisms.[23]

While some missionaries were happy to obey the Church of England clergy, disputes between the missionaries and the official Church of England chaplains began to arise. Rev Marsden, in particular, reacted strongly to any challenge to the privileging of Church of England within the colony. He was responsible for the removal of William Crooke from the Hawkesbury Public school after he celebrated communion from an un-consecrated vessel, and in a rare show of unity Rev Marsden and Governor Macquarie shut down Sunday Schools in Parramatta that were run by dissenters when they competed with the Church of England public schools.[24]

In 1817, the establishment of the Australian Schools Society further challenged the supremacy of the Church of England. The Society was founded to promote the use of the Lancaster Monitorial System of education,[25] later known as the British and Foreign Schools Society System.[26] This system did not teach the Church of England doctrine, instead using non-denominational Bible passages.[27] As a result of this non-denominational focus, the system was preferred by nonconformists and dissenters.[28]

Rev Cowper's Sydney schools

The Church of England dominance in education began to be challenged both at an individual level and at a more organised systematic level. A first attempt to re-establish the Church of England dominance of education can be seen in the rules imposed by Rev Cowper over the schools in the Sydney district.

---

21 Cleverley, above n 10, 69.
22 Ibid. 78.
23 Barcan, above n 11, 12.
24 Cleverley, above n 10, 69.
25 Hyams and Bessant, above n 10, 8.
26 Barcan, above n 11, 24.
27 Albert Gordon Austin, *Australian Education 1788–1900: Church, State and Public Education in Colonial Australia* (Sir Isaac Pitman& Sons Ltd, 1961) 40.
28 Hyams and Bessant, above n 10, 8.

The schools under the Church of England clergyman Rev Cowper's management were required to follow the 'Rules for the management of the Public Schools at Sydney, New South Wales.'[29] The rules included:

> The object of these schools is to afford useful and religious instruction to the children of the poor in general
> [...]
> The Children, according to their ages and improvements, shall be taught Reading, English, Writing, Arithmetic, *and the Catechism of the Church of England.*
> The school-business of every day shall commence and conclude with the singing of a Psalm or Hymn and a short Prayer [emphasis added]

The children were also required to attend Divine Worship on Sunday,[30] give the requirement to teach Church of England Catechisms it can be assumed this was the Church of England service.

While this was just one group of schools, the State, via the colonial office, soon also made an attempt to re-establish a Church of England monopoly over education.

Rev Reddle and the Bell Monitorial System

The first attempt by the State to re-create the Church of England monopoly over education was an attempt by the Colonial office to implement the Bell Monitorial System of education. In 1820 Earl Bathurst instructed Governor Macquarie to implement the Bell Monitorial System, later known as the National System, in all government schools.[31] Unlike the Lancastrian System, discussed above, the Bell system taught the Church of England catechisms. Had the implementation of the Bell system been successful all schools supported by the government would have once again been, in effect, Church of England schools. Earl Bathurst further instructed Governor Macquarie that Rev Thomas Reddle was to take up the role of Superintendent in order to establish the Bell system in the colony.[32] Rev Reddle arrived in 1820 and began attempting to implement the Bell system.[33] He resigned just six years later in February 1826 with the Bell system only partially implemented.[34]

---

29 Frederick Watson (ed), *Historical Records of Australia Series 3, Despatches and papers relating to the settlement of the states* (Library Committee of the Commonwealth Parliament, 1921–1923) vol 2, 356–358.

30 Ibid. 358.

31 Frederick Watson (ed), *Historical Records of Australia Series 1* (Library Committee of the Commonwealth Parliament, 1914–1925) vol 10, 304.

32 Ibid.

33 Barcan, above n 11, 25.

34 Barcan, above n 11, 29. In 1820, Pater Archer Mulgreave was appointed to implement the Bell system in van Diemen's Land. See Frederick Watson (ed), *Historical Records of Australia Series 1* (Library Committee of the Commonwealth Parliament, 1914–1925) vol 10, 372–373. At the time John Thomas Bigge conducted his survey of New South Wales, the

While this first attempt at re-establishing a Church of England monopoly failed, the State did not give up on the idea. Instead, it created the Church and Schools Corporation.

The Church and Schools Corporation

The State's final attempt to establish a Church of England monopoly over education was the creation of the Church and Schools Corporation which came into effect in March 1826.[35] Its creation was a turning point for religion and education in two important ways. First, the Church and Schools Corporation marked the first attempt at creating an overarching system of education.[36] Until now, the creation and administration of schools had been *ad hoc*, relying on local demand and initiative. Second, it formalised the monopoly of the Church of England in education. Prior to the creation of the Corporation attempts at enforcing Church of England supremacy and control of education had limited success.

The Church and Schools Corporation had its genesis in the visit by John Thomas Bigge and Thomas Hobbs Scott to Australia between 1819 and 1821. In 1819 the Colonial Office appointed John Thomas Bigge to conduct an inquiry into the state of the colony in New South Wales. Bigge, along with his secretary Thomas Hobbes Scott, arrived in Sydney in September 1819 and remained until 1821.[37] Bigge wrote three reports that were tabled in the British Parliament in 1822 and 1823. While these reports are generally considered to be a detailed source on the state of the colony in 1820, Bigge devoted just 10 pages to education and religion.[38] Instead, on Bigge and Scott's return to England the Secretary of State, Bathurst, requested Scott to draw up a plan for a system of education in New South Wales.[39] Scott's response was to recommend the creation of what was to become the Church and Schools Corporation.

Scott recommended that one tenth[40] of all colonial land be granted to the Church of England and that the land be used to provide an income to fund both the provision of public schools and pastoral services by Church of England clergy. He further recommended that the system of education to be used in these schools should be the National system. Finally, he recommended that an Archdeacon be appointed for New South Wales and be made Visitor to all public

    only schools using the National System were the two schools in Sydney. See John Thomas Bigge, *Report of the Commissioner of Inquiry on the State of Agriculture and Trade in the Colony of New South Wales* (House of Commons, 1823) 75.

35 For a copy of the Charter see Albert Gordon Austin (ed), *Select Documents in Australian Education 1788–1900* (Sir Isaac Pitman& Sons Ltd, 1963) 10–26.

36 Hyams and Bessant, above n 10, 18.

37 Barcan, above n 11, 26; Austin, *Australian Education 1788–1900*, above n 27, 10–11.

38 Austin, *Australian Education 1788–1900*, above n 27, 10; Bigge, above n 34, 68–78. See Barcan, above n 11, 26.

39 Austin, *Australian Education 1788–1900*, above n 27, 10–11.

40 The actual land granted to the Church and Schools Corporation was one seventh.

schools.[41] Scott himself was appointed Archdeacon for New South Wales and arrived in the colony, with a draft constitution for the new Church and Schools Corporation, in May 1825.[42]

The Church and Schools Corporation effectively endowed the Church of England as the official State provider of education and religion. In effect, the plan was for the State to grant the Corporation land that would then be used to fully fund the provision of public education, which would be provided by the Church of England. Thus, re-creating an official monopoly for the Church of England over education. In creating this monopoly the State was effectively determining the place of religion in public education.

The failure of the Church and Schools Corporation

Ultimately the Church and Schools Corporation was short lived. It is arguable that by the time it was created, the seeds of its downfall had already been sown. The Corporation was neither religiously viable in an increasingly diverse religious landscape, nor was it financially viable in a depressed land market.

By the time the Church and Schools Corporation was created, the Church of England clergy were no longer the only clergy operating in the colony. The Roman Catholics, led by Father Joseph Therry, and the Presbyterians, led by Dr John Dunmore Lang, were the most vocal opponents of the Church and Schools Corporation.[43] They objected to the Corporation on both religious and economic grounds. In Lang's estimation, the Corporation was responsible for,

> repressing emigration, discouraging improvement, secularizing the Episcopal Clergy, and thereby lowering the standard and morals and religion throughout the Territory. [44]

While Lang's main objections appear to be economic, Rev Therry was concerned that the Church of England monopoly created by the Corporation would exclude poor Catholic children from education:

> it may be inferred, that public provision is to be made for Protestant parochial schools exclusively; and that the children of the Catholic poor are to

---

41 Austin, *Australian Education 1788–1900*, above n 27, 10–12. See also Thomas Hobbes Scott, 'Scott to Bathurst, 30 March 1824' in Albert Gordon Austin (ed), *Select Documents in Australian Education 1788–1900* (Sir Isaac Pitman& Sons Ltd, 1963) 6–8.

42 Barcan, above n 11, 26; Austin, above n 27, 13–14.

43 Hyams and Bessant, above n 10, 18–19; Austin, *Select Documents*, above n 35, 26–28.

44 John Dunmore Lang, 'Lindesay to Goderich 18 November 1831' in Albert Gordon Austin (ed), *Select Documents in Australian Education 1788–1900* (Sir Isaac Pitman& Sons Ltd, 1963) 26–27.

be either excluded from the salutary benefits of education, or compelled or enticed to abandon the truly venerable religion of their ancestors.[45]

While the opposition to the Church and Schools Corporation by the non-Church of England denominations was important, the economic difficulty faced by the Corporation may have been more decisive in its downfall. In 1823, just one month after Scott submitted his first report, Earl Bathurst instructed Governor Brisbane to set aside 'Reserves in every district, which may in the future be granted out for the maintenance of both a Clerical and a School Establishment.'[46] Despite this, when the Church and Schools Corporation was established the land had not been fully surveyed, as a result no new land was actually transferred to the Corporation until 1829. Until then the Corporation had to survive on income from small parcels of land that had already been granted, such as vacant glebe land, the assets of the Orphan schools, and government loans.[47] Even after the promised land began to be transferred to the Corporation the income it generated was not enough to defray the costs of providing public education in the colony. The land was of poor quality and an economic recession meant there was little income to be gained from it. As a result, the Corporation continued to rely on funding from the Colonial office.[48]

The Church and Schools Corporation's continued reliance on the Colonial office for funding defeated the purpose for which the Corporation had been formed. The intention had been for the income from land granted to the Corporation to be sufficient to fund Church of England clergy and public schools. Instead, the Colonial office found itself funding these things while land, that might otherwise be profitably used by private individuals, was tied up by the Corporation.[49]

45 Joseph Therry, 'Therry to Editor of the *Sydney Gazette* 14 June 1825' in Albert Gordon Austin (ed), *Select Documents in Australian Education 1788–1900* (Sir Isaac Pitman& Sons Ltd, 1963) 27.

46 Earl Bathurst, 'Bathurst to Brisbane, 3 October 1823' in Frederick Watson (ed), *Historical Records of Australia Series 1* (Library Committee of the Commonwealth Parliament, 1914–1925) vol 11, 139–140.

47 Barcan, above n 11, 26; Austin, *Australian Education 1788–1900*, above n 27, 19.

48 Hyams and Bessant, above n 10, 18–19; Austin, *Select Documents*, above n 35, 19; Barcan, above n 11, 26; Austin, *Australian Education 1788–1900*, above n 27, 19. See also John Dunmore Lang, 'Lindesay to Goderich 18 November 1831' in Albert Gordon Austin (ed), *Select Documents in Australian Education 1788–1900* (Sir Isaac Pitman& Sons Ltd, 1963) 26–27.

49 Frederick John Robinson, 'Goderich to Darling, 14 February 1831' in Albert Gordon Austin (ed), *Select Documents in Australian Education 1788–1900* (Sir Isaac Pitman& Sons Ltd, 1963) 30–31; Third Report of the Commissioner for inquiry into the receipt and Expenditure of the Revenues in the Colonies and Foreign Possession, *Great Britain and Ireland Parliamentary Documents Vol 5 1826–1838*, 1 November 1830, 74–76; Frederick John Robinson 'Goderich to Darling, 14 February 1831' in Frederick Watson (ed), *Historical Records of Australia Series 1* (Library Committee of the Commonwealth Parliament, 1914–1925) vol 16, 81.

In May 1829, the Colonial Office informed Governor Darling of their intention to revoke the Church and Schools Corporation's charter.[50] In June of the following year, the Colonial Office forwarded formal instruction to Governor Darling for the revocation of the Corporation's Charter and the setting up of a temporary commission.[51] The Church and Schools Corporation was finally dissolved in 1833 leaving the colony of New South Wales and Governor Bourke with the question of what to do about education.[52]

Creation of a dual system of education

With the official dissolution of the Church and Schools Corporation on 28 August 1833, the Australian colony and its governors were faced with the problem of what to do about education.[53] The creation of a State-sponsored monopoly by the Church of England had failed, and a new system had to be found. In the following decade, Governors Bourke, Gipps and Fitzroy all attempted to set up systems of State-sponsored education that would be able to provide education for all children, regardless of their religion. It was not until the late 1840s that Governor Fitzroy was finally able to establish a system of education. Even then, it was not a single system for all children but a system divided on the basis of religion.

Creation of the dual system by Governor Fitzroy

The first step on the journey towards secular State-run education was the creation of a dual system of education. Until the creation of this dual system, all schools receiving government support were run by the Churches. Following the collapse of the Church and Schools Corporation, a *de facto* system of education had emerged, with the four dominant Christian denominations each running their own schools. The dual system of education established by Governor Fitzroy added a fifth type of school. Rather than being run by one of the Christian denominations, these schools were run by the State. While the dual system that was established did not itself withdraw State support for church-run schools, it

---

50 George Murray, 'Murray to Darling, 25 May 1829' in Frederick Watson (ed), *Historical Records of Australia Series 1* (Library Committee of the Commonwealth Parliament, 1914–1925) vol 16, 789.

51 Austin, *Australian Education 1788–1900*, above n 27, 23; George Murray, 'Murray to Darling, 30 June 1830' in Frederick Watson (ed), *Historical Records of Australia Series 1* (Library Committee of the Commonwealth Parliament, 1914–1925) vol 15, 560–561. Despite the decision to end the Corporation, it did not come to an end immediately owing to the death of the King, and the subsequent need to conduct elections in England, along with an administrative oversight. See Austin, *Australian Education 1788–1900*, above n 27, 23, 25; Frederick Watson (ed), *Historical Records of Australia Series 1* (Library Committee of the Commonwealth Parliament, 1914–1925) vol 10, 304.

52 Austin, *Australian Education 1788–1900*, above n 27, 31.

53 Barcan, above n 11, 42.

laid the foundation for the eventual removal of State funding to religious schools and the establishment of a State-run system of secular education.[54] The creation of any form of State-run schools was an important first step in the journey; without State-run and therefore State-controlled schools for the colony's children to attend, it would have been very difficult to both withdraw State support from church-run schools and establish a secular system of education.

Prior to Fitzroy

Governor Fitzroy established his Dual Board system of education in 1848, 15 years after the collapse of the Church and Schools Corporation. However, in the intervening years, the issue of education more generally and the place and type of religion in education specifically had not been dormant. Fitzroy's two predecessors – Governors Bourke and Gipps – had both unsuccessfully attempted to establish their preferred systems of education. Governor Bourke had preferred the Irish National System[55] and Governor Gipps had preferred the British and Foreign Schools System with separate schools for Catholic children.[56] However, both proposals had faced significant opposition from the religious leaders in the colony.[57]

Instead the colony developed a system of education where the four major Christian denominations[58] ran their own State-funded schools. In 1836, the *Church Act* was introduced, which provided funding to the four major Christian denominations. This was interpreted to include the funding of schools.[59] However, this system was inefficient and did not adequately provide for the educational needs of all children.[60]

54 The funding of church-run (denominational) schools by the State is often referred to as 'State aid.' This term is also used to refer to more general funding of religion by the State. To avoid confusion, as this book deals with both issues, the term 'State aid' is not used.

55 Richard Bourke, 'Bourke to Stanley, 30 September 1833' in Frederick Watson (ed), *Historical Records of Australia Series 1* (Library Committee of the Commonwealth Parliament, 1914–1925) vol 17, 224–233. The Irish National System was designed to bring children of all religious denominations together, with the education being Christian but non-denominational. The use of the Bible was not permitted. See Albert Gordon Austin, *Australian Education 1788–1900*, above n 27, 35.

56 Barcan above n 11, 47. Gipps recommended a separate system for Catholics on the grounds that they had particular religious objections to the British and Foreign Schools System of education, which was non-denominational but allowed for the free use of the Bible in schools. See Austin, *Australian Education 1788–1900*, above n 27, 42.

57 Austin, *Australian Education 1788–1900*, above n 27, 36–39, 42–45.

58 Church of England, Roman Catholic, Presbyterian and Methodist.

59 Barcan, above n 11, 44.

60 John Strandbroke Gregory, *Church and State: Changing Government Policies Towards Religion in Australia, with Particular Reference to Victoria Since Separation* (Cassell Australia, 1973) 37; Barcan, above n 11, 51–52; Russell Fitcher Doust, *New South Wales Legislative Council 1824–1856: The Select Committees* (Parliament of New South Wales Parliamentary

One of the main reasons for the failure of the unified system proposed by Bourke and Gipps was opposition by religious leaders who could not agree on a system that would be acceptable to all of the major denominations in the colony. The Church of England wanted its monopoly back and the Catholics demanded their own schools, while the Presbyterians and Methodists were at best lukewarm to the various proposals and at worst opposed them.[61] The failure of religious leaders to reach consensus and work together to create an efficient education system that catered for the needs of all children, created the need for a State-run secular system of education. If the churches could not do it, then the State would have to create its own system, and if no form of religious education could be found that was acceptable to all religious denominations, then the solution was to take religion out altogether.

Fitzroy's system

Governor Fitzroy[62] needed to devise a system of education that was different to that proposed by his predecessors. Both Bourke and Gipps had attempted to create a single system that was acceptable to all. This had failed because it had been impossible to design a system that was acceptable to the religious leaders of all of the major Christian denominations. Instead of trying to combine all schools into a single system, Governor Fitzroy proposed a system based around two boards of education: one for the existing church-run schools and one for new State-run schools. In 1848, the National Board of Education was created to oversee the creation and running of government-owned schools based on the Irish National System, along with a Denominational School Board to oversee the distribution of funds to the churches for their various schools.[63]

Fitzroy's solution did not solve all of the problems faced by the education system in the colony. It could be argued that the creation of the Dual Board system was both a significant step along the journey to secular State-run education and no real step at all. Nothing really changed for the four major denominations; their schools continued to receive government funding and continued to compete with one another for students.[64] The multiple systems of education were still inefficient; the creation of State schools merely created a fifth system of education. Unlike later schemes, there was nothing in Fitzroy's scheme to discourage inefficient competition and the creation of new denominational schools.

However, Fitzroy's system was an important first step; for the first time, it created schools run not by religious denominations but by the State. Education was no longer the sole province of the churches and was no longer solely

Library, 2011) 118–119; New South Wales, *Parliamentary Debate*, Legislative Council, 4 October 1844.

61 Austin, *Australian Education 1788–1900*, above n 27, 36–39, 42–45.
62 Governor Fitzroy arrived in the colony in 1848.
63 Barcan, above n 11, 53.
64 Ibid. 53–54.

denominational in character. While general religion was not banned from the classroom in these new government schools, and the Irish National System was far from secular, denominational education in National schools was restricted. Visiting clergy were only permitted to attend the National schools one day per week for the purpose of instructing children in their denomination.[65]

While Fitzroy's system preserved the inefficiencies of the *de facto* system that emerged after the collapse of the Church and Schools Corporation, it laid the groundwork for later changes. In this regard, the most important change introduced by Fitzroy's Dual Board system was the creation of National schools, which broke religion's monopoly over education. The State now competed with the churches in providing education to the colony's children.

From five systems to one State system of secular education

Governor Fitzroy's Dual Board system had effectively established five separate systems of education, which were all funded by the State. However, the Dual Board system had not solved the problem of inefficiency. The eventual solution was to create a single State-run secular system of education. Once this system was established, it remained in place for over 70 years.

The next stage in the creation of a State-run secular system of education involved two steps. First, the Dual Board system was consolidated to a Single Board system, which controlled and oversaw the funding of both State-run schools and schools run by religious denominations. The colonies took two different paths to create their Single Board systems. In Queensland, Victoria and New South Wales, there was a relatively straightforward shift from one board system to another. However, in Tasmania and Western Australia, the path to a Single Board system was more convoluted, with funding being both withdrawn and re-instated to church-run schools.

The second and final step was the removal of funding from religious schools. With this step, the State effectively severed the relationship between the State and religion in education. By Federation, all colonies had abolished State funding to religious schools and entered a period of around 70 years in which State and religion had no relationship in relation to education.

Step One – the Single Board system

The next important change in the education system was the creation of a Single Board system of education. Like Governor Fitzroy's Dual Board system, religion preserved a place in education. Under the Single Board system, church-run schools continued to receive State funding, and in government-run schools,

---

education continued to contain a religious element. However, the ability of the churches to control education was greatly diminished.

Governor Fitzroy's Dual Board system had severed the monopoly of religion over education by giving the State a new role. The State now not only funded education provided by the churches, but it also directly provided education. The Single Board system established in the various colonies took this a step further. Under the Single Board system, the State now took control not only of the educational content and creation of its own National schools, but it also regulated the educational content and creation of church-run schools. This gave an advantage to the State schools.

Two different paths were taken by the colonies to reach this Single Board system. In New South Wales, Victoria and Queensland, the new Single Board system directly replaced the Dual Board system discussed above. Tasmania, Western Australia and South Australia took a different path; none of these colonies had a Dual Board system of education. In Tasmania and Western Australia, the Single Board system was created to replace State-run education systems, while in South Australia, the Single Board system was temporarily created to try to rescue the ailing system of denominational education. In the cases of these colonies, rather than decreasing the involvement of religion in education, the creation of a Single Board system actually increased the relationship between the State and religion.

The changes

The creation of the Single Board system of education brought about two significant changes in education. First, the State imposed restrictions on the creation of new church-run schools, and second, the State imposed restrictions on the content of education in church-run schools. While the Single Board systems in all colonies had similar features, the changes discussed in this section are most applicable in the colonies that moved from the Dual Board system to a Single Board system of education. Therefore, this sub-section will focus on Queensland, Victoria and New South Wales.

Under the Dual Board system, the churches could set up new schools wherever they wanted, and there was little restriction on what they could teach. The *Education Act 1860* (Qld), *Commons Schools Act 1862* (Vic) and *Public Schools Act 1866* (NSW) ('Education Acts') changed this significantly. All three Acts significantly curtailed the ability of churches to set up new denominational schools. In Queensland, no provision was made to fund new denominational schools. In Victoria, a new denominational school could not be established within two miles of an existing government school with less than 200 students.[66] In New South Wales, the distance was five miles and 70 students.[67] The Victorian Act went a step further by empowering the Board to shut down small denominational

66 *Common Schools Act 1862* (Vic) s 10.
67 *Public Schools Act 1866* (NSW) s 9.

schools.[68] For the first time, control of the multiple education systems had truly passed to the States. Under the Dual Board system, the State had control of the establishment of its own National schools, and now it took control of the establishment of church-run schools as well. With restrictions on the funding and creation of new denominational schools, the inefficiencies observed under earlier systems could be curtailed.

Not only did the Single Board system restrict the growth of denominational schools, but it also restricted what could be taught in church-run schools. The Education Acts all required a minimum number of hours of consecutive secular instruction.[69] This was another significant step towards secular education. Previous attempts to control the religious content of education, such as the attempts by Bourke and Gipps to establish single State-run systems of education and the attempts to establish a Church of England monopoly over education, had focused on the type of religion rather than the amount. For the first time, the State now ensured that where it funded education, there was a minimum amount of content that was non-religious.

The effect of both of these changes on the legal relationship between the State and religion was to tip the balance from the churches to the State and from religious education to secular. Like Fitzroy's Dual Board system, these changes were an important incremental step in the overall journey to a State-run system of secular education. The Single Board system and the restrictions imposed on church-run schools effectively set a precedent; that government-run National schools were to be given priority and that education should contain a minimum amount of secular content. The restrictions on denominational schools gave the government schools an advantage. The number of government schools increased while the overall number of denominational schools decreased.[70]

The routes

As discussed above, different colonies took different routes to establish their Single Board systems of education. Queensland, Victoria and New South Wales took a direct route when shifting from the Dual Board system to the Single Board system. Tasmania and Western Australia took a more circular route, with both colonies first attempting to create a single system of State education before re-introducing State funding to church-run schools under a Single Board system. South Australia took a very different route and became the first colony to completely remove State funding for church-run schools.

---

68 *Common Schools Act 1862* (Vic) s 20.
69 *Public Schools Act 1866* (NSW) s 19; *Education Act 1860* (Qld) s 6; *Common Schools Act 1862* (Vic) s 11.
70 Austin, *Australian Education 1788–1900* above n 27, 118–119, 126.

Upon separation from New South Wales, Queensland and Victoria both inherited New South Wales's Dual Board system.[71] All three colonies took a direct path from the Dual Board system to a Single Board education system. While the route from one system to the other was relatively direct, it was not immediate. In the cases of Victoria and New South Wales, the change from the Dual Board system took time. In Victoria, this was due to social conditions created by the gold rush, and in New South Wales, the delay was caused by political instability. In contrast, Queensland moved much more quickly.

The first Dual Board colony to establish a Single Board system was Queensland, which separated from New South Wales on 6 June 1859. Just six months later, in February 1860, Governor Bowen established a temporary National Board to oversee the government schools, but he did not establish a Denominational Board to oversee the church-run schools.[72] In September 1860, Queensland passed the *Primary Education Act 1860* (Qld), which formally abolished the Dual Board system and set the scene for the eventual abolition of funding to denominational schools. While Queensland's change from a Dual Board system to a Single Board system was relatively simple and painless, this was not the case for Victoria and New South Wales. In Victoria, it took until 1862–11 years after separation from New South Wales – and in New South Wales the Single Board system was not established until 1866.

In Victoria, the 11-year delay between separation from New South Wales and the establishment of a Single Board system of education was primarily due to the social turmoil created by the gold rush. In particular, the irreligious attitude of the new migrants spurred the State and the churches to work more closely together to overcome the perceived evils that this entailed.[73]

In education, this manifested in increased State support for denominational schools and decreased support for National schools. Upon separation from New South Wales, Superintendent La Trobe did not establish a National Board to oversee the government schools. Instead, he handed control of these schools to the Denominational School Board.[74] While this arrangement did not last long, it set the tone of the relationship between the government schools, the denominational schools and the State. Even after a National Board was established, the Board and the government schools it supervised remained the poor cousins to the Denominational Board and its schools.[75] The lack of support for government schools led to three attempts to abolish them altogether. Despite this, they survived.[76]

---

71 Barcan, above n 11, 102, 106.
72 Ibid. 103.
73 Austin, *Australian Education 1788–1900*, above n 27, 121–124.
74 Ibid. 120.
75 Ibid. 121–124.
76 Their survival was largely due to the work of George William Rusden. See Austin, *Australian Education 1788–1900*, above n 27, 125–126; see also Ann Blainey and Mary Lazurus,

The eventual creation of the Single Board system in Victoria was largely due to a change in public sentiment, which shifted over time to support State-run secular education.[77] As the population spread out as a result of the gold rush, the need to unify the two school systems to prevent inefficiencies became more apparent.[78] This was achieved via the *Common School Act 1862* (Vic).[79]

The last of the Dual Board colonies to move to the Single Board system was New South Wales. In New South Wales, the delay was the result of political instability. As early as 1855, a Select Committee recommended the institution of a Single Board system. The Committee condemned the Dual Board system as inefficient and the conditions of the denominational schools in particular as inadequate. However, no action was taken to reform the school system.[80]

Over the next 11 years, there were at least 10 further attempts to reform education in New South Wales.[81] Much of the failure of these attempts can be attributed to the political instability of the colony. In this climate, few politicians were willing to seriously tackle a divisive issue such as education reform, despite the fact that the need for reform was growing more evident.[82] On 1 January 1866, political opponents James Marks and Henry Parks formed a coalition, which finally created the political stability needed to tackle educational reform.[83] In September 1866, the New South Wales Parliament finally passed the *Public Schools Bill 1866* (NSW), which abolished the Dual Board system and replaced it with a Single Board system.[84]

Tasmania and Western Australia took a very different path from the eastern mainland colonies in their journey to a Single Board system of education. Neither colony had to deal with the creation and collapse of the Church and Schools Corporation; nor did they inherit the Dual Board system created in New South Wales. Despite this, Tasmania and Western Australia both eventually developed a single system with features similar to that in place in the eastern mainland colonies.

In the eastern mainland colonies, the creation of the Single Board system increased State control over religion in education by controlling both creation and the content of education provided in church-run schools. In contrast, in Tasmania and Western Australia, the creation of Single Board-style education systems was the result of the re-introduction of State funding to denominational

Rusden, George William (1819–1903) (January 2018) Australian Dictionary of Biography http://adb.anu.edu.au/biography/rusden-george-william-4523/text7405>.

77 Austin, *Australian Education 1788–1900*, above n 27, 126.

78 Barcan, above n 11, 105–106.

79 *Common School Act 1862* (Vic) cl 5.

80 Barcan, above n 11, 82–85.

81 Ibid. 109–112.

82 Ibid. 11; Austin, *Australian Education 1788–1900*, above n 27, 109–112.

83 Austin, *Australian Education 1788–1900*, above n 27, 117; Barcan, above n 11, 111–112.

84 *Public Schools Act 1866* (NSW) ss 1–6; Austin, *Australian Education 1788–1900*, above n 27, 118–119.

schools. They were also both created as a compromise to appease the competing interests of the Church of England and the Roman Catholic Church.

Tasmania reached the solution of a Single Board-style system of education before the eastern mainland colonies. The first step in Tasmania's journey towards the Single Board-style system came in 1839 under Governor Franklin, with the establishment of Tasmania's first formal system of education. Unlike Governors Bourke and Gipps in New South Wales, Governor Franklin was successful in establishing a single State-run system of education based on the British and Foreign Schools System. In addition to establishing a single system of education, this effectively removed State funding to denominational schools.[85] All schools receiving State funding were now government-run. Had this innovation lasted, Tasmania would have been the first colony to remove funding to denominational schools.

Almost immediately, this new State-run system of education came under attack first from competition from the new Roman Catholic schools and more influentially from the Church of England hierarchy, who objected to the British and Foreign Schools System's non-denominational nature.[86] The conflict continued to increase until in May 1845, when the Colonial Secretary ordered an inquiry into the state of education in Tasmania.[87] Despite the fact that the inquiry concluded that the state of government schools was not as bad as had been reported by the Church of England hierarchy, the Colonial Secretary ordered the Governor to allocate funding to denominational schools.[88] This both ended Tasmania's experiment with a single State-run education system and created its Single Board-style system of education. However, it is important to note that this step in the journey towards the eventual creation of a secular State education system was happening in the opposite direction to that in the eastern mainland colonies. While New South Wales, Queensland and Victoria decreased the role of the churches in education, Tasmania had reached the Single Board-style system by increasing the churches' involvement. Tasmania was not unique in this experience; Western Australia established its Single Board-style system via a similar process.

Like Tasmania, Western Australia eventually created a Single Board-style system of education. As with Tasmania, the creation of the Single Board-style system followed the removal of State funding to church-run schools and was introduced as a compromise with the Church of England and the Roman Catholic Church. However, Western Australia's journey to the Single Board-style system was much longer and more convoluted than in Tasmania due to the very different starting position.

For the first 20 years of the Western Australian colony, the government did very little for education.[89] It was not until 1848 that the first government-funded

85 Barcan, above n 11, 62–63.
86 Ibid. 63–65; Austin, *Australian Education 1788–1900*, above n 27, 73–78.
87 Austin, *Australian Education 1788–1900*, above n 27, 78–79.
88 Ibid. 79; Barcan, above n 11, 65–66.
89 Barcan, above n 11, 69–70.

schools were established. Like Tasmania, the system that was initially established was based on State-run non-denominational schools. The aim of creating these schools was to provide an alternative to the existing Roman Catholic schools, which dominated education in the colony despite the fact that they received no government funding.[90]

Western Australia's first attempt at a Dual Board system occurred when Governor Fitzroy provided funding to Roman Catholic schools as well as continuing funding to the existing State schools.[91] This system was different to the dual systems in all other colonies in that it created a dual system of State schools and one other type of religious school. In all other colonies, multiple denominations received funding for their schools under the dual model.[92]

This dual government–Catholic system lasted until 1855, when Governor Kennedy abolished funding to Catholic schools. The main reason given for this decision was that the colony was in a dire financial situation.[93] In the following years, Roman Catholics continuously lobbied for a return of funding to their schools. These pleas were ignored until the arrival of the Roman Catholic Governor Weld in 1869.[94]

Upon his arrival in the colony, Governor Weld began to explore options for returning funding to Roman Catholic schools. His initial proposals were met with hostility, especially from Protestants who supported the existing government schools. Weld's plans were also frustrated by the first Legislative Council elections, at which most successful candidates opposed making any changes to the existing system.[95] The Anglican Bishop Hale finally broke the deadlock between the Roman Catholics and the Protestants by proposing that rather than giving funding to just Roman Catholic and government schools, the funding was given to all denominational schools. Governor Weld accepted this suggestion and the Legislative Council passed the *Elementary Education Act 1871* (WA).[96]

Like Tasmania, the compromise in Western Australia, which created its Single Board-style system of education, saw an increase in the interaction between the State and religion in relation to education. Church-run schools, which had either previously had their funding removed, such as the Roman Catholic schools, or had never received any funding at all, now received State funding alongside the State-run schools.

South Australia took a very different path to all other colonies. It was neither a Dual Board colony, nor did it have a tug-of-war between the denominational schools and government schools. Further, unlike the other colonies, the form that education was going to take was planned from the start. In 1836, the same

90 Ibid. 70; Austin, *Australian Education 1788–1900*, above n 27, 84–88.
91 Austin, *Australian Education 1788–1900*, above n 27, 90–93.
92 This system was similar to that proposed by Governor Gipps. See also Barcan, above n 11, 71.
93 Austin, *Australian Education 1788–1900*, above n 27, 144–150.
94 Ibid. 151.
95 Ibid. 151–154.
96 Ibid. 154–156.

year that the colony was settled, the South Australian School Society was founded in order to provide funding to schools in South Australia. This funding was to come from private subscriptions rather than the government, and the schools were to be non-denominational. The society opened its first school on 28 May 1838.[97] From the start, South Australia showed a preference for a limited interaction between the State and religion in the field of education; the plan was that both should be excluded.

One reason that South Australia was so different from the other colonies was the character of the early colonists. The majority of those who initially settled in South Australia believed in civil liberty, equality for all religions and voluntarism. Many were religious dissenters and non-conformists.[98] Thus, they believed that education should be non-denominational, voluntary and supported by voluntary subscriptions. However, the reality of colonial life did not live up to the ideal. In August 1843, the Society's first school became private, and as the years progressed, it became increasingly apparent that government funding would be needed to support both churches and schools.[99]

In 1846, the newly appointed Governor of South Australia, Governor Robe, announced a plan to fund both churches and their schools.[100] The new plan created controversy within the colony, with many churches debating internally whether they should accept the funding on offer. The controversy and confusion lasted only a few years.[101] The election in 1851 was dominated by the issue of whether the State should fund religion, including religious education.[102] Those in support of abolishing State funding to religion won the election, and at the end of the first week of sittings, the newly elected Legislative Council refused to renew State grants to the churches.[103] Later in the same year, a Select Committee on education recommended the abolition of funding to denominational schools and suggested funding only those schools that provided 'good secular instruction based on the Christian religion, apart from all theological and controversial differences on discipline and doctrine and no denominational catechisms shall be used.'[104] With the adoption of the Select Committee's recommendations, South Australia became the first colony to abolish all funding to church-run schools.[105]

As with the other colonies, the government-run schools funded by the State in South Australia were not yet secular in nature. The funding was to go to schools that provided 'good secular instruction based on the Christian religion.'

---

97 Barcan, above n 11, 71–72.
98 Austin, *Australian Education 1788–1900*, above n 27, 93–96.
99 Barcan, above n 11, 72; Austin, *Australian Education 1788–1900*, above n 27, 93–98.
100 Austin, *Australian Education 1788–1900*, above n 27, 98–100.
101 Ibid. 100–101.
102 Douglas Pike, *Paradise of Dissent: South Australia 1829–1857* (Melbourne University Press, 2nd ed, 1967) 421–426.
103 Ibid. 421–426, 436–437.
104 Austin, *Australian Education 1788–1900*, above n 27, 101–102.
105 Ibid. 102, 156–160.

The real difference from the other Colonies was that denominational schools were excluded from State funding. With the establishment of their Single Board systems of education, the other colonies had taken another important step in the journey towards a State-run system of secular education; however, their systems still funded not only Christian education, but also denominational education.

The last step on the journey

The final step on the journey to State-run secular education systems for all colonies was the creation of a truly secular education system and, with the exception of South Australia, the final removal of all funding to denominational schools. After funding had been removed in each colony, it was not re-introduced for over 70 years.

The first colony with a Single Board system to remove funding from denominational schools was Victoria, which removed all government funding to church-run schools on 1 January 1872.[106] The other colonies followed and, by 1895, all colonies had abolished State funding to denominational Schools.[107]

A number of factors contributed to the eventual removal of State funding to church-run schools. While no single factor can be said to have caused this important change, three of the most important factors include the public's changed attitude towards the role of religion in society, changed views regarding who was responsible for education, and increased sectarian tension between Protestants and Roman Catholics. When taken together, these factors produced the necessary catalyst for the State to take the final step towards a State-run secular education system and to remove State funding from all church-run schools.

Change in public's attitude towards religion

The significant change that had taken place in the public's attitude towards religion cannot be underestimated as a factor that led to the creation of secular education systems in the Australian colonies. In the early colony, education was seen as a way to save children from the degradation of their parents. The method of attaining this salvation was through Christian religious education. By the 1870s and 1880s, attitudes regarding the place of religion had changed significantly. The changed attitude of the public in relation to religion can be seen in how Victoria responded to a situation that had led to the increased involvement of religion in education in the early New South Wales colony.

---

106 Barcan, above n 11, 133.
107 Ibid. 151, 175, 197; Michael Cathcart (ed), *Manning Clark's History of History of Australia* (Melbourne University Press, 1993) 333; see *Public Instruction Act 1880* (NSW) ss 7, 17, 18; *Education Act 1875* (Qld) ss 12, 13, 22; *Education Act 1875* (SA); *Education Act 1885* (Tas); *Education Act 1872* (Vic) ss 10, 12; *Elementary Education Act 1871* (WA) s 24; *Assisted Schools Abolition Act 1885* (WA).

In Victoria, a dramatic increase in the number of school-aged children was one of the factors that led to education reform. 'Hordes' of idle children were seen on the streets of Melbourne and other colonial cities. To policy-makers, this was a deplorable situation that would lead to an increase in crime and a disruption to society. As in the early colony, it was the parents who seen to be to blame for this deplorable state of affairs. Unlike the early colony, the solution was not religious education, but compulsory education.[108] The religious education of children was now seen as the responsibility of the churches and the parents.[109]

In previous decades, the solution may have been to increase funding to the denominational schools and churches. Instead, at the very time that there was a dramatic increase in the child population, Victoria removed funding to denominational education and began the process of making education in State schools free and compulsory.[110]

Who should be responsible for education?

Despite these changed notions of the place of religion in education, religion was not excluded from government schools. All of the colonial Education Acts of the 1870s–1890s provided for at least some form of religious instruction.[111] The change in beliefs about the place of religion in education was more than that religious instruction should be undertaken by someone other than the school master. The change also involved a change in understanding about the institutions that should be responsible for education. In the early colony, the Church of England, and later the other Christian denominations, saw one of their major roles as being the education of children. The State was happy for them to occupy this role to such an extent that no real provision was made for education with the arrival of the First Fleet. By the 1870s and 1880s, this attitude had changed dramatically. There was now a belief that the State was responsible for the education of children, and the experience of the past few decades had shown colonial politicians that the denominational system was inefficient. Politicians and the community more generally now believed that only the State was capable of providing an effective education system for the colonies' children.[112] The debate was therefore as much about who provided education as it was about whether education should be secular or religious.

108　Bob Bessant, 'Free Compulsory, and Secular Education: The 1872 Education Act, Victoria, Australia' (1984) 24(1) *Paedagogica Historica: International Journal of the History of Education* 5, 6–10.

109　Victoria, *Parliamentary Debates*, Legislative Assembly, 12 September 1872, 1344 (J. W. Stephen), quoted in Barcan, above n 11, 132.

110　Hyams and Bessant, above n 10, 9.

111　Austin, *Australian Education 1788–1900*, above n 27, 168.

112　Ibid. 177.

Sectarian tensions

Increased sectarian conflict also influenced the removal of government funding to denominational schools. As discussed above, the inability of the various religious denominations to agree had led to the creation of public schools in the first place. The continuing sectarian conflict made the next step of removing support from denominational schools almost inevitable.

In 1864, Pope Pius IX published his *Syllabus of Errors*.[113] Among many other perceived evils of the modern world, the Pope condemned Roman Catholic support of mixed Christian schools run by the State.[114] In the decades following the publication of the *Syllabus of Errors*, the Roman Catholic hierarchy in Australia became increasingly militant in their opposition to the creation of any single mixed school system and increasingly vocal in their calls for the support of their own schools. The difficulty faced by the Roman Catholic hierarchy was that it had supported mixed schools in the past and many lay people sent their children to government schools.[115] To try and counter these issues, the Australian Roman Catholic bishops cajoled and encouraged their followers to send their children to Catholic schools. Some bishops went so far as to threaten to ex-communicate any parents who did not send their children to a Roman Catholic school.[116] As Roman Catholic militancy on the issue of education grew, so too did Protestant resistance to Roman Catholic calls for their own government-funded school system.

The sectarian conflict over education was made worse by the fact that the *Syllabus of Errors* had also condemned liberal values held by many Protestant leaders, including political leaders in Australia. In theory, these liberal values would not allow politicians who held them to discriminate against a religious group because of their beliefs. These beliefs would in theory have supported the continued funding of Roman Catholic schools because of their belief that they could not attend mixed schools. Austin argues that as Roman Catholic militancy on the issue of education grew, Protestants, including those who held liberal beliefs, began to feel under attack. They also saw the threats of the bishops towards their own followers as little more than tyranny. In response to this attack, the Protestant political leaders removed funding from denominational schools, including Roman Catholic schools. It could be argued that the Education Acts of the 1870s–1890s were partially motivated by a desire to prevent the Roman Catholic assault on liberal values from being funded with the government's own money.[117]

By the turn of the century, all of the colonies had taken the final step on the journey towards a State-run secular education system by removing State funding

---

113 For the history and background to the *Syllabus of Errors*, see Owen Chadwick, *A History of the Popes 1830–1914* (Oxford University Press, 1998) 168–181.
114 Pope Pius IX, *Syllabus of Errors* (Vatican, 1864) error 45.
115 Austin, *Australian Education 1788–1900*, above n 27, 193–204.
116 Ibid. 203.
117 Ibid. 196–197.

to denominational schools. All education funded by the State was now run by the State along secular lines.[118] The journey towards this position had been one of incremental steps. While each individual change may not have been revolutionary, together they combined to transform the education system. In the 100 or so years since the arrival of the First Fleet, the education system in the Australian colonies had transformed from a system of effectively religious education run by the Church of England clergy with some support from the State to a system of secular education run and funded by the State.

A period of stability

In 1895, Western Australia became the last colony to remove State funding to church-run schools. The preceding 100 years had been a period of constant change in the system and structure of education. While there had been some lengthy periods between actual change, such as the 15 years between the collapse of the Church and Schools Corporation and the creation of Fitzroy's Dual Board system, and 18 years between the creation of Fitzroy's Dual Board system and the creation of a Single Board system in New South Wales, these were not periods of stability in terms of the issues of the place of religion in education; it remained a live issue. By contrast, the following 70 years[119] were a period of stability.

For 70 years, the State ran and funded only its own schools, and the churches were left to their own devices. Church-run schools – especially Roman Catholic schools – continued to exist, but they received no support from the State.[120] One potential reason for the period of stability in relation to religion in education may be that the population was relatively homogeneous in terms of religious belief. The period of stability may also have come to an end for similar reasons. As will be discussed below, the outbreak of World War Two and the resulting population changes contributed to the re-introduction of State funding for church-run schools. Stability, however, did not last forever. As will be discussed below, in 1964 the federal government re-introduced State funding for church-run schools. While the initial funding was small in scale, its introduction was the first step in a journey back towards a significant interaction between the State and religion in relation to education.

It is important to note that while education funded by the State during this period was secular this did not mean religion was completely excluded from the

---

118 However, all of the colonial Education Acts permitted a small number of hours each week for segregated voluntary religious instruction.
119 The 70 years is calculated from the removal of State funding in Western Australia in 1895 to the introduction of the School Science Laboratories scheme in 1964. For colonies that removed State funding to church schools earlier, the gap is even larger: 92 years for Victoria and 113 years for South Australia.
120 For a discussion of church schools, including Roman Catholic schools, during this period, see Austin, *Australian Education 1788–1900*, above n 27, 200–202; Barcan, above n 11, 141–143.

classroom. All of the Education Acts provided for some form of religious instruction.[121] This situation continues today. While most of the State's modern Education Acts refer to secular education,[122] they also provide for specific religious instruction of one form or another.[123]

The first step: capital grants

For over 70 years, the interaction between the State and religion in relation to education remained unchanged. This period of stability came to an end in the 1960s, when the issue of State funding for church-run schools re-emerged, leading to the creation of the School Science Laboratories Scheme. This federally funded scheme became the first step in the return journey towards an increased relationship between the State and religion in relation to education. While it is not argued that a complete return to a church-run system of education is either likely or possible, however incremental changes in the interaction between the State and religion that have occurred since the re-introduction of State funding for religion reversed many of the changes that led to the State-run secular education system that existed at Federation. This reversal has had three steps: first, the re-introduction of State funding via capital grants schemes; second, the creation of per-capita grants schemes; and third, the introduction of a State-sponsored religious programme into otherwise secular State schools.

As with the journey towards a State-run secular education system, the reasons for the return journey are complex. Perhaps most importantly, in the second half of the twentieth century Australia was a very different place compared to when the colonies had established the secular education system. Also important was the political situation in the 1960s, with the newly formed Democratic Labor Party (DLP) effectively holding the balance of power.[124] Given the DLP's Roman Catholic supporter base, as well as the changed attitudes towards Roman Catholicism and the crisis facing the Roman Catholic education system, the time was ripe to re-introduce funding to religious schools.

---

121 Austin, *Australian Education 1788–1900*, above n 27, 168.
122 *Education Act 2004* (ACT) s 28; *Education Act 1990* (NSW) s 30; *Education Act 2016* (Tas) s 125; *Education and Training Reform Act 2006* (Vic) s 2.2.10; *School Education Act 1999* (WA) s 68.
123 *Education Act 2004* (ACT) s 29; *Education Act 1990* (NSW) ss 32, 33; *Education Act 2015* (NT) ss 86, 87; *Education (General Provisions) Act 2006* (Qld) s 76; *Education Act 1972* (SA) s 102; *Education Act 2016* (Tas) s 126; *Education and Training Reform Act 2006* (Vic) s 2.2.11; *School Education Act 1999* (WA) ss 69, 71; see also Cathy Byrne, *Religion in Secular Education* (Brill, 2014) 167–174.
124 P. N. Gill, 'The Federal Science Grant: An Episode in Church and State Relations, 1963–1964' (1964) 7(1) *Melbourne Studies in Education* 271, 282; James Jupp, *Australian Party Politics* (Melbourne University Press, 2nd ed, 1968) 83.

School Science Laboratories Scheme (SSLS)

In the lead-up to the 1963 federal election, Prime Minister Robert Menzies announced the creation of a new funding scheme for both government and non-government schools. Menzies announced:

> there is a special need for the improved science teaching in the secondary schools, if we are to keep in step with the march of science.
>
> As some recognition of this need, we will make available £5M. per annum for the provision of building and equipment facilities for science teaching in secondary schools. The amount will be distributed on a school population basis, and will be available to all secondary schools, government or independent, without discrimination.[125]

In just a few short sentences, Menzies swept away 70 years of opposition to the direct funding of non-government schools. While the amount of funding was targeted and relatively small, it was an important first step in the federal government's funding of education for two reasons. First, it was the federal government's first foray into the direct funding of either government or non-government schools. The federal government had previously maintained that it had no role in the direct funding of schools. Second, and more important, it was the first time since the establishment of the principle of 'free, compulsory and secular' education that a government of any level had created a scheme to provide direct funding to non-government schools.

On 21 May 1964, the *States Grants (Science Laboratories and Technical Training) Act 1964* (Cth) was passed by the Commonwealth Parliament in fulfillment of Menzies' election promise.[126] The SSLS allocated £5million per year of Commonwealth funds to the building and equipping of science laboratories in government and non-government, including religious, secondary schools.[127]

Reasons for the School Science Laboratories Scheme

As referred to above, the creation of the SSLS is remarkable because it broke with several longstanding conventions regarding the relationship between the State and religion; that is, that the States fund education rather than the federal government, and that only government secular schools would receive funding. As late as November 1962, Prime Minister Menzies maintained that the

---

125 Robert Menzies, 'Federal Election, 1963 Policy Speech' (Speech delivered in Melbourne, 12 November 1963).
126 Ian Wilkinson et al., *A History of State Aid to Non-Government Schools in Australia* (Department of Education, Science and Training, 2007) 19.
127 The provisions relating to the SSLS can be found in Section 2 of the Act. The Act also set up a scheme that provided £5 million per year for the funding of technical training (Section 3).

Commonwealth could not and would not provide funding to schools, including non-government schools.[128] In 1960, in answer to the question:

> whether his Government favours the provision of financial assistance for denominational schools throughout the Commonwealth?[129]

Menzies replied simply:

> The honourable [sic] member puts to me a question that is outside the jurisdiction of this Government.[130]

Given this, the question that has to be answered is why the Menzies Government changed its mind? As alluded to above, the answer is complex and involves a number of factors, including a crisis in the education system, political capital that could be gained by the creation of the scheme and the changed nature of Australia's attitude towards religion.

A crisis in (Catholic) education

One important factor that contributed to the timing of the introduction of the SSLS was a crisis in funding facing both the Roman Catholic school system and the government school system in the 1950s and 1960s. The 1950s saw a boom in the number of school-aged children as a result of the post-War baby boom, post-War migration, higher school retention and higher school-leaving ages.[131] This created immense pressure on the education systems.[132]

The Roman Catholic education system was under particular pressure. In the period 1948–1960, the Catholic school system across Australia saw a 98% increase in enrolments.[133] The Catholic School system was also facing increased wages, as teachers in their schools now demanded to be paid the same wages as

---

128 Gough Whitlam, *The Whitlam Government 1972–1975* (Viking, 1985) 296–297; Anne O'Brien, *Blazing a Trail: Catholic Education in Victoria 1963–1980* (David Lovell Publishing, 1999) 30.

129 Commonwealth of Australia, *Parliamentary Debates*, House of Representatives, 30 August 1960, 514 (Mr James).

130 Ibid. (Robert Menzies, Prime Minister). Arthur Calwell (Leader of the Opposition) reminded Menzies of this answer during the debate on the *States Grants (Science Laboratories and Technical Training) Act 1964* (Cth); see Commonwealth of Australia, *Parliamentary Debates*, House of Representatives, 14 May 1964, 1930 (Arthur Calwell).

131 Wilkinson et al., above n 126, 22.

132 L. Warren Louden and R. K. Browne, 'Developments in Education Policy in Australia: A Perspective on the 1980s' in Hedley Beare and William Lowe Boyd (eds), *Restructuring Schools: an international perspective on the movement to transform the control and performance of schools* (The Falmer Press, 1993) 108.

133 Barcan, above n 11, 316–317.

teachers at government schools. This was exacerbated by a shift away from teachers who were members of religious orders towards the use of lay teachers.[134]

The crisis facing the Roman Catholic education system was brought to the public's attention when the Auxiliary Bishop of Canberra-Goulburn, John Cullinane, closed all Roman Catholic schools in his diocese on 16 July 1962. The dramatic closures were in response to demands by the New South Wales Health Authorities that the toilet facilities at Our Lady of Mercy Preparatory School be improved and expanded. The school did not have the funds and resented being told how to spend its limited resources. As a result of meetings with parents at other Roman Catholic schools in the diocese, a decision was made to close all schools in solidarity with Our Lady of Mercy Preparatory School and to attempt to enrol the children in the local government primary schools.[135] While the protest was short-lived, it garnered significant attention from the press and the public more generally.[136] The Goulburn closure, along with the more general crisis facing education, meant that more funding was needed; however, changes to the tax system in 1942 meant that the States and territories simply did not have the funds.

Prior to 1942, both the States and the Commonwealth collected income tax. In 1942, the Commonwealth wanted to increase the tax it collected to help fund World War Two. Simply increasing the percentage collected by the Commonwealth would have placed an unequal burden on citizens in different States and had drastic political implications because of the large increase needed to adequately fund the War effort. To try and avoid these difficulties, the Commonwealth used a number of heads of power in the *Constitution* and effectively excluded the States from this area of revenue.[137]

As a result, the States now had less revenue but needed more funds to cater for the increasing number of students in their education systems. In the end, the federal government responded to the crisis by introducing the SSLS. As with Governor Fitzroy's Dual Board system of education, the SSLS did not solve the crisis in the existing system of education because it funded just one small area of education. However, as with Fitzroy's Dual Board system, it was an important first step because it set the precedent that the federal government could fund education and religious schools, just as Fitzroy's system had set the precedent that there could be State-run schools.

---

134 Wilkinson et al., above n 126, 40; Barcan, above n 11, 368–371.
135 Of the 2,070 Catholic school children in Goulburn, 640 were enrolled at the State primary and secondary schools.
136 Wilkinson et al., above n 126, 26–29.
137 Sarah Joseph and Melissa Castan, *Federal Constitutional Law: A Contemporary View* (Thomson Reuters, 3rd ed, 2010) 329–330.

Changed attitudes towards religion and education

At the end of the nineteenth century, one of the factors that contributed to the removal of State funding of church-run schools and the creation of a State-run secular system of education was a change in the community's attitude towards religion in education. Public attitudes had changed again by the 1960s, and now a reduction in sectarian conflict contributed to the re-introduction of State funding for church-run schools.

Demographic change was an important contributor to this change in public sentiment. In the 70 years since the removal of funding to religious schools, the religious demographics of Australia had shifted. Importantly, Roman Catholics no longer made up a small lower class.[138] At the time of the 1961 census, there were 2,620,011 Catholics[139] in Australia compared to 3,668,931 Church of England adherents.[140] While they were not yet a majority – a feat that Roman Catholics achieved in the 1986 census[141] – they were well on their way and at the very least made up a sizable, growing and important minority.[142]

The sentiments of non-Roman Catholics towards the State funding of non-government schools had also shifted in the 70 years since the removal of State funding to church-run schools. Polls conducted around the time that the SSLS was introduced show that there was support for the introduction of State funding for non-government schools. In all bar one Gallop polls conducted in this period, there was an absolute majority in favour of the re-introduction of such funding. Given that Roman Catholics were still a minority, this indicates that Protestants were now prepared to support the funding of religious schools even though the majority of any such funding would go to Roman Catholic schools.[143]

Political capital

Another important factor in the timing of the creation of the SSLS was the political capital to be gained by the Menzies Liberal Government as a result of creating the scheme. At the time the scheme was introduced, the Menzies Government was able to exploit two political factors to its own advantage. First, the creation of the SSLS enabled the Menzies Government to highlight significant internal

138 Barcan, above n 11, 319.
139 This figure is obtained by combining those who described themselves as 'Catholic' and those who described themselves as 'Roman Catholic' on the census form.
140 Gill, above n 124, 276.
141 Ian Castles, *Religion: Census of Population and Housing 30 June 1986* (Australian Bureau of Statistics, Commonwealth of Australia, 1991) 1–2, available at <www.ausstats.abs.gov.au/ausstats/free.nsf/0/804F27A83754B481CA2574D500165929/$File/25100_1986_Religion_in_Australia.pdf>.
142 Barcan, above n 11, 319; Gill, above n 124, 275–276.
143 Gill, above n 124. In 1961, 82% of non-Government schools in Australia were Roman Catholic; see Australian Bureau of Statistics, *Year Book of the Commonwealth of Australia No.49–1963* (Commonwealth Bureau of Census and Statistics, 1963) 729.

conflict within the Australian Labor Party (ALP). Secondly, the Scheme enabled the Menzies Government to garner the support of the Democratic Labor Party (DLP) and its predominantly Roman Catholic supporter base.

Not long before the announcement of the 1963 election and therefore the announcement of the SSLS, the State Labor Government in New South Wales had been engaged in a very public argument with the federal branch of the Labor Party on the issue of funding schemes for students at non-government schools. There was great political capital to be gained by the Federal Liberal Party in offering a funding scheme that the Labor Party could not.

In 1963, the New South Wales State Labor Conference recommended that the NSW State Labor Government fund science laboratories in all schools and provide bursaries for secondary school students. However, these policies conflicted with the national ALP policy adopted in 1957.[144] With the next national conference just two months away, the New South Wales branch of the ALP decided to wait and see how the ALP National Conference and the National Executive would respond to its proposed funding programme. At the 1963 National Conference, direct funding of non-government schools was ruled out.[145] However, the Conference supported a system of scholarships for students of both government and non-government schools, provided that the payment was made directly to the student.[146] This meant that the planned NSW science classroom scheme was no longer permissible. However, the NSW Labor Government interpreted the second policy on education as permitting its new bursary scheme. The Federal ALP Executive took a different view.[147] The problem was that the National Labor policy permitted the payment of bursaries directly to students, while the NSW scheme paid the bursary to parents, which in effect reimbursed them for fees already paid to non-government schools.[148]

The NSW State Labor Party and the Federal Labor Executive were at an impasse. After two hurried negotiations, a settlement was finally reached that allowed the New South Wales Government to keep its proposed bursary scheme.[149] While the bursary scheme remained, it did so only after very public and fraught negotiations

144 Henry Albinski, *The Australian Labor Party and the Aid to Parochial Schools Controversy* (Pennsylvania State University, 1966) 11–13.
145 'Labour Party Clarifies Policy on Aid to Schools,' *The Sydney Morning Herald* (Sydney), 2 August 1963, 1.
146 Albinski, above n 144, 18.
147 Whitlam, above n 128, 298.
148 'State Aid Plan Under Attack: Contrary to ALP Federal Policy,' *The Age* (Melbourne), 4 October 1963, 3.
149 See 'Compromise Proposal to Avert Rift Over School Aid,' *The Sydney Morning Herald* (Sydney), 4 October 1963, 1; 'Labor Party Disunity on Two Major Issues,' *The Sydney Morning Herald* (Sydney), 4 October 1963, 2; 'State Aid Plan Under Attack,' above n 148, 3; 'State Govt. Wins on School Aid; Federal Envoy Drop Attack,' *The Sydney Morning Herald* (Sydney), 9 October 1963, 1; 'Askin Attacks Aid Decisions,' *The Sydney Morning Herald* (Sydney), 9 October 1963, 5.

between the NSW State Labor Party and the National Executive.[150] As *The Sydney Morning Herald* editorial noted, the Federal Executive was made to look 'remarkably foolish.'[151]

Not long after this very public dispute between Federal and State Labor, the then Liberal/Country Prime Minister Menzies announced an early election for 30 November 1963.[152] The Liberal/Country Party won the election. While education was not the only factor in the election, the issue served to highlight internal divisions within the ALP as well as the so-called '36 Faceless Men' of the Labor Executive.[153]

As well as highlighting internal division within the ALP, the announcement of the SSLS enabled the Liberal Party to garner support from the DLP. The very existence of the DLP and its particular position in the political landscape of the 1960s played an important role in the timing of the re-introduction of State funding to church-run schools.

The DLP split from the ALP in 1954–1955.[154] While the DLP had little parliamentary representation, it effectively held the balance of power via its flow of preferences to the Liberal Party. Prior to the 1963 election, the Liberal Government held the lower house of federal Parliament by a majority of just one vote.[155] Perhaps more importantly, the Liberal Party had attained many of the seats it held courtesy of the DLP's second preference flows.[156] In order to retain government, the Liberal Party needed to retain the flow of the DLP's second preferences. One of the DLP's key policy issues was education. It was particularly concerned by the low level of funding.[157] At the 1963 election, the DLP's policy on education was to immediately increase Commonwealth assistance to all forms of education.[158] By announcing the SSLS and extending it to cover both government and non-government schools, including Roman Catholic schools, the Liberal Party was able to offer the DLP a way to achieve one of its policy objectives. The Scheme would also have appealed to the DLP voters, who were predominantly Roman Catholic.[159]

---

150 Albinski, above n 144, 20–22.
151 'NSW Labour Victory on State Aid,' *The Sydney Morning Herald* (Sydney), 9 October 1963, 2.
152 Whitlam, above n 128, 299.
153 See Gill, above n 124, 300–304; Ross Fitzgerald and Stephen Holt, *Pressman Par Excellence: Alan 'the Red Fox' Reid* (University of New South Wales Press, 2010) 153–164.
154 Wilkinson et al., above n 126, 31. This split also led the ALP to change its policy regarding education from one that supported the funding of non-Government schools to one that did not; see Whitlam, above n 128, 297.
155 Gill, above n 124, 282.
156 Jupp, above n 124, 83.
157 'DLP Puts Foreign Policy and Defence in Forefront,' *The Age* (Melbourne), 8 November 1963, 6–7.
158 Ibid; Gill, above n 124, 274.
159 Gill, above n 124, 282.

During the debate surrounding the SSLS, there was no suggestion from the Federal Liberal Government or Prime Minister Menzies that the Scheme heralded the beginning of a wider funding programme for either government or non-government schools.[160] They did not see it as the first step in a return journey back towards a close relationship between the State and religion in education. As far as the architects of the Scheme were concerned, it was a one-off programme and the federal government had no intention to further interfere in the arena of education.[161] Despite this, the SSLS holds the historical position as the first step in the journey towards greater Commonwealth involvement in education generally and funding of non-government schools specifically.

The School Libraries Scheme

The next incremental step in the journey towards an increased relationship between the State and religion in relation to education occurred in 1968, with the creation of the Federal School Libraries Scheme.[162] The Scheme provided $27million over three years, which was distributed along the same lines as the SSLS.[163]

Unlike the SSLS, the introduction of the School Libraries Scheme for secondary schools was not a surprise.[164] The Scheme was preceded by extensive lobbying from interest groups and public support for such a programme.[165] It also made further funding seem more likely. The federal government had now taken two tentative steps along the return journey towards the re-introduction of ongoing funding for religious schools. The SSLS, which had been a point, had now become a line that could turn into a pattern of federal funding to schools.

Ongoing capital grants

So far, direct funding to non-government schools had been via non-recurring grants. The School Libraries Scheme was specified to run for just three years; in theory, the SSLS could have been phased out at any time.[166] These schemes

---

160 See Commonwealth of Australia, *Parliamentary Debates*, House of Representatives, 14 May 1964, 1971 (Kim Beazley), 1950 (Malcolm Mackay).

161 Don Smart, *Federal Aid to Australian Schools* (University of Queensland Press, 1978) 78.

162 *States Grants (Secondary school Libraries) Act 1968* (Cth), as repealed by *Statute Law Revision Act 1973* (Cth) sch 3.

163 Commonwealth of Australia, *Parliamentary Debates*, House of Representatives, 14 August 1968, 142 (Malcolm Fraser, Minister for Education and Science).

164 Smart, *Federal Aid to Australian Schools*, above n 161, 73.

165 Ibid. 73–96; Don Smart, 'Origins of the Secondary Schools Library Scheme' in Douglas Alan Jecks (ed), *Influences in Australian Education* (Carroll's Pty Ltd, 1974) 105–127.

166 According to the Karmel report, these schemes were due to finish on 31 December 1974 and 30 June 1975 respectively; see Interim Committee for the Australian Schools Commission, *Schools in Australia: Report of the Interim Committee for the Australian Schools Commission* (Interim Committee for the Australian Schools Commission, 1973) 6.

were far from being permanent funding that non-government schools could rely on. Permanency came in 1973 with the creation of ongoing capital funding for non-government schools. In 1972, the federal government had created a capital grants scheme for government schools.[167] The following year, the federal government extended it to apply to non-government schools as well.[168] Non-government schools now had a more reliable and flexible source of capital funding – even if they already had a suitable science block and library, they could now apply for funding for other urgent capital works.[169]

The second step: per-capita grants

The second step in the journey towards an increased interaction between the State and religion in relation to education was the creation of a system of per-capita grants for non-government schools. This step produced three important changes. First, for the first time, it created per-capita rather than capital grants. Second, the per-capita grants scheme created an ongoing interaction between the State and religion that non-government schools could rely upon as a source of funding. Finally, the funding was exclusively between the State and non-government schools, unlike the SSLS, Libraries Scheme and capital grants schemes State-run government schools were not included.

The amount of recurrent funding and the way in which the amount received by each school was determined changed several times in the decades following the initial introduction of per-capita grants. Initially, the funding was a set dollar amount per student, which was changed to a percentage per student before being completely re-invented as a system of funding based on 'need.' While each of these funding modes have different implications, the most important step was the initial creation of recurrent per-capita-based funding. While important, the changes and amendments are simply different ways of achieving the same aim of ongoing funding of religious schools by the State. This ongoing funding of non-government schools has continued into modern Australia and is arguably the basis of modern Australia's dual system of education. The most recent examination of the way in which funds are allocated to schools, including non-government schools, are the Gonski Reviews.[170]

---

167 *States Grants (Capital Assistance) Act 1971–1972* (Cth).
168 Commonwealth of Australia, *Parliamentary Debate*, House of Representatives, 11 May 1972, 2456 (William McMahon); Interim Committee for the Australian Schools Commission, above n 166, 40.
169 Commonwealth of Australia, *Parliamentary Debate*, House of Representatives, 14 September 1972, 1397–1399 (Malcolm Fraser, Minister for Education and Science).
170 David Gonski et al., *Review of Funding for Schooling: Final Report* (Australian Government, Department of Education, Employment and Workplace Relations, 2011). As of May 2017, it was announced that David Gonski would head another panel to produce a report assessing the allocation of funds to schools. This report is due to be provided to the government on March 2018. For more information see Gabrielle Chan and Paul Karp, '"Gonski 2.0" review to allocate resources as funding is cut to private schools,'

Creation of per-capita funding

The crisis in Roman Catholic education, as discussed above, had not abated as a result of the introduction of the various capital works schemes. As Prime Minister Malcolm Fraser pointed out, there was a very real danger of the government school system being flooded with students if the non-government schools collapsed.[171] The solution was the introduction of per-capita grants to non-government schools.

An important aspect of this step in the journey was that it only applied to non-government schools. The SSLS, School Libraries Scheme and the Capital Funding Scheme had all provided funding to both government and non-government schools. The new per-capita grants programme only provided funding to non-government schools, which were predominantly religious and predominantly Roman Catholic. Prime Minister Fraser specifically rejected any argument that similar grants should be made to government schools as well. In the government's opinion, it already provided over 50% of the States' recurrent expenditure, and as such, it had already supplied 50% of the funding of government schools.[172]

Fixed rate grants

The first version of the per-capita grants to be introduced was based on a fixed dollar amount per student. In the 1969/70 budget, the Commonwealth government announced that it would provide per-capita grants to non-government schools of $35 per primary school student and $50 per secondary school student.[173] The initial grants were not enough to alleviate the crisis; in 1972, the amount of the per-capita grants was increased to $50 per primary school student and $68 per secondary school student.[174]

The small amount and fixed nature of the grants left the schools vulnerable to increased costs if the fixed amounts were not increased each year. At the time, the cost of educating a child in a government primary school was over $300 per

The Guardian (online), 2 May 2017 <www.theguardian.com/australia-news/2017/may/02/gonski-review-allocate-resources-funding-cut-private-schools>; Australian Government, Department of Education and Training, *Review to Achieve Educational Excellence in Australian Schools* (17 November 2017) www.education.gov.au/review-achieve-educational-excellence-australian-schools>.

171 Commonwealth of Australia, *Parliamentary Debate*, House of Representatives, 13 August 1969, 186 (Malcolm Fraser).
172 Ibid. 187 (Malcolm Fraser).
173 Ibid. 185–186 (Malcolm Fraser); see *States Grants (Independent Schools) Act 1969* (Cth); Commonwealth of Australia, *Parliamentary Debate*, House of Representatives, 16 September 1969, 1413–1414 (Malcolm Fraser); Commonwealth of Australia, *Parliamentary Debate*, House of Representatives, 23 September 1969, 1743–1762, 1767–1791.
174 Commonwealth of Australia, *Parliamentary Debate*, House of Representatives, 9 December 1971, 4435 (William McMahon). At the same time, the Government announced a general capital grants programme worth $20 million for Government schools.

year, and the cost of educating a child in a secondary government school was over $500.[175] The per-capita grants to the non-government schools represented just 17% and 14% respectively of the cost of educating a child.[176] However, the creation of the fixed-sum grants was an important step that set the precedent of continued ongoing funding for non-government schools.

Percentage-based grants

While the creation of fixed-sum per-capita grants had set the precedent of an ongoing funding, without a procedure to increase the funding as the costs of providing education grew, the step may have become pointless, as Roman Catholic schools may have still collapsed under the ever-increasing funding costs.

In late 1972, the federal government changed the per-capita grants scheme from a fixed dollar amount per student to a percentage.[177] Under the new scheme, grants were calculated at 20% of the average cost of educating a student in a government primary or secondary school.[178]

The reason given for this change was, as Prime Minister McMahon explained, to provide non-government schools with 'assurances for the future.'[179] By tying the per-capita grants to the costs of educating a child in a government school, non-government schools were provided with certainty that the current level of funding would be maintained even if the costs of providing education increased significantly.[180]

While the principle of ongoing per-capita funding had been established, the method of determining the amount of funding received by various schools underwent one final change. In the 1970s, the newly elected Whitlam Labor Government changed the system of funding for non-government schools from a uniform per-capita rate to a system based on 'need.'

A 'needs-based' approach

While the per-capita grants programme for non-government schools introduced by the Fraser Liberal Government is arguably one of the most important steps on the return journey towards an increased relationship between the State and

175　Ibid. 4435 (William McMahon).
176　Ibid. 4437 (Kim Beazley Snr).
177　See *States Grants (Schools) Act 1972* (Cth). The Act also authorised a five-year capital grants scheme that provided grants to both government and non-government schools.
178　Commonwealth of Australia, *Parliamentary Debate*, House of Representatives, 11 May 1972, 2455–2458 (William McMahon); Interim Committee for the Australian Schools Commission, above n 166, 41.
179　Commonwealth of Australia, *Parliamentary Debate*, House of Representatives, 11 May 1972, 2456 (William McMahon).
180　See Commonwealth of Australia, *Parliamentary Debate*, House of Representatives, 14 September 1972, 1399–1400 (Malcolm Fraser, Minister for Education and Science).

religion in relation to education, it did not last long. In 1972, the ALP, led by Gough Whitlam, defeated the Federal Liberal Government. While the ALP no longer actively opposed State funding to non-government schools, it did have a significantly different approach to the issue. Rather than favouring uniform per-capita grants to all non-government schools, the ALP favoured a 'needs-based' approach. While in opposition, it had continually championed this position; now that it was in government, it had the opportunity to put its views into action.[181]

The creation of a needs-based funding model was a long-lasting and significant step in the journey. As discussed above, per-capita funding for non-government schools has continued through to modern Australia. The recent Gonski Reviews of school funding, *inter alia*, recommended the continuation of a funding model for non-government schools based on relative needs.[182]

The Karmel Report[183]

On 12 December 1972, just 11 days after taking office, Whitlam announced the 11 members of the Interim Committee for the Australian Schools Commission, along with its terms of reference. The terms of reference for the Interim Committee required, *inter alia*, for the Committee to:

> Make recommendations to the Minister for Education and Science as to the *immediate financial needs* of schools, priorities within those needs, and appropriate measures to assist in meeting those needs [emphasis added].[184]

The Interim Committee determined 'need' on the basis of the amount of resources used by a particular school in conjunction with any special disadvantages suffered by pupils at that school.[185] It used this measure of need to create an index of resources used in a school with a base of 100 as the average resources used in a government school in Australia.[186]

---

181 See Commonwealth of Australia, *Parliamentary Debate*, House of Representatives, 23 September 1969, 1743–1749 (Lance Barnard); Commonwealth of Australia, *Parliamentary Debate*, House of Representatives, 9 December 1971, 4436–4437 (Kim Beazley); Commonwealth of Australia, *Parliamentary Debate*, House of Representatives, 26 September 1972, 1936–1940 (Kim Beazley). The Liberal Government had specifically rejected a needs-based approach to the allocation of funding on the basis that it would penalise schools whose parents and supporters worked hard to improve their schools; see Commonwealth of Australia, *Parliamentary Debate*, House of Representatives, 14 September 1972, 1399 (Malcolm Fraser). For other funding models considered by the Liberal Government, see O'Brien, above n 128, 48–49.
182 See Gonski et al., above n 170, xxi (Recommendation 4).
183 Professor Peter Karmel was the Chair of the committee.
184 Interim Committee for the Australian Schools Commission, above n 166, 3.
185 Ibid. 49–50.
186 Ibid. 57.

All Catholic parochial school systems scored below 100;[187] however, the scores of non-Catholic non-government schools varied significantly. While some had resources below the level of government schools, others had resources significantly above that of government schools.[188] The Interim Committee split these schools into eight categories based on their score and recommended that each category receive a different level of funding.[189] It also recommended that grants to schools with the highest level of resources be phased out by 1976.[190]

Following the release of the Karmel Report, the Whitlam Government moved quickly to implement the Interim Committee's recommendations.[191] However, instead of phasing out funding to the non-government schools with the highest level of resources, the Cabinet decided to end funding to these schools immediately.[192]

The Acts

The Interim Committee's recommendations, including those relating to the funding of non-government schools, were put into effect via two Acts: the *Schools Commission Act 1973* (Cth) and the *States Grants (Schools) Act 1973* (Cth). Both *Acts* had a stormy passage through Parliament. While the Liberal opposition did not reject the principles contained in the Acts, they objected to certain provisions, including the immediate withdrawal of all funds to the wealthiest schools and the method of appointing Commissioners.[193]

The deadlock was broken via a compromise between the Labor Government and the Country Party. The Country Party agreed to cross the floor and support both Bills if the government was prepared to continue a minimum level of per-capita funding to the wealthiest non-government schools.[194]

With the successful passage of the *Schools Commission Act 1973* (Cth) and the *States Grants (Schools) Act 1973* (Cth), another important step in the journey towards increased relationship between the State and religion had been taken.

---

187 Ibid. 61, 67 (Tables 6.1 and 6.3).
188 Ibid. 69–71.
189 Ibid. 71.
190 Ibid.
191 Patrick Weller, 'The Establishment of the Schools Commission: A Case Study in the Politics of Education' in Ian Birch and Don Smart (eds), *The Commonwealth Government and Education 1964–1976: Political Initiatives and Development* (Drummond, Victoria, 1977) 57.
192 Ibid. 57.
193 See Commonwealth of Australia, *Parliamentary Debates*, House of Representatives, 11 October 1973, 1982–1987; Commonwealth of Australia, *Parliamentary Debates*, House of Representatives, 27 November 1973, 3886 (Malcolm Fraser); Commonwealth of Australia, *Parliamentary Debates*, House of Representatives, 27 November 1973, 3931–3932; Kim Beazley, 'The Labor Party in Opposition and Government' in Ian Birch and Don Smart (eds), *The Commonwealth Government and Education 1964–1976: Political Initiatives and Development* (Drummond, 1977) 99–100.
194 Smart, *Federal Aid to Australian Schools*, above n 161, 112.

The needs-based funding model also signified a side step in the journey, as the debate moved from being about State funding and religious schools to needs and wealthy schools.

A change of focus

In the debate around earlier funding schemes, such as the SSLS, there had been a focus on the crisis faced by Roman Catholic schools. The funding allocated was divided between government, Roman Catholic and other non-government schools. As a result, there was a focus on the religious aspect of the problem. Susan Pascoe has argued that the transition to needs-based funding shifted the debate from one about State funding to religious schools, to one about government funding to wealthy schools.[195] The Karmel report repeated the practice of dividing schools into government, Catholic and other non-government schools. However, the focus was not so much on funding government as opposed to non-government – predominantly Roman Catholic – schools. Instead, the focus was on how much to fund the wealthiest schools compared to the poorest schools.

The change in emphasis is demonstrated by the Hawke Labor Government's attempt to remove funding from the 50 wealthiest non-government schools. Over the years of the Liberal Fraser Government, the amount of federal funding to non-government schools had increased by 87.2% in real terms, while federal funding to government schools had decreased by 24.3% in real terms. There had also been a rationalisation of the categories of 'need' from eight to just three.[196] This, *inter alia*, had led to a resurgence of the debate about the State funding of non-government schools.

Just a few months after taking office in 1983, the new Labor Education Minister, Senator Ryan, announced that funding to the wealthiest non-government schools would be reduced by 25%.[197] Prior to the election, the ALP had announced that if it won the election, it would reduce the amount received by the 50 wealthiest non-government schools over 1984 and 1985, with the implication that funding to these schools would eventually be phased out entirely.[198] The proposed reduction and potential phasing out of funding to these schools met immediate opposition and was eventually dropped.[199] The importance of this temporary renewal of the debate about State funding to non-government schools is that at no time did the Hawke Labor Government suggest that State

---

195 Susan Pascoe, 'Non-Government Schools in Australia' (Paper presented at Australian Council for Education and Research Conference: Schools in Australia 1973–1998 The 25 Years Since The Karmel Report, Sydney, 9–10 November 1998) 5.

196 Don Smart, 'The Hawke Labor Government and Public–Private School Funding Policies in Australia, 1983–1986' in William Boyd and James Cibulka (eds), *Private Schools and Public Policy: International Perspectives* (The Falmer Press, 1989) 128–129.

197 Ibid. 131.

198 Ibid. 130.

199 Ibid. 131–136.

funding be removed from all non-government schools. Instead, the focus was only on those schools that could be considered 'wealthy.' In an attempt to calm the waters, after announcing the phasing out of funding to these wealthy schools, Hawke assured the public that there was no intention to remove funding from all non-government schools.[200]

The needs-based funding model had effectively cemented an ongoing relationship between the State and religion in the field of education by taking the public focus off religion and putting it instead on need. The opposition to the Hawke Government's plan also demonstrated how far the journey had come. One hundred years earlier, the proposal to remove State funding to all denominational schools had been successful and had resulted in a period of 70 years during which the State refused to fund schools run by religious denominations. Now, the Hawke Government's proposal to simply reduce funding to the wealthiest schools was met with so much opposition that it was dropped.

Despite how far the journey had come, there was still one very significant roadblock that needed to be overcome. Questions had been raised regarding the constitutionality of the federal government providing funding to religious schools.[201] While the focus had shifted to the needs of non-government schools, rather than their religiosity, most were still, and continue to be in modern Australia, religious. Section 116 of Australia's *Constitution*, *inter alia*, prohibits the Commonwealth from making 'any law for establishing any religion.' If funding religious schools amounted to 'establishing any religion,' then all of the funding programmes for non-government schools – from the SSLS to Whitlam's needs-based funding model – were unconstitutional.

The DOGS High Court challenge

As discussed above, one of the significant elements of the SSLS was that it was a federally funded programme. State funding for church-run schools had been removed prior to Federation; therefore, all funding for these schools had come from the local colonial governments. The various colonies had not been subject to constitutions containing provisions similar to Section 116, and there was therefore no constitutional question regarding any of the funding schemes for church-run schools in the nineteenth century. However, the federal government was subject to Section 116. The question therefore needed to be answered regarding whether Section 116 prohibited the federal government from funding religious schools.

---

200 Ibid. 131.
201 See Melvin J. Ely, *Erosion of the Judicial Process: An Aspect of Church–State Entanglement in Australia: the struggle of citizens to be heard in the Australian full High Court on the state aid issue, 1956–1980* (Defence of Government Schools Victoria, 1981) 7, 9; Ian Birch, 'State-aid at the Bar: The DOGS Case' (1984) *Melbourne Studies in Education* 31, 35; Commonwealth of Australia, *Parliamentary Debates*, House of Representatives, 14 May 1964, 1930–1931 (Arthur Calwell, Leader of the Opposition).

Questions regarding the constitutionality of the re-introduction of State funding to religious schools were raised almost as soon as the funding was re-introduced. In 1964, the Defence of Government Schools (DOGS) organisation was formed with the intention of bringing a court action to challenge the constitutionality of the federal funding of religious schools.[202] The DOGS argued that such funding was in breach of the establishment clause of Section 116 of the *Australian Constitution* and therefore unconstitutional. The DOGS was not alone in this view.[203] During the debate of the legislation introducing the Menzies' Government's SSLS in 1964, the ALP leader Arthur Calwell mooted the possibility of challenging the constitutionality of the programme.[204] In 1966, the ALP Executive set up a committee to investigate the possibility of challenging the constitutionality of the SSLS, but the investigation was abandoned a few months later.[205] Others held a different view. In articles published in 1963 and 1964 Clifford Pannam and Patrick Lane respectively, both questioned the success of any such challenge.[206] With two competing views, the only way an answer could be reached would be via a High Court decision on the issue. The DOGS decided to go ahead and launched its intended High Court challenge at a public rally in Melbourne on 21 September 1971.[207] The question of the constitutionality of the various federal funding schemes was eventually answered a decade later, on 10 February 1981, when the High Court handed down its decision in *Attorney General (Vic); ex rel Black v. The Commonwealth*.[208]

---

202   Ely, above n 201, 9; Birch, 'State-aid at the Bar,' above n 201, 35.

203   The Victorian Protestant Federation also explored the option of challenging an earlier programme that assisted non-government, mostly Catholic, schools in the ACT. This challenge was abandoned, as the Victorian Protestant Federation and its members did not have standing before the High Court and could not convince a relevant Attorney General to grant them fiat; see Ely, above n 201, 7; Birch, 'State-aid at the Bar,' above n 201, 35.

204   Commonwealth of Australia, *Parliamentary Debates*, House of Representatives, 14 May 1964, 1930–1931 (Arthur Calwell, Leader of the Opposition); Birch, 'State-aid at the Bar,' above n 201, 35.

205   Ely, above n 201, 9.

206   Clifford Pannam, 'Traveling Section 116 with a U.S. Road Map' (1963) 4(1) *Melbourne University Law Review* 41; Patrick Lane, 'Commonwealth Reimbursement for Fees at Non State Schools' (1964) 38 *Australian Law Journal* 130.

207   Ely, above n 201; Jean Ely, *Contempt of Court: Unofficial Voices from the DOGS Australian High Court Case 1981* (Dissenters Press, 2010) 171–172. Between 1964 and 1971, the DOGS ran candidates in State and federal elections and by-elections and participated in protests against State aid to non-government schools; see Allan Roy Horton, 'DOGS in New South Wales 1969–1971' in Douglas Alan Jecks (ed), *Influences in Australian Education* (Carrol's Pty Ltd, 1974) and Jean Ely, *Contempt of Court: Unofficial Voices From the DOGS Australian High Court Case 1981* (Dissenters Press, 2010) ch 5.

208   (1981) 146 CLR 559. The case is often referred to as the DOGS case because of the involvement of the Defence of Government Schools Organisation. The DOGS had been forced to bring its case to the High Court as a relator action because it was believed at the time that it did not have standing to bring the case itself. However, the DOGS drove the case and should be considered the real plaintiffs. See for example, Jean Ely, *Contempt of Court*, above n 207, 8, ch 10.

The High Court of Australia held in a 6–1 decision that the various federal school funding schemes[209] that provided funding to religious schools did not infringe the establishment clause of Section 116 of the *Australian Constitution*. The majority judges (Barwick CJ, Gibbs, Stephen, Mason and Wilson JJ) all held that 'establishing' should be defined using the 'natural' meaning of the word and that there was no ambiguity to be resolved.[210] All five concluded that 'establishing' required to a greater or lesser extent the setting up of a State church or religion. While each judge came to a slightly different conclusion as to what would constitute 'establishing' in the Australian context, all five concluded that the non-discriminatory funding of religious schools was not enough.[211] The Court also considered the meaning of the word 'for' in the phase 'for establishing any religion.' The majority held that 'for' meant that the relevant law must have the purpose of 'establishing' religion.[212] Since the various school funding schemes did not have the establishment of religion as their purpose, they were not unconstitutional. Justice Murphy was the only judge in dissent, holding the contrary view that the federal school funding schemes were unconstitutional. Murphy gave a wider interpretation to the term 'establishment' than the majority, interpreting the word to include State sponsorship and support of religion, which therefore precluded the State from funding religious schools.[213]

The National School Chaplaincy Programme (NSCP)

In October 2006 Prime Minister John Howard announced the creation of a chaplaincy programme for both government and non-government schools.[214] Five and a half years later,[215] the High Court of Australia handed down its decision in the case of *Williams v The Commonwealth* (*Williams*)[216] holding that the NSCP was unconstitutional. Despite this finding, the NSCP has continued. As with the *Jehovah's Witnesses case* discussed above, the finding of unconstitutionality did not relate to the religious nature of the programme. Rather, the High Court found

---

209 The cases considered the constitutionality of the following Acts: *State Grants (Schools) Act 1972–1974* (Cth), *State Grants (Schools) Act 1976* (Cth), *State Grants (Schools Assistance) Act 1976* (Cth), *State Grants (Schools Assistance) Amendment Act 1977* (Cth), *States Grants (School Assistance) Amendment Act 1978* (Cth), *States Grants (School Assistance) Act 1978* (Cth) and *Schools Commission Act 1973* (Cth).

210 *Attorney General (Vic); ex rel Black v. The Commonwealth* (1981) 146 CLR 559, 579 (Barwick CJ), 597 (Gibbs J), 606 (Stephen J), 653 (Wilson J).

211 Ibid. 582 (Barwick CJ), 603–604 (Gibbs J), 610 (Stephen J), 612 (Mason J), 653 (Wilson J).

212 Ibid. 579 (Barwick CJ), 609 (Stephen J), 653 (Wilson J). While not discussing the meaning of 'for' in detail, Gibbs J (604) also seems to assume that the purpose of the legislation must be to establish a religion.

213 Ibid. 622–623 (Murphy J).

214 John Howard, 'National School Chaplaincy Program' (Media Release, 29 October 2006).

215 20 June 2012.

216 [2012] HCA 23 (20 June 2012).

that the programme was unconstitutional because of the way in which the funding had been structured. However, it is the religiosity of the programme that has caused the greatest controversy.

The content of the NSCP

The NSCP commenced in 2007.[217] Under the programme, government and non-government schools could apply for grants of up to $20,000[218] to fund the provision of chaplaincy services.[219] The purpose of the programme was to 'assist . . . schools in providing greater pastoral care and supporting the spiritual wellbeing of their students.'[220] John Howard envisaged that chaplains would:

> provide pastoral care, general religious and personal advice and comfort and support to all students and staff, irrespective of their religious beliefs. A Chaplain might support school students and their wider school community in a range of ways, such as assisting students in exploring their spirituality; providing guidance on religious, values and ethical matters; helping school counsellors and staff in offering welfare services and support in cases of bereavement, family breakdown or other crisis and loss situations.[221]

In defence of the proposed scheme John Howard did not shy away from the use of the word 'chaplain,' stating:

> Yes I am calling them chaplains because that has a particular connotation in our language.. . . And as you know I'm not overwhelmed by political correctness. To call a chaplain a counsellor is to bow to political correctness. Chaplain has a particular connotation, people understand it, they know exactly what I'm talking about.[222]

He also acknowledged that the majority of chaplains were likely to be from Christian denominations.[223] As predicted, by February 2011 98.52% of chaplains funded came from Christian churches. [224]

---

217 Australian Government, 'National School Chaplaincy Program' (Discussion Paper, Australian Government, 2011) 3.
218 The government initially committed $30 million per year for three years.
219 John Howard, 'National School Chaplaincy Program,' above n 214.
220 Ibid.
221 Ibid.
222 'Federal Govt to Fund Chaplains in Schools' *ABC News* (online), 29 October 2006 < >http://bananas-in-pajamas.com/news/stories/2006/10/29/1776009.htm?site=news>.
223 John Howard, 'This is no attempt to force-feed religion to children,' *The Age* (online), 1 November 2006 www.theage.com.au/news/opinion/not-an-attempt-to-forcefeed-religion/2006/10/31/1162278138800.html>.
224 Australian Government, 'National School Chaplaincy Program,' above n 217, 8.

The religious nature of the programme, both in its design and implementation is significant. The NSCP places religious workers (called chaplains), paid with funds provided by the State, into both government and non-government schools. While the programme was amended between 2007 and 2014 to allow for secular pastoral care workers, at its inception it was exclusively religious. This is important, as for the first time the federal government has effectively endorsed religion in government schools. While the federal government, and to a lesser extent State and territory governments, have funded religious non-government schools for many decades, this is very different from funding religion in government schools. Parents sending their children to religious non-government schools do so knowing of the religious content of the schools. They accept it as part of their children's education. On the other hand, Australia has had a long history of providing secular education in its government schools. While the NSCP does not change the secular nature of the educational content provided by government schools and enshrined in most States and territories in legislation, it does place a religious element within the school.

There are two arguments that could be mounted to refute the significance of the change in the legal relationship between the State and religion brought about by the creation of the NSCP. First, the programme is voluntary, both in terms of a school and individual student's participation, and second that religious programmes were already present in many government schools prior to the introduction of the NSCP.

It is a voluntary programme

The NSCP is entirely voluntary, with school communities applying for funds and choosing the chaplain they wish to have at their school.[225] This includes the ability to choose a chaplain from a religion of their choice. While participation in the programme is voluntary, it has had a high take up rate,[226] meaning that for many children they will have little option but to attend a government school which participates in the NSCP.

The programme is also voluntary in terms of an individual student's participation.[227] However, there is not a uniform system of recoding parental consent to

225 John Howard, 'National School Chaplaincy Program,' above n 214.

226 See Australian Government, 'National School Chaplaincy Program,' above n 217, 3; Australian Government, Department of Education, Employment and Workplace Relations, *National School Chaplaincy and Student Welfare Programme – Continuation of Service National Statistics* (8 February 2013) <https://web.archive.org/web/20130921144258/http://deewr.gov.au/national-school-chaplaincy-and-student-welfare-program-successful-schools-expansion-rounds>.

227 See NSCP Guidelines clause 5.1 and Clause 2 of the Code of Conduct for school Chaplains re-produced in Northern Territory Ombudsman, *Investigation Report on the Operation of the Chaplaincy Services within Five Government Rural Schools of the Northern Territory* (Northern Territory Ombudsman, 2010) 84. See also Commonwealth Ombudsman,

a child's participation in the NSCP. Some States operate an opt-in system, while others operate an opt-out system.[228] In practice, either opting-in or opting-out may not always be practical due to the chaplains' participation in a broad range of school activities such as sports days and school camps.[229]

Religion was already a part of government school education

As stated above, the secular nature of education in government schools is enshrined in State and territory legislation.[230] This does not mean that religion has been totally excluded from government schools. Secular instruction in most States and territories included general religious education, as distinct from dogmatic or denominational religious education.[231] Further, all States and territories provide for denominational religious education to be offered to students, usually at the request of parents, by a visiting religious instructor.[232] In addition, at the time the NSCP was introduced in 2007 there were chaplains working in State schools in all Australian States and territories, except New South Wales.[233] The existing chaplaincy programmes were already growing rapidly prior to the announcement of the NSCP.[234]

It cannot be doubted that religion was present in government schools prior to the creation of the NSCP. What is different between these programmes and the NSCP is the level of endorsement, the scale of the programme, and the tier of government involved. Chaplaincy programmes and religious education prior to the NSCP was predominantly funded by donations and/or staffed by volunteers, and as a result the State did not 'endorse' the programmes. The public nature of the announcement of the NSCP also showed a high level of endorsement by the federal government inextricably linking it to the State. As a national programme the NSCP is also much larger in scale than those that existed prior

Administration of the National School Chaplaincy Program, Report No 06/2011 (2011) 12–14.

228 Commonwealth Ombudsman, above n 227, 12–14.

229 Australian Government, 'National School Chaplaincy Program,' above n 217, 9.

230 *Education Act 2004* (ACT) s 28; *Education Act 1990* (NSW) ss 30, 33; *Education Act 2016* (Tas) s 125(1); *Education and Training Reform Act 2006* (Vic) s 2.2.10; *School Education Act 1999* (WA) s 68(1)(a).

231 *Education Act 2004* (ACT) s 28(2); *Education Act 1990* (NSW) s 30; *School Education Act 1999* (WA) s 68(2).

232 *Education Act 2004* (ACT) s 29; *Education Act 2015* (NT) s 86; *Education Act 1990* (NSW) s 32; *Education (General Provisions) Act 2006* (Qld) s 76; *Education Act 1972* (SA) s 102; *Education Act 2016* (Tas) s 126; *Education and Training Reform Act 2006* (Vic) s 2.2.11; *School Education Act 1999* (WA) s 69.

233 David Pohlmann, *School Chaplaincy in Queensland State schools: A Case Study* (PhD Thesis, Griffith University, 2010) 58; New South Wales, *Parliamentary Debates*, Legislative Council, 16 November 2006, 4132 (Gordon Moyes and John Hatzistergos).

234 Christopher Venning, 'Chaplaincy in the State Schools of Victoria' (2005) 48(1) *Journal of Christian Education* 9, 14; Jill Clements, 'Chaplaincy in the States Schools of Western Australia' (2005) 48(1) *Journal of Christian Education* 19, 20.

to its introduction. Further, as a national programme, the NSCP is endorsed by the federal government, while programmes in existence prior to the NSCP were State-based programmes.

The creation of the NSCP

The NSCP was originally conceived by Peter Rawlings, treasurer of his local chaplaincies committee on the Mornington Peninsula, Victoria. Having seen the positive result of chaplains, funded by voluntary donations, in his local community, he saw the potential for chaplains in schools around the nation.[235] He put the idea to the Prime Minister, with the encouragement of his local Member of Parliament, Gregory Hunt, who raised the matter in federal Parliament on 13 June 2006.[236] In explaining his reasons for the scheme, Peter Rawlings said, 'I have seen the results in young families and families that work – the potential for that to be replicated around this nation.'[237] Similarly, Gregory Hunt said, when referring to the exiting programme in his electorate, 'Experience to date has been of an extraordinary engagement with students. These programmes have come at the behest of the schools, the school communities and the parents.'[238] Other supporters of the programme, including Prime Minister John Howard, also referred to the success of existing programmes funded via voluntary donations, and to a lesser extent State government funding.[239] In a speech to Parliament on 31 October, Federal Member of Parliament David Fawcett emphasised that the NSCP was created in response to demand for already successful chaplaincy programmes in government schools.

> So who has actually been calling for it? Most of the critics are saying that it is the government trying to ram some agenda down people's throats. But I have to say that this has been in response to a call from the community, who are already seeing the benefits of existing chaplaincy programmes around Australia. They exist right now in state schools and are benefiting students. In South Australia, this programme has been running for well over 20 years,

235 Jill Rowbotham, 'Grassroots idea grows into $90million Scheme,' *The Australian* (online), 31 October 2006 <www.theaustralian.com.au/news/nation/grassroots-idea-grows-into-90-million-scheme/news-story/683948b09d5da45f819f43a11538b1ee>.
236 Commonwealth of Australia, *Parliamentary Debate*, House of Representatives, 13 June 2006, 140 (Gregory Hunt, Member for Flinders).
237 Rowbotham, above n 235.
238 Commonwealth, *Parliamentary Debates*, House of Representatives, 13 June 2006, 140 (Gregory Hunt).
239 Ibid; See also Commonwealth of Australia, *Parliamentary Debates*, House of Representatives, 30 October 2006, 36 (Julie Bishop); Commonwealth of Australia, *Parliamentary Debates*, House of Representatives, 31 October 2006, 126 (Gregory Hunt); Commonwealth of Australia, *Parliamentary Debates*, House of Representatives, 1 November 2006, 155 (Christopher Pearce); John Howard, 'This is no attempt to force-feed religion to children,' above n 223.

and the South Australian government already gives some $50,000 each year to it. In Victoria, the state government already gives some $25,000 per chaplain to the programme and in Queensland the state government gives some $10,000 per group.

What is the programme? Let me make it very clear that it is not a programme about religious education. As someone who has spent over 22 years in the military, I am very aware of the role of chaplains, and the role is not about religious education. It is for the same reason that we have chaplains in hospitals, in industry, in the military, as I have mentioned, in police services and in correctional services. There are chaplains in schools around Australia, except, I believe, in New South Wales, and they are even in sporting teams. They are there for a range of good reasons but not for religious education.[240]

The NSCP received bi-partisan support with then opposition leader Kim Beazley, and education spokeswoman Jenny Macklin, supporting the programme; although some Labor MPs opposed the scheme.[241] Labor Prime Ministers Kevin Rudd and Julia Gillard also supported the NSCP, announcing extended funding of the programme during their terms.[242]

Changes to the NSCP

Since the introduction of the NSCP in 2007, it has undergone a series of reviews, including a departmental review, and two ombudsman's reports. These reviews have led to a number of changes in the NSCP, including increased minimum qualifications, ongoing professional development requirements, increased funding and improved complaint handling procedures.[243] The most significant change was the temporary introduction of secular pastoral care workers. The inclusion of secular pastoral care workers as part of the NSCP, saw a rebrand of the NSCP into the National School Chaplaincy and Welfare Programme (NSCWP) in 2011.

240 Commonwealth of Australia, *Parliamentary Debate*, House of Representatives, 31 October 2006, 113–114 (David Fawcett).
241 Jewel Topsfield, 'Chaplains Cause Rift in Labor Ranks,' *The Age* (Melbourne), 1 November 2006.
242 In November 2009 Kevin Rudd announced an additional $42.8 million dollars extending the programme until December 2011, see Kevin Rudd, 'Speech to the Australian Christian Lobby's national conference' (Speech Delivered at Australian Christian Lobby's national conference, Hyatt Hotel, Canberra, 22 November 2009) <http://parlinfo.aph.gov.au/parlInfo/search/display/display.w3p;query=Id%3A%22media%2Fpressrel%2FE7MV6%22>. In the 2011/12 Budget an additional $222million was announced to extend the NSCP to December 2014 see Peter Garrett, 'National School Chaplaincy Program' (Budget 2011–12 Media Release, 10 May 2011) www.capmon.com/budget2011/eewr/p110510006b. PDF>.
243 Peter Garrett, 'Schools Given Greater Choice Under Expanded Chaplains Program' (Media Release, 7 September 2011); Peter Garrett, 'Applications Open for School Chaplaincy and Welfare services' (Media Release, 30 September 2011).

This changed the programme from being an exclusive interaction between the State and religion, to an interaction that included a non-religious element.

Initially, secular pastoral care workers were introduced to fill a 'skills shortage' in chaplaincy. In 2007, the new Labor Minister for Education, Julia Gillard, announced that she would amend the programme to allow for 'secular pastoral care workers.'[244] However, secular pastoral care workers were only able to be employed under the NSCP if no suitable chaplain could be found.[245] The reason for the change was not to secularise the programme. Rather, the change was made to respond to difficulties faced by some schools in finding a suitable chaplain; there was 'almost a skills shortage in chaplaincy.'[246] While this change to the NSCP could be seen as a move away from the religious character of the programme, it is important to note that schools could not simply opt to have a 'secular pastoral care worker' instead of a chaplain. The school had to first attempt to find a chaplain and only if they were unable to do so would they be permitted to use the funds to support a secular pastoral care worker.

Secular pastoral care workers were not initially introduced as an alternative to chaplains. However, in 2011 Minister for School Education, Early Childhood and Youth, Peter Garret, announced that the NSCP would be re-branded as the National School Chaplaincy and Welfare Programme (NSCWP), and that the re-named programme would allow schools to choose to employ either a chaplain or a secular welfare worker.[247] The change was made in response to 'strong feedback for the programme to be extended to qualified secular welfare workers, which will empower principals and school communities to choose the right person for the needs and circumstances of their schools.'[248] Unlike the introduction of secular pastoral care workers in 2007, schools would now be able to choose whether to employ a religious chaplain or a secular pastoral care worker. They would no longer be required to attempt to first employ a chaplain before seeking out a suitable secular pastoral care worker. This is an important change in the programme, as this change meant that the NSCP was no longer exclusively religious. However, the programme still allowed for the employment of chaplains – with all the associated religious connotations of that word.

The inclusion of secular welfare workers has however been short lived. In the 2014–15 Budget the Liberal Government announced that '[t]he . . . programme

244 Ben Packham, 'Chaplaincy programme goes secular in Rudd overhaul,' *Herald Sun* (Online), 14 January 2008, < >www.eagles-lair.org/local_content/Melbourne_Herald-Sun/Chaplaincy-program-goes-secular-in-Rudd-overhaul.html>; Commonwealth Ombudsman, above n 227, 4.
245 Evidence to Standing Committee on Education, Employment and Workplace Relations, Commonwealth of Australia Senate, Canberra, 20 February 2008, 50–56 (Chris Sheedy).
246 Ibid. 52 (Lisa Paul).
247 Peter Garret, 'Schools Given Greater Choice Under Expanded Chaplains Program,' above n 243; Peter Garret, 'Applications Open for School Chaplaincy and Welfare services,' above n 243.
248 Ibid.

will be returned to its original intent; to provide funding for school chaplains'[249] in effect ending the inclusion of secular welfare workers.

Williams v The Commonwealth

As with the federal funding of non-government Schools the NSCP faced Constitutional Challenge. On 21 December 2010, Queensland father Ronald Williams issued a Writ of Summons in the High Court challenging the constitutionality of the NSCP.[250] A year and half later[251] the High Court handed down its decision declaring in a majority decision that the NSCP was unconstitutional. While the NSCP was declared unconstitutional, the Court's decision was not based on the religious nature of the programme. Instead, the Court's decision rested on the funding method used by the Commonwealth.[252]

While Williams won the overall case, he was unsuccessful in relation to his two arguments that the NSCP contravened Section 116. First, that chaplains held an 'office . . . under the Commonwealth' and secondly that the NSCP imposed a 'religious test' for this office.[253] If the High Court had accepted these arguments the NSCP would have been contrary to the fourth limb of Section 116 and therefore unconstitutional. The High Court unanimously rejected these arguments.

Only two of the judgments in *Williams (No 1)* discussed the Section 116 arguments in any detail, the joint judgment of Gummow and Bell JJ, and the dissenting judgment of Heydon J (although he was not in dissent on this point).[254] The remaining four Justices agreed with the reasoning in the joint judgment, making no further comments.[255] Both the joint and dissenting judgments considered the meaning of 'officer . . . under the Commonwealth.' In both cases they determined that the relationship between the chaplains and the Commonwealth was

---

249 Scott Ryan, 'Keeping our commitments: Funding a National School Chaplaincy Programme' (Media Release, 13 May 2014) <https://ministers.education.gov.au/ryan/keeping-our-commitments-funding-national-school-chaplaincy-programme>.

250 See High Court of Australia, *Case S307/2010 Williams v. Commonwealth of Australian and Ors* (2010) www.hcourt.gov.au/cases/case-s307/2010>.

251 20 June 2012.

252 For a discussion of the arguments relating the funding of the NSCP see Graeme Orr and William Isdale, 'Responsible government, Federalism and the School chaplaincy Case: God's okay, it's Mammon that's Troublesome' (2013) 38(1) *Alternative Law Journal* 3, 6; Nicholas Mirzai, 'Power to Legislate and the Financial Framework Legislation Amendment Act' (2012) 36 *Australian Bar Review* 171; Benjamin Saunders, 'The Commonwealth and the Chaplains: Executive Power After Williams v Commonwealth' (2012) 23(3) *Public Law Review* 153; Amanda Sapienza, 'Using Representative Government to Bypass Representative Government'(2012) 23(3) *Public Law Review* 161.

253 *Williams v The Commonwealth* [2012] HCA 23 (20 June 2012) [107] (Gummow and Bell JJ), [442]–[443] (Heydon J).

254 Ibid. [107]–[110] (Gumow and Bell JJ), [305]–[307] (Heydon J), [442]–[448] (Heydon J).

255 Ibid. [9] (French CJ), [168] (Hayne J), [476] (Crennan J), [597] (Kiefel J).

not close enough to establish that the chaplains were in fact officers under the Commonwealth.[256]

Heydon J determined that ' "[a]n office" is a position under constituted authority to which duties are attached,' and that this required a direct relationship with the Commonwealth.[257] Chaplains employed under the NSCP were in no such direct relationship. The chaplains were in a relationship with the chaplaincy provider, who in the case under consideration, was Scripture Union Queensland (SUQ),[258] who was in turn in a contractual relationship with the Commonwealth.[259] The Commonwealth could not 'appoint, select approve or dismiss' the chaplains employed under the NSCP,[260] meaning that the Commonwealth could not direct them. Williams had argued that the fact that chaplains had to comply with a code of conduct imposed by the Commonwealth meant that the Commonwealth in effect exercised supervision or control over the chaplains.[261] The Court rejected this argument, preferring a narrower reading. The joint judgment also adopted this position, pointing out that the fact that the Commonwealth was the source of funding for the chaplains' employment was not enough to 'render a chaplain . . . the holder of an office under the Commonwealth.'[262] Both judgments stopped short of outlining exactly what would be required for a person to hold an 'office . . . under the Commonwealth,' simply stating that the relationship between the chaplains employed under the NSCP and the Commonwealth did not meet the required threshold.[263]

After determining that the chaplains employed under the NSCP were not officers 'under the Commonwealth,' both Gummow and Bell JJ, in the joint judgment, and Heydon J, in the dissenting judgment, found it unnecessary to discuss the plaintiff's second Section 116 argument, that the qualification for being a chaplain imposed a religious test.[264] This leaves the tantalising possibility that there may in fact have been a 'religious test' imposed.[265] However, Heydon J points out that 'neither the NSCP nor the qualification for "chaplains" had much to do with religion in any specific or sectarian sense. The work described could have been done by persons who met a religious test. It could equally have been

---

256 Ibid. [109] –[110] (Gummow and Bell JJ), [444]–[447] (Heydon J).
257 Ibid. [444] (Heydon J).
258 The chaplaincy provider varies between States and even between schools.
259 *Williams v The Commonwealth* [2012] HCA 23 [109] (Gummow and Bell JJ), [445] (Heydon J).
260 Ibid. [445] (Heydon J).
261 Ibid. [443] (Heydon J).
262 Ibid. [109] (Gummow and Bell JJ).
263 Ibid. [110] (Gummow and Bell JJ), [447] (Heydon J).
264 Ibid. [442] (Heydon J), [448] (Heydon J). The joint judgment makes no mention of the Plaintiff's second argument.
265 For a discussion on the meaning of 'religious test' see Luke Beck, 'The Constitutional Prohibition on Religious Tests' (2011) 35(2) *Melbourne University Law Review* 323.

done by persons who did not.'[266] So perhaps even if the Court had considered the issue, it would have found that there was no religious test anyway.

Williams was successful in his arguments relating to the way in which the NSCP had been funded. The NSCP was not created via legislation; instead it was created and funded directly by the Executive. The High Court found that this arrangement was unconstitutional because the Federal Executive did not have the power to spend money on programmes like the NSCP without legislative support.[267] In response to this decision the federal government passed the *Financial Framework Legislation Amendment Act (No 2) 2012* (Cth) which purported to fix this problem for the NSCP and other government programmes.[268]

In response to the passage of the *Financial Framework Legislation Amendment Act (No 2) 2012* (Cth) Williams again launched High Court action challenge the constitutional validity of this legislation as a mechanism to fund the NSCP.[269] On 19 June 2014 the High Court handed down its second judgment finding the funding mechanism for the NSCP to be unconstitutional.[270] The religious nature of the NSCP programme is notably absent from this second decision. Section 116 is not discussed at all and the words religion, or any derivation thereof, does not appear anywhere in the judgment.

Williams (No 2) has not, however, spelled the end of the NSCP. In November 2014 the federal government announced that it had reached agreements with all States and territories. Like funding of non-government religious schools, the federal government would provide the funds to the States and territories who would then run and administer the programme.[271]

In the end the *Williams* cases have not been a victory for those who have criticised the NSCP. While the NSCP was found to be unconstitutional, the federal government has been able to remedy this defect, and the High Court found no constitutional problem with the religious nature of the programme.

Conclusion

The relationship between the State and religion in relation to education has undergone dramatic changes across Australia's history since colonisation. From being effectively neglected by the State, and therefore left to the clergy of the

---

266 *Williams v The Commonwealth* [2012] HCA 23 [306] (Heydon J).
267 The impact of this decision goes far beyond the NSCP and will affect a wide range of Government spending programmes. See Orr and Isdale, above n 252; Mirzai, above n 252; Sapienza, above n 252.
268 Orr and Isdale, above n 252, 6.
269 Renae Barker, A Critical Analysis of Religious Aspects of the Australain Chaplaincy Cases' (2015) 4(1) *Oxford Journal of Law and Religion* 26, 48.
270 *Williams v Commonwealth of Australia* [2014] HCA 23 (19 June 2014).
271 Australian Government, Department of Education and Training, *Student Resilience and Wellbeing Resources – National School Chaplaincy Programme* (17 November 2017) www.education.gov.au/national-school-chaplaincy-programme>.

colony by default, to a formal system encompassing four different systems of religious education alongside a State-run secular education system, through to a single secular education system before returning to a system that embraces both State funded religious and secular education. While many of these different systems have come about as a result of political expediency, rather than as a deliberate decision to alter the relationship between the State and religion, they demonstrate the remarkable variety and change that can take place in just one area of the relationship between the State and religion.

Today education continues to be an important component of the State–religion relationship. The federal government continues to fund schools run by religious organisations. These now encompass not only Christian schools but also schools from a number of smaller religious groups such as Judaism and Islam. The issue of religion in ostensibly secular government runs schools continues to be important. The National School Chaplaincy Programme along with religious instruction are important issues. However, new issues are also beginning to emerge such as the right of parents to withdraw children from classes, particularly those relating to sexuality, which conflict with their religious beliefs. During the parliamentary debate on the Marriage Amendment (Definition and Religious Freedoms) Bill 2017 an attempt was made to include an amendment which would have permitted parents to withdraw children from classes which were inconsistent with the parent's 'traditional' view of marriage.[272] The inclusion of an issue related to education rather than marriage during debate on same-sex marriage highlights the importance of the relationship between the State and religion in this area. As highlighted in the opening lines of this chapter, the education of the nation's young is something which both the State and religious organisations are likely to continue to prioritise into the future.

272 See Commonwealth, *Parliamentary Debates*, Senate, 28 November 2017, 9061 (James Paterson).

9 Funding religion

Introduction

During the Constitutional convention debates Edmund Barton, later to become Australian first prime Minister and then founding Justice of the High Court, confidently asserted that: 'you have only two powers of spending money and a church could not receive the funds of the commonwealth under either of them.'[1] Barton was speaking in defence of his position that a clause, similar to what became Section 116 of the *Australian Constitution,* was unnecessary because, in his words:

> We are a Christian community we ought to have advanced so much since the days of State aid and the days of making a law for the establishment of a religion, since the days for imposing religious observance or exacting a religious test as a qualification for any office of the state, as to render any such dangers practically impossible.[2]

Despite Barton's assertion, Tony Blackshield has suggested that, on the reasoning presented by the High Court in the *Attorney General (Vic); ex rel Black v The Commonwealth,*[3] the Commonwealth could provide funding directly to a religious organisation, for example, for the building of a Cathedral.[4]

The funding of religion by the State has been an issue of controversy from the earliest days of the Australian colony. Whether it be too little funding, inequitable funding, too much funding, unquantifiable funding or the accusation that non-believers are being forced to subsidies believers, the issue has never been off the table for long.

---

1 *Official Record of the Debates of the Australasian Federal Convention,* Melbourne, 2 March 1898, 1772 (Edmund Barton).
2 *Official Record of the Debates of the Australasian Federal Convention,* Melbourne, 2 March 1898, 1771 (Edmund Barton).
3 (1981) 146 CLR 559.
4 Tony Blackshield, 'Religion and Australian Constitutional law' in Peter Radan, Denise Meyerson and Rosalind F. Atherton (eds), *Law and Religion: God, the State and the Common Law* (Taylor& Francis, 2005) 75, 91.

In the early colony, Rev Richard Johnston, the Church of England clergyman and chaplain, complained of a lack of financial support for religion.[5] As a result, he was forced to undertake the construction of the first church in the colony himself and then faced a four-year delay and dispute with the Lieutenant Governor before being reimbursed. However, the under-provision of funding for religion was remedied in 1863 by the institution of the *Church Acts*. These provided funding to the main Christian denominations in the colony.[6] The inclusion of denominations other than the Church of England was in large part due to complaints from the other dominant denominations about the privileging of the Church of England under the previous, largely ad hoc arrangements.[7]

By the time of the Constitutional Conventions, and Barton's confident assertion that the Commonwealth could not spend money on religion, State aid via the *Church Acts* had been abolished.[8] Arguably both the removal of State aid and the inclusion of Section 116 in the *Australian Constitution* were symptoms of a wider societal move away from direct State involvement in religious affairs.

However, the funding of religion by the State did not end with the removal of direct State aid. Religious organisations today continue to be indirectly funded by the State in the form of tax exemptions.[9] While these exemptions do not give new money to religions, they do leave money in the hands of religious organisations that would otherwise be collected in tax. These, like the early provision of direct State aid, have been criticised on a number of grounds, not least of which because in effect non-believers are being asked to subsidise believers.[10]

This chapter traces the evolution of the relationship between the State and religion in relation to funding of religion from the early *ad hoc* funding of the Church

5 Richard Johnson, 'Rev Richard Johnson to Governor Phillip, 29 February 1792' in Jean Woolmington (ed), *Religion in Early Australia The Problem of Church and State* (Cassell Australia, 1976) 1–2; James Cook (author), Britton Alexander and Frank Murcott Bladen (eds), *Historical Records of New South Wales* (Government Printer, 1892–1901) vol 2, 594. See also Richard Johnson, 'Rev Richard Johnson to Henry Fricker 5 November 1788' in George Mackaness (ed), *Some Letters of Rev Richard Johnson BA First Chaplain of New South Wales* (Review Publications, 1978) pt I, 25; Richard Johnson, 'Rev Richard Johnson to Henry Fricker, 4 October 1791' in George Mackaness (ed), *Some Letters of Rev Richard Johnson BA First Chaplain of New South Wales* (Review Publications, 1978) pt I, 42; Richard Johnson, 'Rev Richard Johnson to Anonymous 23 March 1982' in George Mackaness (ed), *Some Letters of Rev Richard Johnson BA First Chaplain of New South Wales* (Review Publications, 1978) pt I, 46–47.

6 *Church Act 1836* (NSW); *Church Act 1837* (VDL).

7 See, for example, Bernard Keith Hyams and Bob Bessant, *Schools for the People? An Introduction to the History of State Education in Australia* (Longman, Victoria, 1972) 18–19; Albert Gordon Austin, *Australian Education 1788–1900 Church, State and Public Education in Colonial Australia* (Sir Isaac Pitman& Sons Ltd, Melbourne, 1961) 26–28.

8 State funding of religion had been phased out through the implementation of different acts throughout the colonies such as the *State Aid Abolition Bill 1860* (Qld), *State Aid Distribution Act 1862* (Tas), *Public Worship Prohibition Act 1862* (NSW), *State Aid to Religion Abolition Act 1871* (Vic) and *Ecclesiastical Grant Abolition Act 1895* (WA).

9 Australian Government, Australian Taxation Office, *Religious institutions: access to tax concessions* (12 October 2016) <www.ato.gov.au/Non-profit/Getting-started/In-detail/Types-of-charities/Religious-institutions-access-to-tax-concessions/>.

10 See, for example, David Marr, *The High Price of Heaven* (Allen and Unwin, 1999).

of England thorough to the creation of the Australian Charities and Not-for-Profit Commission which today regulates the charities sector, including religious organisations. The relationship can best be characterized as a tug-of-war between the State and religion. Both attempting to wrestle control of funding from each other.

Funding of religion in the early days of the colony

For most of the early colonial period the funding of religion, at all levels, was on an *ad-hoc* basis. This included, to a certain extent, the funding of religious ministers. The first chaplain Rev Richard Johnson received a stipend of £182 10s, which would have been at least partially made up of endowments.[11] In 1824, the longest serving chaplains were granted an increase in their stipends. Rev Marsden's stipend was increased to £400, Rev Cowper and Rev Cartwright's to £300, and Rev Fulton's £250.[12] What is important to note about these increases is that they were not part of a structured system of funding; rather the increases were determined and granted at the instructions of the Colonial Secretary.

For most of this period, the largest share of funding went to the Church of England.[13] This is not surprising, as the Roman Catholic Church did not have permanent official chaplains until 1820. The first Presbyterian Minister, Rev John Dunmore Lang, did not arrive until 1823, and was not officially appointed as a Chaplain of the colony until 1826.[14] However, even after religious leaders from other religious denominations began to arrive, the Church of England continued to receive the largest share, this would have been due to the superior number of the Church of England clergy, but it was also due to the inequitable amount of funds granted to the non-Church of England clergy. The Roman Catholic Chaplains were initially given stipends of just £100, compared to the £250 available to the Protestant clergy at the time.[15] Similarly, Rev Lang was initially granted only £100 compared to £150 available for the Church of England clergy at the

---

11 Ross Border, *Church and State in Australia 1788–1872 A Constitutional Study of the Church of England in Australia* (Society for Promoting Christian Knowledge, London, 1962) 17.

12 See Lord Bathurst, 'Despatch Lord Bathurst to Governor Brisbane, 24 September 1824' in Frederick Watson (ed), *Historical Records of Australia Series 1* (Library Committee of the Commonwealth Parliament, 1914–1925) vol 11, 370–371.

13 John Barrett, *That Better Country, The Religious Aspects of Life in Eastern Australia, 1835–1850* (Melbourne University Press, 1966) 29.

14 William Westbrooke Burton, *The State of Religion and Education in New South Wales* (J. Cross/Simpkin, Marshall, 1840) 12–13; Donald William Archibald Baker, *Days of Wrath: A Life of John Dunmore Lang* (Melbourne University Press, 1985) 32–36.

15 Earl Bathurst, 'Despatch Earl Bathurst to Governor Macquarie, 20 October 1819' in Frederick Watson (ed), *Historical Records of Australia Series 1* (Library Committee of the Commonwealth Parliament, 1914–1925) vol 10, 204. According to Manning Clark the reason for this discrepancy was ". . .because Bathurst knew they did not require more, as the Catholic laity were more generous than others in supporting their clergy." When Earl Bathurst first informed Governor Macquarie of the appointment of two Catholic priests the amount they were to be paid was £250. See Lord Bathurst, 'Despatch Lord Bathurst to Governor Macquarie, 24 August 1818' in Frederick Watson (ed), *Historical Records of Australia Series 1* (Library Committee of the Commonwealth Parliament, 1914–1925) vol 9, 833.

time. He was also forced to choose between receiving a stipend and funds for the building of a church.[16]

Rev Johnson's Church

The *ad-hoc* nature of the funding available for religion is highlighted by the dispute between Rev Richard Johnson and Lieutenant-Governor Grose over the funding of the first church building in the colony. The details surrounding the building of the church are usually included in histories of the early colony to demonstrate the difficulties Rev Richard Johnson encountered in trying to carry out his ministry, or to demonstrate the neglected state of religion in the early colony. While the incident does demonstrate these things, it is included here to demonstrate both the power of the State over religion in relation to funding, and the *ad-hoc* nature of funding available to religion in the early colony when compared to the structured system created under the later *Church Acts*.

The lack of a church building

Despite being instructed to 'take such steps for the due celebration of publick [sic] worship as circumstances will permit,'[17] Australia's first Governor, Arthur Phillip, did not build a church or chapel during his time in the colony. Rev Johnson complained about this situation to both Governor Philip and his friends back in England to no avail.[18]

In the end the solution was for Rev Richard Johnson to build the first Australian church himself. He began on 10 June 1793 as recorded by David Collins.[19]

> The clergyman, who suffered as much inconvenience as other people from the want of a proper place for the performance of divine service, himself undertook to remove the evil, on finding that, from the pressure of other

16 R. B. Walker, 'The Abolition of State Aid to Religion in New South Wales' (1962) 10 *Historical Studies Australia and New Zealand* 165, 165.

17 James Cook (author), Britton Alexander and Frank Murcott Bladen (eds), *Historical Records of New South Wales* (Government Printer, 1892–1901) vol 1, pt 2, 90.

18 Richard Johnson, 'Rev Richard Johnson to Governor Phillip, 29 February 1792' in Jean Woolmington, *Religion in Early Australia: The Problem of Church and State* (Cassell Australia, 1976) 1–2; James Cook (author), Britton Alexander and Frank Murcott Bladen (eds), *Historical Records of New South Wales* (Government Printer, 1892–1901) vol 2, 594. See also Richard Johnson, 'Rev Richard Johnson to Henry Fricker 5 November 1788' in George Mackaness, *Some Letters of Rev Richard Johnson BA First Chaplain of New South Wales* (Review Publications, 1978) pt 1, 25; Richard Johnson, 'Rev Richard Johnson to Henry Fricker, 4 October 1791' in George Mackaness, *Some Letters of Rev Richard Johnson BA First Chaplain of New South Wales* (Review Publications, 1978) pt 1, 42; Richard Johnson, 'Rev Richard Johnson to Anonymous 23 March 1982' in George Mackaness, *Some Letters of Rev Richard Johnson BA First Chaplain of New South Wales* (Review Publications, 1978) pt 1, 46–47.

19 Deputy Judge-Advocate and Lieutenant Governor. See *Collins, David (1756–1810)* (January 2018) Australian Dictionary of Biography http://adb.anu.edu.au/biography/collins-david-1912>.

works it was not easy to foresee when a church would be erected. He accordingly began one under his own inspection, and chose the situation for it at the back of the huts on the east side of the cove. The front was seventy-three feet by fifteen; and at right angles with the centre projected another building forty feet by fifteen. The edifice was constructed of strong posts, wattles, and plaster, and was to be thatched. Much credit was due to the Rev Mr. Johnson for his personal exertions on this occasion.[20]

After the completion of the building and the first service on the 25 August 1793,[21] Rev Johnson wrote to the Under Secretary of State, Henry Dundas, informing him of the building of the church and enclosing a table setting out the cost of the work.[22]

> As Chaplain to this distant Colony, I humbly beg leave to state to you these following circumstances,
> [...]
> That publick [sic] works of different kinds have been and still continue to be, so urgent that no place of any kind has yet been erected, for the purpose of performing divine Service.
> [...]
> That in these and such like considerations, I have at length deemed it advisable, and even expedient, on my own accord, and account, to run up a temporary shelter, which would serve the above important purpose until a better can be provided.[23]

It appears that Rev Johnson both expected the works he had undertaken to be approved of and to be reimbursed for the expenses he had personally incurred. Unfortunately for Rev Johnson, Lieutenant-Governor Grose did not agree. The dispute that followed demonstrated both the power of the State over religion in relation to funding and the *ad-hoc* nature of funding. The dispute was not settled and Rev Johnson was not reimbursed until 1797, four years after the church was opened.

The dispute

Rev Johnson gave his letter and estimate of costs to Lieutenant-Governor Grose to be included in his next dispatch to England. Rather than endorsing the

---

20 David Collins, *An Account of the English Colony in New South Wales from its First Settlement in January 1788 to August 1801* (Cadell and Davies, 2nd ed, 1804) 218.

21 For an account of the first service conducted in the new Church see Collins, above n 20, 223–224.

22 Richard Johnson, 'Rev Richard Johnson to Under Secretary of State Dundas September 1793' in George Mackaness, *Some Letters of Rev Richard Johnson BA First Chaplain of New South Wales* (Review Publications, 1978) pt 1, 47–48. For a copy of the table of expenses see James Cook (author), Britton Alexander and Frank Murcott Bladen (eds), *Historical Records of New South Wales* (Government Printer, 1892–1901) vol 2, 66.

23 Richard Johnson, 'Rev Richard Johnson to Under Secretary of State Dundas September 1793' in George Mackaness, *Some Letters of Rev Richard Johnson BA First Chaplain of New South Wales* (Review Publications, 1978) pt I, 47–48.

expenditure and re-imbursement of Rev Johnson, Lieutenant Governor Grose included his own letter in which he cast dispersions upon Rev Johnson's character, and made the following comments in relation to Rev Johnson's request for reimbursement:

> His charge for this Church is infinitely more than it ought to have cost, and his attempt to make a charge of it at all surprises me exceedingly; for on his applications to myself for a variety of little articles with which he has been furnished from the stores, he has invariably stated that as he was building this church at his own expense he hoped to be obliged, and on this account generally was accommodated with whatever he came to ask.[24]

Despite the Lieutenant Governor's assertions above, throughout the building of the church Rev Johnson had encountered problems, as aid promised by the Lieutenant Governor was withdrawn or never provided. As a result, he was forced to pay for labour, rather than use convict labour, and use his own servants and equipment.[25] Perhaps it should not have come as a surprise that Lieutenant Governor Grose then refused to reimburse Rev Johnson.[26] What the refusal demonstrates is the absolute power of the State over religion in relation to funding. At this very early stage of the colony Rev Johnson had few others he could turn to in order to fund the building of the church. The colony was largely made up of convicts, the military, and State officials, so he had little chance of raising funds locally from private subscriptions. What he required in terms of funding had to be provided by the State. There was no one else. In this situation, with the State's refusal of funding, Rev Johnson was powerless, the funding of religion was effectively at the whim of the Governors and the authorities back in England.

Rev Richard Johnson was eventually reimbursed for the church in 1797. However, it was burnt down on 2 October 1798.[27]

The *Church Acts*

As discussed in Chapter 8, the Church and Schools Corporation was intended to provide an end to the *ad-hoc* funding and to endower the Church of England so that it could provide for the religious needs of the colony. However, it was officially dissolved in 1833 after it failed to achieve its objectives.[28] With the collapse

---

24 James Cook (author), Britton Alexander and Frank Murcott Bladen (eds), *Historical Records of New South Wales* (Government Printer, 1892–1901) vol 2, 64.

25 Neil Macintosh, *Richard Johnson Chaplain to the Colony of New South Wales His Life and Times 1755–1827* (Library of Australian History, 1978) 68–69.

26 For a discussion of the wider dispute between Lieutenant Governor Gross and Rev Richard Johnson see Macintosh, above n 25, 62–82.

27 Macintosh, above n 25, 70, 87; James Cook (author), Britton Alexander and Frank Murcott Bladen (eds), *Historical Records of New South Wales* (Government Printer, 1892–1901) vol 2, 881.

28 Albert Gordon Austin, *Australian Education 1788–1900: Church, State and Public Education in Colonial Australia* (Sir Isaac Pitman& Sons Ltd, 1961) 31.

of the Corporation, a new system for funding of religion was needed. Unlike education, which was to take many years and several Governors, before a new system could be developed and accepted, the problem of funding was solved relatively quickly. The solution was the *Church Acts,* which were to become an integral feature of the relationship between the State and religion for decades to come.

In September 1833 Governor Sir Richard Bourke[29] sent a dispatch to the Colonial Secretary Lord Stanley setting out his proposal for the funding of religion in the colonies.[30] Bourke's plan was to fund the 'Three Grand Divisions of Christianity,' namely the Church of England, Roman Catholic Church and Presbyterian Church, using a co-contribution scheme.[31] This plan became the *Church Acts* and was a radical departure from the prevailing system of funding.

The background to the Church Acts

One of the most significant changes brought about by the *Church Acts* was the break in the exclusive relationship between the State and the Church of England. For most of early colonial period the State and the Church of England had an exclusive relationship in relation to funding, because, as with education, the Church of England was the only religion to have a significant official presence in the colony. The *Church Acts* officially ended this exclusive relationship. While the *Church Acts* did not provide funding to all religions, being restricted to the 'Three Grand Divisions of Christianity,' it was a step away from the traditional monopoly of the Church of England.

The colony now had several different religious denominations.[32] One of Governor Bourke's concerns, therefore, was that his new system of State funding for religion be equitable. In his opinion, the population of New South Wales would not support the establishment of the Church of England, and that if an attempt were made to establish it, the people may turn away from religion completely.[33]

Governor Bourke's view was supported by numerous petitions complaining of the amount of funding received by the Church of England. Even prior to the Church and Schools Corporation, the Church of England had received the majority of State funding. Instead of continuing to solely fund the Church of England, Governor Bourke proposed that the 'Three Grand Divisions of Christianity' should all receive State funding, although he expressed the hope that in the future State funding may be able to be removed altogether.[34] He is reported

---

29 Governor Bourke arrived in New South Wales in December 1831. See Manning Clark, *A History of Australia* (Melbourne University Press, 1962) vol 2, 183.
30 Frederick Watson (ed), *Historical Records of Australia Series 1* (Library Committee of the Commonwealth Parliament, 1914–1925) vol 17, 224–233.
31 Ibid. 226–8.
32 Ibid. 225.
33 Ibid. 226–227.
34 Ibid.

to have said that he looked forward to a time when the churches would 'roll off State support like saturated leeches.'[35]

A response to Governor Bourke's plan was delayed due to successive changes of government in England.[36] The new Colonial Secretary, Lord Glenelg, finally replied to Governor Bourke's plan for State funding for religion in New South Wales on 30 November 1835. Lord Glenelg expressed the British government's attachment to the Church of England but acknowledged that in New South Wales it was not appropriate for it to be the established Church of Australia.[37]

On receiving Lord Glenelg's reply, Governor Bourke wasted no time in getting his *Church Act* on the statute Books.[38] The Bill was placed before the Legislative Council on 22 July 1836 and *An act to promote the building of Churches and Chapels and to provide for the maintenance of Ministers of Religion in New South Wales* was passed just seven days later.[39]

Van Diemen's Land followed New South Wales and Governor Bourke's lead, introducing its own *Church Act; The Support of Certain Christian Ministers and Erection of Places of Divine Worship Act*,[40] in November 1837.[41]

The structure and regulatory features of the Church Acts

The *Church Acts* created a structured system of funding subject to oversight by the State. Prior to the creation of the Church and Schools Corporation funding, even to the Church of England, had been *ad-hoc*. Now the Church of England, the Roman Catholic Church and the Presbyterian Church had access to a structured and consistent system of funding.

The *Church Acts 1836* (NSW) had two main limbs: the first for the provision of funds for the building of churches and chapels; and the second for the provision of stipends for Ministers of Religion. In relation to the first limb, the *Church Acts* created a co-contribution scheme for the building of churches, chapels and ministers' dwellings. Where the local congregation could raise more than £300 by private subscription the government would provide an equal amount, up to £1,000.[42] In relation to the second limb, the *Church Acts 1836* (NSW) set out a scale, based on the number of adherents, for the payment of stipends to

35 Jack Gregory, 'State Aid to Religion in the Australian Colonies 1788–1895' (1999) 70(2) *Victorian Historical Journal* 128, 131.

36 in Frederick Watson (ed), *Historical Records of Australia Series 1* (Library Committee of the Commonwealth Parliament, 1914–1925) vol 18, 201.

37 Ibid. 202–203.

38 Jack Gregory, above n 35, 131.

39 Barrett, above n 13, 34. The Act is generally referred to as the *Church Act 1936* (NSW) although it is sometimes referred to as the *Church Building Act 1936* (NSW). Regulations to accompany the Act were gazetted on 4 October 1836. See New South Wales, *New South Wales Government Gazette*, No 243, 12 October 1836, 762–764.

40 1 Vict, No 16; In this paper referred to as the *Church Act 1837* (VDL).

41 Barrett, above n 13, 37–40.

42 *Church Act 1836* (NSW) s 1.

Ministers of Religion.[43] In the case of 100 adherents the minister would be paid £100, for 200 adherents £150, and for 500 adherents £200.[44]

As well as providing the amount of funds available for building works and ministers' salaries, the *Church Acts* also created a system of State oversight as to how the money provided was spent. In relation to church buildings, the *Church Acts* required that trustees be appointed to hold the church land and that these trustees were required to provide an account to the State that would be reviewed by an architect to determine the quality of the building, and that the claimed amount had actually been spent.[45] Ministers of Religion who received stipends under the Act where required to provide proof that they were ministering to the community for which they received their stipend.[46]

The *Church Acts* as a structures system

As has been referred to above, the *Church Acts* created a structured system of funding which contrasts with the *ad-hoc* nature of the funding system prior to the *Church Acts*. While the Church and Schools Corporation was arguably meant to be a structured system of funding it was a short lived and failed scheme.

The *Church Acts* in both New South Wales and Van Diemen's Land were very effective in promoting the growth of religion in the colony. As will be detailed below, both the number of clergy and the number of church buildings grew dramatically in the years following the introduction of the *Church Acts*. However, this growth highlighted a potential flaw in the scheme – that is that there was no cap on the total amount of funding that the State could be required to provide to religion. While the *Church Acts* determined the amount any individual church or cleric could receive, there was no limit on the total that could be applied for. In effect, as long as the various religious denominations met the co-contribution and adherent number requirements, State funding of religion was unlimited.

As well as being an unlimited funding scheme, the *Church Acts* also placed the control of funding in the hands of religion. This is in stark contrast to the situation that persisted prior to the creation of the *Church Acts*. As was discussed above, prior to the creation of the *Church Acts* funding for religion was *ad-hoc*

---

43 Ibid. s 2.
44 Ibid. Where there was a Church or Chapel but the requirement for at least 100 adherents could not be met, the Governor had the discretion to provide a stipend of £100, if 'under the special circumstances of the case the said Governor and Executive Council shall deem it expedient.' Where there was no Church or Chapel but at least £50 could be raised privately, the Government would pay an amount equal to the amount raised privately, up to £100, towards a stipend for a Minister of Religion. See *Church Act 1836* (NSW) ss 3, 5.
45 *Church Act 1836* (NSW) ss 7–10; New South Wales, *New South Wales Government Gazette*, No 243, 12 October 1836, 763.
46 *Church Act 1836* (NSW) s 6. Clause 7 of the regulations made under the Act provided that a certificate from the Lord Bishop of Australia in the case of the Church of England (Bishop Broughton), the Moderator in the case of the Presbyterians and the Roman Catholic Bishop (Bishop Polding) would satisfy this clause. See New South Wales, *New South Wales Government Gazette*, No 243, 12 October 1836, 763.

and at the whim of the State. This created difficulties for the early chaplains and inequality between the various religious denominations. In creating an egalitarian, structured and unlimited system of funding, the State also in effect handed control over to religion. It was religion that now determined how much funding the State provided, although the State retained control of how that funding could be spent.

The success of the Church Acts

Prior to the introduction of the *Church Acts* in New South Wales and Van Diemen's Land religion was relatively poorly catered for. By contrast, just a few years after the introduction of the *Church Acts,* there was almost an oversupply of religion in the colony. If the success of the *Church Acts* was to be measured in terms of how well it promoted the growth in the number of clergy and church buildings in the colony then it should be judged a remarkable success.

In 1836, New South Wales had 17 active Church of England clergy with nine more in Van Diemen's Land. The Roman Catholics did little better with five priests in New South Wales and another two in Van Diemen's Land. Other denominations had a similarly small number of clergy. By 1836, the Wesleyan Methodists had four clergy.[47] The Presbyterians (Church of Scotland) had five ministers in each of the colonies making a total of 10.[48] The Independent (Congregational) Church had three ministers in New South Wales and one in Van Diemen's land, while the Baptists had one minister in each colony.[49]

In the four years before the *Church Act 1836* (NSW) was passed, the number of clergy in the colony varied from 27 to 32, while in 1841, four years after the introduction of the *Church Act 1836* (NSW), the number had risen to 84, more than a two-and-a-half-fold increase.[50] Van Diemen's Land saw a similar increase in clergy with around 50 ministers in 1841, 35 of whom were supported by the State.[51]

As well as leading to an increase in the number of clergy, the *Church Acts* also lead to an increase in the number of church buildings and ministers' dwellings. The table below, taken from a despatch from Governor Gipps to Lord Russell in 1841, demonstrates the remarkable increase in religious building activities.

47 Barrett, above n 13, 13.
48 Ibid.
49 Ibid. 14.
50 Frederick Watson (ed), *Historical Records of Australia Series 1* (Library Committee of the Commonwealth Parliament, 1914–1925) vol 21, 219.
51 Barrett, above n 13, 43.

Table 9.1 Churches and parsonages built under the *Church Act 1836* (NSW) for the years 1836 to 1841[52]

Religious Group	Churches Completed	Parsonages Completed	Cost of completed buildings £ s. d.	Churches in progress	Parson-ages in Progress	Cost of buildings in progress £
Church of England	15	6	13,155 15 2	24	11	56,467
Presbyterian	6	1	2,335 17 7	6	1	10,420
Wesleyan	3	0	1,577 4 9	6	1	14,872
Congre-gational	2	0	433 8 3	2	1	2,545
Roman Catholic	5	0	2,490 8 9	6	0	8,792
Total	30	7	19,992 14 6	44	14	93.096

While the *Church Acts* were successful in promoting growth in the numbers of clergy and church buildings, all this growth was expensive. As more difficult financial times set in, it soon became apparent that the unlimited nature of the *Church Acts* was going to cause problems for the colony's finances.

Unlimited funding poses a problem for the State

With the dramatic growth in the number of churches, parsonages, and religious ministers, a flaw in the scheme soon became evident. While the *Acts* prescribed how much a single congregation could get to build a church, or the amount a single minster could receive per year, no cap was placed on the overall amount that could be granted to fund religion. As the number of churches and religious minsters grew, so too did the cost of funding religion. In effect, the *Church Acts* had given the churches control of their own funding. As long as they could meet the co-funding and number of adherents' requirements the various religious denominations could claim as much funding as they wished, and the State had no way of limiting it. As the colonies entered a depression, this problem became acute and the colonial governments looked for ways to take back control of the funding of religion.

In 1837, the New South Wales government had paid just £19,167 in grants to religion. Under the *Church Act 1836* (NSW), this grew to £35,981 by 1841, an 88% increase in just 4 years.[53] The *Church Act 1836* (NSW) had been introduced in boom times, however economic depression soon set in. Land sales fell

52 Frederick Watson (ed), *Historical Records of Australia Series 1* (Library Committee of the Commonwealth Parliament, 1914–1925) vol 21, 218–219.
53 Jack Gregory, above n 35, 135.

dramatically from £316,626 in 1840, to £90,388 in 1841, and to just £14,575 in 1842.[54] Even before the depression began, Governor Gipps was concerned about deficit budgets. Wool prices were falling, and a drought began in 1838, this along with an increasing demand for government services meant that the colony's finances were in trouble.[55]

Like New South Wales, Van Diemen's Land also began to feel the financial strain of an unlimited *Church Act*. On one side of the equation Van Diemen's Land faced an economic depression, falling wool prices, small land sales, a shortage of coin, an adverse balance of payments, and an expensive immigration programme, while on the other the amount of funds claimed under the *Church Act* rose alarmingly from £12,000 in 1837, to £15,000 in 1842.[56]

The State takes back control

While the State – via the co-contribution requirements in the *Church Acts* – had control of how State funding for religion was spent, the *Church Acts* placed no upper limit on the quantum of funding that could be claimed. With a wholesale repeal of the *Church Acts* unlikely,[57] other solutions needed to be found.

The initial solution was a limit on the quantum of funding that could be provided to religion by the State via a constitutional cap. The institution of a constitutional cap on the amount of funding gave the State control of the quantum of funding and maintained an ongoing financial relationship with religion. While the constitutionally enshrined nature of State funding for religion made it difficult to remove, eventually the State exercised its ultimate control over the funding relationship by removing all direct grants to religion.

Controlling the quantum

The first change to take place was the restriction on the amount of funding that was available. In both New South Wales and Tasmania, this was achieved via the creation of a constitutional provision of a set amount for the funding of 'public worship.' While this cap enabled the State to take back control of State funding for religion, simply putting a cap in place did not solve all the issues that had been created via the unlimited system of funding established under the *Church Acts*. Two further issues needed to be resolved: first, how that cap could be reconciled with the apparently unlimited funding available under the *Church Acts*, and

---

54 Barrett, above n 13, 46.

55 Ibid.

56 Ibid, 45, 47, 53–54.

57 The Attorney-General J.H Plunkett had advised that any attempt to amend the Act prior to elections would be unadvisable and that the only real way to limit the operation of the Act would be to repeal it altogether. See Frederick Watson (ed), *Historical Records of Australia Series 1* (Library Committee of the Commonwealth Parliament, 1914–1925) vol 23, 732–733.

second, how the now limited funding should be distributed between the various Christian denominations.

The constitutional cap

In 1842, the British government passed the *Australian Constitution Act 1842* (Imp) 5& 6 Vict. c 7, and in 1850, it passed the *Australian Constitution Act 1950* (Imp), creating the foundation for democratic and responsible government in New South Wales and Tasmania respectively. Additionally, the *Acts* set out the amount that was to be made available for 'public worship.' In New South Wales, a sum of £30,000 was stipulated; in Tasmania, the amount was £15,000.[58]

The amount that could be spent on religion now had an upper limit. This meant that the most problematic element of the *Church Acts* – the unlimited nature of the available funding – had been resolved. It also handed the control of funding back to the State. While funding had been unlimited, religion had effectively been in control. Now that a cap had been set, the State had control of both the quantum and how the money was spent.

Reconciling the cap with the Church Acts

For New South Wales, the answer to the question of how to reconcile the new constitutional cap on State funding for religion was to be found in the *Church Act 1836* (NSW). On re-examining the *Church Act*, the Attorney-General JH Plunkett rediscovered apparently overlooked wording in Clauses 1 and 2. In the case of funding of church buildings, the grant could only be made '*with the advice of the Executive Council,*' and in Clause 2, large grants could only be made '*with the consent of the Legislative Council.*' This meant that the unlimited nature of the *Church Act* could be circumvented by the Executive or the Legislative Council, disapproving applications in excess of the £30,000 cap.[59]

However, in the end, it was not this rediscovered control mechanism that gave the State back control of the quantum of religious funding. Instead, the depression, combined with the original control mechanism of co-contributions, was enough to bring the amount of funding claimed under the *Church Act* under the £30,000 cap. As a result of the depression, local congregations were unable to raise the co-contribution amounts required to make claims. In 1844, the amount actually claimed was just £26,000, making the Legislative Council's assertion of control a moot point.[60]

---

58 *Australian Constitutions Act 1842* (Imp), 5& 6, Vict, c 7, sch C; *Australian Constitution Act 1850* (Imp); see also Barrett, above n 13, 47, 55; Jack Gregory, above n 35, 135.

59 Frederick Watson (ed), *Historical Records of Australia Series 1* (Library Committee of the Commonwealth Parliament, 1914–1925) vol 33, 734–735; Walker, above n 16, 165.

60 Barrett, above n 13, 48. When Victoria separated from New South Wales in 1851, the amount available to fund religion in New South Wales was reduced to £28,000. See Walker, above n 16.

Tasmania's *Church Act 1837* (VDL) did not originally contain a provision analogous to Clauses 1 and 2 in New South Wales, making its *Church Act* truly unlimited. In 1840, the Tasmanian Government remedied this by passing the *Support of Certain Christian Ministers and Erection of Places of Divine Worship Amendment 1840* 4 Vict., No. 16. The amendment permitted the Governor and Executive Council to refuse funding where it was sought for a church or house that was not necessary.[61] By itself, this amendment proved to be insufficient and estimates of expenditure for religious funding in Tasmania continued to climb.[62]

Unlike New South Wales, Tasmania was unable to bring the actual amount of State funding for religion below the constitutional cap. As will be discussed below, a further attempt to bring the amount of funding below the constitutional cap was made in 1862, and while this gave the State in Tasmania a little more control of the quantum of funding, it was not until all direct funding to religion was actually removed, that the State was able to truly take control of funding.

The distribution

The second issue that needed to be settled before the State could fully take back control of funding of religion in New South Wales was how the £30,000 was to be distributed. Under the unlimited *Church Act*, the quantum that each denomination received was determined by their ability to meet the co-contribution requirements. In an unlimited funding environment, this second element was of less concern; however, with a cap now in place, the division of the fixed sum of money available became very important.

Two different distribution models were proposed, one by the Roman Catholic Church and the other by the Church of England. On behalf of the Roman Catholic Church, Bishop Polding recommended that the money be distributed in accordance with the number of adherents of the various churches.[63] On behalf of the Church of England, Bishop Broughton rejected this as a departure from the principle of the *Church Acts*, instead recommending that the money be distributed in proportion to the amount received prior to the cap.[64] Rather than deciding himself, Governor Gipps referred the matter to the Colonial Secretary.[65]

The Colonial Secretary, Lord Stanley, eventually approved the *uti possiditis* method of distribution. The amounts each denomination received would be determined by reference to the number of adherents in a selected census year rather than in the year of distribution.[66] While this method was introduced in 1844, it was not until 1853 that a census year was finally selected for this purpose.

---

61 Barrett, above n 13, 53.
62 Ibid. 55.
63 Frederick Watson (ed), *Historical Records of Australia Series 1* (Library Committee of the Commonwealth Parliament, 1914–1925) vol 18, 346–351.
64 Ibid. 346–352.
65 Ibid. 348–349.
66 Ibid. 734; Walker, above n 16.

The reason given for the delay was the rapid increase in the population and the significant changes in the proportion of the population claimed by each church. Finally, in 1853, the census of 1851 was selected, thus settling the question after nine years of debate.[67]

The State in New South Wales now had control of the quantum of funding, which religious denominations received that funding and how that funding could be spent. In one view, the State had won the tug-of-war for control of State funding of religion; however, State provision of funding for religion was constitutionally enshrined. This appeared to guarantee that the financial relationship would continue into the future. As will be discussed below, this relationship did not last forever, and changing attitudes towards religion eventually led to the removal of the constitutionally enshrined funding for religion not just in New South Wales but also in all other Australian colonies.

Before analysing the removal of all direct funding to religion, the creation and level of State control of State funding to religion in the other colonies needs to be considered. Subtly different local circumstances produced subtly different changes in each colony. While all colonies, except Queensland, developed a *Church Act*-like scheme of funding, the actual implementation of that scheme was subtly different.

The other colonies

Like New South Wales and Tasmania, all of the other Australian colonies faced the issue of how best to fund religion. While all colonies eventually developed a *Church Act*-like funding scheme, the development and implementation of the scheme differed in every colony. This was primarily due to different local circumstances and different starting points. While each is subtly different, they can be divided into two broad categories based on the starting point of the relationship: first, those that directly inherited the principle of State funding for religion upon separation from New South Wales, and second, those that had little or no initial provision for State funding of religion.

In the case of the first category, the creation of State funding for religion was simply a function of the colonies' separation from New South Wales. In effect, it only changed which colonial authority religion had a relationship with, rather than the character or nature of that relationship. Victoria and Queensland both fall into this first category. Upon separation from New South Wales,[68] both colonies had a sum for religious worship set out in their founding Constitution. Schedule B of the *Australian Constitution Act 1850* (Imp) initially provided

---

67 Walker, above n 16, 166–167.
68 Victoria separated from New South Wales in July 1851 and Queensland separated in December 1859. See John Stradbroke Gregory, *Church and State: Changing Government Policies Towards Religion in Australia; with Particular Reference to Victoria since Separation* (Cassell Australia, 1973) 44.

£6,000 per year for 'Public worship in Victoria,'[69] while the amount in Queensland was £1,000 per year.[70]

In contrast, the colonies that fall into the second category did not inherit the principle of State funding of religion from New South Wales. Instead, they developed this principle on their own, in response to local conditions after initially having little or no provision for State funding of religion.

Western Australia and South Australia

Western Australia and South Australia did not separate from New South Wales and therefore did not inherit the principle of State funding for religion. As a result, the principle developed independently in these two colonies. While they have this feature in common and both eventually developed a *Church Act*-like scheme of funding, they also have some important differences. Four of the most important are the initial intentions of the founders of the colonies, the principle upon which State funding of religion was distributed once it was provided, the operation of the schemes in practice and the controls placed on the schemes by the State.

The initial intentions of the founders of Western Australia and South Australia in relation to State funding of religion were very different. In Western Australia, it was intended that religion be provided for in a similar way to New South Wales, while in South Australia, the intention was that no State funding would be provided to religion. While the eventual creation of a system of State funding in both colonies was the same, the implications of that change were very different. In Western Australia, the creation of a system of State funding for religion effectively conformed to what the colony founders intended, while in South Australia, the creation of State funding was an abandonment of the principles upon which the colony was founded.

The instructions to Governor Stirling, founding Governor of Western Australia, were that religion was to be provided for in a similar way to New South Wales upon its establishment over 40 years earlier:[71]

> You will bear in mind, that in all locations of Territory, a due proportion must be . . . as well as for the maintenance of the Clergy, Support for the Establishments for the purposes of Religion, and the education of youth.[72]

---

69 Ibid. In Victoria, the Constitutional cap on State funding for religion was increased to £30,000 on 18 January 1853. See *An Act more effectually to promote the erection of Buildings for Public Worship and to provide for the Maintenance of Ministers of Religion in the colony of Victoria 1853* (Vic); 'Legislative Council,' *The Argus* (Melbourne), 1 December 1852, 4–5; John Stradbroke Gregory, above n 68, 51.

70 Jack Gregory, above n 35, 139.

71 Rowan Strong, 'Church and State in Western Australia: Implementing New Imperial Paradigms in the Swan River Colony, 1827–1857' (2010) 61(3) *Journal of Ecclesiastical History 517*, 521.

72 Ibid.

However, as with education, the actual provision of religion in the Swan River colony was initially very slight.[73] Initially, grants were made on an *ad-hoc* basis, and it was not until 1840 that a scheme of State funding for religion was established under the *Church Act 1840* 4 Vict., No. 6. The *Act* was nearly identical to Governor Bourke's New South Wales *Church Act*, but the grants available were much smaller.[74]

In contrast, in South Australia, the initial intention of the founders was that there be no provision for State funding of religion. As discussed in Chapter Eight, this included State funding of schools. Unlike the other colonies, many of the original settlers in South Australia were from dissenting Christian denominations who believed in voluntarism.[75] However, the principle of voluntarism left many churches in a desperate situation, with religion and education poorly catered for in many areas.[76] The solution was State funding for religion.

State funding for religion was eventually introduced in 1845 by the newly appointed Lieutenant-Governor Frederick Robe.[77] Two days later, the new Legislative Council passed a resolution that a grant from special revenue be made for religion for all Christian denominations that would accept it.[78]

Even after a scheme of State funding for religion was created in South Australia and Western Australia, they continued to have a subtly different relationship between the State and religion in relation to State funding of religion from both each other and the other Australian colonies. One way in which the subtle difference manifested itself was the way in which the funds were distributed. In Western Australia, an almost exclusive relationship between the State and the Church of England developed, while in South Australia, the founding principles of the colony manifested itself in being the only colony to provide State funding for non-Christian religions.

On paper, the relationship between the State and religion in relation to State funding of religion in Western Australia was the same as in the eastern mainland colonies. Like the New South Wales *Church Act*, Western Australia's funding scheme provided funding to all of the dominant Christian denominations.[79] In practice, the Church of England received the bulk of the funding under the *Act*. By 1843, the Wesleyans had received just £200, while the Roman Catholics had to wait until 1852 for a stipend to be paid to any of their ministers.[80] In theory,

---

73 Jack Gregory, above n 35, 133.
74 Strong, above n 71, 525–526.
75 Jack Gregory, above n 35, 134; Douglas Pike, *Paradise of Dissent South Australia 1829–1857* (Melbourne University Press, 2nd ed, 1967) 3. Voluntarism is the principle that religion should not be funded by the State and instead should be funded by voluntary contributions from adherents.
76 Pike, above n 75, 351–357, 359.
77 Ibid. 359–360.
78 Ibid. 361.
79 Church of England, the Roman Catholic Church and the Wesleyans.
80 Strong, above n 71, 526–528.

there was a relationship between the State and all three Christian denominations; however, in practice, the relationship that developed was a nearly exclusive one between the State and the Church of England. This relationship became even stronger with the arrival of the first convicts in 1850.[81] Convicts were initially brought to Western Australia to help alleviate the desperate financial circumstances of the colony and this continued until 1868. During this period, the Church of England clergy developed an even closer relationship with the State. They spent so much of their time ministering to and supervising the convicts that they became indistinguishable from prison chaplains, with many receiving a large proportion of their income from this work.[82] While all Christian denominations had in theory been on an equal footing since the passage of the *Church Act 1840* (WA), in reality, the convict era served to strengthen the dominance of the Church of England. It was not until 1871 that State funding of religion in Western Australia was finally distributed equally to all denominations.[83]

In contrast, in South Australia, not only were all Christian denominations treated equally in terms of the available funding, but so too were non-Christian denominations. While this book uses the term 'religion,' in effect, the relationship in relation to State funding to religion had been a relationship between the State and Christianity only. South Australia was the only colony to truly have a relationship between the State and all religions in the colony.

On the same day that funding was granted to Christian denominations in South Australia, the motion to grant religious funding was amended to include Jews. Those in support of the amendment insisted that despite the fact that there were only 58 Jews in the colony, there might be more in the future and they wanted to establish the principle of equity from the start. When challenged that this principle would also allow Mohomedans[84] and Pagans to receive government funding, the supporters of Jewish funding agreed that all could potentially be included.[85]

As highlighted above, in relation to both the *Church Acts* in Tasmania and New South Wales, the funding schemes under the *Church Acts* were potentially unlimited, giving religion control of the quantum of funding available. In the eastern colonies, the State took back control by placing a constitutional cap on the amount of funding available for religion. While this created a new constitutional relationship, it gave the State control of the quantum of funding, at least on paper. Western Australia and South Australia also faced the issues of a scheme

---

81 Marian Verley, 'Western Australian Society: The Religious Aspect 1929–1895' in Charles Thomas Stannage (ed), *A New History of Western Australia* (University of Western Australia Press, 1981) 589.

82 Ibid. 590–592.

83 Ibid. 592.

84 Muslims.

85 Jack Gregory, above n 35, 138. For a comprehensive discussion of the treatment of Jews in the Australian colonies, see Israel Getzler, *Neither Toleration nor Favour* (Melbourne University Press, 1970).

of funding that was unlimited, at least in theory. In each colony, the State took back control using different methods.

While it is arguable that South Australia was the most reluctant colony to introduce State funding for religion due to its founding principles of voluntarism, it in fact introduced the most unlimited funding scheme of all colonies. An amount of two shillings per head was granted to each denomination that would accept it.[86] Therefore, the more people in each denomination, the more funding they were entitled to. Like the original Bourke *Church Acts*, religion was in control of the quantum of funding – the more adherents a religion could claim, the greater the amount of funding it could claim from the State. With no cap in place, the only limiting factor in the amount that each denomination could receive would have been the population of the colony. The initial funding scheme in South Australia was also unlimited in another way. There were no controls placed on how the granted funds could be spent. The denominations were simply given their allotted funds and it was left to them to determine how this money was to be spent.[87] This gave the religious denominations even more control than they had in New South Wales and Tasmania.

While the South Australian funding scheme was initially different from the original *Church Acts* the State in South Australia quickly developed a *Church Act*-like scheme of funding. In doing so, the State took back control of funding of religion by determining how that funding should he spent. From 1848, funds were awarded on a co-contribution basis in a similar way to the *Church Acts* in other colonies.[88]

While the State in South Australia eventually exercised control in the same way as under the *Church Acts* – by creating a co-contribution purpose-based scheme of funding for religion – religion exercised control over funding in South Australia in a different way to all other colonies by refusing to accept the funding on offer. Four Christian denominations claimed their entitlement under the 1846 ordinances.[89] The remaining non-conformist denominations refused to accept the funding allotted to them, meaning that in the first 18 months of the scheme, only £2,629 of the available £3,336 was used.[90]

In theory, the Western Australia *Church Act* was also unlimited. Like South Australia, Western Australia did not have a constitutional cap on funding. The solution in Western Australia to the apparently unlimited nature of the *Church Act* funding scheme was administrative rather than legal. From the very beginning of the scheme, the State exercised control over religion in relation to funding in the way in which the funding scheme was administered. For example, the government would not pay a stipend or church building grants to an itinerant

---

86 Pike, above n 75, 363; the Jews, with only 58 adherents, were entitled to £2 18s.
87 Ibid.
88 Ibid. 371–372; £150 was available for a Church building where there was a private subscription of £50, and £50 was available for any clergy who had 50 pew holders.
89 Church of England, Church of Scotland, Roman Catholic Church and Wesleyans.
90 Pike, above n 75, 369.

preacher, where there were no fixed service times, where the signatures gathered came from non-adherents of that denomination, or where the minister received funds from a source external to the colony.[91] These restrictions were not part of the *Act* itself, but were applied as an administrative restriction. The reason for the restrictions and small funding amounts may have been the desperate financial situation in the colony. In December 1843, the financial situation was so bad that the colonial government was forced to suspend the *Church Act 1840* (WA).[92] The administrative measures and the suspension of the *Church Act* in Western Australia suggest that despite the theoretically unlimited funding scheme created by Western Australia's *Church Act*, religion was never in control because the State in Western Australia could never afford to let it be.

Removal of funding to religion

All the colonies eventually reached a situation where the State had taken back most of the control in the relationship between the State and religion in relation to funding. In all colonies, a system had been established where the State controlled how much funding the various denominations received and how that funding could be spent. It could be argued that the State therefore had all of the control; however, an obligation still existed – via their legislation and constitutions – to fund religion.

The eventual removal of direct State funding of religion can be seen in two ways. First, it could be argued that the removal of funding was the ultimate act of control by the State. While the various schemes existed, religion could exercise some control, but the very existence of the schemes was in the hands of the State rather than religion. Any control that religion may have had in the past was arguably illusory in that the State could have exercised ultimate control at any time by changing or abolishing any of the colonial funding schemes. Second, the removal of State funding of religion could be seen as religion taking back control. All of the various funding schemes eventually reached a position where the State directed how funds were to be spent. This would have had the effect – via the co-contribution requirements – of influencing how the various denominations operated. By providing funding only for clergy and churches built on a co-contribution basis, the various denominations had an incentive to concentrate their activities in these areas. As highlighted above, the *Church Acts* were very effective in promoting both the arrival of new clergy in the colonies and constructing church buildings. In removing direct State funding, State control, via incentives to concentrate activity in certain areas, was removed. In effect, the churches could now set their own priorities unencumbered by State incentives to behave in particular ways.

The final abolition of direct State funding for religion in the Australian colonies was drawn out over four decades. In 1851, South Australia became the first

91 Strong, above n 71, 526–528.
92 Ibid. 528–529.

colony to abolish State funding for religion, and 44 years later, in 1895, Western Australia became the last. The details of the removal of State funding in each colony vary depending on local conditions, but they can be divided into three broad categories. First, in South Australia and Queensland, the abolition of State funding occurred relatively quickly and painlessly. Second, in New South Wales, Tasmania and Victoria, the process was protracted mainly as a result of political factors. Finally, in Western Australia, the abolition appears to be predominantly a case of catching up with the eastern colonies. The details of the abolition of State funding are less important than the fact that it was eventually abolished. With its abolition, the State effectively severed a relationship that had existed since the very early days of the colony.

A brief experiment with State funding

In Queensland and South Australia, State funding for religion was removed relatively quickly and painlessly. In both cases, direct State funding for religion did not last long enough to become an entrenched feature of the colony. In Queensland, it lasted just one year. On 1 August 1860, after a failed attempt to increase State funding for religion,[93] the *State Aid Abolition Bill 1860* (Qld)[94] was passed by the Legislative Council, ending State funding to religion in Queensland just over one year after the colony separated from New South Wales.[95]

South Australia's direct funding scheme lasted a little longer – just under a decade. While Lieutenant Governor Robe had been successful at initiating State religious funding in South Australia, his scheme faced significant opposition from the beginning. Voluntarists organised petitions and public meetings in opposition to religious funding. While these were met by similar moves from those in support of religious funding, the underlying opposition did not go away.[96] The end of religious funding in South Australia seemed inevitable when, prior to the 1851 election, the old Legislative Council turned down applications for funding based on the 1847 Ordinance on the basis that new legislation was needed to authorise

---

93 See P. C. Gawne, 'State Aid to religion and Primary Education in Queensland, 1860' (1976) 9(1) *Journal of Religious History* 50, 55.
94 Some sources refer to it as the *State Aid Discontinuance Bill* 1860.
95 Queensland separated from New South Wales in June 1859; for the debate on the Bill, see 'Queensland Parliament,' *The Moreton Bay Courier* (Brisbane), 2 August 1860, 2. The Bill passed its third reading in the Legislative Council with seven votes to four. It had passed its third reading in the Legislative Assembly on 24 July 1860 with 16 votes to six; see 'Queensland Parliament,' *The Moreton Bay Courier* (Brisbane), 26 July 1860, 2. For the debate on the Bill, see 'Queensland Parliament,' *The Moreton Bay Courier* (Brisbane), 12 July 1860, 2–4; 'Queensland Parliament,' *The Moreton Bay Courier* (Brisbane), 19 July 1860, 3; 'Queensland Parliament,' *The Moreton Bay Courier* (Brisbane), 28 July 1860, 2; 'Queensland Parliament,' *The Moreton Bay Courier* (Brisbane), 26 July 1860, 2; 'Queensland Parliament,' The Moreton Bay Courier (Brisbane), 2 August 1860, 2–3.
96 For a detailed discussion of the debate surrounding religious funding in South Australia, see Pike, above n 75, 361–362.

any new funding.[97] The refusal to grant new funding by the Legislative Council effectively ended religious funding in South Australia. This effective end became a formal end when the newly elected Legislative Council formally rejected a Bill to continue State funding of religion on its first reading, 13 votes to 10.[98]

A more turbulent removal

While the removal of State funding to religion was relatively straightforward in South Australia and Queensland, the issue took much longer to resolve in the other colonies. In New South Wales, Victoria and Tasmania, State funding had become an entrenched feature of the colony and was enshrined in their constitutions. As a result of this and political turmoil, the eventual removal of direct State funding to religion took longer in these colonies.

In Tasmania, the actual removal of State funding to religion was relatively straightforward. In 1868, with no actual campaign underway for the removal of State funding to religion, Tasmania passed the *State Aid Commutation Act 1868* (Tas), commuting the constitutionally enshrined yearly funding of £15,000 to a single lump sum payment of £100,000.[99] As the Governor General explained, the issue had been raised several times in recent years, and until the issue was finally addressed, this would continue to happen.[100]

However, to reach this point, Tasmania first had to confront the continuing control that religion had over State funding of religion. As discussed above, unlike the other colonies, the State in Tasmania had never been truly successful in taking control of the quantum of funding provided. In a final attempt to exert control, Tasmania passed the *State Aid Distribution Act 1862* (Tas). The Act attempted to take back control by re-asserting the constitutional cap and it provided a mechanism by which the amount of funding actually provided would reduce over time until it fell below that constitutional cap.[101] However, this was only a compromise and the eventual abolition of all State funding for religion six years later arguably finally gave the State in Tasmania control over State funding of religion by abolishing it.

---

97 Ibid. 423.

98 Ibid. 436–437.

99 *State Aid Commutation Act 1868* (Tas) ss 2–5.

100 'Parliament of Tasmania,' *The Mercury* (Hobart), 14 August 1968, 2–3; see also Richard Davis, *State Aid and Tasmanian Politics 1868–1920* (University of Tasmania, 1969) 29–31; see also 'Parliament of Tasmania,' *The Mercury* (Hobart), 21 August 1868, 2–3; 'Parliament of Tasmania,' *The Mercury* (Hobart), 5 September 1868, 3; for debate on the Bill, see 'Parliament of Tasmania,' *The Mercury* (Hobart), 14 August 1868, 2–3; 'Parliament of Tasmania,' *The Mercury* (Hobart), 19 August 1868, 2–3; 'Parliament of Tasmania,' The Mercury (Hobart), 21 August 1868, 2.

101 'State Aid Redistribution,' *The Mercury* (Hobart), 26 September 1862, 4. The Act attempted to do this by listing the clergy who could receive stipends under the Act and disallowing further stipends. As a result, it was thought that the amount of funding would drop as clergy receiving stipends died or retired.

In New South Wales and Victoria, the process was more politically difficult. In New South Wales, the main problem was political instability. As with the creation of the Single Board system of education discussed in Chapter 8, continuing political instability meant that multiple attempts to abolish State funding for religion failed.[102] Finally in 1862, the government was successful in passing the *Publish Worship Prohibition Act 1862* (NSW), effectively abolishing State funding for religion.[103]

In Victoria, the delay in removing State funding for religion was also caused by political turmoil – in this case, the constitutionally enshrined nature of State funding for religion. In order to repeal the provision relating to State funding for religion, the Constitution required an absolute majority in both houses of parliament.[104] Over 15 years, several attempts were made to abolish State funding for religion; however, on most occasions, the Bill passed the Legislative Assembly only to be blocked by the Legislative Council or to pass by such a slim majority as to not constitute the absolute majority required.[105] Finally, in 1871, in a resigned decision, the now deeply unpopular Legislative Council passed the *State Aid to Religion Abolition Act 1871* (Vic), 18 votes to seven.[106] As Thomas A'Beckett stated:

> I do not think it will be contended that when, by the people, a most emphatic and repeated approval of the principle of a Bill has been pronounced, it is proper that we should, year after year and season after season, refuse our assent to it.[107]

Playing catch-up

Western Australia was the last colony to abolish direct State funding to religion. It finally did so in 1895, 44 years after South Australia and 24 years after the last of the eastern Colonies, Victoria.[108] In many respects, Western Australia was playing catch-up. The last Governor, Sir John Forrest, had maintained that the special character of Western Australia warranted the continuation of direct State funding of religion.[109] However, with growing public and political sentiment against this continuing and with the arrival in the colony of migrants from colonies in

---

102 Walker, above n 16, 168.
103 Ibid. 169. The Act did not abolish clergy stipends immediately. As a result, New South Wales continued to pay the stipends of Ministers of Religion into the twentieth century. The last minister to be paid a stipend under this provision, the Rev. Septimus Hungerford, died in 1927, although he had given up his stipend a few years earlier when he retired; see 'Last Recipient of State Stipend,' *The Sydney Morning Herald*, 7 July 1927, 10.
104 *Victorian Constitution Act 1855* (Imp) cl 60.
105 John Stradbroke Gregory, above n 68, 76–123.
106 Ibid. 122–123.
107 Ibid. 123.
108 Although Victoria abolished State funding in 1871, it did not take effect until 1875, reducing the gap to 20 years.
109 Jack Gregory, above n 35, 142.

which State funding for religion had long been abolished, Forrest was forced to concede that the time had come to remove State funding for religion in Western Australia.[110]

The *Ecclesiastical Grant Abolition Act 1895* (WA) gave a payout of £35,420 to the four predominant Christian denominations in lieu of ongoing grants.[111] With the passage of the *Ecclesiastical Grant Abolition Act 1895* (WA), the last vestiges of direct State funding of religion were abolished in Australia.

Indirect funding of religion

Today religions in Australia no longer receive ongoing direct funding from the State.[112] However, charities, including religious charities, are exempt from, or receive a rebate on, a wide range of taxes including income tax, capital gains tax, fringe benefits tax, the Goods and Services Tax (GST), Payroll Tax, Land Tax, Stamp Duty and Rates.[113] In 2009, it was estimated that that this amounted to over $1 billion.[114] This significant amount of forgone government revenue can be seen as indirect funding of charities, including religious organisations. While taxation exemptions do not place new money in the hands of charities, they do leave money in the hands of charities which would otherwise be payable to the government. The government therefore, in effect, is funding the charity to the amount of the exemption, or as Senator Xenophon would put it, 'effectively making donations on our behalf through tax exemptions.'[115] Religious organisations receive a significant proportion of this funding. In Australia, religious based charities or those with religious origins dominate the charity sector.[116] The basis

---

110 Verley, above n 81, 596.

111 See *Ecclesiastical Grant Abolition Act 1895* (WA) s 2.

112 Religious organisations that contract with the State as service providers do receive ongoing direct funding from the State, however, this funding is received as a consequence of their status of a service provider, not a religious organisation. The State does on occasion also make direct financial contributions to religious organisations in relation to specific projects or events. For example, both the federal and New South Wales governments provided funding for World Youth Day celebrations in 2008 see New Matilda, *Who's Paying for World Youth Day?* (27 March 2008) NewMatilda.com https://newmatilda.com/2008/03/27/whos-paying-world-youth-day/>.

113 Gino Evans Dal Pont, *Law of Charity* (LexisNexis Butterworths, 2010) 144–153.

114 Parliament of Australia, Senate Economics Legislation Committee, *Tax Laws Amendment (Public Benefit Test) Bill 2010* (Senate Printing Unit, Parliament House, 2010) 12. See also Max Wallace, *The Purple Economy: Supernatural Charities, Tax and The State* (Australian National Secular Association, 2007) 31–33; Ian Sheppard, Robert Fitzgerald and David Gonski, *Report of the Inquiry into the Definition of Charities and Related Organisations* (The Treasury, 2001) 52.

115 Commonwealth, *Parliamentary Debates*, Senate, 13 May 2010, 2843–2844 (Nicholas Xenophon).

116 Kerry O'Halloran, 'Charity and Religion: International charity law reform outcomes and the choices for Australia' (2011) 17(2) *Third Sector Review* 29, 31.

for this indirect funding was laid with the introduction of the first direct income taxes in the late nineteenth and early twentieth century.

The creation of indirect funding

Exemptions for religious organisations from direct taxation in Australia, including income tax, can be traced back to the very first Australian income tax introduced in South Australia in 1884.[117] Direct funding for religion had been removed in South Australia in 1851, 33 years earlier. However, in Western Australia, direct aid was abolished in 1895, and income tax, including exemptions, was introduced in 1907.[118]

Just as the foundations of the indirect funding model for religion were being laid, at the same time, that direct funding was being removed, the creation of these exemptions, however, does not appear to have become an issue for some time. The first serious discussion of exemptions as something akin to funding did not occur until 1936. During the parliamentary debate on the *Income Tax Assessment Act 1936* (Cth), several speakers expressed concern about the advantage that religious organisations were receiving as a result of tax exemptions.[119]

The transfer of the relationship

Income taxes, and therefore exemptions for religious organisations, were initially applied only at the State level. However, in 1942, the federal government took over the levying of income tax in an attempt to increase federal funds to support the war effort during World War Two.[120] While this is the point at which the change became permanent, it was not the first time the federal government had levied income tax. It had first levied income tax in 1915 as a way to raise revenue to fund World War One. Between 1915 and 1942, both the States and territories and the federal government levied income tax. This ceased in 1942 in a move that was challenged and eventually found to be constitutional in the first and second *Uniform Tax Cases*.[121] All subsequent federal income tax acts have included exemptions for religious organisations.[122] Today the exemption applies

---

117 *Taxation Act 1884* (SA) s 7(III); Wallace, above n 114, 35; Myles McGregor-Lowndes, 'Does Charity Begin and End at Home for Tax Exemptions?' (1998) 5 *Canberra Law Review* 221.

118 *Land and Income Tax Assessment Act 1907* (WA) ss 11(c), 19(6).

119 See, for example, Commonwealth, *Parliamentary Debates*, Senate, 20 May 1936, 1893–1898.

120 Sarah Joseph and Melissa Castan, *Federal Constitutional Law: A Contemporary View* (Thomson Reuters, 3rd ed, 2010) 329–330.

121 Cynthia Coleman and Margaret McKerchar, 'A History of Progressive Tax in Australia' in John Tiley (ed), *Studies in the History of Tax Law, Volume 3* (Hart Publishing, 2009) 40–42; *South Australia v Commonwealth* (1942) 65 CLR 373; *Victoria v Commonwealth* (1957) 99 CLR 575.

122 Australian Parliament, Joint Standing Committee on Foreign Affairs, Defence and Trade, *Conviction with Compassion: A Report on Freedom of Religion and Belief* (The Committee,

to all registered charities.[123] As discussed below, religious organisations including churches, temples, mosques etc. can register as a charity for the advancement of religion and thus continue to have access to federal income tax exemptions.

The expansion

In 2003, the federal government proposed to amend the definition of charity via the *Charities Bill 2003* (Cth). The Bill was a response to the *Report of Inquiry into the Definition of Charities and Related Organisations*. If it had passed, it would have achieved a number of changes in the legal relationship between the State and religion. Most importantly, it would have created a legislative definition of charity that included a positive public benefit test for all charities.[124] The Bill also created a definition of religion based on a series of indicia.[125] Arguably, like the more general definition of charity, had this change gone ahead, religions may have been subtly influenced to amend their practices and beliefs in order to meet this definition. However, the government abandoned the Bill on the advice of the Board of Taxation.[126]

While the government had abandoned the major recommendation from the *Report of Inquiry into the Definition of Charities and Related Organisations*, it did not abandon the Report altogether, opting instead to implement a more limited reform. This amounted to two relatively small changes: first, it extended tax exemptions to closed contemplative orders; and secondly, it created a requirement for charities to be endorsed by the Commissioner of Taxation.

Extending the definition of charity to closed or contemplative religious orders was necessary if they were to receive tax exemptions as a result of the common law definition of charity. Under common law, a charity needed to be able to show a public benefit. While this was presumed for charities for the advancement of religion, there were instances where this presumption had been rebutted. One example of this was in relation to closed or contemplative religious orders. Such orders did not meet the 'public' requirement of the public benefit test.[127] The *Report of Inquiry into the Definition of Charities and Related Organisations* recommended that the law be amended to remove this exclusion.[128] The recommendation

---

2000) 188–190. See also the *Income Tax Assessment Act 1997* (Cth) s 50–5 prior to the amendments made by the *Australian Charities and Not-for-profit Commission (Consequential and Transitional) Act 2012* (Cth) for explicit reference to religious organisations.

123 See *Income Tax Assessment Act 1997* (Cth) s 50.5, table item 1.1 (this provision must be read in conjunction with *Income Tax Assessment Act 1997* (Cth) s 995–1 and *Australian Charities and Not-for-profits Commission Act 2012* (Cth) s 25–5(5)).

124 *Charities Bill 2003* (Cth) ss 4, 7.

125 Ibid. s 12.

126 Board of Taxation, *Consultation on the Definition of a Charity* (Canprint Communications, 2003).

127 Commonwealth, *Parliamentary Debates*, House of Representatives, 16 June 2004, 30487 (David Cox); Dal Pont, *Law of Charity*, above n 113, 242–245.

128 Sheppard, Fitzgerald and Gonski, above n 114, 127.

was acted upon with the passage of the *Extension of Charitable Purposes Act 2004* (Cth).

The consistent concerns regarding the existence of tax exemptions for religious organisations highlighted below suggest that the extension of the exemption to closed religious orders whose public benefit is questionable would have been objected to. However, the parliamentary debate on the *Act* only refers to this aspect of the *Act* very briefly and in neutral or even positive terms.[129] No politician criticised the extension of the definition of charity to cover closed or contemplative religious orders in any way. Instead, the debate focused on the extension of the definition of charity to include self-help groups and child care as well as criticisms of the government for not carrying through with more of the recommendations from the *Report of Inquiry into the Definition of Charities and Related Organisations.*[130]

Another small change in the relationship between the State and religion recommended in the *Report of Inquiry into the Definition of Charities and Related Organisations* also came in 2004. The *Tax Laws Amendment (2004 Measures No. 1) Act* (Cth), *inter alia*, enacted the second part of Recommendation 26[131] by requiring that 'charities . . . be endorsed by the Commissioner of Taxation in order to access all relevant taxation concessions.'[132] While this change can be seen as a subtle shift in the relationship between the State and charities, including religious charities. The State was in effect taking back some control by requiring charities to be endorsed by the Commissioner of Taxation. In this way, there was effectively a check to see whether charities were 'real,' which has been an ongoing concern for the State when dealing with tax exemptions for charities and religious organisations.[133] It can also be seen as the first step towards the creation of a national register of charities. Which was eventually achieved in December 2012 with the creation of the Australian Charities and Not-For-Profit Commission (ACNC).

129   Commonwealth, *Parliamentary Debates*, House of Representatives, 16 June 2004, 30487 (David Cox), 30491, 30498; Commonwealth, *Parliamentary Debates*, Senate, 23 June 2004, 24643 (Nick Sherry), 24645 (John Cherry).
130   Commonwealth, *Parliamentary Debates*, House of Representatives, 27 May 2004, 29319 (Ross Cameron, Parliamentary Secretary to the Treasurer); Commonwealth, *Parliamentary Debates*, House of Representatives, 16 June 2004, 30485–30506; Commonwealth, *Parliamentary Debates*, Senate, 16 June 2004, 23975–23976 (Eric Abetz); Commonwealth, *Parliamentary Debates*, Senate, 22 June 2004, 24606–24607 (Nick Sherry); Commonwealth, *Parliamentary Debates*, Senate, 23 June 2004, 24643–24661.
131   Sheppard, Fitzgerald and Gonski, above n 114, 294.
132   Commonwealth, *Parliamentary Debates*, House of Representatives, 19 February 2004, 25239 (Ross Cameron, Parliamentary Secretary to the Treasurer).
133   See, for example, Commonwealth, *Parliamentary Debates*, Senate, 20 May 1936, 1893–1894.

Criticisms of tax exemptions for religious organisations

Criticism of whether and to what extent the State should provide tax exemptions for religious organisations has emerged several times since the introduction of the exemptions at the turn of the century. The criticisms can be classified into three main areas. First, religious organisations that derive income from 'commercial activities' have a competitive advantage over organisations that do not receive a tax exemption and therefore exemptions should be restricted to 'core activities.' Second, religion should not be treated differently to other organisation; in treating them differently, non-believers are effectively being asked to subsidies believers. Third, all charities, including religious charities, should be subject to a positive public benefit test before being eligible for tax exemptions.

While income tax exemptions are the largest source of indirect State funding for religious organisations, it is not the only source. Religious organisations and other charities also receive exemptions from a range of other federal, State and local government taxes.[134] The exemptions provided for religious organisations in relation to these taxes have generally been criticised on the same grounds as income tax exemptions. Criticisms of tax exemptions for the various local, State and federal taxes are therefore dealt with together.

Tax exemptions for 'commercial activities'

The first criticism to emerge relates to the 'commercial activities' of religious organisations.[135] In many cases, tax exemptions do not discriminate between activities of religious organisations that directly relate to the core activities of the organisation and other activities undertaken, including commercial activities. As a result, religious organisations receive tax exemptions on what would otherwise be considered a commercial enterprise. It has been argued on several occasions throughout the twentieth century that this gives religious organisations an 'unfair' advantage over commercial enterprises.

It is important to note that the criticism is not of exemptions for religious organisations in general, but in relation to their commercial activities specifically. Those criticising exemptions for the commercial activities of religious organisations often express the desirability of exemptions for religious organisations generally.

The first criticism of tax exemptions for the commercial activities of religious organisations emerged during the debate on the *Income Tax Assessment Act 1936*

---

134 Dal Pont, *Law of Charity*, above n 113, 144–153.
135 Recent data suggest that charities, including religious charities, are increasingly relying on income derived from commercial sources. However, as noted by Ian Murray, 'commercial activities' have not been definitively defined in the context of charities. See Ian Murray, 'Charitable Fundraising Through Commercial Activities: The Final Word or a Pyrrhic Victory' (2008) 11(2) *Journal of Australian Taxation* 138, 140–141, 144–148.

(Cth).[136] During the debate several members of Parliament raised concerns that some organisations might commit fraud by claiming to be religious when in fact their main activity was commercial. However, the government declined to attempt to restrict access to tax exemptions as they believed that any attempt to catch some organisations would inevitably catch all, including those that made significant contributions to the welfare of the community.[137]

The issue was raised again in 1941, this time in relation to the *Local Government Bill 1941* (Vic). On this occasion, the main issue of contention was the interpretation of a provision granting exemption from rates to land on which there was a church, hall or other buildings connected with public worship.[138] While there was significant dispute as to the breadth of the clause, both sides of Parliament agreed that land owned by religious organisations but used for commercial activities should not be exempt from rates.[139] In the end, the government agreed to amend the clauses to put the issue beyond doubt.[140]

The issues re-emerged again in the 1980s in the wake of the *Scientology*[141] and *DOGS*[142] cases. In its 1984 Report, *Discrimination and Religious Conviction*, the New South Wales Anti-Discrimination Board noted the significant community concern about the issues of tax exemptions for the commercial activities of religious organisations. The report noted that commercialism was 'endemic in organised religion' and quoting Murphy J's comments in his dissenting judgment in the *Scientology Case*:[143]

> The organised religions are big business. They engage in large scale real estate investment, money dealing and other commercial ventures.[144]

However, the Board made no specific recommendations on the issue.

More recently, concern regarding tax exemptions for the commercial activities of religious organisations occurred over a series of reports and inquiries in the

---

136 Commonwealth, *Parliamentary Debates*, Senate, 20 May 1936, 1893–1894.
137 Ibid.
138 Victoria, *Parliamentary Debates*, Legislative Assembly, 15 October 1941, 1262–1298; Victoria, *Parliamentary Debates*, Legislative Assembly, 5 November 1941,1592, 1601–1603; Victoria, *Parliamentary Debates*, Legislative Council, 3 December 1941, 2252–2273, 2277–2278.
139 See, for example, Victoria, *Parliamentary Debates*, Legislative Assembly, 15 October 1941, 1284 (Ian MacFarlane).
140 Victoria, *Parliamentary Debates*, Legislative Assembly, 18 November 1941, 1826–1831.
141 *Church of the New Faith v Commissioner of Pay Roll Tax (Vic)* (1983) 154 CLR 120.
142 *Attorney General (Vic); ex rel Black v The Commonwealth* (1981) 146 CLR 559.
143 New South Wales Anti-Discrimination Board, *Discrimination and Religious Conviction: a report of the Anti-Discrimination Board in accordance with Section 119 (a) of the Anti-Discrimination Act 1977* (New South Wales Anti-Discrimination Board, 1984) 171.
144 Ibid.

1990s and 2000s.[145] Prior to these reports, there appears to have been an assumption that tax exemptions on the commercial activities of religious organisations gave them an advantage over their commercial competitors. In 1995, the Industry Commission Report into Charitable Organisations attempted to analyse this presumed advantage. It concluded that for both unrelated fundraising activities and core activities, income tax exemptions did not provide charitable organisations with a competitive advantage.[146] Later inquires such as the Productivity Commission's 2000 report '*Contribution of the Not-for-profit Sector: Research Report*'[147] and Ken Henry's 2010 report '*Australia's Future Tax System*'[148] concurred with this finding.

However, the Industry Commission Report determined that exemptions from input taxes, such as fringe benefit tax, can provide charities with an advantage over their for-profit competitors.[149] Again the Productivity Commission and Henry Reports reached similar conclusions.[150]

Non-believers should not subsidise believers

While the argument that income tax exemptions provide a competitive advantage to the commercial activities of religious organisations is arguably dead, this is not the only criticism that has been made of tax exemptions for religious organisations. The exemptions have also been subject to a much more fundamental objection. By providing indirect funding via tax exemptions, non-believers and their organisations that have to pay tax are subsidising believers and their organisations, which do not pay the same tax.

Tax exemptions are effectively an indirect method of funding religion. While exemptions do not directly put extra funds into the hands of religion, the

---

145 Industry Commission, *Charitable Organisations in Australia* (Australian Government Publishing Service, 1995); Human Rights and Equal Opportunity Commission, *Article 18 Freedom of Religion and Belief* (Human Rights and Equal Opportunity Commission, 1998); Australian Parliament Joint Standing Committee on Foreign Affairs, Defence and Trade, *Conviction with Compassion: A Report into Freedom of Religion and Belief* (The Committee, 2000); Sheppard, Fitzgerald and Gonski, above n 114; Board of Taxation, above n 126; Desmond Cahill, Gary Bouma, Hass Dellal and Michael Leahy, *Religion Cultural Diversity and Safeguarding Australia: A Partnership under the Australian Government's Living in Harmony Initiative* (Department of Immigration and Multicultural and Indigenous Affairs, and Australian Multicultural Foundation, 2004); Senate Standing Committee on Economics, *Disclosure Regimes for Charities and Not-for-profit Organisations* (The Committee, 2008); Productivity Commission, *Contribution of the Not-for-profit Sector: Research Report* (Productivity Commission, 2010); Senate Economics Legislation Committee, above n 114; Australian Human Rights Commission, *Freedom of Religion and Belief in 21st Century Australia* (Australian Human Rights Commission, 2011).
146 Industry Commission, above n 145, 312.
147 Productivity Commission, above n 145, 203–205.
148 Ken Henry, *Australia's Future Tax System: Final Report* (The Treasury, 2010) 208–209.
149 Industry Commission, above n 145, 312–313.
150 See Productivity Commission, above n 145, 206–208; Henry, above n 148, 206–208, 211.

exemptions mean that they get to keep funds that they would otherwise have to pay to the government in tax. From the government's point of view, this means that they forgo revenue to the amount of the tax that would be payable if the exemptions did not exist. The State therefore has less revenue than it might otherwise have to carry out the functions of government – a greater proportion of which arguably comes from non-believers whose equivalent organisations do not enjoy the same tax exemptions. Many have argued that this arrangement is unfair and discriminatory.[151]

The first time the argument against exemptions for religious organisation was raised, it was not about the effect of these exemptions on non-believers, but about the resentment that exemptions may create towards the churches. During the 1941 debate on the Victorian *Local Government Bill 1941* (Vic), two members of Parliament expressed concern that providing an exemption for religious organisations would further antagonise the section of the community that is opposed to the churches and that this would be bad for the churches.[152]

The next time the issues was raised it had evolved to be about equality, but not between believers and non-believers. This time, the focus was on equality between organisations of a 'similar' type. In 1967, the New South Wales *Report of the Royal Commission of Inquiry into Rating, Valuation and Local Government Finance*[153] was asked to consider which land owned by religious organisations should be exempt from rates. The Commission concluded that exemptions should be confined to:

> Land on which is erected a church or building use solely for public worship or a hall used for religious teaching or training in connection with such church or building, together in each case with a reasonable curtilage of land surrounding such church, building or hall.[154]

This excluded land used as the residence of religious ministers, which was further than submissions to the Commission had recommended.[155] However, as the Commission pointed out, Crown land used for residential proposes was not exempt; as such, they could see no reason why land owned by a religious organisation should be treated differently.[156]

It was not until 1980s that the argument finally evolved to being a comparison between believers and non-believers. In 1984, the New South Wales

---

151 See, for example, David Marr, *The High Price of Heaven* (Allen and Unwin, 1999).

152 Victoria, *Parliamentary Debates*, Legislative Assembly, 15 October 1941, 1294–1295; Victoria, *Parliamentary Debates*, Legislative Council, 3 December 1941, 2267–2268. They also argued that State support is bad for religion generally.

153 Rae Else-Mitchell, S. Haviland and R. S. Luke, *Report of the Royal Commission of Inquiry into Rating, Valuation and Local Government Finance* (Government Printer, 1967).

154 Ibid. 133.

155 Ibid. 132.

156 Ibid. 132–133.

Anti-Discrimination Board Report *Discrimination and Religious Conviction*[157] noted that there was an argument in favour of removing all ratings exemptions for religious organisations. Other organisations were capable of, and did in fact provide, welfare services. Instead, the local council should collect all rates and then provide welfare services as needed, rather than granting exemptions. As the Board put it:

> This approach has the advantage that non-believers would not subsidise the religious activities of other members of the community, whom they may not want to support and, indeed, may actively oppose.[158]

While the Board stopped short of recommending that this approach be adopted, it recognised that the provision of tax exemptions to religious organisations and not to other organisations was arguably discriminatory.[159] The Board proposed two possible solutions. First, it recommended that the available exemptions be widened to include 'purposes that are anti-religious or can very broadly termed religious, on the grounds that together [with religious purposes] promote mental or moral improvement.'[160] In effect, this recommendation was that organisations run for, or by, non-believers, which filled the same place as religion in the lives of believers, should be treated in the same way as believers. Second, the Board suggested that exemptions could be restricted so that they were only available for 'identifiable social purposes, such as the promotion of health, education or some other charitable form of social welfare.'[161] While the issue of non-believers effectively subsiding believers has been raised several times since 1984, no official government report or inquiry has gone as far as the New South Wales Report in suggesting that tax exemptions could be removed from religious organisations.[162] Most reports simply notes the concerns raised by atheist and humanist groups without making any specific recommendations.[163] The 2001 *Report of the Inquiry into the Definition of Charities and Related Organisations* even went so far as to assert that tax exemptions should be retained as 'it is clear that a large proportion of the population have a need for spiritual sustenance.'[164] The assertion that there was a need for 'spiritual sustenance' was not supported in the Report by any evidence nor did it explain why tax exemptions necessary to provide for this need, if it existed.

---

157 New South Wales Anti-Discrimination Board, above n 143.
158 Ibid. 141.
159 Ibid. 170, 172.
160 Ibid. 172.
161 Ibid. 172.
162 See Australian Parliament Joint Standing Committee on Foreign Affairs, Defence and Trade, above n 145, 185–186, 192–193; Sheppard, Fitzgerald and Gonski, above n 114, 175–179; Senate Standing Committee on Economics, above n 145, 83–84; Senate Economics Legislation Committee, above n 114, 20–21; Australian Human Rights Commission, above n 145, 25, 39, 47, 55.
163 See for example Australian Parliament Joint Standing Committee on Foreign Affairs, Defence and Trade, above n 145, 185–186.
164 Sheppard, Fitzgerald and Gonski, above n 114, 179.

There should be a 'public benefit' test

The most recent argument against the continuation of wholesale tax exemptions for religious organisations is that a positive 'public benefit test' should be imposed on any organisation claiming tax exemptions. This would require charities, including religious charities, to prove that they provided a benefit to the public. Under existing law, charities for the advancement of religion are presumed to be for the public benefit.[165] The argument that charities, and especially religious charities, should prove they are for the public benefit is premised on the presumption that some religions do not in fact benefit the public and may in fact be harmful.[166]

The suggestion for a positive public benefit test was first raised in 2001 in the *Report of the Inquiry into the Definition of Charities and Related Organisations.*[167] In response to the Report's recommendations, the government proposed to create a statutory definition of Charity which would have included a public benefit test.[168] However, the government abandoned its attempt to legislatively define charity, opting instead to continue with the common law definition.[169]

The issue was raised again in 2010 when Senator Xenophon introduced the T*ax Laws Amendment (Public Benefit Test) Bill 2010* (Cth).[170] The Bill was referred to the Economics Legislation Committee,[171] which recommended, *inter alia*, that

---

165 Dal Pont, '*Law of Charity*' above n 113, 234–245.
166 See particularly the comments by Senator Xenophon in the Explanatory Memorandum, Tax Laws Amendment (Public Benefit Test) Bill 2010 (Cth); Commonwealth of Australia, *Parliamentary Debate*, Senate, 13 May 2010, 2843 (Nicholas Xenophon); Senate Economics Legislation Committee, above n 114, 45–49; Senate Community Affairs Legislation Committee, Parliament of Australia, *Australian Charities and Not-for-profits Commission Bill 2012 [Provisions], Australian Charities and Not-for-profits Commission (Consequential and Transitional) Bill 2012 [Provisions] and Tax Laws Amendment (Special Conditions for Not-for-profits Concessions) Bill 2012 [Provisions]* (Senate Printing Unit, Parliament House, 2012) 48.
167 Sheppard, Fitzgerald and Gonski, above n 114, 111–129.
168 See *Charities Bill 2003* (Cth).
169 Gary Johns, 'Charity Reform in Australia' (2004) 11(4) *Agenda* 293, 297–298; Peter Costello, 'Final Response to the Charities Definition Inquiry' (Media Release, No 31, 11 May 2004); in common law, charity was defined by reference to the *Statute of Charitable Uses 1601* (UK) 43 Eliz I, c 4 and the four heads of charity laid down in the *Commissioner for Special Purposes of the Income Tax v. Pemsel* [1891] AC 531 ('*Pemsel*'). These are the relief of poverty, age or impotence, the advancement of education, the advancement of religion and any other purpose beneficial to the community. See Pauline Ridge, 'Religious Charitable Status and Public Benefit in Australia' (2011) 35(3) *Melbourne University Law Review* 1071, 1074; Gino Evans Dal Pont, 'Charity Law and Religion' in Peter Radan, Denise Megerson and Rosalind F. Croucher (eds), *Law and Religion: God, the State and the Common Law* (Routledge, 2005) 220; Dal Pont, *Law of Charity*, above n 113, 17, 213–214.
170 Commonwealth of Australia, *Parliamentary Debates*, Senate, 13 May 2010, 2843 (Nicholas Xenophon).
171 Ibid. 2844, 2971.

the government develop a public benefit test for charities.[172] In the Committee's view, there was a need for a higher level of accountability in the sector, and that a public benefit test would be an appropriate way of achieving this.[173]

At the time, the government supported this recommendation, stating that as part of the 2010 election campaign, it had committed to reform of the sector and that the Treasurer had been tasked with a scoping study for the establishment of a National Commission.[174] However, as discussed below, the legislative definition of charity created at the time of the creation of the ACNC and the subsequent legislative definition created in the *Charities Act 2013* (Cth) do not create a positive public benefit test. Instead, both specifically preserve the presumption of public benefit for charities for the relief of poverty, age or impotence, the advancement of education and the advancement of religion.[175]

The Australian Charities and Not-for-profit Commission

The Australian Charities and Not-for-profit Commission (ACNC) was formally launched on 10 December 2012, over a decade after a national charity regulator was first proposed.[176]

As discussed above, charities, including religious charities, are exempt from, or receive a rebate on, a wide range of taxes including income tax, capital gains tax, fringe benefits tax, the Goods and Services Tax (GST), Payroll Tax, Land Tax, Stamp Duty and Rates.[177]

The ACNC requires that charities, including religious charities, wishing to take advantage of income tax exemptions register with the ACNC.[178] Registration with the ACNC imposes ongoing reporting requirements and regulatory

---

172 Senate Economics Legislation Committee, above n 114, 17–29.

173 Ibid. 29.

174 Parliament of Australia, *Senate Economics Legislation Committee Inquiry into Tax Laws Amendment (Public Benefit Test) Bill 2010 Government Response* <www.aph.gov.au/Parliamentary_Business/Committees/Senate/Economics/Completed%20inquiries/2008-10/public_benefit_test_10/index>.

175 *Australian Charities and Not-for-profits Commission Act 2012* (Cth) s 25–5(5); *Charities Act 2013* (Cth) s 7.

176 David Bradbury and Mark Butler, 'New Era For Charities Sector Begins' (Joint Media Release, No 163, 10 December 2012) <http://ministers.treasury.gov.au/DisplayDocs.aspx?doc=pressreleases/2012/163.htm&pageID=003&min=djba&Year=&DocType=0>. A National regulator for the Charities sector was first proposed in 2001: see Sheppard, Fitzgerald and Gonski, above n 114. Since then the creation of a national regulator for the charities sector has been recommended in a number of reports including Recommendations 3 and 4 by the Senate Standing Committee on Economics in Senate Standing Committee on Economics, '*Disclosure Regimes for Charities and Not-for-profit Organisations* (The Committee, 2008) 137; Recommendation 6.5 in Productivity Commission, above n 145, 152; Ken Henry, above n 148, 212.

177 Dal Pont, *Law of Charity*, above n 113, 144–153.

178 *Income Tax Assessment Act 1997* (Cth) s 50.5, table item 1.1 'registered charities.' Note this section was amended, as of 3 December 2012, by *Australian Charities and Not-for-profit*

compliance. Failure to do so can result in de-registration of a charity, and therefore exclusion from income tax exemptions. This high level of oversight by the ACNC was a significant change in the fiscal relationship between the State and religion. Prior to the creation of the ACNC very little was required in terms of reporting or compliance from the charities sector in return for the indirect funding they received from the government. The ACNC changed this.

Registration

A significant change in the charity sector, brought about by the creation of the ACNC, is the requirement that all charities, including religious charities, must register in order to access income tax exemptions.

The first change brought about by the requirement for registration is a definitional change as to which charities are entitled to income tax exemptions. Prior to the creation of the ACNC, organisations that were exempt from income tax were listed in Section 50.5 *Income Tax Assessment Act 1997* (Cth). These included charitable institutions[179] and religious institutions.[180] Charitable institutions included charities for the advancement of religion. Many religious organisations would also have been eligible as other types of charitable institutions. After the introduction of the ACNC, charitable institutions and religious institutions have been condensed to be just one item, 'registered charities.'[181] This meant that any charity wishing to access income tax exemptions must be a registered charity with the ACNC. Without this small, but important definitional change, many of the other changes brought about by the ACNC would be ineffective, as it is this definitional change that creates the incentive to register with the ACNC. Registration with the ACNC is voluntary, therefore without an incentive many charities may have chosen not to register, particularly given the reporting and regulation requirements that come with registration.[182]

The second change brought about by the requirement for charities to register in order to access income tax exemptions is the creation and publication of the register. Prior to the creation of the ACNC there was no publicly available list of all charities receiving tax exemptions. While those organisations receiving tax

---

Commission *(Consequential and Transitional) Act 2012* (Cth) as part of the creation of the Australian Charities and Nor-for-profit Commission, discussed in more detail below.

179 s 50.5, item 1.1 as repealed by *Australian Charities and Not-for-profits Commission (Consequential and Transitional) Act 2012* (Cth) cl 30 and substituted with 'registered charity.'

180 s 50.5, item 1.2 as repealed by *Australian Charities and Not-for-profits Commission (Consequential and Transitional) Act 2012* (Cth) cl 30.

181 Ibid. s 50.5 item 1.1 *"registered charity"* means an entity that is registered under the *Australian Charities and Not-for-profits Commission Act 2012* (Cth) as the type of entity mentioned in column 1 of item 1 of the table in subsection 25-5(5) of that Act. See *Income Tax Assessment Act* 1997 (Cth) s 995-1.

182 Revised Explanatory Memorandum, *Australian Charities and Not-for-profits Commission Bill 2012; Australian Charities and Not-for-profits Commission (Consequential and Transitional) Bill 2012,* 29–30.

exemptions were required to be endorsed by the ATO, this list was not necessarily available to the public. The newly created register is publicly available on the internet.[183] The type of information that is available to the public includes the name, address, and ABN number of the charity, along with the type and sub type of the entity, the entity's governing rules, any financial reports that have been provided by the entity, and details of any enforcement proceedings undertaken against the entity by the ACNC.[184]

Reporting

As referred to above, there is an extensive list of information that will be included in the register of charities maintained by the ACNC. In order to keep this information up-to-date, the *Australian Charities and Not-for-profits Commission Act 2012* (Cth) provides for a reporting regime. This ongoing reporting regime has two important effects. First, it puts into the public domain, in many cases for the first time, detailed information about charities. Second, it is envisaged that the reporting regime will streamline the reporting requirements of charities.

Prior to the creation of the ACNC, the amount of forgone taxation as a result of exemptions given to charities was unquantifiable; as entities exempt from income tax do not lodge income tax returns. As a result, there is no publicly available data on the income of most charities, making estimates of the amount of income and other taxes forgone impossible to calculate. In 2009 the Federal Treasury estimated that the forgone revenue from charities was around $1 billion, but officially listed the amount forgone as unquantifiable.[185] In 2010, the Productivity Commission estimated that the revenue forgone as a result of these tax exemptions was at least $4 billion, and could be as much as twice that figure.[186] While the two figures do measure slightly different things, they both demonstrate the uncertainty around the amount of indirect funding given to charities, including religious charities, by the government and the possibility for that figure to be substantial. The ACNC reporting regime has the potential to bring some certainty in estimates of the amount of revenue forgone by the government and therefore the amount of indirect funding received by charities.

---

183 Ibid. 51–54. The list can be accessed at Australian Government, Australian Charities and Not-for-Profits Commission, *Find a charity on the ACNC Register* <www.acnc.gov.au/ACNC/FindCharity/Search_the_ACNC_Register/ACNC/OnlineProcessors/Online_register/Search_the_register.aspx?hkey=4cffc3e0-00db-4548-91a8-bb2860e8d137>. There is a search database allowing those responsible for a charity to check and update the charity's details. Otherwise, the database allows members of the public to check information on certain charities.

184 Revised Explanatory Memorandum, *Australian Charities and Not-for-profits Commission Bill 2012; Australian Charities and Not-for-profits Commission (Consequential and Transitional) Bill 2012*, 51–54.

185 Senate Economics Legislation Committee, above n 114, 11–12.

186 Productivity Commission, above n 145, 76.

There are two types of reports that registered charities will be required to pro-vide – annual information statements and financial reports. It is the latter of these that has the potential to clarify the amount of indirect funding received by chari-ties. All large and medium charities registered with the ACNC entities will be required to provide annual financial statements.[187] While small charities and basic religious charities are not required to provide annual financial statements, they may do so voluntarily.[188] While the exclusion of small and basic religious chari-ties means that a complete picture of the amount of indirect funding received by religious charities will not be able to be gained from these financial statements they will go a long way towards addressing the uncertainty around the amount of revenue forgone by the government as a result of tax exemptions.

In 2015 and 2016, religious activity was the most common activity reported by charities with 31% and 30.8% respectively of all charities reporting this as their main activity.[189] This however does not capture all religious charities as charities may register multiple activities in addition to their main type. For example, a reli-gious school is likely to have registered their main activity as education and may in addition register other activities including the advancement of religion. Fur-ther, Knight and Gilchrist, in their report on the 2013 ACNC annual information statements, noted that a 'large number of charities established by and still operat-ing under the auspices of a religious organisation did not identify any religious affiliation in either their purpose or activities.'[190] They were unable, however to identify an underlying cause of this under reporting.[191]

There is also potential for the information provided in annual information statements to be used to challenge the charitable status of registered entities. As will be discussed in more detail below, the definition of charity presumes in many cases, including in the cases of charities for the advancement of religion, that the charity is for the 'public benefit.' If an entity is not for the 'public benefit' then it is not a charity. However, the presumption means that many charities do not need

---

187 *Australian Charities and Not-for-profits Commission Act 2012* (Cth) s 60–10. A large charity is one with an annual revenue of $1million or more, a medium charity is one with an annual revenue between $250,000 and $1million. See s 205–25.

188 Australian Charities and Not-for-profits Commission Act 2012 (Cth) s 60–60(2). A small charity is one with revenue of less than $250,000 per year: s 205–25. According to s 205–35, a basic religious charity is one that is registered and complies only with the subtype of entity mentioned in column 2 of item 3 of the table in subsection 25–5(5).

189 N. Cortis, A. Young, A. Powell, R. Reeve, R. Simnett, K. Ho, and I. Ramia, *Austral-ian Charities Report 2015* (University of New South Wales, Centre for Social Impact and Social Policy Research Centre, 2016) 11, 28 available at www.csi.edu.au/media/Austral-ian_Charities_Report_2015_Web_ND8DU2P.pdf>; A. Powell, N. Cortis, I. Ramia, and A. Marjolin, *Australian Charities Report 2016* (University of New South Wales, Centre for Social Impact and Social Policy Research Centre, 2017) 27 available at <http://aus-traliancharities.acnc.gov.au/wp-content/uploads/2017/12/Australian-Charities-Report-2016-FINAL-20171203.pdf>.

190 Penny Knight and David Gilchrist, *Australia's Faith based Charities; A Study Supplementing the Australian Charities 2013 Report* (Curtin University, 2015) 2.

191 Ibid.

to prove this public benefit. One effect of the reporting regime is that the annual information statements may provide members of the public, the government, or other organisations the information needed to rebut this presumption.

Even if the information provided in annual information statements is not used to challenge the charitable status of registered entities, it may affect charities' behaviour. As discussed above, there is an incentive to being a registered charity and subject to these reporting requirements. If a charity is concerned that their activities may be challenged, they may adjust their operations in order to make sure that the information made public about them reveals a public benefit in order to justify their registration as a charity.

The second effect of the reporting requirements is the streamlining of contact between the Commonwealth government and charities. It is intended that it will be a 'report once, use often' system. This means that charities will report only to the ACNC and that other Commonwealth and State agencies will access any information they need from the register held by the Commission. Prior to the introduction of the reforms many charities were required to report to several different government agencies and needed to 'prove their bona-fides' each time they dealt with a new agency. It is hoped that this kind of duplication will be eliminated by the creation of the register.[192] While this is a relatively small change, it will mean that charities, including religious charities, will now interact with the State via fewer government agencies. Some duplication may still occur, especially if State and territory governments do not adopt registration with the ACNC as the definition of a charity,[193] but overall there will be a streamlining of the interaction between the State and religion in relation to charitable status and tax exemptions.

Regulation

Prior to the creation of the ACNC, charities were governed by a variety of different governance standards, depending on the structure of the charity, the industry in which they operated, and their level of interaction with government.[194]

---

192 Revised Explanatory Memorandum, *Australian Charities and Not-for-profits Commission Bill 2012; Australian Charities and Not-for-profits Commission (Consequential and Transitional) Bill 2012*, 95–96; House of Representatives Standing Committee on Economics, Parliament of Australia, *Report on the Exposure Draft of the Australian Charities and Not-for-profits Commission Bills 2012* (2012) 36–38.

193 So far only South Australia and the Australian Capital Territory have announced changes to their laws to incorporate registration with the ACNC. See David Bradbury, Mark Butler and John Rau, 'Government Delivering Real Reductions in Red Tape for Charities' (Media Release, 11 October 2012) <http://ministers.treasury.gov.au/DisplayDocs. aspx?doc=pressreleases/2012/116.htm&pageID=003&min=djba&Year=&DocType=0>; David Bradbury, Mark butler and Andrew Barr, 'ACT signs up to New Charities Regulator' (Media Release, 11 March 2013) <http://assistant.treasurer.gov.au/DisplayDocs. aspx?doc=pressreleases/2013/030.htm&pageID=003&min=djba&Year=&DocType=>.

194 Revised Explanatory memorandum, *Australian Charities and Not-for-profits Commission Bill 2012; Australian Charities and Not-for-profits Commission (Consequential and Transitional) Bill 2012* 58.

It is possible that some charities, including charities for the advancement of religion, would have had no requirement to comply with any set of governance standards, although they may have done so voluntarily. This means that some of the charities that were receiving indirect government funding, courtesy of tax exemptions, were not required to comply with any externally imposed governance standards.

Basic religious charities

The registration, reporting, and regulation requirements created by the ACNC will apply to most religious charities. However, the *Australian Charities and Not-for-profit Commission Regulation 2013* (Cth) provides some exceptions for 'basic religious charities.'

A basic religious charity is defined in the *Australian Charities and Not-for-profits Commission Act 2012* (Cth) as a registered entity that is entitled to be registered as a charity for the advancement of religion, and is not entitled to be registered as any other subtype.[195] However, where an organisation meets these requirements but is incorporated, is a deductible gift recipient, is part of a reporting group, or received a government grant of more than $100,000 in a finial year, it will not qualify as a basic religious charity.[196]

If a charity for the advancement of religion meets all of the requirements to be defined as a basic religious charity, it will be exempt from submitting annual financial statements and complying with the Governance Standards.[197] In addition, the Charities Commissioner cannot suspend the responsible entity of a basic religious charity for non-compliance with the *Charities Acts*.[198] In effect, this means the Commissioner cannot suspend the leader of a religion.

In 2013 80% of the 12,254 who listed advancement of religion as their purpose self-identified as a basic religious charity. This is significantly higher than the anticipated 20% of religious charities.[199] As 2013 was the first year that charities were required to report to the ACNC, it is likely that many religious charities misidentified themselves as basic religious charities. These errors appear to be continuing, however. In response to the 2015 Annual information statements,

---

195 *Australian Charities and Not-for-profits Commission Act 2012* (Cth) s 205–35(1).
196 Ibid. s 205–35(2)-(5).
197 *Charities and Not-for-profits Commission Act 2012* (Cth) ss 45–10(5), 60–60(1); Revised Explanatory Memorandum, *Australian Charities and Not-for-profits Commission Bill 2012; Australian Charities and Not-for-profits Commission (Consequential and Transitional) Bill 2012* 59, 74–75.
198 *Charities and Not-for-profits Commission Act 2012* (Cth) s 100–5(3). A responsible entity is defined in s 205–30 for more details on responsible entities and the Commissioners powers of suspension. See Revised Explanatory Memorandum, *Australian Charities and Not-for-profits Commission Bill 2012; Australian Charities and Not-for-profits Commission (Consequential and Transitional) Bill 2012* 148–161, 221–222.
199 Knight and Gilchrist, above n 190, 2.

the ACNC contacted a number of charities advising them that they incorrectly self-identified as a basic religious charity.[200]

Where a charity for the advancement of religion is also entitled to be registered as another subtype of charity, they will not qualify as a basic religious charity. In their submission to the Parliamentary Joint Committee on Corporations and Financial Services inquiry, Moore Stephens Accountants and Advisers pointed out the many churches and religious institutions engage in pastoral care and ancillary activities that go beyond the advancement of religion.[201] The explanatory memorandum for the *Australian Charities and Not-for-profits Commission Act 2012* (Cth) indicated that some ancillary activities would be permitted before a charity for the advancement of religion crossed the threshold of being entitled to register as another subtype. However, the example given in the explanatory memorandum appears to set this threshold very low.[202]

> For example, a church. . . . Occasionally provides clothes and food vouchers to families that attend their church services and that are experiencing poverty. This service is not provided frequently, and is merely incidental to the registered entity's activities to advance religion.[203]

If a church provided a regular soup kitchen, opportunity shop or food program they may breach the threshold as it is described in the explanatory memorandum. As Moore Stephens points out:

> A strict reading of s205–35(c) would place significant restrictions on these activities, which are ancillary or incidental to the advancement of religion.[204]

If the *Australian Charities and Not-for-profits Commission Act 2012* (Cth) is read as Moore Stephens suggests, charities for the advancement of religion may be influenced to restrict their ancillary activities in order to fall within the definition of a basic religious charity. This exclusion also points to an understanding of religion that implies that it can be separated out from other charitable activities.

---

200 Australian Government, Australian Charities and Not-For-Profits Commission, *FAQs: Reporting errors in the 2015 Annual Information Statement – Basic Religious Charities* www.acnc.gov.au/ACNC/FAQs/BRCErrors.aspx>.

201 Moore Stephens, Submission No 30 to Parliamentary Joint Committee on Corporations and Financial Services, *Australian Charities and Not-for-profits Commission Bill 2012; Australian Charities and Not-for-profits Commission (Consequential and Transitional) Bill 2012; Tax Laws Amendment (Special Conditions for Not-for-profit Concessions) Bill 2012* (2012), 30 August 2012, 10.

202 Revised Explanatory Memorandum, *Australian Charities and Not-for-profits Commission Bill 2012; Australian Charities and Not-for-profits Commission (Consequential and Transitional) Bill 2012* 222.

203 Ibid. 222.

204 Moore Stephens, above n 201, 10.

Given the high number of charities in Australia that have historical affiliation with religious organisations, this is a strange position to take.[205]

Some of the other exclusionary items have also been criticised;[206] however, they may be explainable by reference to the purpose of the ACNC. As discussed above, one of the main aims of the ACNC is to create a 'one-stop-shop' for all government agencies that require information about charities. Classification as a basic religious charity exempts a religious organisation from providing some of this information. In the case of the exclusions listed in Sections 205–25(2)-(5), the charity would be required to report to a government agency. For example, those charities that have structured themselves as a corporation would need to report to ASIC, and those who receive large government grants would need to report to the government agencies providing those grants. If these exclusions were not included in the qualification for classification as a basic religious charity the 'one-stop-shop,' 'report once, use often' system would be useless, as the ACNC would not have the information needed by the other government agencies.

The definition of charity

One important change introduced by the ACNC is a statutory definition of charity. Prior to the creation of the ACNC charity was defined by the common law. At common law, an entity is a charity if it is for the public benefit, and is within the 'spirit and intendment of the Statute of Elizabeth.'[207] The 'spirit and intendment of the Statute of Elizabeth' was interpreted in *Commissioner for Special Purposes of Income Tax v Pemsel*[208] as consisting of four heads of charity:

1   The relief of poverty, age or impotence;
2   The advancement of education;
3   The advancement of religion; and
4   Any other purpose beneficial to the community.[209]

---

205 O'Halloran, above n 116, 31.
206 See Moore Stephens, above n 201, 25–27.
207 Sheppard, Fitzgerald and Gonski, above n 114, 111. The preamble of the Statute of Elizabeth – also known as the *Charitable Uses Act 1601* (UK) – stated that charity included: the relief of the aged, impotent and poor people; the maintenance of sick and maimed soldiers and mariners, schools of learning, free schools and scholars in universities; the repair of bridges, ports, havens, causeways, churches, sea-banks and highways; the education and preferment of orphans; the relief, stock or maintenance of houses of correction; the marriages of poor maids; the supportation, aid and help of young tradesmen, handicraftsmen and persons decayed; the relief or redemption of prisoners or captives; and the aid or ease of any poor inhabitants concerning payment of fifteens, setting out of soldiers and other taxes. See Dal Pont, *Law of Charity*, above n 113, 1.
208 [1891] AC 531, 538.
209 Dal Pont, *Law of Charity*, above n 113, 17.

In the cases of the first three heads, including the advancement of religion, public benefit is presumed.[210]

The ACNC definition

At the time of its creation, the ACNC legislation included a statutory definition of charity, however, it did not substantially alter the common law. Section 25–5(6) of the *Australian Charities and Not-for-profits Commission Act 2012* (Cth) as passed, stated that,

> The object of column 2 of items 1, 2, 3 and 4 of the table in subsection (5) is to describe entities that are covered by the 4 heads of charity traditionally recognised by the courts.

Section 25–5(5) of the *Australian Charities and Not-for-profits Commission Act 2012* (Cth), as passed, defined charities as:

1   Entity with a purpose that is the relief of poverty, sickness or the needs of the aged;
2   Entity with a purpose that is the advancement of education;
3   Entity with a purpose that is the advancement of religion;
4   Entity with another purpose that is beneficial to the community;
5   Institution whose principal activity is to promote the prevention or the control of diseases in human beings;
6   Public benevolent institution; or
7   Entity with a charitable purpose described in Section 4 of the *Extension of Charitable Purpose Act 2004* (provision of child care services).

The first four categories are the four heads of charities set down in *Pemsel*. The final three categories all relate to entities that, prior to the reforms, were listed separately as receiving taxation exemptions or concessions. Including them in the statutory definition of charity simply streamlines taxation legislation and as a result does not significantly alter the definition of charity in any way.[211]

Section 25–5(5) and 26–5(6) were repealed and replaced by the *Charities (Consequential Amendments and Transitional Provisions) Act 2013* (Cth) as part of the implementation of the new *Charities Act 2013* (Cth) which came into effect on 1 January 2014.

---

210   Sheppard, Fitzgerald and Gonski, above n 114, 111–112.
211   Revised Explanatory Memorandum, *Australian Charities and Not-for-profits Commission Bill 2012; Australian Charities and Not-for-profits Commission (Consequential and Transitional) Bill 2012* 35, 242–243.

Charities Act 2013 (Cth) definition

The *Charities Act 2013* (Cth) commenced on 1 January 2014.[212] The Act created a standalone statutory definition of charity.

Section 5 of the Act defines charity:[213]

> Charity means an entity:
> That is not-for-profit;
> All of the purposes of which are:
> Charitable purposes (see part 3) that are for the public benefit (see Division 2 of this Part); or
> Purposes that are incidental or ancillary to, and in furtherance or in aid of, purposes of the entity covered by subparagraph (i); and
> None of the purposes of which are disqualifying purposes (see division 3); and
> That is not an individual, a political party or a government entity.

While the requirement in Section 5(b)(i) that the entity be for the 'public benefit' would seem to create a positive public benefit test, the effect of this Section is negated by Section 7 which states that certain charitable purposes are presumed to be for the public benefit, including *inter alia* 'the purpose of advancing religion.'[214] This is despite the fact that there have been several recommendations to alter the definition of charity in relation to the 'public benefit' requirement.[215]

Charitable purposes are listed in Section 12. This list is much broader than the four heads of charity provided for at common law and the seven originally included in the ACNC legislation. However, in relation to religion there is little change, as 'advancing religion' is included on the list.[216]

As a result, the creation of a statutory definition of charity has had no practical impact on which religious organisation qualify as a charity, the definition has simply been moved from the common law to a statute. Those organisations that qualified before the creation of the ACNC will still qualify.

Conclusion

As the old saying goes 'Money makes the world go round' and while it may not be as exciting or appear to be as crucial as freedom of religion, terrorism or education, the funding of religion by the State is an important aspect of the relationship between the State and religion. In Australia this relationship has been

---

212 *Charities Act 2013* (Cth) s 2.
213 *Charities Act 2013* (Cth) s 5.
214 Ibid. s 7(e).
215 See most recently Senate Economics Legislation Committee, above n 114.
216 Ibid. s 12(1)(e).

characterised by an ongoing tussle for control of both the quantum of that funding and how that funding may be spent.

Prior to Federation, the Australian colonies tried a number of methods of funding religion, from *ad-hoc* funding through to structured schemes with set amounts available for certain styles of religious activities and denominations. One advantage of all these schemes was that the amount of funding provided by the State to religion could be seen on a balance sheet. Whether the State or religion was in control the amount of the funding was, at the very least, transparent. While the removal of State aid at the end of the nineteenth century could be seen as a win for the separation of church and State, it has been replaced by a funding method which is less transparent. Today, religious organisations receive exemptions from a range of local, State and federal taxes. The exact amount of taxation revenue forgone as a result of these exemptions is unclear, meaning that the State does not know to what extent they are funding religion. While the creation of the ACNC, and in particular its reporting requirements, have increased overall transparency for the whole charities sector Basic Religious Charities and Small Charities are not required to provide full financial details – so while the picture is getting clearer it is still very opaque.

With an increasing proportion of the population self-identifying as having no religion, the continued provision of funding to religious organisations via tax exemptions is likely to continue to be a source of debate. Religious organisations are unlikely to give up their tax exemptions voluntarily and 'roll off State support like saturated leeches'[217] as predicted by Governor Bourke when proposing the *Church Acts*. As a result, the tug-of-war for control is likely to continue long into the future.

217 Jack Gregory, 'State Aid to Religion in the Australian Colonies 1788–1895' (1999) 70(2) *Victorian Historical Journal* 128, 131.

Part III
Conclusion

10 Conclusion

The relationship between the State and religion has changed significantly across Australia's history. On the continuum of potential State–religion relationships at various points, the relationship could have been described as establishment, plural establishment, pragmatic pluralism and plural establishment.[1] The relationship has waxed and waned and often been far more complex than the labels ascribed to the various models of State–religion relationships would suggest.

Today the relationship would best be described as pragmatic pluralism,[2] although that is something of an oversimplification. Australia is a secular multicultural and multi-faith democracy with a significant proportion of the population who self-identify as having no religion.[3] At the same time religion continues to plays an important role in public policy debates, as exemplified in the recent debate around the legalisation of same-sex marriage.[4] Australia does not have a Bill or Charter of Rights containing an express freedom of religion[5] and its Constitutional protection for religion found in Section 116 has been interpreted by the High Court as a check on federal governmental legislative power, rather than as an individual express right.[6] Legal protections for freedom of religion are therefore limited and tend to be found in anti-discrimination laws and exemptions to general provisions in those laws.[7] Yet Australians enjoy a comparatively

---

1 Stephen V. Monsma and J. Christopher Soper, *The Challenge of Pluralism: Church and State in Five Democracies* (Rowman& Littlefield Publishing Group, 1st ed, 1997) 93.
2 Ibid. ch. 5.
3 Renae Barker, *Religion and the Census: Australia's Unique Relationship to Faith and Unbelief* (5 July 2017) ABC, Religion and Ethics www.abc.net.au/religion/articles/2017/07/05/4696888.htm>; Renae Barker, *Australians have an increasingly complex, yet relatively peaceful, relationship with religion* (21 December 2016) The Conversation <https://theconversation.com/australians-have-an-increasingly-complex-yet-relatively-peaceful-relationship-with-religion-70328>.
4 See Chapter 6.
5 Louise Chappel, John Chesterman and Lisa Hill, *The Politics of Human Rights in Australia* (Cambridge University Press, 2009) 27–29.
6 See *Adelaide Company of Jehovah's Witnesses Inc v The Commonwealth* (1943) 67 CLR 116.
7 See *Discrimination Act 1991* (ACT); *Australian Human Rights Commission Act 1986* (Cth); *Anti-Discrimination Act 1992* (NT); *Anti-Discrimination Act 1991* (Qld); *Equal Opportunity*

high level of personal religious freedom.[8] Australia's relationship with religion is therefore both complex and uniquely Australian.[9]

The relationship between the State and religion today stands in stark contrast to that which existed at the beginning of European colonisation. The Church of England arrived in Australia in 1788 as the *de facto*, if not the *de jure*, established church of the new colony.[10] The Church of England Chaplain, Rev Richard Johnston, was the only religious leader in the colony, the Roman Catholic's having been denied permission to send their own chaplain.[11] It was in essence a penal colony ruled over by autocratic governors. There was no freedom of religion. The only religion on offer was that provided by the Rev Richard Johnston, and wherever possible the Governors made attendance at his services compulsory for all convicts, including those of other faiths and denominations.[12] Attendance at Church of England services was even made part of the punishment metered out to those involved in the Vinegar Hill uprising in 1789.[13] Religion, however, did not have it all its own way. It was the State, personified in the Governor, which was very much in charge of the relationship. The extent to which Rev Johnston and his successors were able to minister to their flocks was dependant on the will and cooperation of the Governor of the day.[14]

In the intervening years between colonisation and today, the relationship has evolved both at a macro 'nationwide' level and in relation to individual issues as Australia's religious demographics and expectations about the place and role of religion have changed. While the secularisation thesis predicted that religion would overtime become increasingly irrelevant to matters of public policy,[15] this

---

Act 1984 (SA); *Anti-Discrimination Act 1998* (Tas); *Equal Opportunity Act 2010* (Vic); *Equal Opportunity Act 1984* (WA).

8 Ian Vásquez and Tanja Porčnik, *The Human Freedom Index 2016 – A Global Measurement of Personal, Civil and Economic Freedom* (Cato Institute, 2016) 5 also available at <https://object.cato.org/sites/cato.org/files/human-freedom-index-files/human-freedom-index-2016-update-3.pdf>.

9 Barker, *Religion and the Census: Australia's Unique Relationship to Faith and Unbelief*, above n 3; Barker, *Australians Have an Increasingly Complex, yet Relatively Peaceful, Relationship with Religion*, above n 3.

10 See Chapter 3.

11 Manning Clark, *A History of Australia* (Melbourne University Press, 1962) vol 1, 78; James Cook (author), Britton Alexander and Frank Murcott Bladen (eds), *Historical Records of New South Wales* (Government Printer, 1892–1901) vol 1, pt 1, 119; Patrick Francis Cardinal Moran, *History of the Catholic Church in Australasia From Authentic Sources* (The Oceanic Publishing Company, 1896) 5–6; James Waldersee, *Catholic Society in New South Wales 1788–1860* (University of Sydney Press, 1974) 2–3.

12 Tom Luscombe, *Builders and Crusaders* (Lansdowne Press, 1st ed, 1967) 3.

13 Lynette Ramsay Silver, *The Battle of Vinegar Hill: Australia's Irish Rebellion, 1804* (Doubleday, 1st ed, 1989) 114.

14 See Chapter 2.

15 See Tom Frame, *Losing My Religion Unbelief in Australia* (University of New South Wales Press, 2009), 272.

prediction has not been born out in many of the areas of interaction in the Australian State–religion relationship.

For example, the interaction between the State and religion in relation to education has seen some of the most dramatic change. That change has not been one directional. Far from being a steady march towards the removal of all religion from education, or even just from publicly funded education, Australia has seen an increase in the interaction between the State and religion in relation to education since the middle of the twentieth century. By Federation all of the colonies had removed State funding of religious schools.[16] During the Constitutional Convention debates Edmund Barton assured delegates that churches could not receive federal funding under the *Australian Constitution*, stating emphatically 'you have only two powers of spending money, and a church could not receive the funds of the Commonwealth under either of them'.[17] Today, however, non-government schools, including those run by religious organisations, receive funding from the federal government and federally funded chaplains operate in both secular State schools and non-government schools. The Constitutional validity of funding non-government religious schools was confirmed in *Attorney General (Vic); ex rel Black v. The Commonwealth (*the *DOGS case).*[18] While the school chaplaincy programme was found to be unconstitutional in *Williams v The Commonwealth No 1*[19] and *No. 2*[20] this was on the basis of the funding model, not the religiosity of the programme or the receipt of government funds by religious organisations.[21] The funding model has since been rectified, allowing the chaplaincy programme to continue to operate.[22]

It is easy to assume that an increase in the interaction between the State and religion is a net positive for religion, however increased restrictions on religious practice also involve an increase in interaction. Chapter 7 considered several examples of restrictions on religious practice by the State. For Roman Catholics, Jehovah's Witnesses, Scientologists and Muslims the interaction during the relevant periods were far from positive. For example, both the Church of Scientology and Jehovah's Witnesses had to fight attempts to ban their organisations. The increasing interaction between the State and Australian Muslims is another example where the interaction is not wholly positive. The question of when and where

16 Renae Barker, 'Under Most Peculiar Circumstances: The Church Acts in the Australian Colonies as a Study of Plural Establishment' (2016) 3(3) *Law& History* 28, 50.

17 Tony Blackshield, 'Religion and Australian Constitutional Law' in Peter Radan, Denise Meyerson and Rosalind F. Croucher (eds), *Law and Religion: God, the State and the Common Law* (Routledge, 2005) 89.

18 (1981) 146 CLR 559.

19 [2012] HCA 23 (20 June 2012).

20 [2014] HCA 23 (19 June 2014).

21 Renae Barker, 'A Critical Analysis of Religious Aspects of the Australian Chaplaincy Cases' (2015) 4(1) *Oxford Journal of Law and Religion* 26, 41–49.

22 Australian Government, Department of Education and Training, *Student Resilience and Wellbeing Resources – National School Chaplaincy Programme* (17 November 2017) www. education.gov.au/national-school-chaplaincy-programme>.

a Muslim woman can wear a face covering for religious reasons has been raised in a number of contexts.[23] In terms of the State–religion interaction, one of the most significant negative interactions was the temporary ban in 2014 on people wearing face coverings entering the public gallery of Federal Parliament. While the ban was short lived it was symbolically important. It said 'more than "we need to identify interjectors". It says to Muslim women "you are not welcome here, you cannot be trusted, like school children you must be kept behind glass".'[24]

Freedom of religion is not an absolute. As identified by Latham CJ in *Adelaide Company of Jehovah's Witnesses Inc v Commonwealth*,[25] religious belief and practice covers a wide spectrum of human endeavour:

> almost any matter may become an element in religious belief or religious conduct. The wearing of particular clothes, the eating or the non-eating of meat or other foods, the observance of ceremonies, not only in religious worship, but in the everyday life of the individual - all of these may become part of religion.[26]

As a result, it is inevitable that the State will need to intervene to restrict some religious practices in the interests of society as a whole or the protection of vulnerable individuals. Some level of negative interaction between the State and religion is therefore to be expected. It is easy to assume that the best way to achieve this, and therefore maximise freedom of religion is via a wholly secular State. However, freedom of religion is not necessarily positively correlated with increased secularity.

Durham has suggested viewing the spectrum of possible State religion relationships as a loop provides a better depiction of the relationship between the various models and freedom of religion.[27] In the most 'secular States' such as those operating under secular world view, secular control or abolitionist models of State religion relationship, there is little to no freedom of religion. In these States the State's negative interaction with religion is high in that the State takes positive steps to exclude, marginalise and even eliminate religion. Similarly, in those States with a high level of positive interaction such as States operating under theocratic, erastian and religious establishment models there is very limited freedom of religion. In these States the positive interaction with religion is so high as to identify

---

23 See Renae Barker, 'Rebutting the Ban the Burqa Rhetoric: A Critical Analysis of the Arguments for a Ban on the Islamic Face Veil in Australia' (2016) 37(1) *Adelaide Law Review* 191.
24 Ibid. 216.
25 (1943) 67 CLR 116.
26 Ibid. 124 (Latham CJ).
27 W. Cole Durham Jr, 'Perspectives on Religious liberty: Acomparative Framework' in Johan D. van der Vyver and John Witte Jr (eds), *Religious Human Rights in Global Perspective: Legal Perspectives* (Martinus Nijhoff Publishers, 1st ed, 1996) 18–25.

the State with the chosen religion and as a consequence effectively exclude other options.[28]

Maximum freedom of religion is found somewhere between the extremes of complete positive interaction and complete negative interaction. Where on the continuum freedom of religion is maximised for a given State will vary depending on a number of factors.[29] In Australia, balance has, for now, been found in a pragmatic pluralism model. Pluralism is not a matter of principle in Australia, but rather a pragmatic response to a multi-cultural and therefore multi-faith society in which multiple faiths exist alongside a significant proportion of the population who identify as having no religion.[30] Whether or not this is the 'right' model to maximise freedom of religion, including the freedom not to have a religion, is a matter of debate.

As outlined above, the relationship between the State and religion in Australia has changed significantly over time. In debating whether or not the current relationship is the best outcome for Australia as a whole, understanding not only how dramatic that shift has been but also how persistent issues relating to religion have been is fundamentally important. In Chapters 7 through 9, this book considered three case studies in the relationship between the State and religion: State restriction on religion, education and funding. Individually, each chapter traced the history of each case study outlining the major changes in law and government policy. When taken together they demonstrate the remarkable persistence, evolution and importance of the interaction and relationship between the State and religion. In every decade since European colonisation the State has had to grapple with at least one important issue in its interaction with religion.

The relationship between the State and religion is dynamic and ever-changing. While the law and government policies in relation to any one issue may remain constant for extended periods of time, it will inevitably be evolving in others. When these changes are added together over time and across discreet issues they make up the totality of the macro relationship between the State and religion. What that relationship will look like in 10, 20, 50 or even 100 years' time is difficult to predict. Just as Barton was unable to foresee the federal government ever providing funding directly to religious organisations politicians, policy makers, religious and community leaders are unlikely to be able to fully predict how the Australian State–religion relationship will evolve. If current demographic trends continue, more and more Australians will identify as having no religion while at the same time the religious diversity of the population will continue to increase. This will pose significant challenges not only for the State

---

28 Ibid.
29 W. Cole Durham Jr and Brett G. Scharffs, *Law and Religion: National, International and Comparative Perspectives* (Wolters Kluwer, 2010) 117.
30 Rex Ahdar and Ian Leigh, *Religious Freedom in the Liberal State* (Oxford University Press, 2nd ed, 2013) 111–112.

but also for religious leaders of Christian denominations who have historically been in the majority. How that will play out, how the relationship will evolve and whether the model of State–religion relationship that emerges in the future is the 'right' one is going to be an ongoing matter of debate. What we can be assured of is that it will be a uniquely Australian solution, a uniquely Australian State–religion relationship.

Index